W9-BQK-821

The Teen's Guide to Sex, Relationships, and Being a Human

LET'S TALK ABOUT IT

Erika Moen
Matthew Nolan
Layout Assistance by Maria Frantz

Also by Erika Moen and Matthew Nolan

Drawn to Sex: The Basics
Oh Joy Sex Toy, Volumes 1 to 4

This book was written in Google Documents, drawn digitally using Clip Studio Paint, and colored and edited in Photoshop. It utilizes a homemade font of Erika Moen's handwriting in addition to Agilis, Lobster, Raleway, Futura Handwritten, and TektonPro.

The material in this book is for informational purposes only. Although every effort has been made to provide the most up-to-date information, the facts and the science in the subject areas covered by this book and the information about sex, relationships, and being a human will evolve over time. No book can replace the experience, expertise, and personalized advice of a trusted medical professional, so please consult with a health-care provider before making any decisions that affect your health, particularly if you suffer from a medical condition or have a symptom that may require treatment.

The authors and publisher expressly disclaim responsibility for any adverse effects that may result from the use or application of the information contained in this book.

Cover art, text, and interior illustrations copyright © 2021 by Erika Moen Comics & Illustration LLC

All rights reserved. Published in the United States by RH Graphic, an imprint of Random House Children's Books, a division of Penguin Random House LLC, New York.

RH Graphic with the book design is a trademark of Penguin Random House LLC.

Visit us on the Web! RHKidsGraphic.com • @RHKidsGraphic

Educators and librarians, for a variety of teaching tools, visit us at RHTeachersLibrarians.com

Library of Congress Cataloging-in-Publication Data is available upon request.
ISBN 978-1-9848-9314-7 (pbk.) — ISBN 978-0-593-12531-1 (trade) —
ISBN 978-1-9848-9315-4 (lib. bdg.) — ISBN 978-1-9848-9316-1 (ebook)

MANUFACTURED IN SINGAPORE
10 9 8 7 6 5 4 3 2 1
First Edition

Random House Children's Books supports the First Amendment and celebrates the right to read.

Penguin Random House LLC supports copyright. Copyright fuels creativity, encourages diverse voices, promotes free speech, and creates a vibrant culture. Thank you for buying an authorized edition of this book and for complying with copyright laws by not reproducing, scanning, or distributing any part in any form without permission. You are supporting writers and allowing Penguin Random House to publish books for every reader.

A comic on every bookshelf.

To whoever needs it, whatever your age

Contents

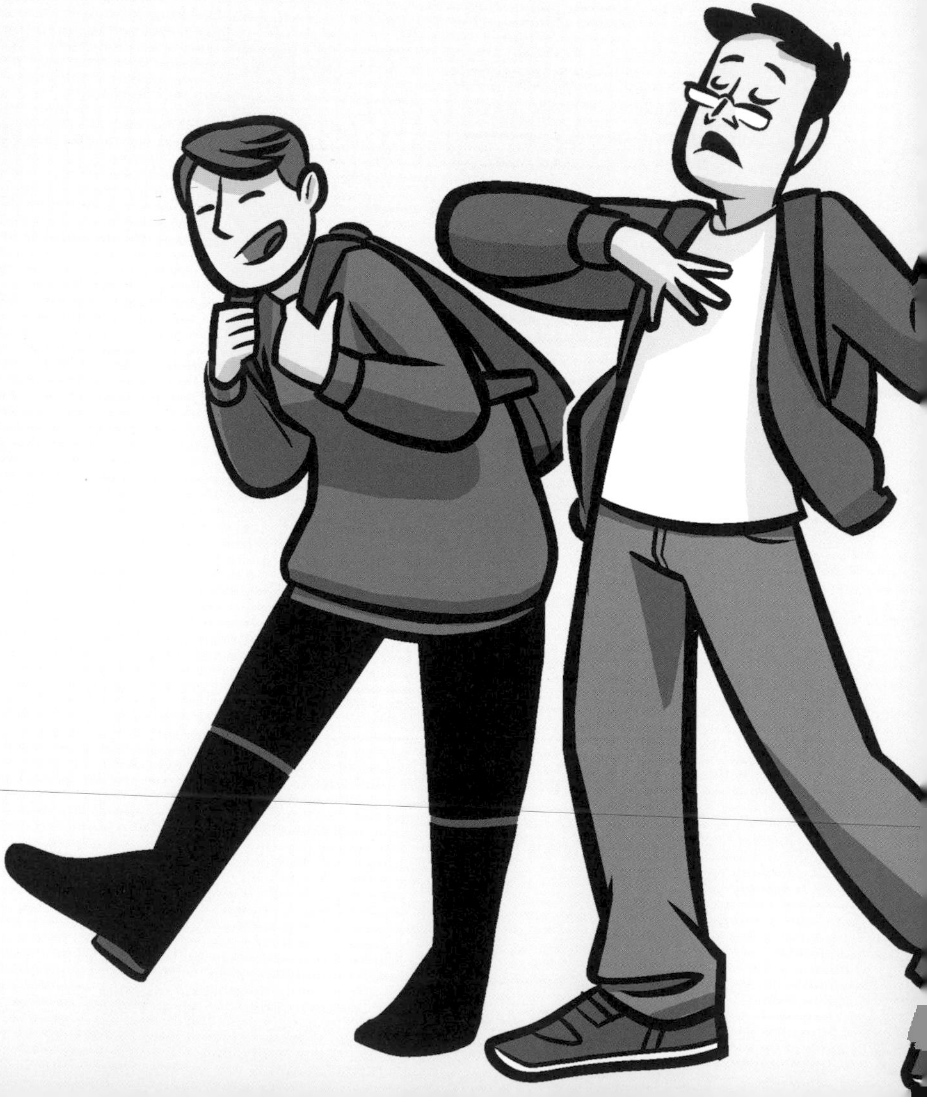

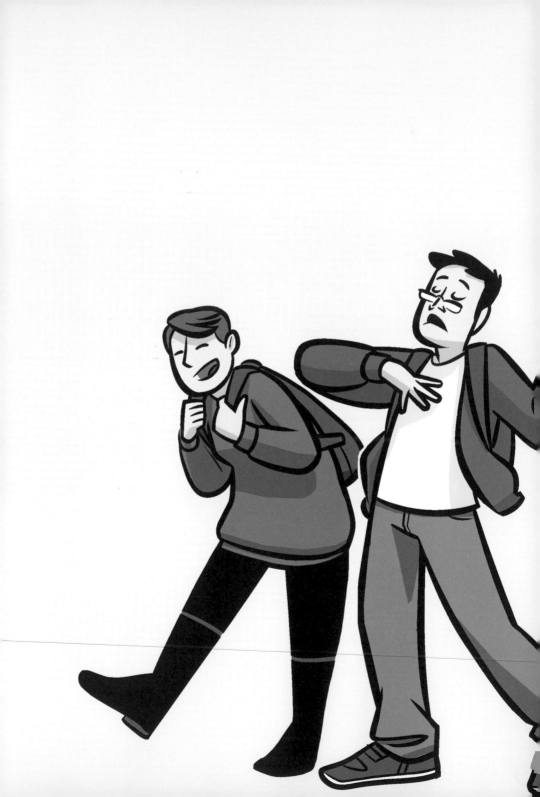

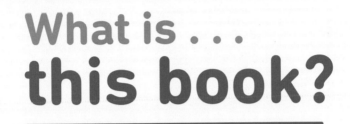

What is . . . this book?

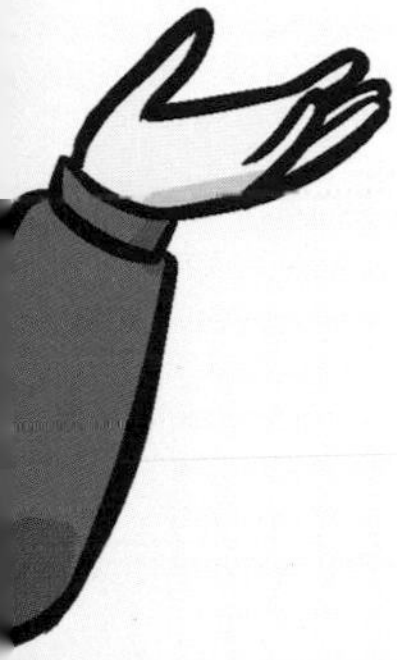

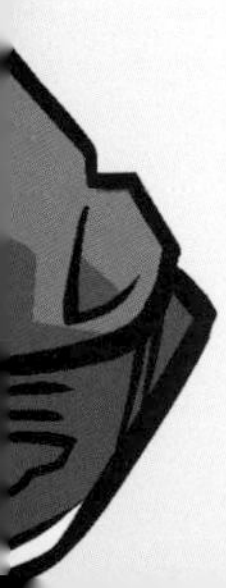

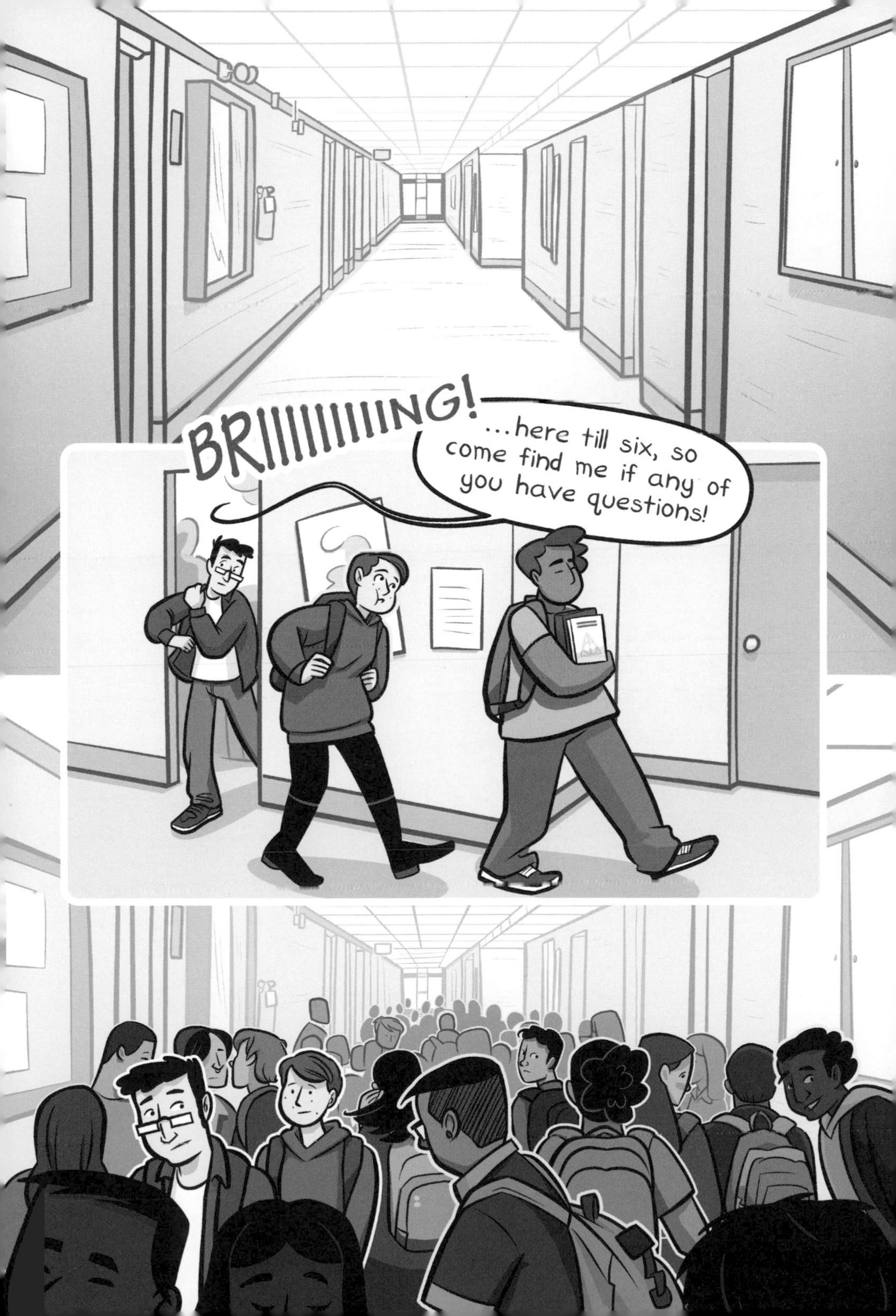
BRIIIIIIIIIING!
...here till six, so come find me if any of you have questions!

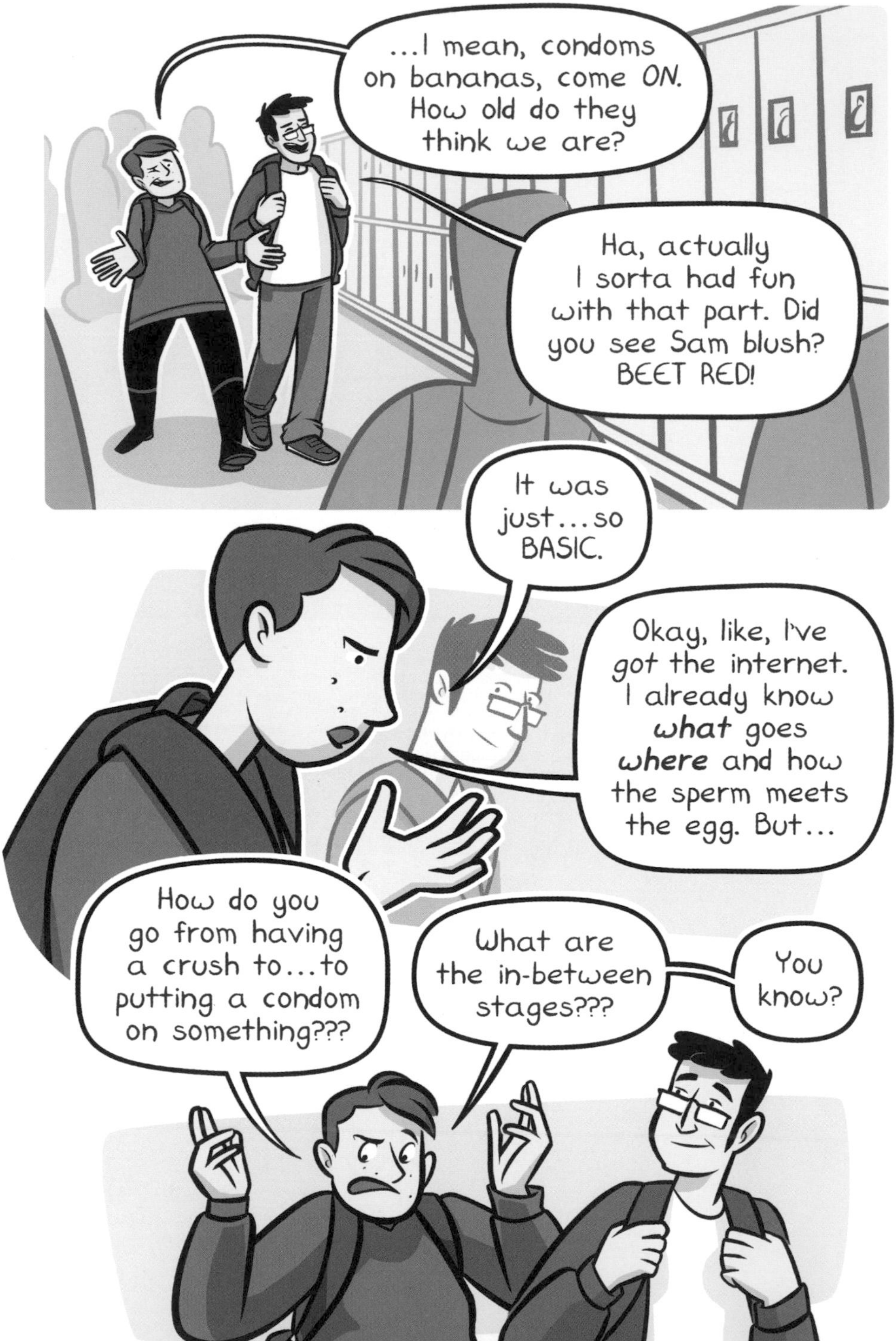
...I mean, condoms on bananas, come ON. How old do they think we are?
Ha, actually I sorta had fun with that part. Did you see Sam blush? BEET RED!
It was just...so BASIC.
Okay, like, I've *got* the internet. I already know ***what*** goes ***where*** and how the sperm meets the egg. But...
How do you go from having a crush to...to putting a condom on something???
What are the in-between stages???
You know?

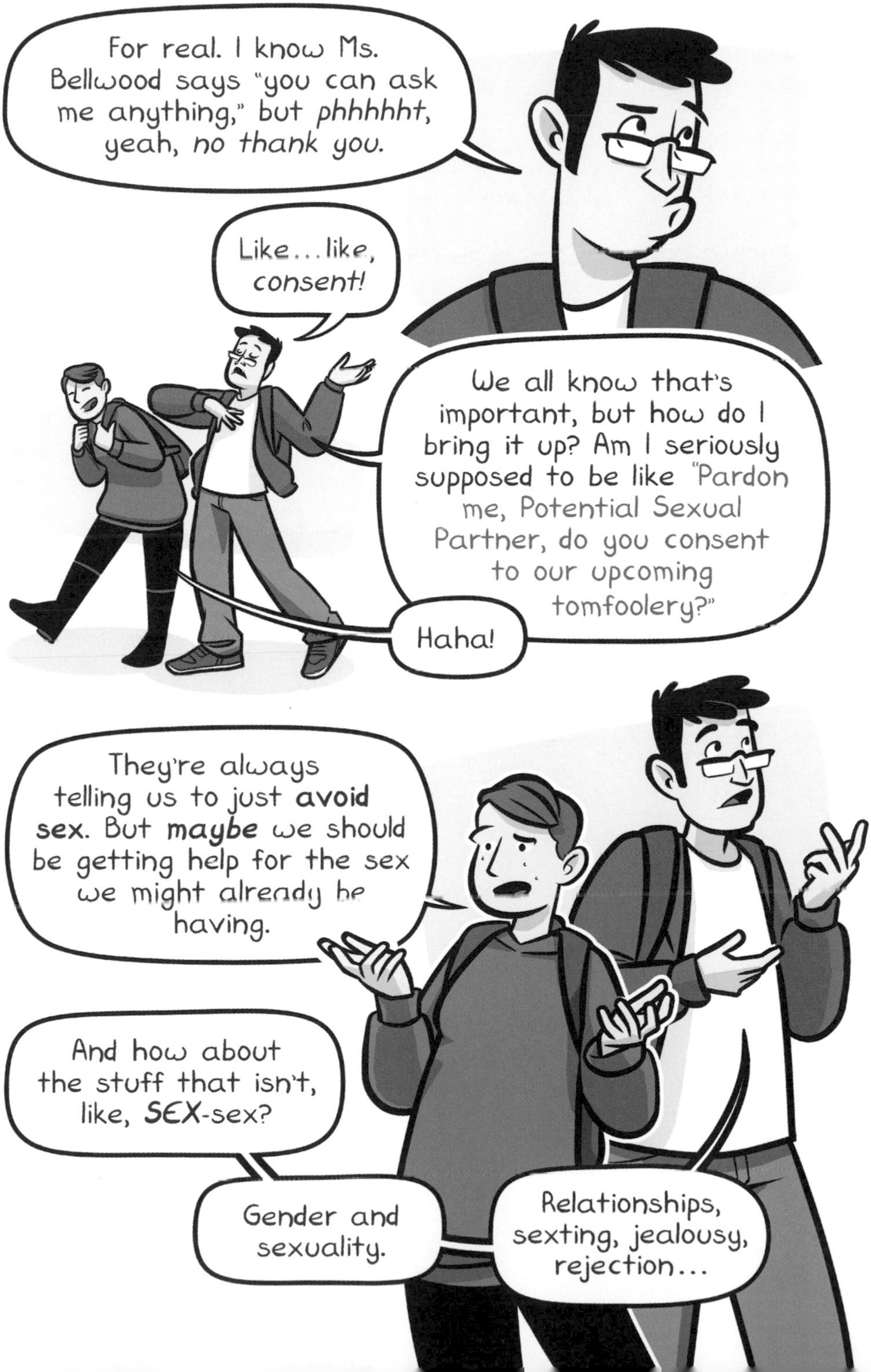
For real. I know Ms. Bellwood says "you can ask me anything," but *phhhhht*, yeah, *no thank you.*
Like...like, *consent!*
We all know that's important, but how do I bring it up? Am I seriously supposed to be like "Pardon me, Potential Sexual Partner, do you consent to our upcoming tomfoolery?"
Haha!
They're always telling us to just **avoid sex**. But **maybe** we should be getting help for the sex we might already be having.
And how about the stuff that isn't, like, **SEX**-sex?
Gender and sexuality.
Relationships, sexting, jealousy, rejection...

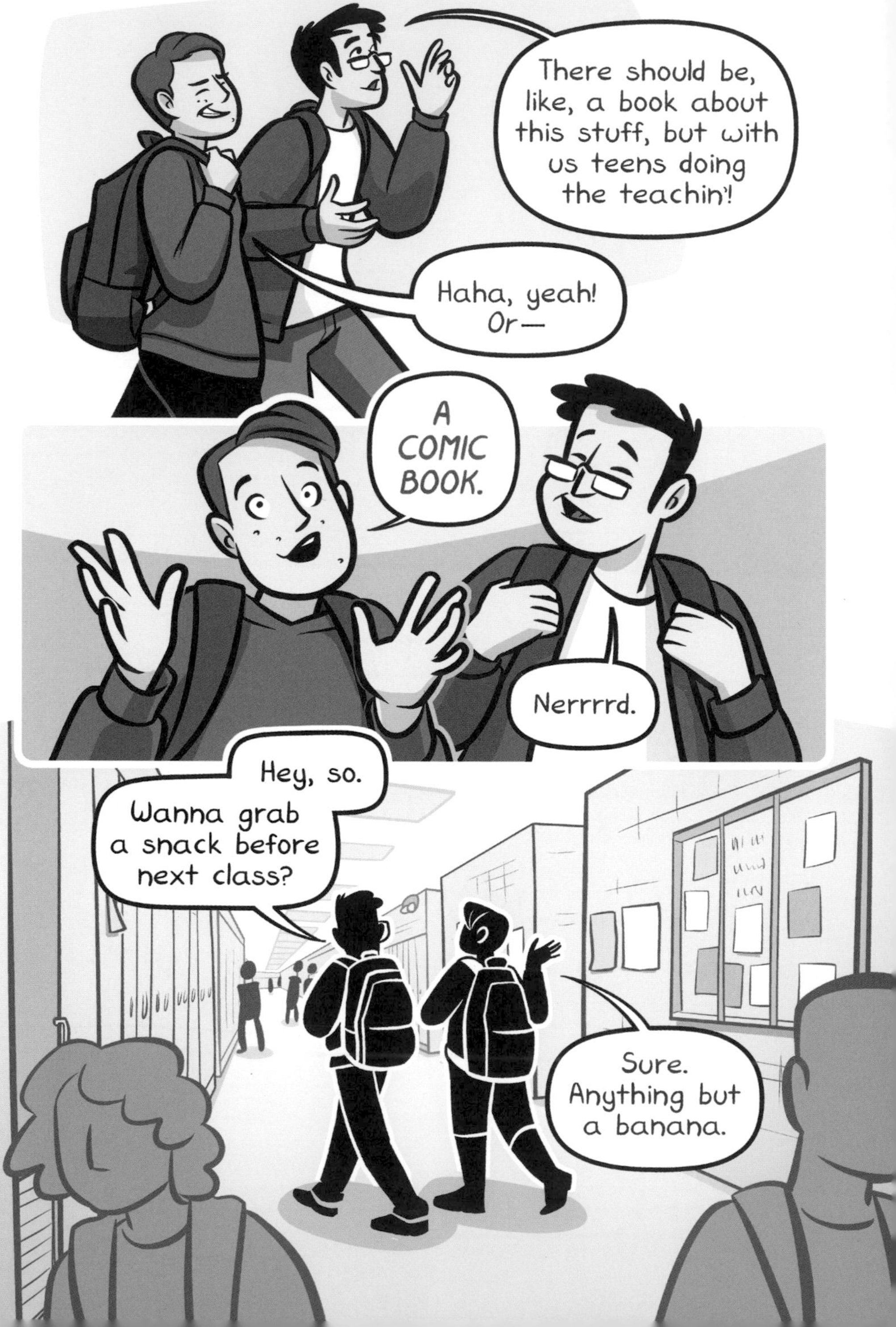
There should be, like, a book about this stuff, but with us teens doing the teachin'!
Haha, yeah! Or—
A COMIC BOOK.
Nerrrrd.
Hey, so.
Wanna grab a snack before next class?
Sure. Anything but a banana.

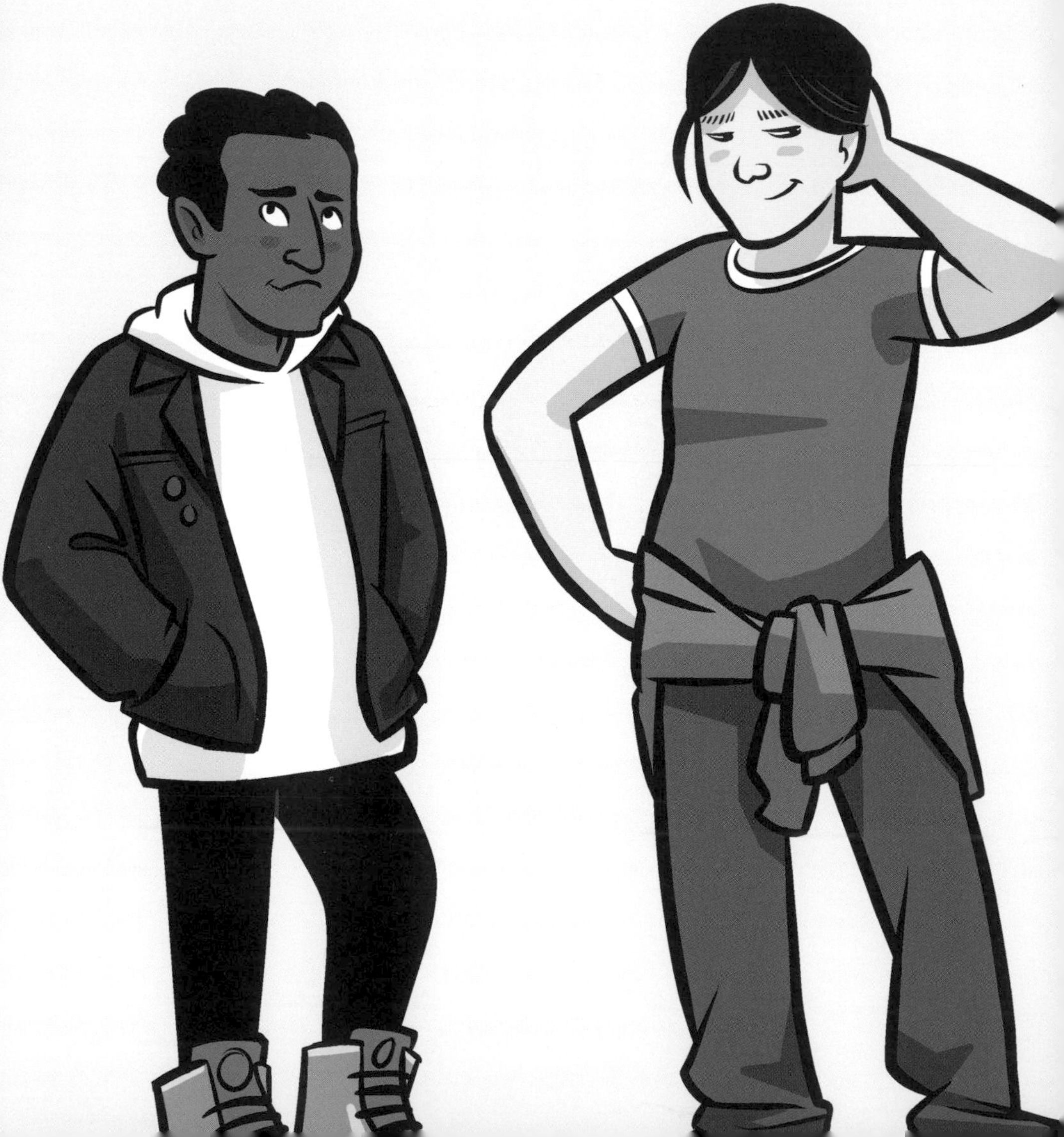

What is . . . first?

What do you do? How do you know you're ready? No, but how do you make absolutely sure? How do you talk about whether you're ready? How do you make sure your partner is ready? Why is this all so complicated?

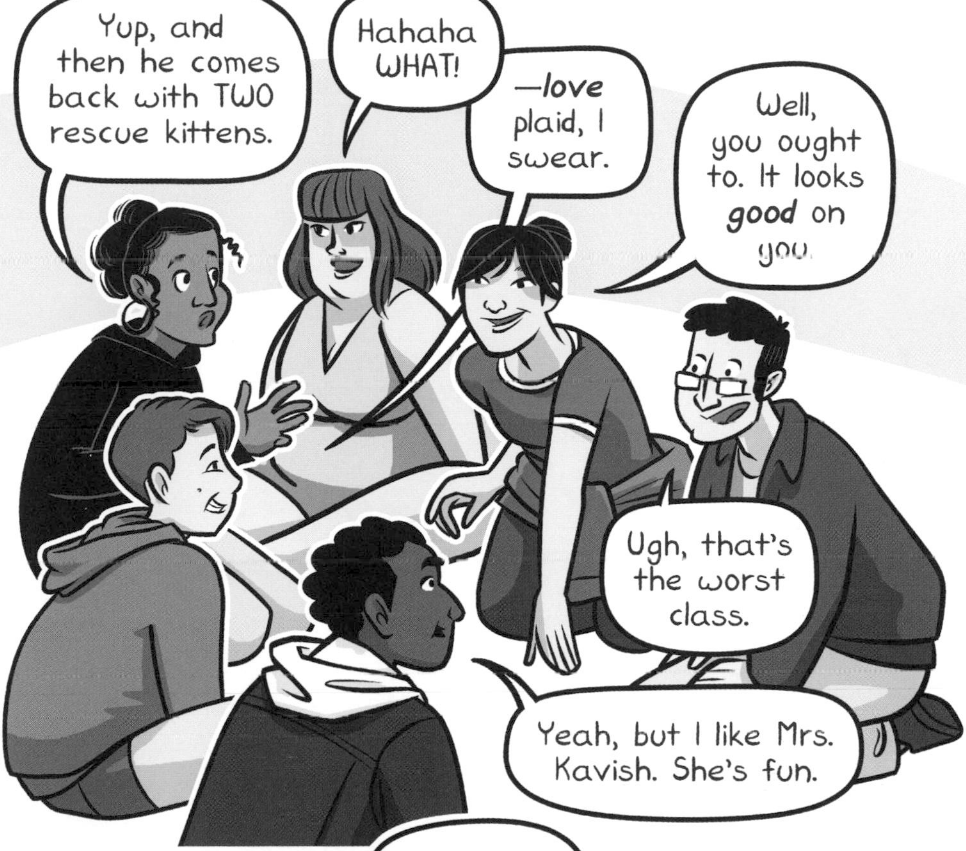
Yup, and then he comes back with TWO rescue kittens.
Hahaha WHAT!
—*love* plaid, I swear.
Well, you ought to. It looks **good** on you.
Ugh, that's the worst class.
Yeah, but I like Mrs. Kavish. She's fun.

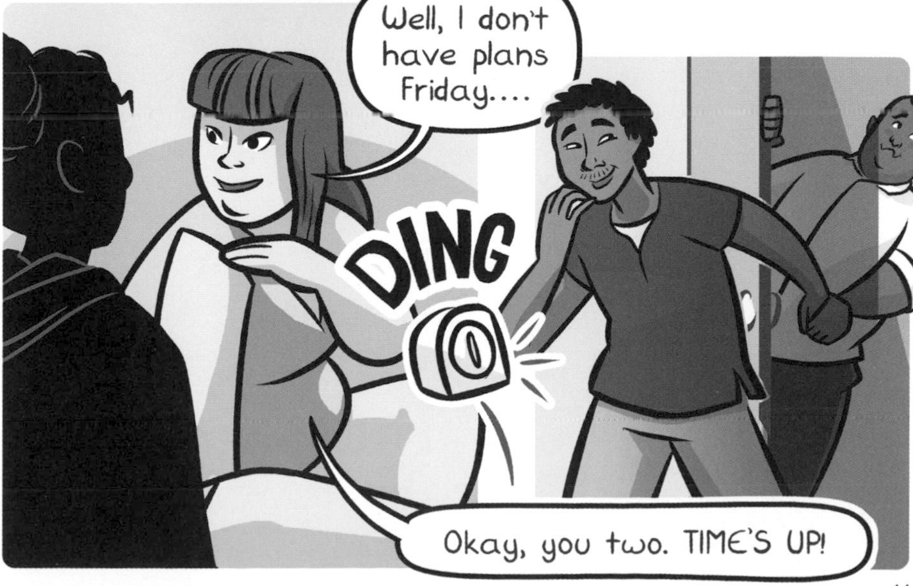
Well, I don't have plans Friday....
DING
Okay, you two. TIME'S UP!

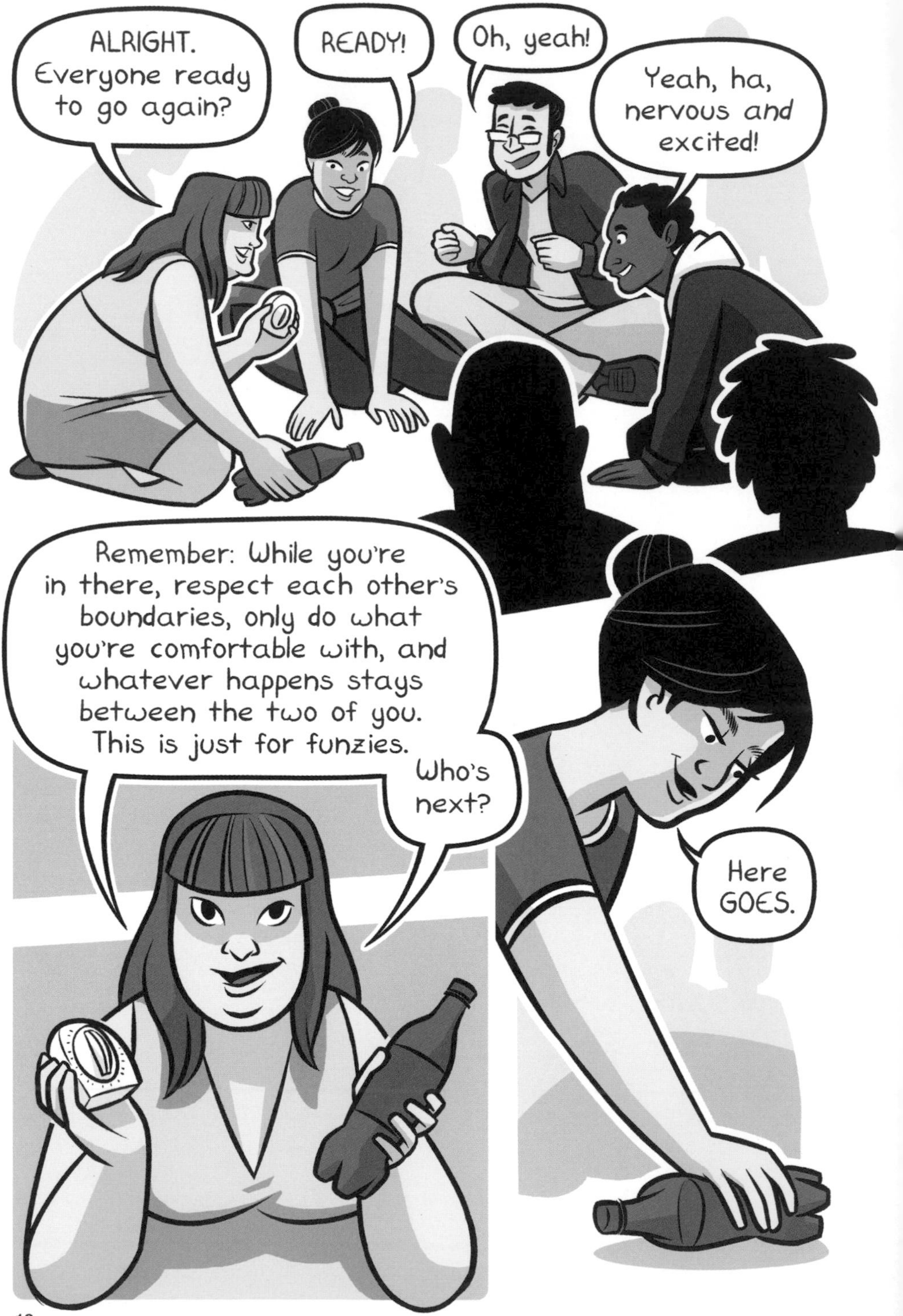
ALRIGHT. Everyone ready to go again?
READY!
Oh, yeah!
Yeah, ha, nervous and excited!
Remember: While you're in there, respect each other's boundaries, only do what you're comfortable with, and whatever happens stays between the two of you. This is just for funzies.
Who's next?
Here GOES.

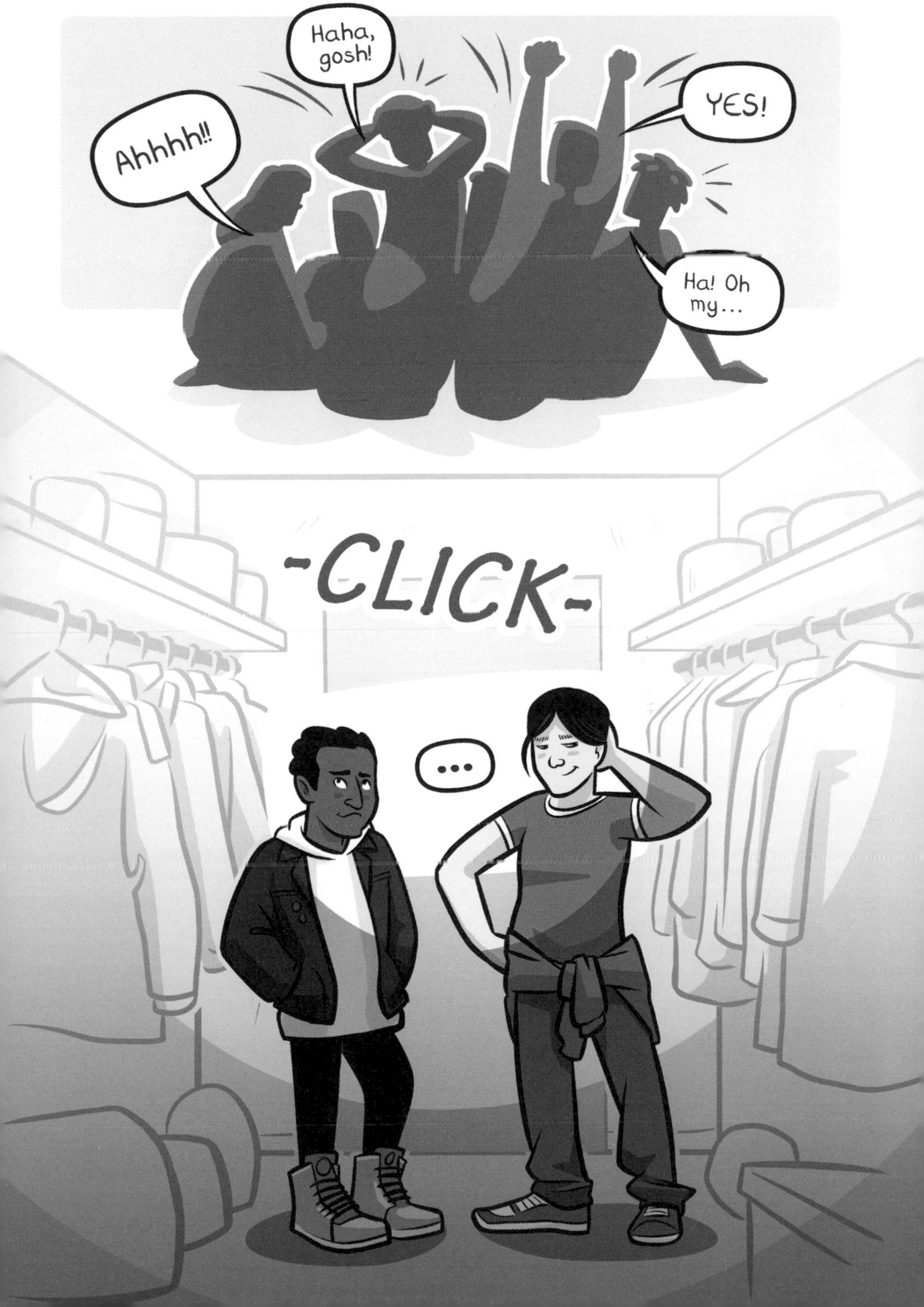
Ahhhh!!
Haha, gosh!
YES!
Ha! Oh my...
-CLICK-
...

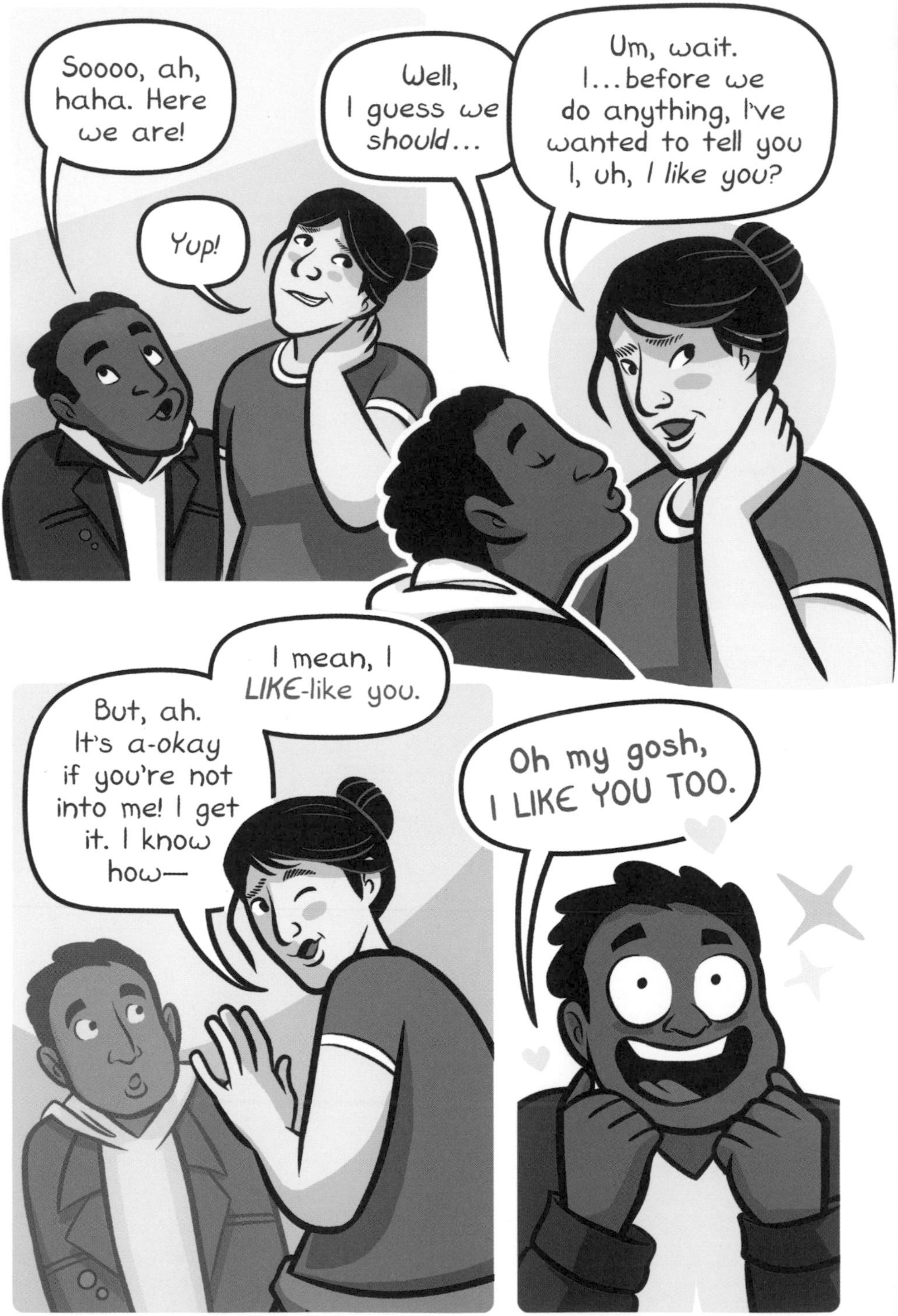
Soooo, ah, haha. Here we are!
Yup!
Well, I guess we should...
Um, wait. I...before we do anything, I've wanted to tell you I, uh, I *like you?*
I mean, I *LIKE*-like you.
But, ah. It's *a-okay* if you're not into me! I get it. I know how—
Oh my gosh, I LIKE YOU TOO.

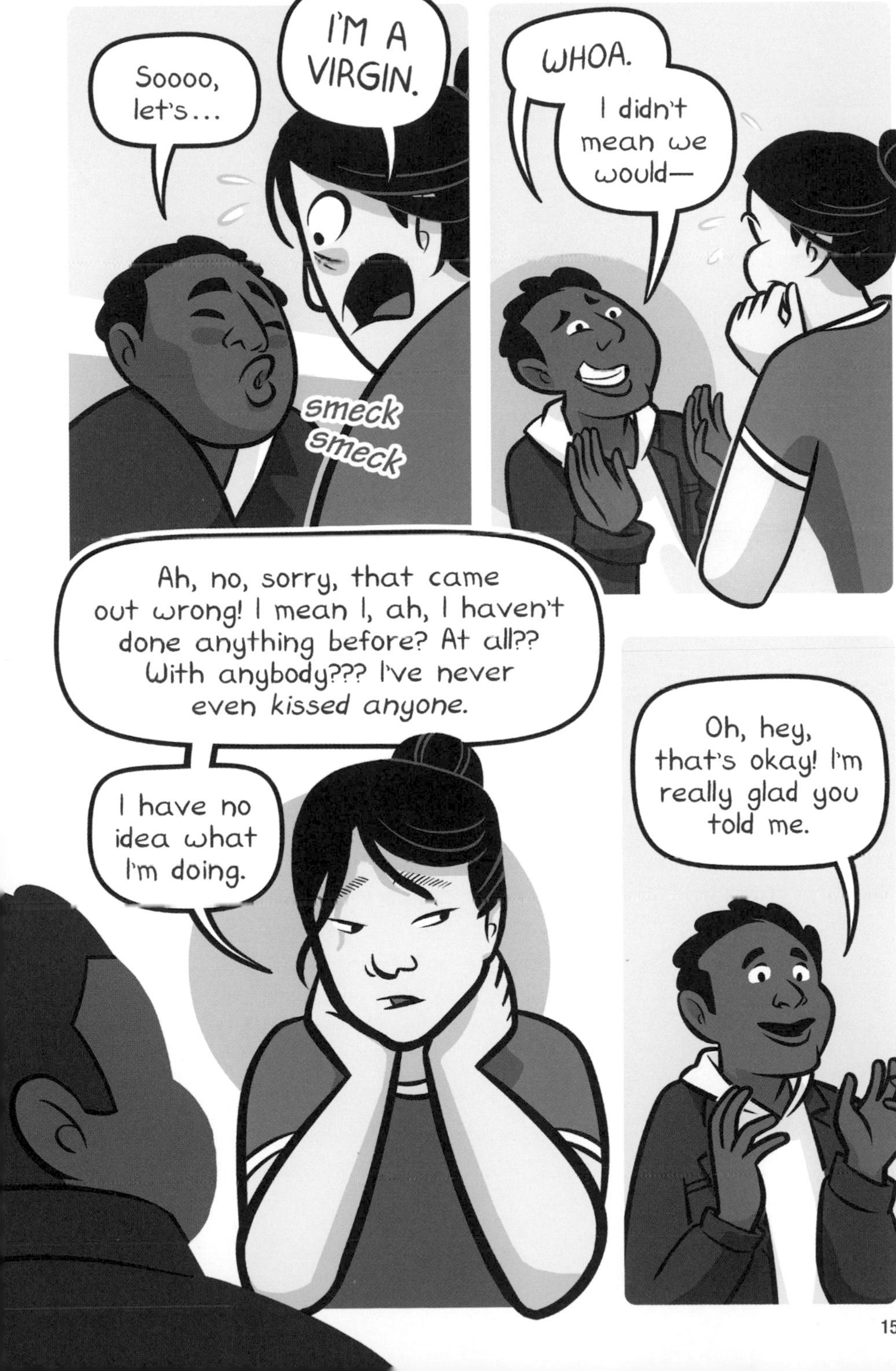

Soooo, let's...
I'M A VIRGIN.
smeck smeck
WHOA.
I didn't mean we would—
Ah, no, sorry, that came out wrong! I mean I, ah, I haven't done anything before? At all?? With anybody??? I've never even kissed anyone.
I have no idea what I'm doing.
Oh, hey, that's okay! I'm really glad you told me.

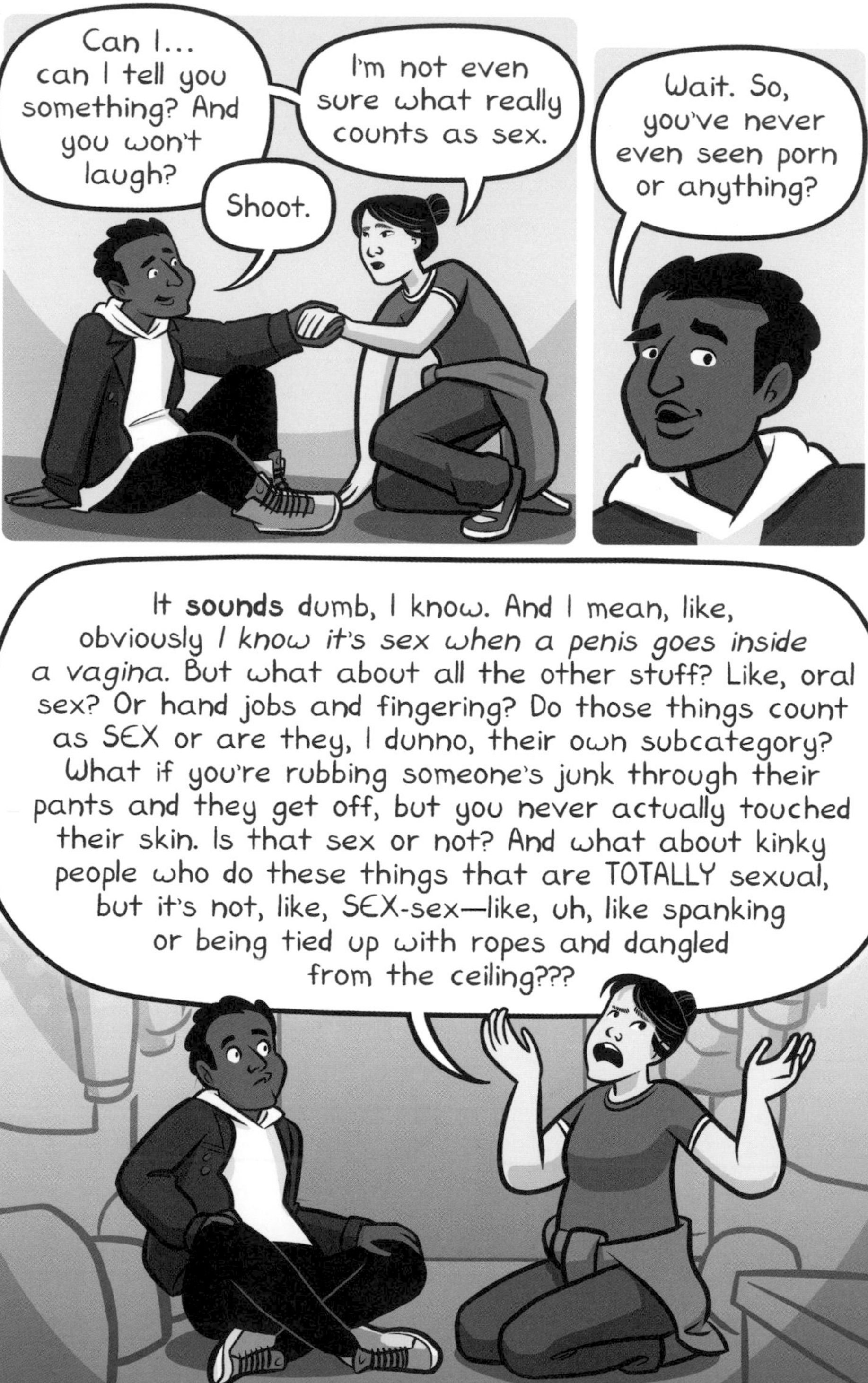
Can I... can I tell you something? And you won't laugh?
Shoot.
I'm not even sure what really counts as sex.
Wait. So, you've never even seen porn or anything?
It **sounds** dumb, I know. And I mean, like, obviously *I know it's sex when a penis goes inside a vagina.* But what about all the other stuff? Like, oral sex? Or hand jobs and fingering? Do those things count as SEX or are they, I dunno, their own subcategory? What if you're rubbing someone's junk through their pants and they get off, but you never actually touched their skin. Is that sex or not? And what about kinky people who do these things that are TOTALLY sexual, but it's not, like, SEX-sex—like, uh, like spanking or being tied up with ropes and dangled from the ceiling???

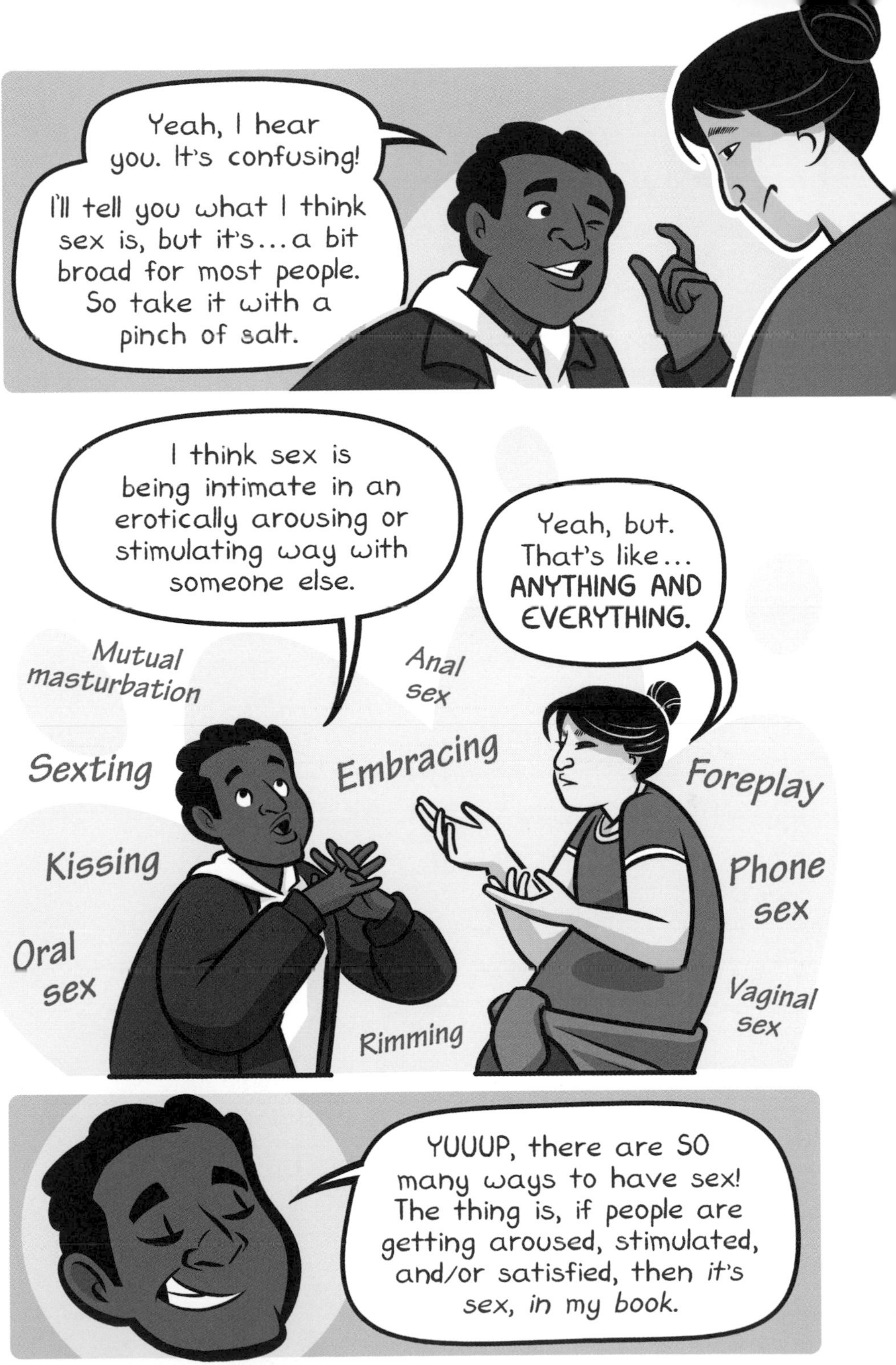
Yeah, I hear you. It's confusing!
I'll tell you what I think sex is, but it's... a bit broad for most people. So take it with a pinch of salt.
I think sex is being intimate in an erotically arousing or stimulating way with someone else.
Yeah, but. That's like... **ANYTHING AND EVERYTHING.**
Mutual masturbation
Anal sex
Sexting
Embracing
Foreplay
Kissing
Phone sex
Oral sex
Vaginal sex
Rimming
YUUUP, there are SO many ways to have sex! The thing is, if people are getting aroused, stimulated, and/or satisfied, then *it's sex, in my book.*

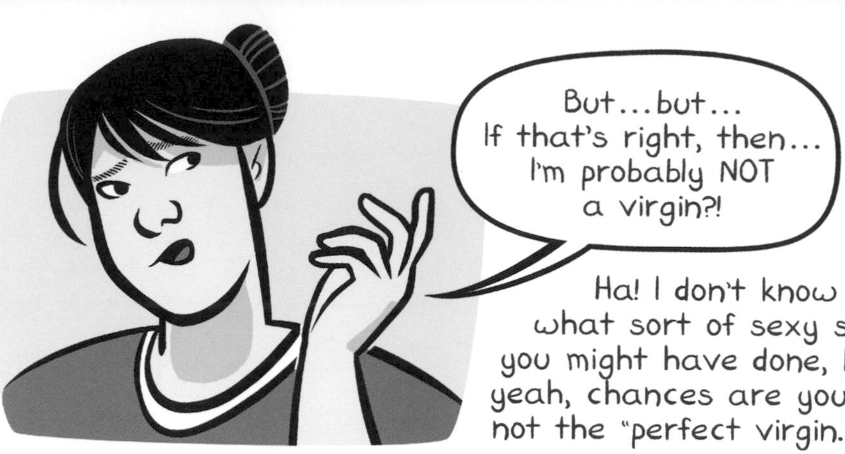
But...but... If that's right, then... I'm probably NOT a virgin?!

Ha! I don't know what sort of sexy stuff you might have done, but yeah, chances are you're not the "perfect virgin."

See, "virginity" is this silly label people came up with to describe a person who hasn't done a *specific sexual act*, traditionally, a cisgender man or woman who hasn't yet had penis-in-vagina intercourse.

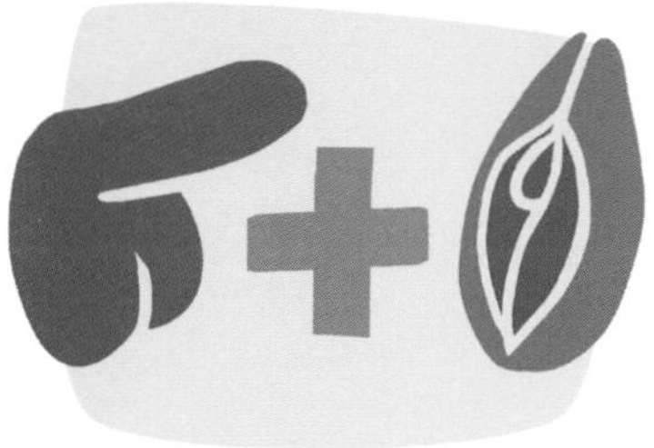

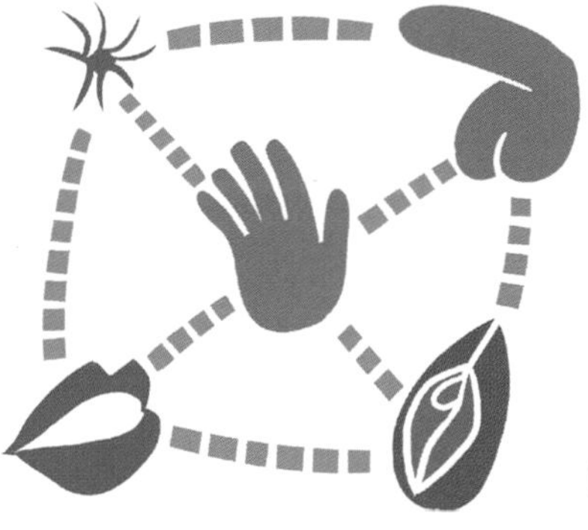

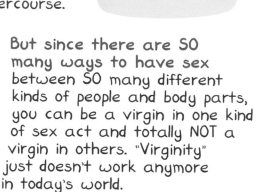

But since there are SO many ways to have sex between SO many different kinds of people and body parts, you can be a virgin in one kind of sex act and totally NOT a virgin in others. "Virginity" just doesn't work anymore in today's world.

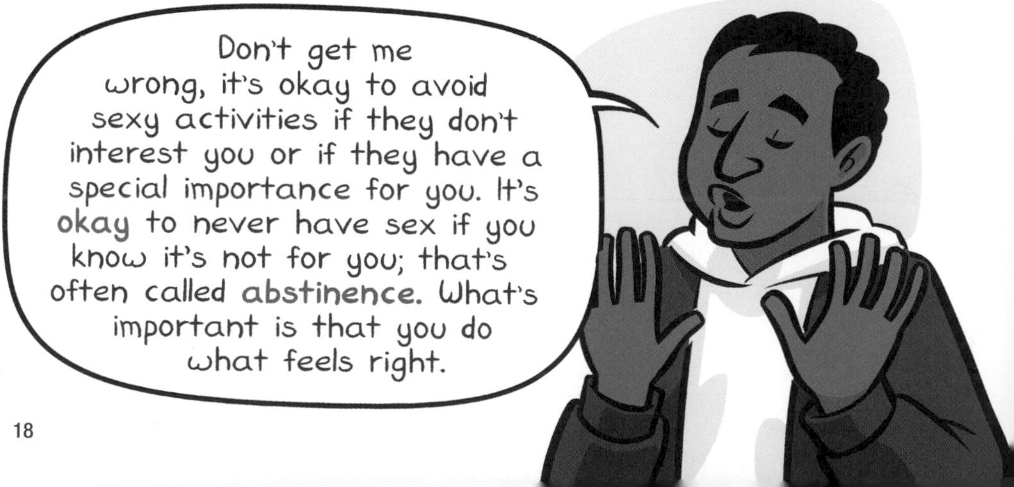
Don't get me wrong, it's okay to avoid sexy activities if they don't interest you or if they have a special importance for you. It's okay to never have sex if you know it's not for you; that's often called **abstinence**. What's important is that you do what feels right.

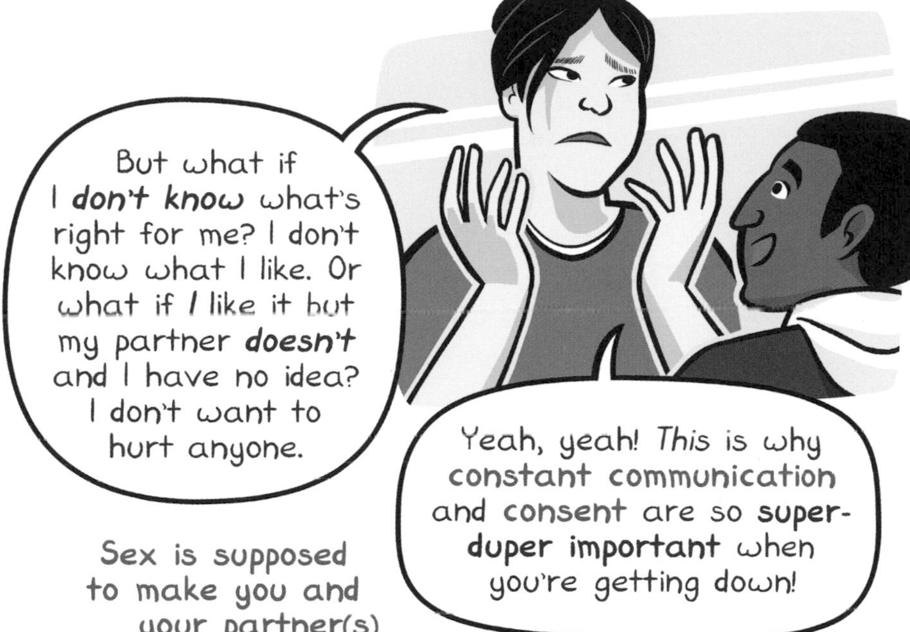
But what if I **don't know** what's right for me? I don't know what I like. Or what if *I* like it but my partner **doesn't** and I have no idea? I don't want to hurt anyone.
Yeah, yeah! *This* is why **constant communication** and **consent** are so **super-duper important** when you're getting down!

Sex is supposed to make you and your partner(s) happy, and that requires trust, concern, compassion, and care! To be a good partner, you need to be thoughtful and kind.

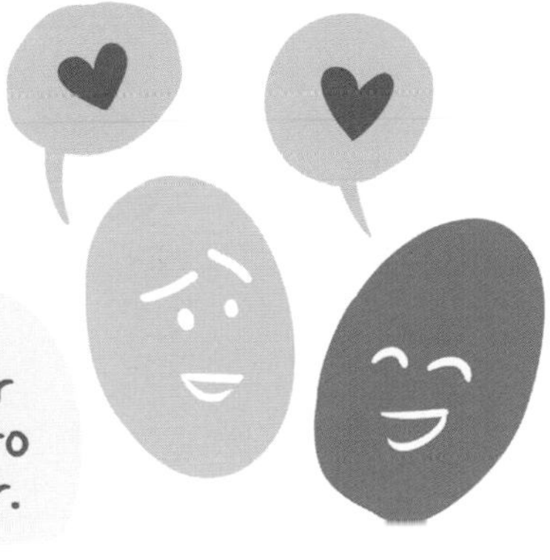

Consent during sexual activities is an ongoing eager agreement between people to do something sexy together.

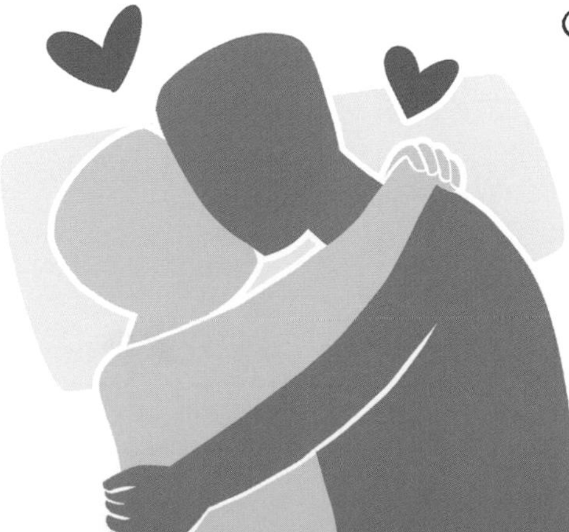

Consent is usually treated like a black-or-white permanent YES or NO, but it can actually have some shades of gray. It's given freely, it's reversible, and it's essential for sex.

Consent is **communication and respecting boundaries.** It's getting to a place where you and the people you're about to fool around with are on **the same page, feeling informed, in agreement, and ready** for what's about to happen.

Start with some good leading questions.

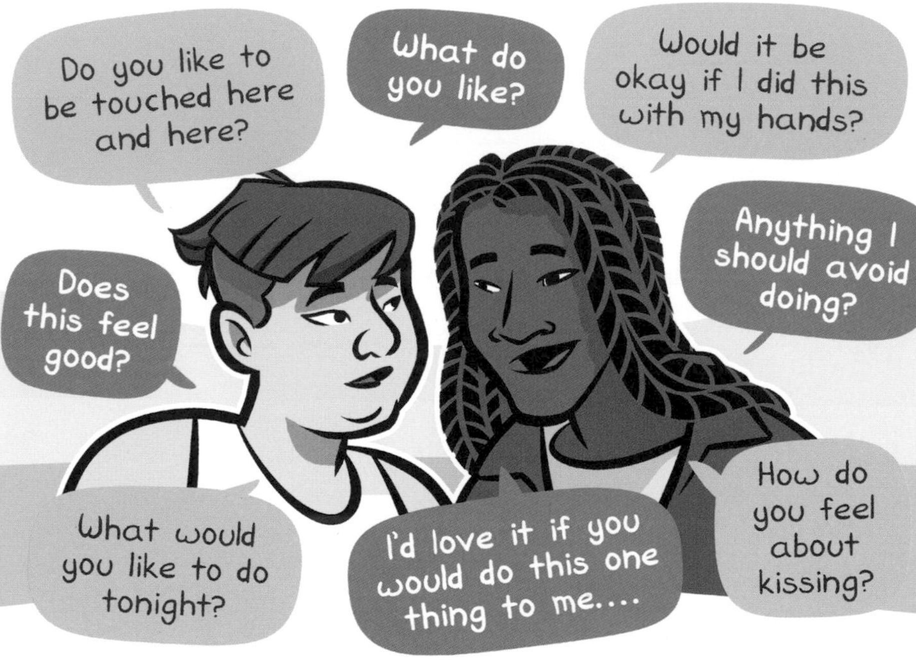

Do you like to be touched here and here?
What do you like?
Would it be okay if I did this with my hands?
Does this feel good?
Anything I should avoid doing?
What would you like to do tonight?
I'd love it if you would do this one thing to me....
How do you feel about kissing?

Don't be shy about what's on your mind. The more you get out there, the better it'll be. And be cool about what you hear back.

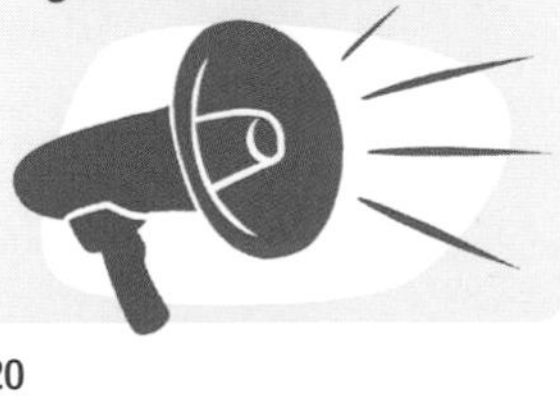

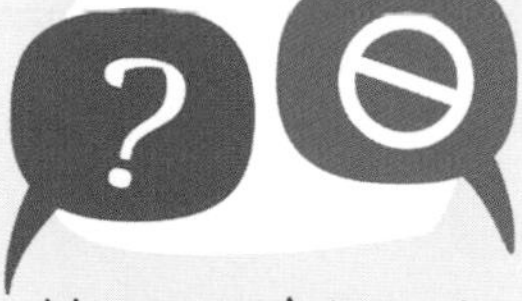

?

You might not hear what you wanted, but it's better to get that out in the open before you get down.

When you all know what everyone does and does not want to do, it's so much easier to have a fun time.

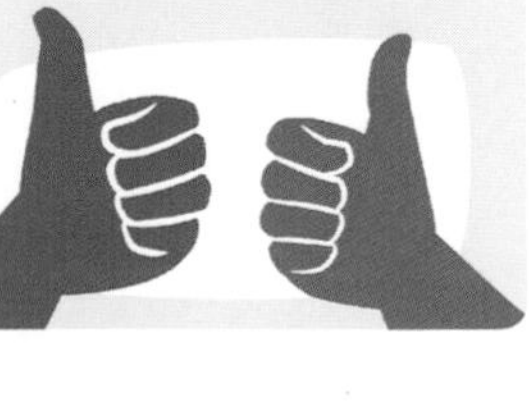

Remember that consent is given freely. With that in mind, here are some things that **consent is NOT:**

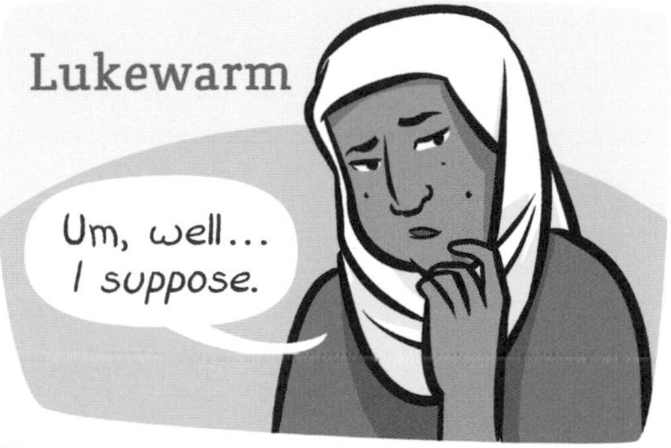
Lukewarm
Um, well... I suppose.

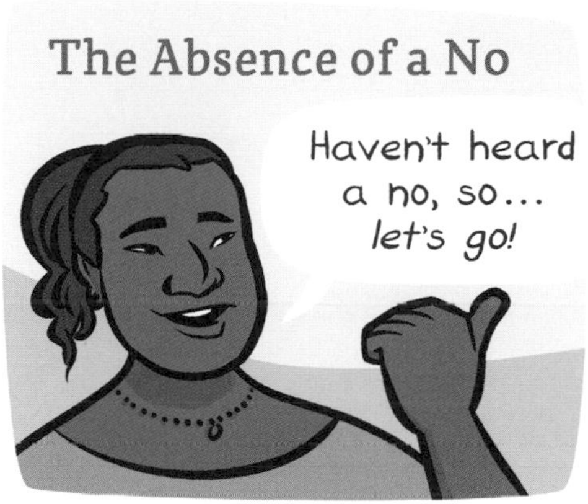
The Absence of a No
Haven't heard a no, so... *let's go!*

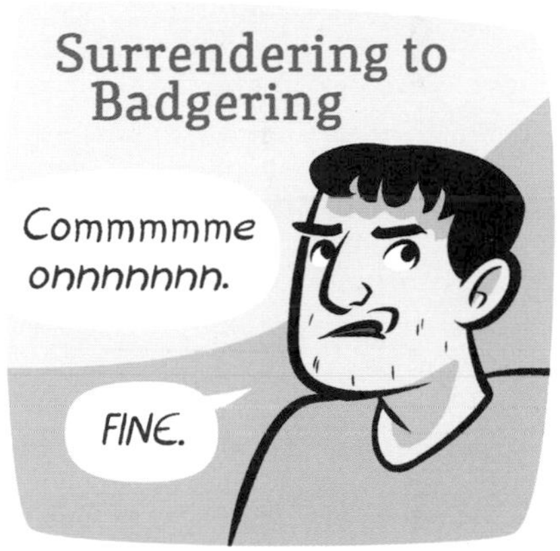
Surrendering to Badgering
Commmmme onnnnnnn.
FINE.

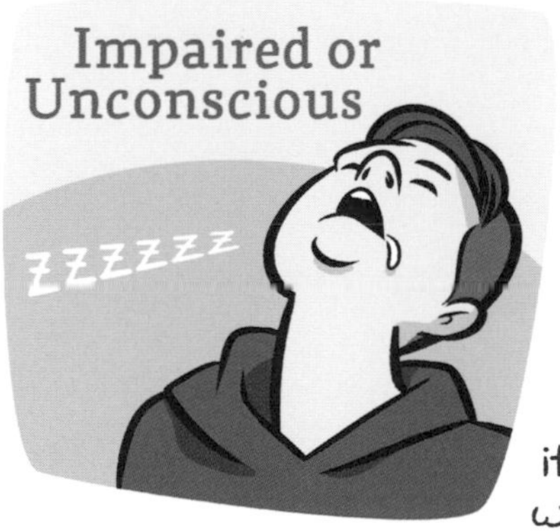
Impaired or Unconscious
ZZZZZZ

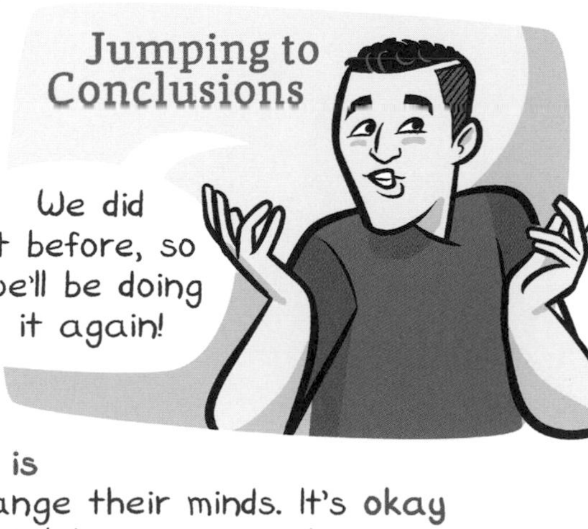
Jumping to Conclusions
We did it before, so we'll be doing it again!

Even with all the boxes ticked and both of you ready, **consent is flexible.** People change their minds. It's **okay** to speak up and to pause or stop.

Handy Check-In Words

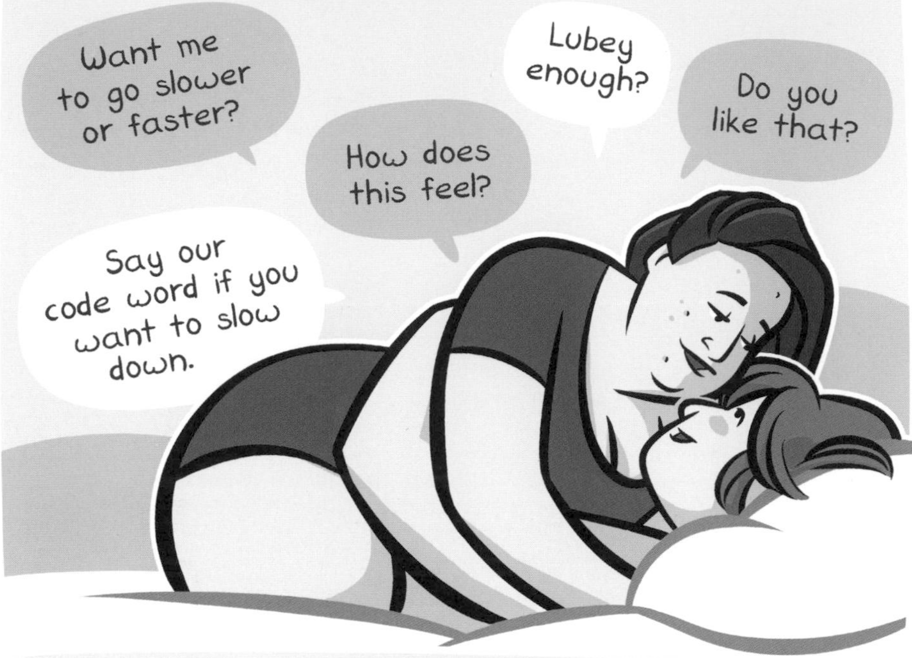

Want me to go slower or faster?
How does this feel?
Lubey enough?
Do you like that?
Say our code word if you want to slow down.

Handy Words to Change What's Happening

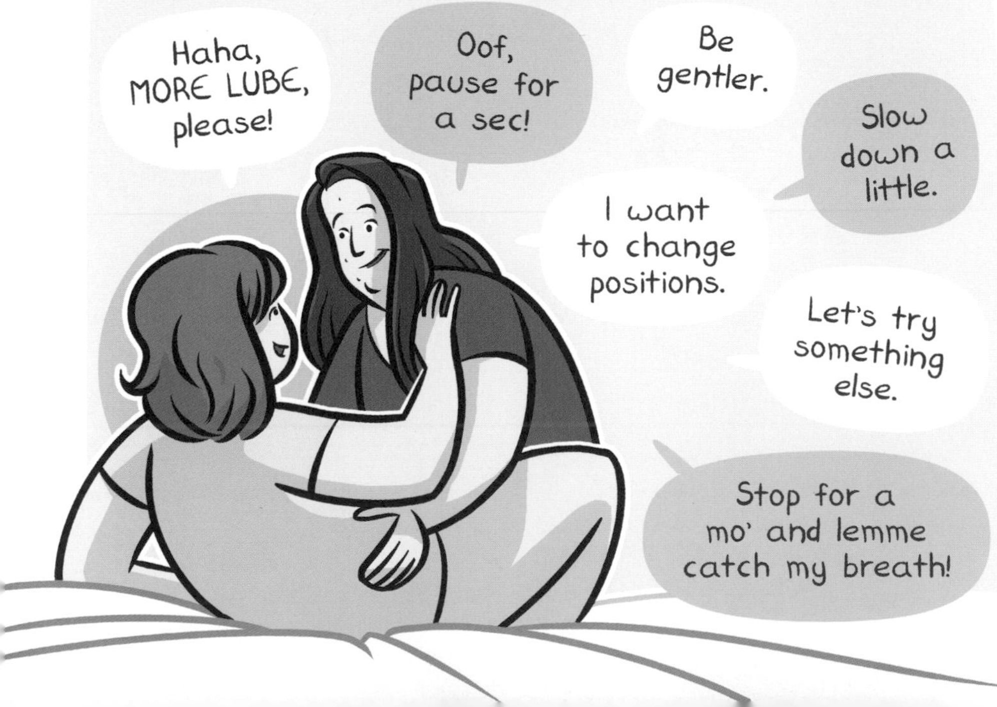

Haha, MORE LUBE, please!
Oof, pause for a sec!
Be gentler.
Slow down a little.
I want to change positions.
Let's try something else.
Stop for a mo' and lemme catch my breath!

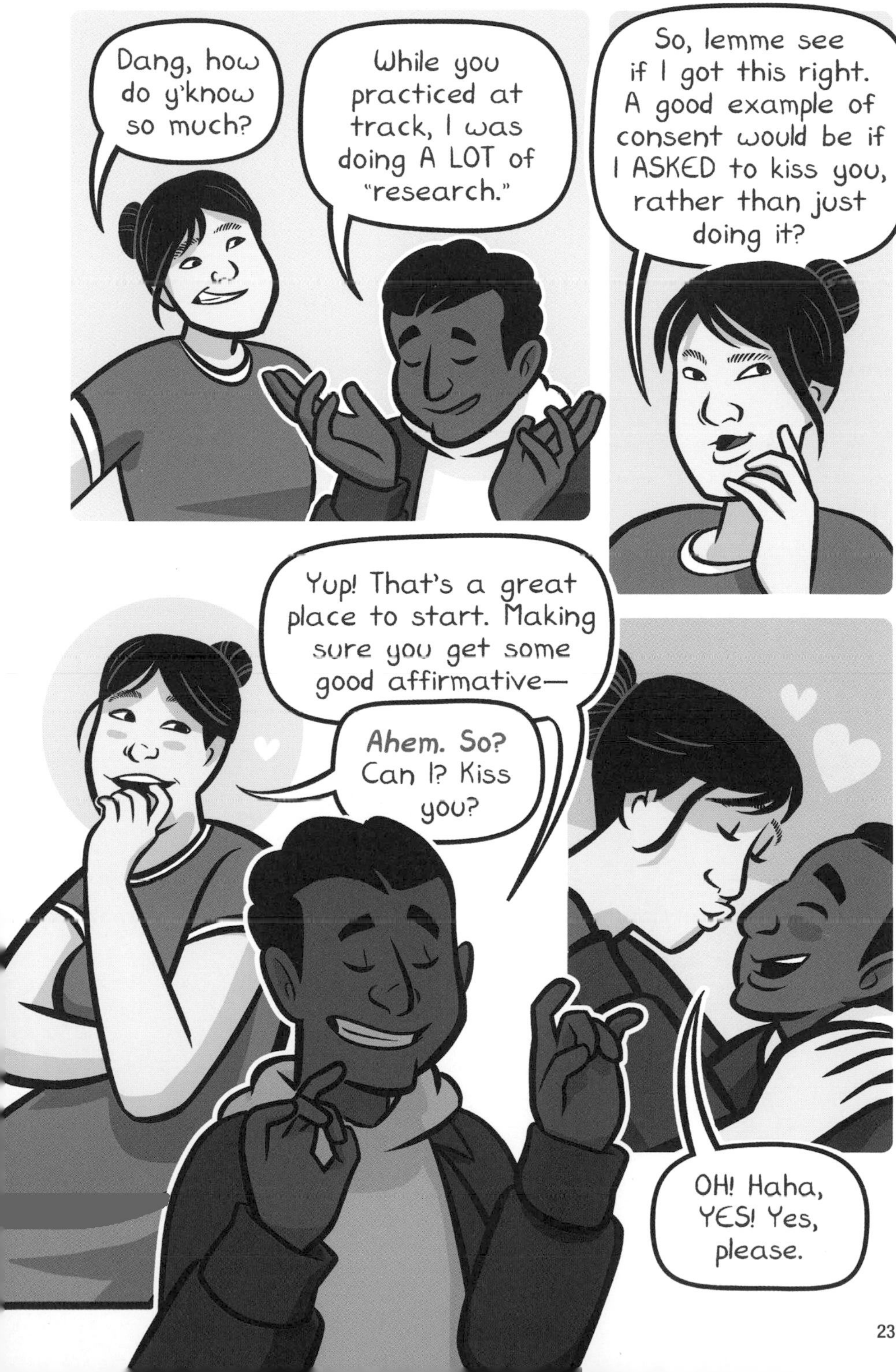
Dang, how do y'know so much?
While you practiced at track, I was doing A LOT of "research."
So, lemme see if I got this right. A good example of consent would be if I ASKED to kiss you, rather than just doing it?
Yup! That's a great place to start. Making sure you get some good affirmative—
Ahem. So? Can I? Kiss you?
OH! Haha, YES! Yes, please.

What is . . .
a relationship?

Dating! What . . . exactly . . . is
involved? How do you get from
flirting to dating? What kinds of
relationships are there? How do you
know which type you're in? Why is it
so hard to talk about all this?

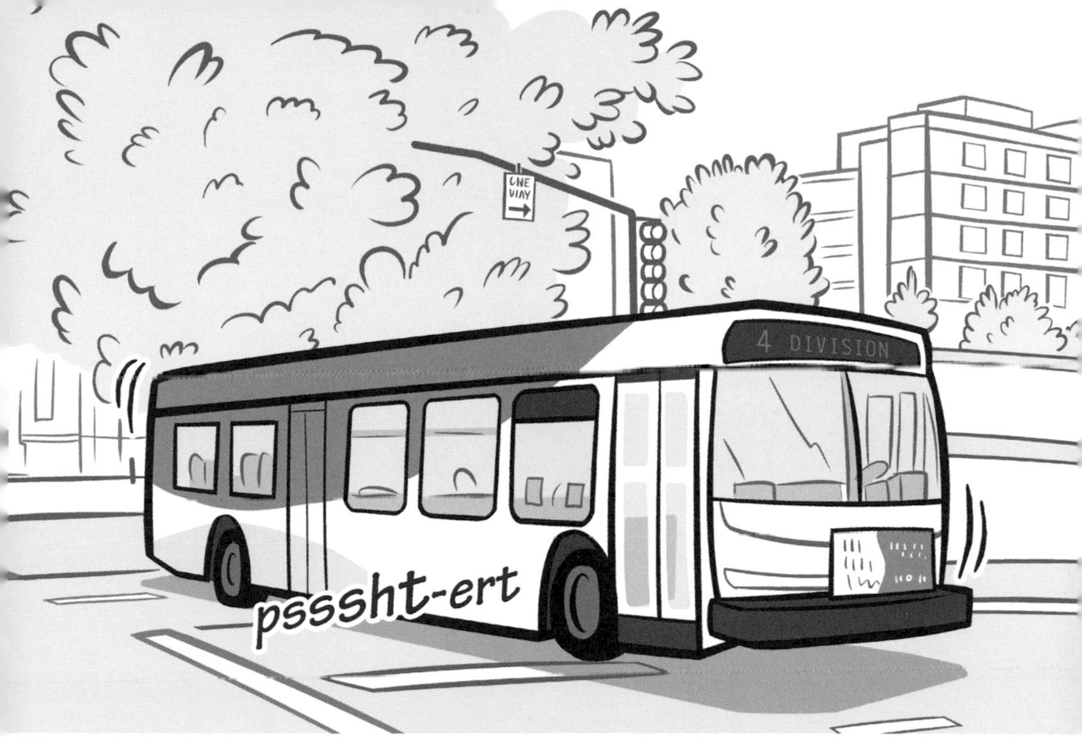
ONE WAY
4 DIVISION
pssssht-ert

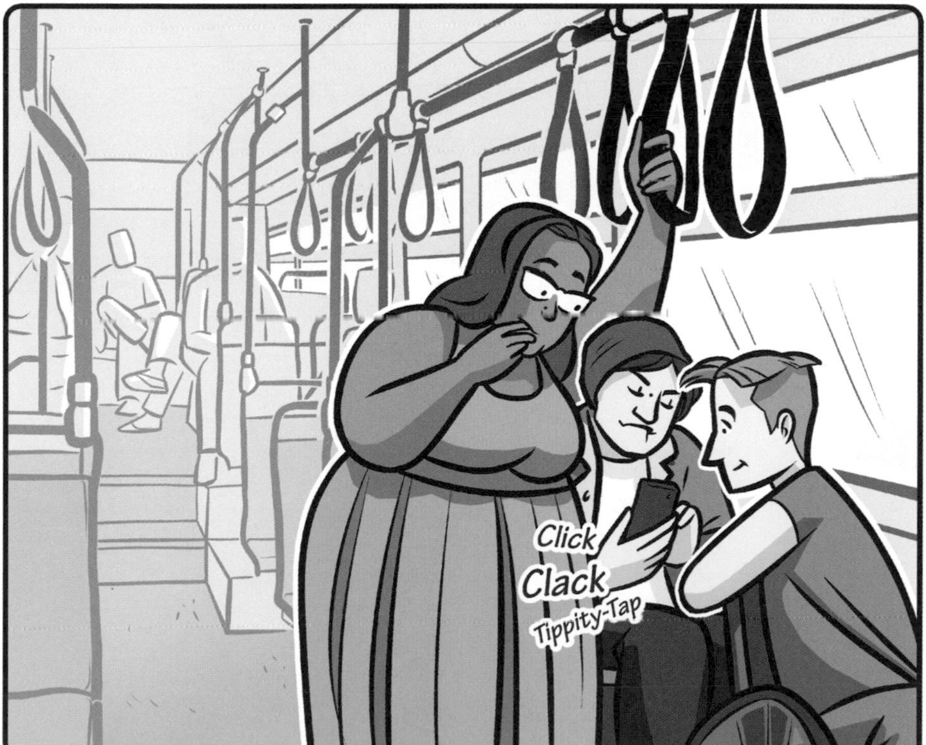
Click
Clack
Tippity-Tap

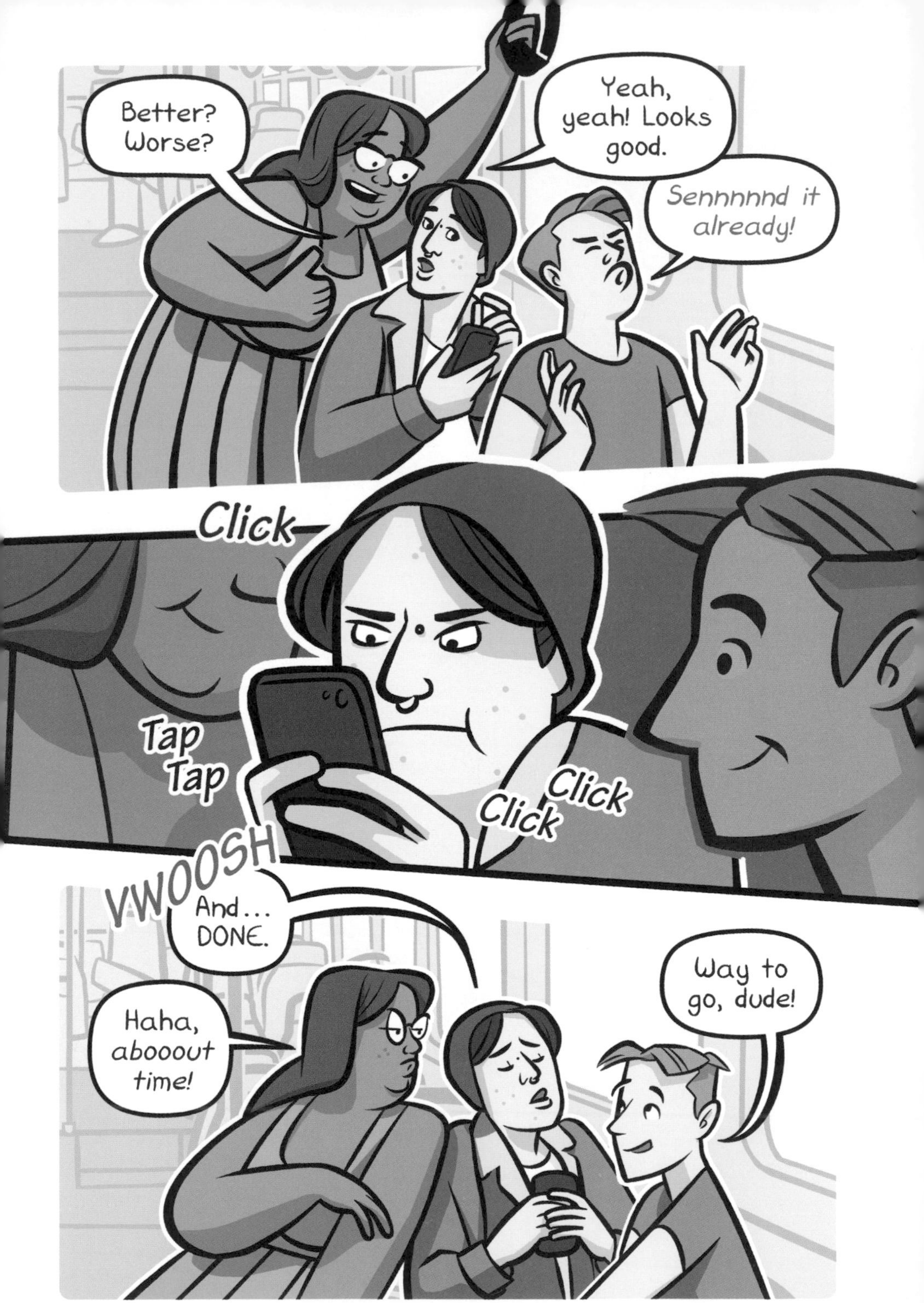
Better? Worse?
Yeah, yeah! Looks good.
Sennnnnd it already!
Click
Tap Tap
Click
Click
VWOOSH
And... DONE.
Haha, aboooout time!
Way to go, dude!

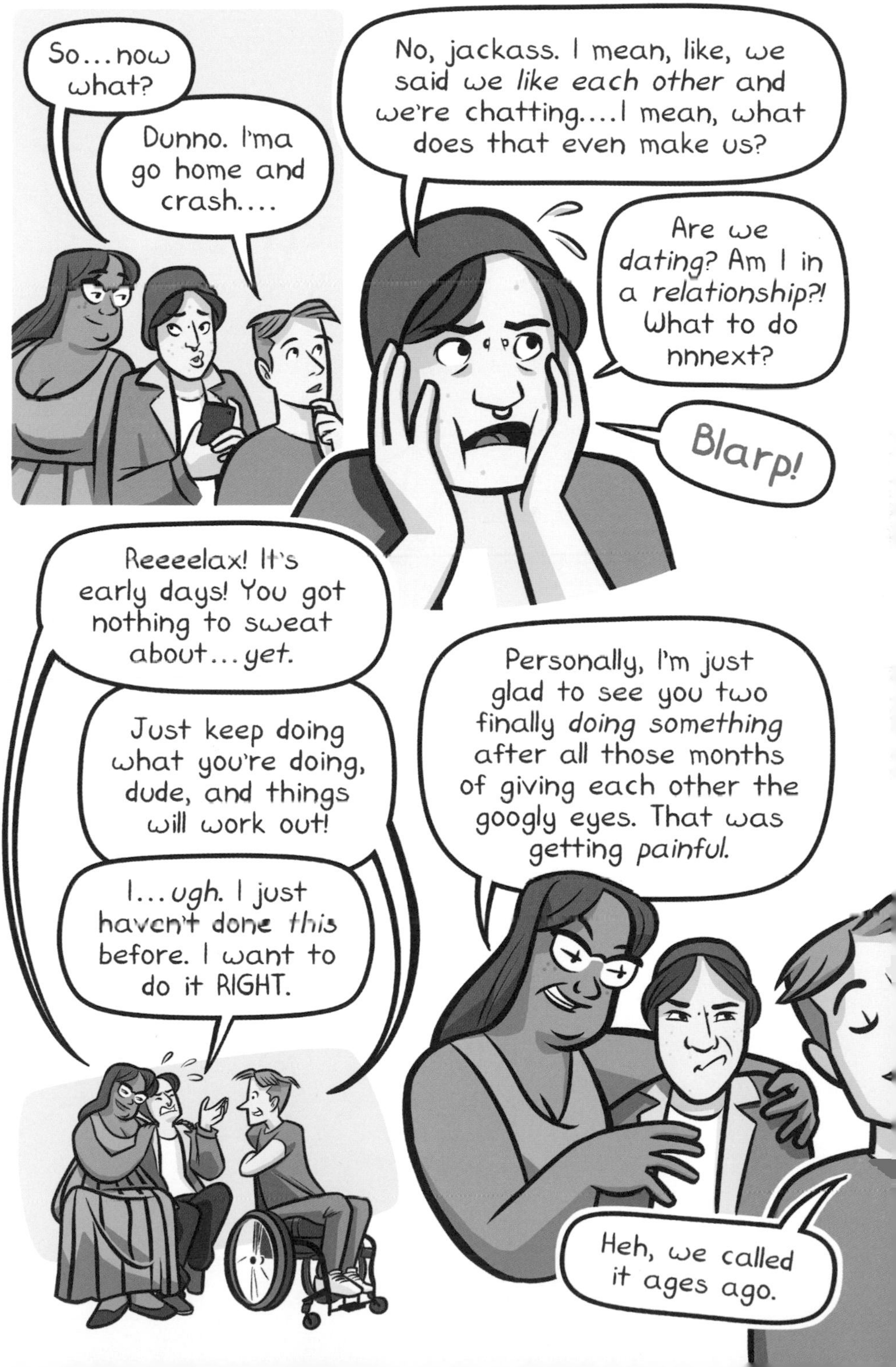
So...now what?
Dunno. I'ma go home and crash....
No, jackass. I mean, like, we said we *like each other* and we're chatting....I mean, what does that even make us?
Are we *dating*? Am I in a *relationship?!* What to do nnnext?
Blarp!
Reeeelax! It's early days! You got nothing to sweat about...*yet*.
Just keep doing what you're doing, dude, and things will work out!
I...*ugh*. I just haven't done *this* before. I want to do it RIGHT.
Personally, I'm just glad to see you two finally *doing something* after all those months of giving each other the googly eyes. That was getting *painful*.
Heh, we called it ages ago.

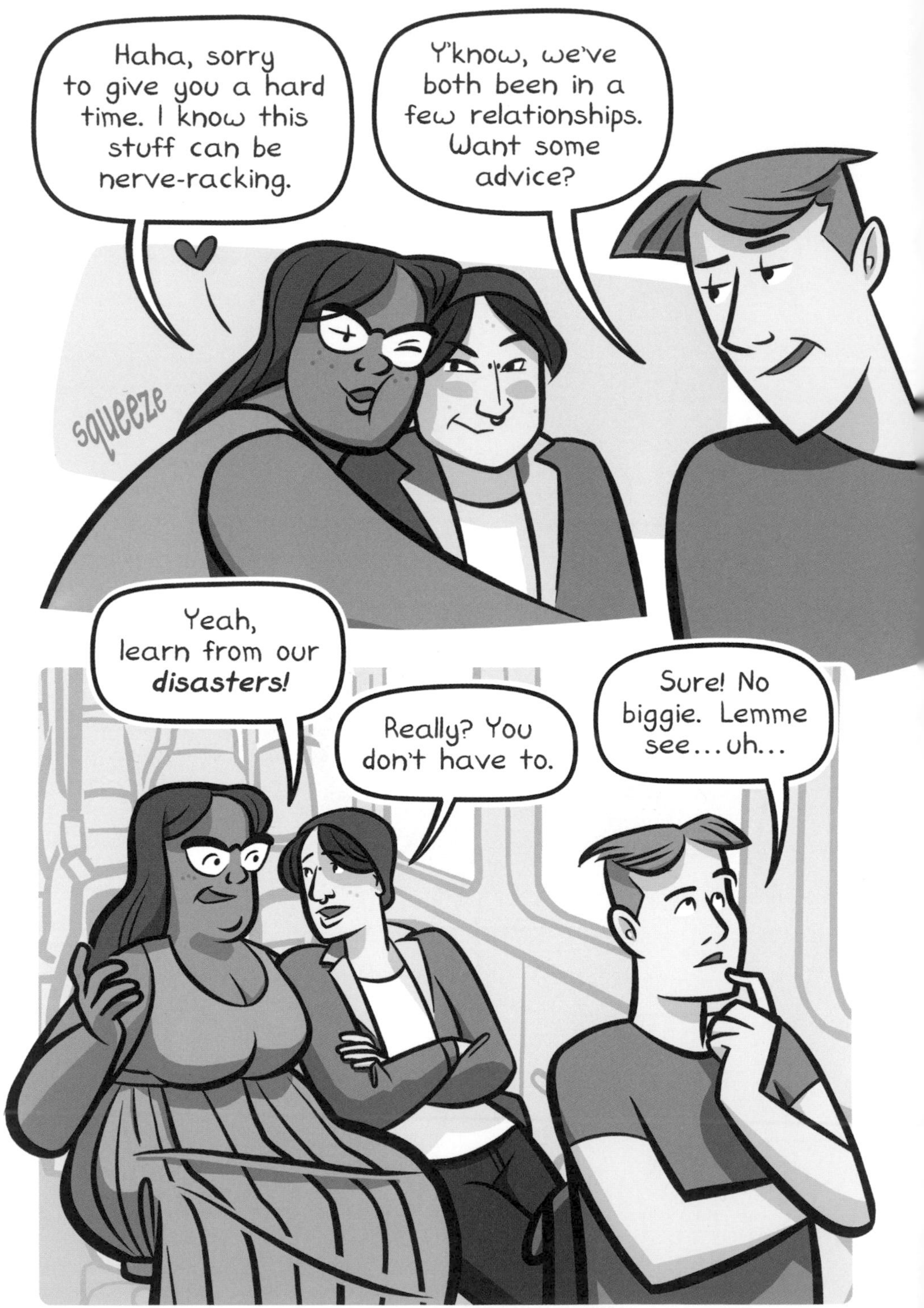
Haha, sorry to give you a hard time. I know this stuff can be nerve-racking.
Y'know, we've both been in a few relationships. Want some advice?
squeeze
Yeah, learn from our **disasters!**
Really? You don't have to.
Sure! No biggie. Lemme see... uh...

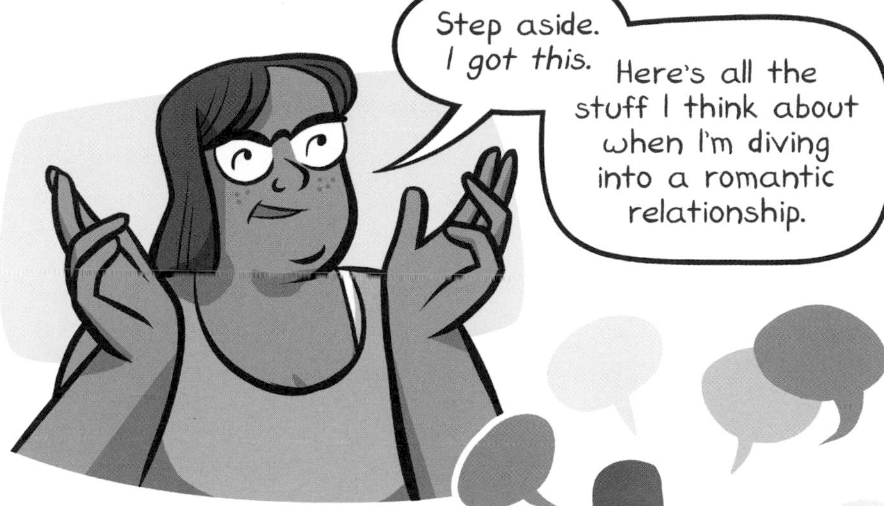
Step aside. I got this.
Here's all the stuff I think about when I'm diving into a romantic relationship.

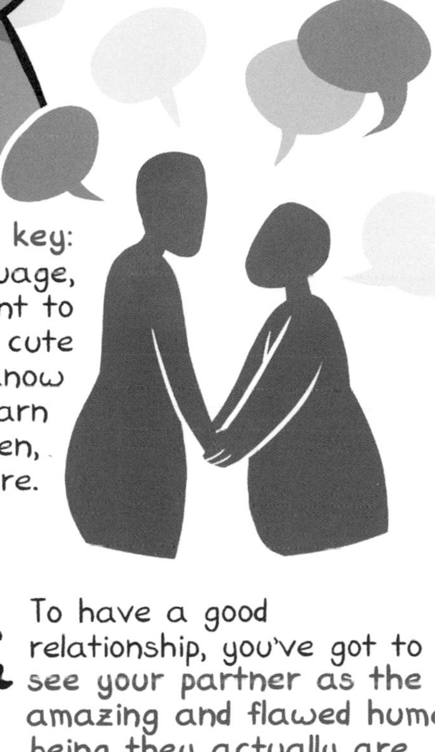

Communication is key: talking, texting, body language, and everything else. Want to start something with a cute someone and really get to know them? Well, you have to learn to open up, listen, and share.

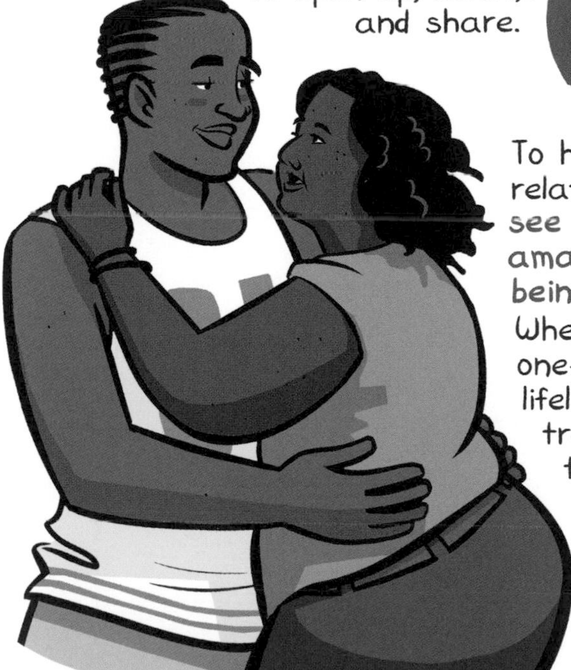

To have a good relationship, you've got to see your partner as the amazing and flawed human being they actually are. Whether you're having a one-night stand or you're lifelong soul mates, try to treat those around you the way you want to be treated, and expect the same in return.

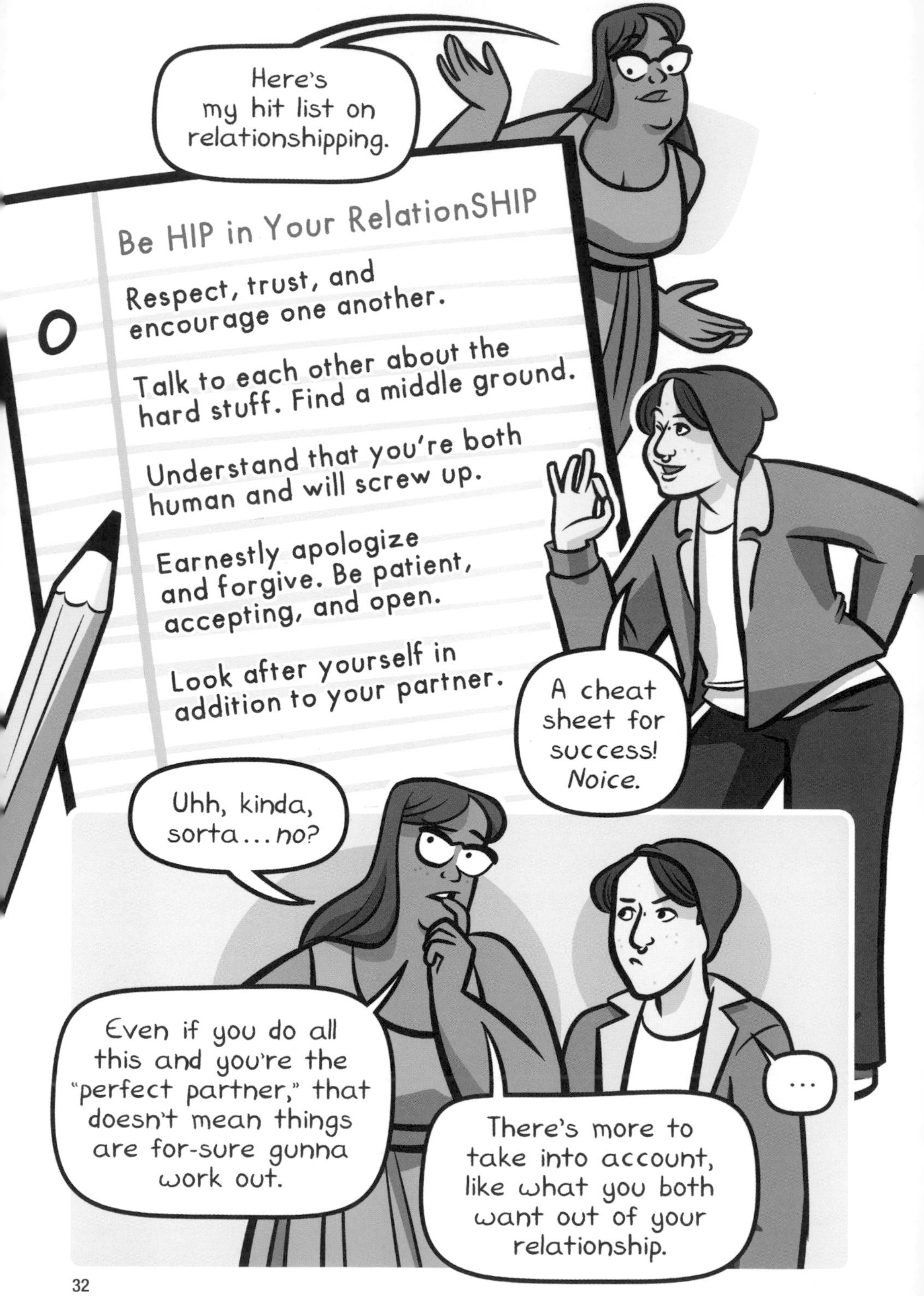
Here's my hit list on relationshipping.
Be HIP in Your RelationSHIP
Respect, trust, and encourage one another.
Talk to each other about the hard stuff. Find a middle ground.
Understand that you're both human and will screw up.
Earnestly apologize and forgive. Be patient, accepting, and open.
Look after yourself in addition to your partner.
A cheat sheet for success! Noice.
Uhh, kinda, sorta... *no?*
Even if you do all this and you're the "perfect partner," that doesn't mean things are for-sure gunna work out.
...
There's more to take into account, like what you both want out of your relationship.

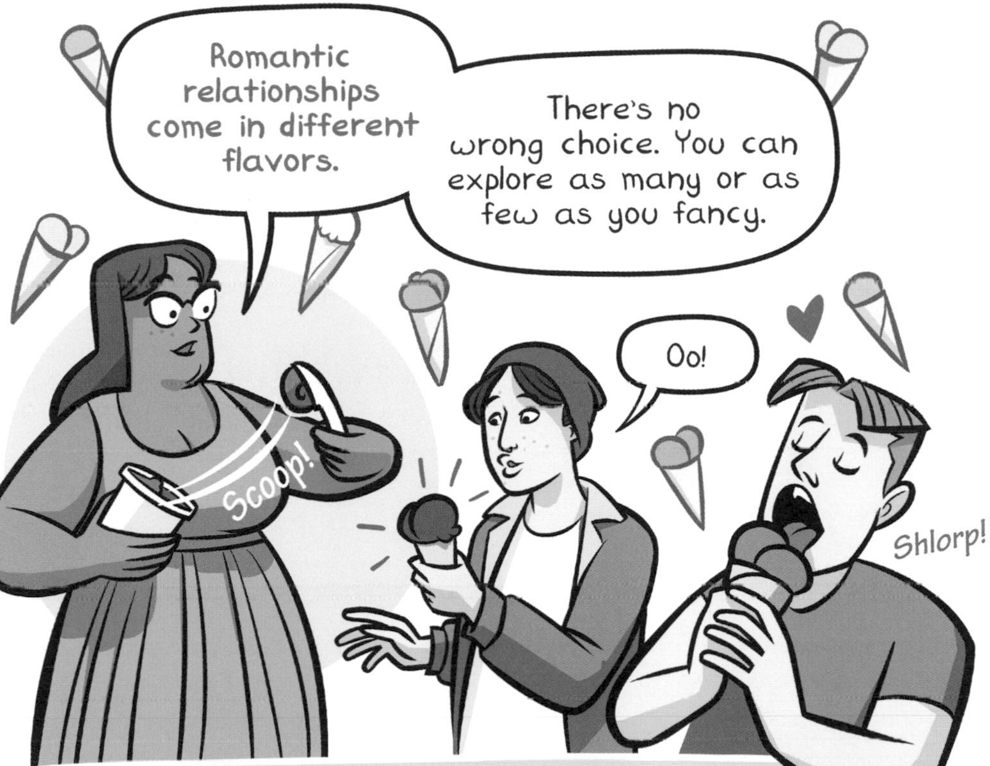
Romantic relationships come in different flavors.
There's no wrong choice. You can explore as many or as few as you fancy.
Scoop!
Oo!
Shlorp!

Monogamous Relationships

Being Exclusive

Probably the most traditional relationship type out there. Two people are romantic and intimate with each other and no one else.

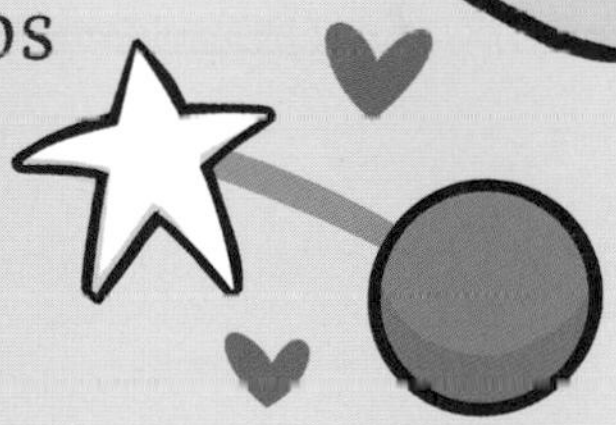

Polyamorous Relationships

Poly, Polyam

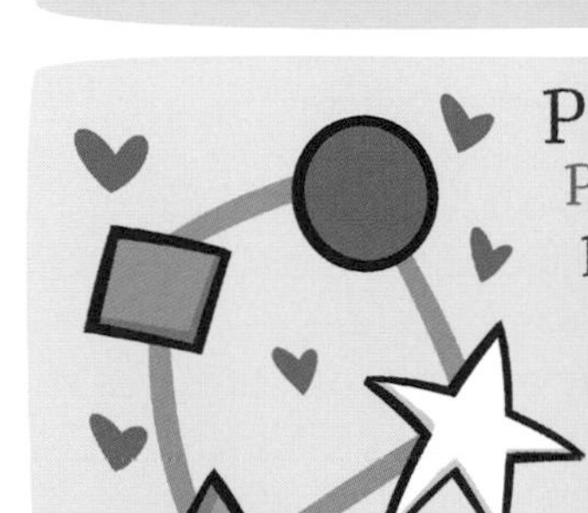

People in polyamorous relationships can have romantic, intimate, and loving connections with more than one partner. How these relationships are structured is different from person to person and group to group.

Open Relationships
Open, Monogamish, Swinging

Folks in committed open relationships may still have sexual or intimate experiences with others, while staying focused on each other.

Casual Relationships
Friends with Benefits, Hookup, Fling

People in casual relationships have fewer expectations and commitments to one another, often focusing on the more sexual side of things.

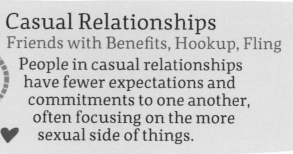

Companionate Relationships

People in this kind of relationship are focused on the romance or intimacy they have with each other and have little or no interest in the physical and sexual side.

And then there's the most important relationship you'll ever have: the one you have with **yourself!**

Make sure to extend the same kindness, care, and forgiveness to yourself that you share with others. You deserve love, especially from yourself. Relationships will come and go. But you? You're with yourself for life.

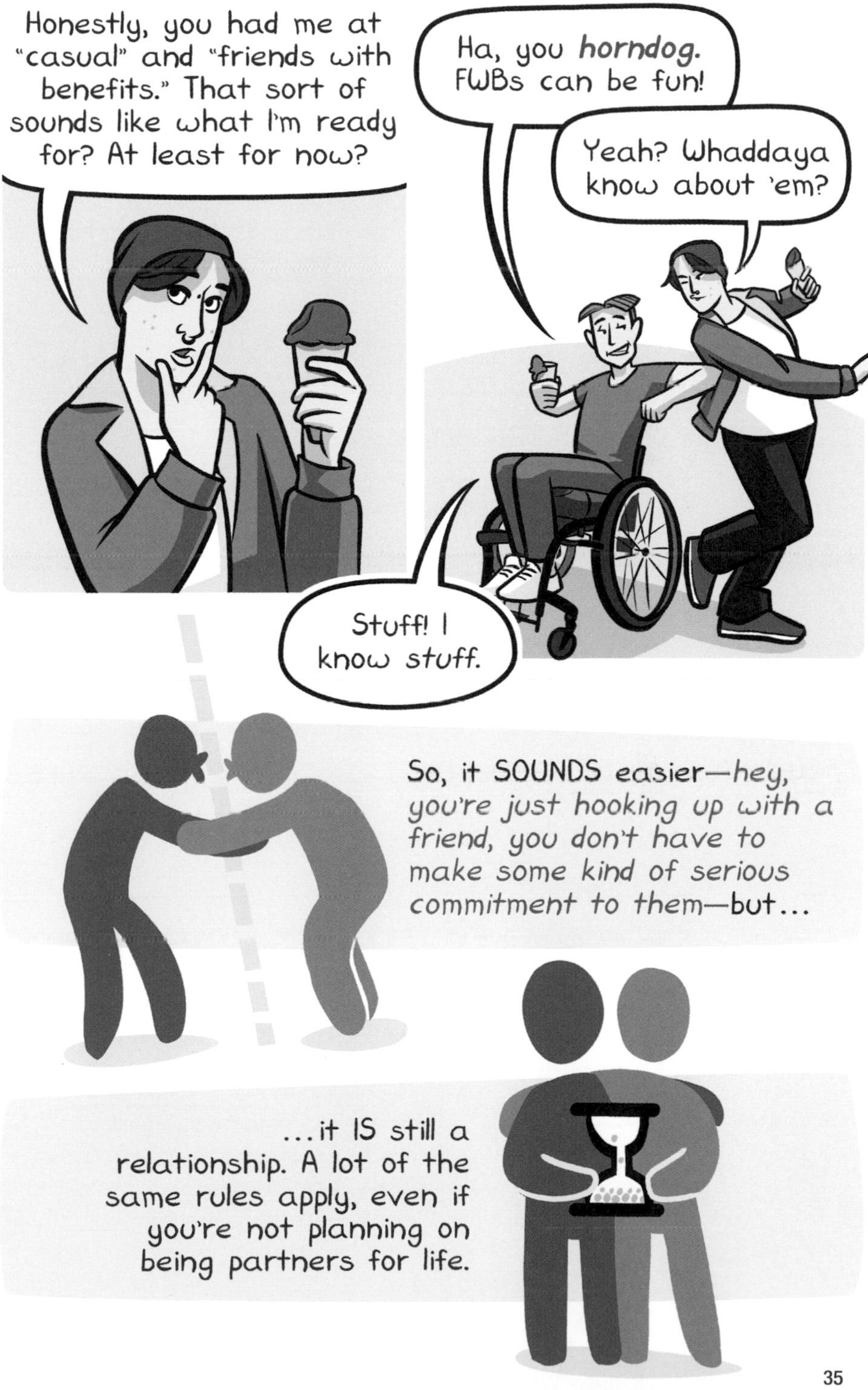
Honestly, you had me at "casual" and "friends with benefits." That sort of sounds like what I'm ready for? At least for now?
Ha, you **horndog.** FWBs can be fun!
Yeah? Whaddaya know about 'em?
Stuff! I know stuff.
So, it SOUNDS easier—*hey, you're just hooking up with a friend, you don't have to make some kind of serious commitment to them*—**but**...
...it IS still a relationship. A lot of the same rules apply, even if you're not planning on being partners for life.

To avoid getting hurt or unintentionally hurting your potential partner, you'll need to do some talking!

If you two don't chat about your boundaries and exactly how much you can give to each other, you might find yourself going in with unreasonable expectations, developing feelings that aren't reciprocated, or hurting one another.

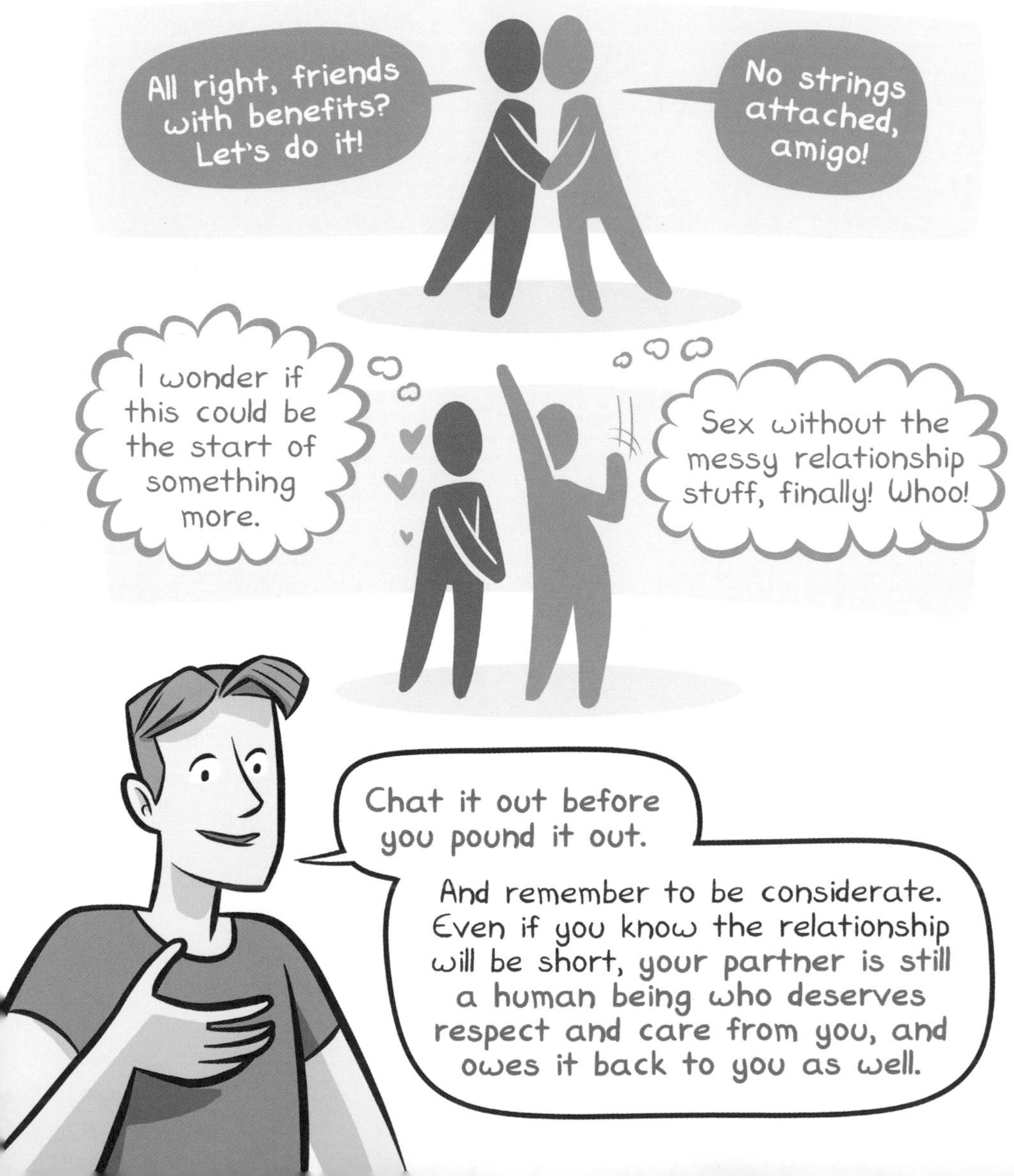

All right, friends with benefits? Let's do it!
No strings attached, amigo!
I wonder if this could be the start of something more.
Sex without the messy relationship stuff, finally! Whoo!
Chat it out before you pound it out.
And remember to be considerate. Even if you know the relationship will be short, your partner is still a human being who deserves respect and care from you, and owes it back to you as well.

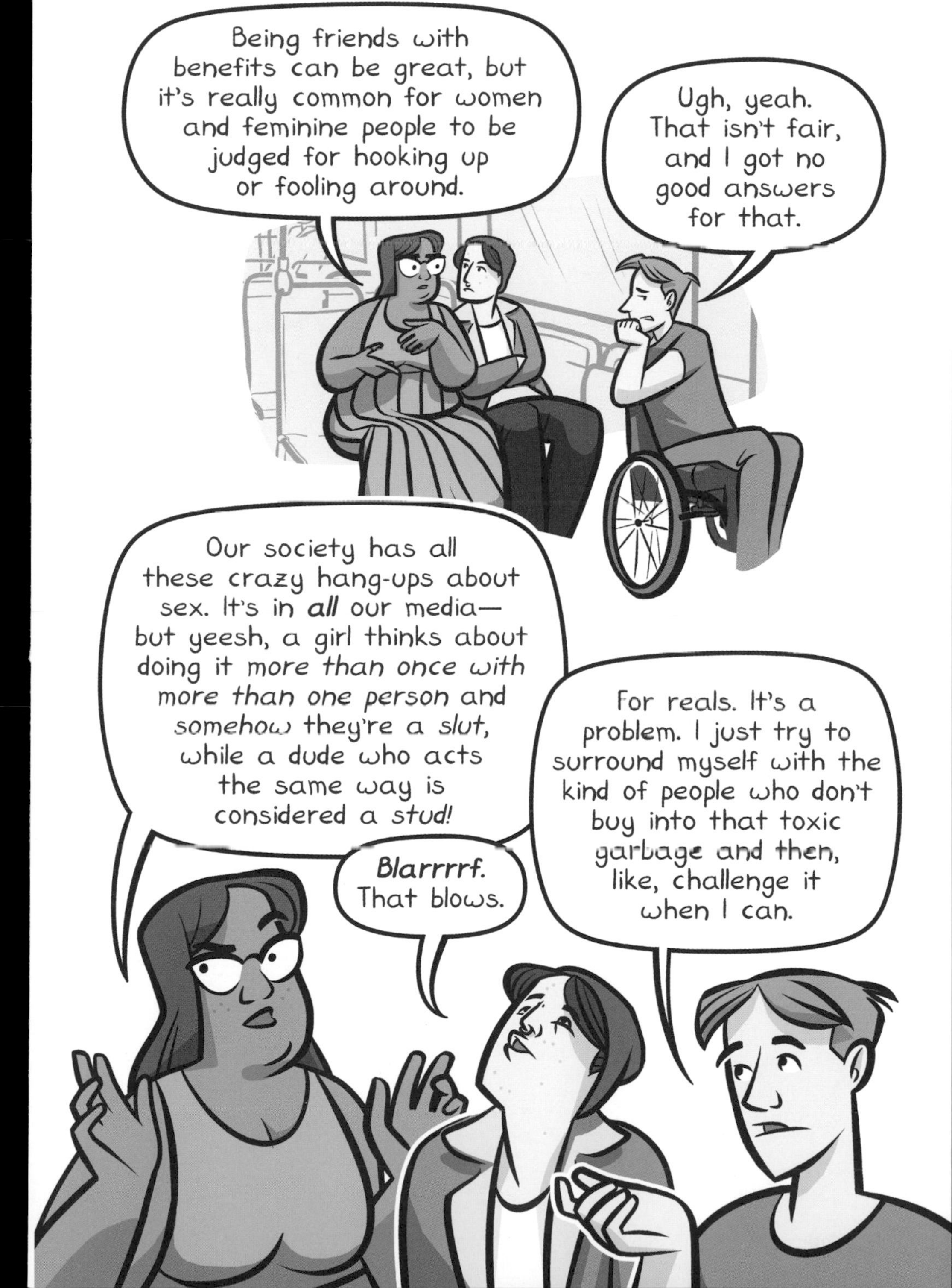
Being friends with benefits can be great, but it's really common for women and feminine people to be judged for hooking up or fooling around.
Ugh, yeah. That isn't fair, and I got no good answers for that.
Our society has all these crazy hang-ups about sex. It's in *all* our media—but yeesh, a girl thinks about doing it *more than once* with *more than one person* and *somehow* they're a *slut*, while a dude who acts the same way is considered a *stud!*
Blarrrrf. That blows.
For reals. It's a problem. I just try to surround myself with the kind of people who don't buy into that toxic garbage and then, like, challenge it when I can.

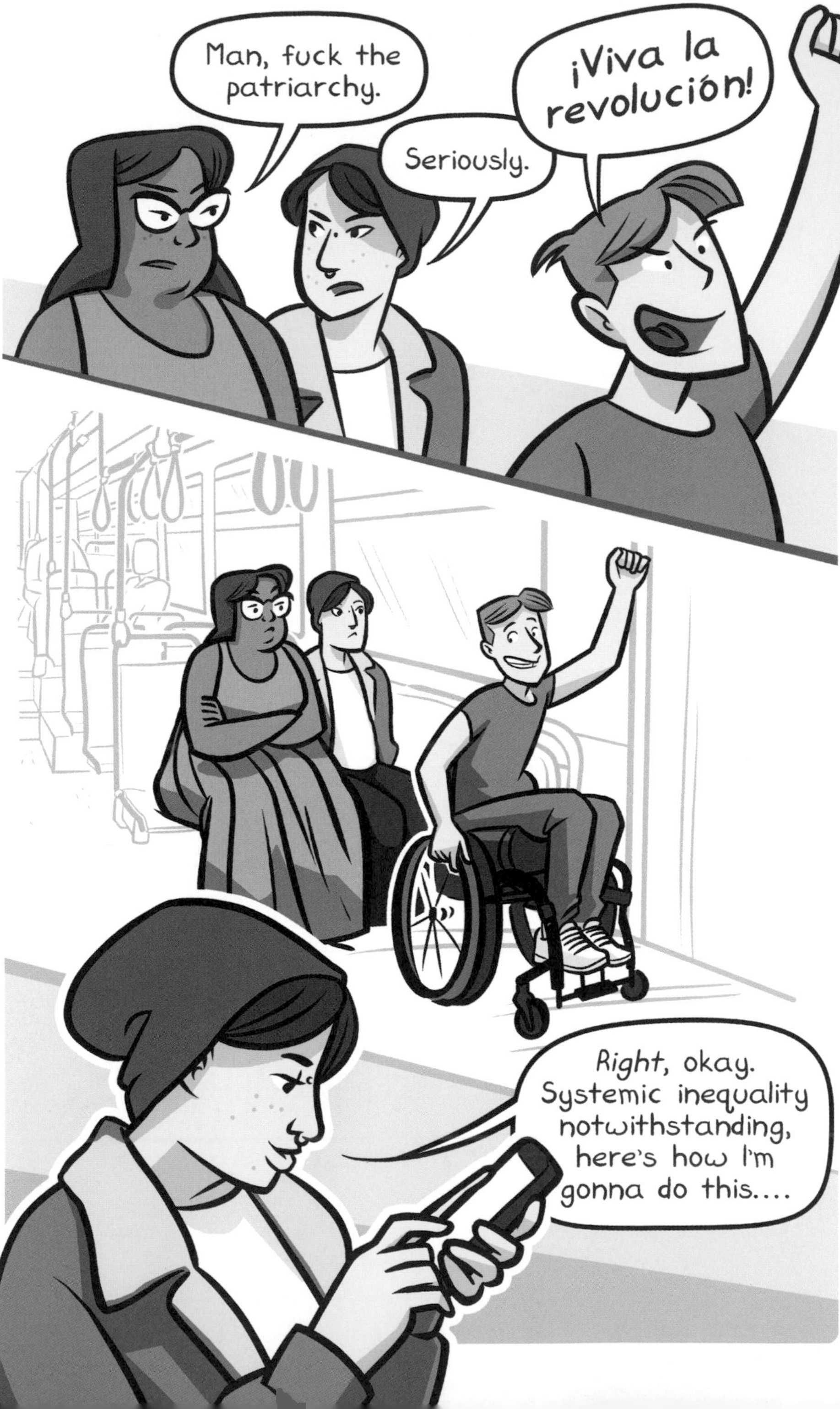
Man, fuck the patriarchy.
Seriously.
¡Viva la revolución!
Right, okay. Systemic inequality notwithstanding, here's how I'm gonna do this....

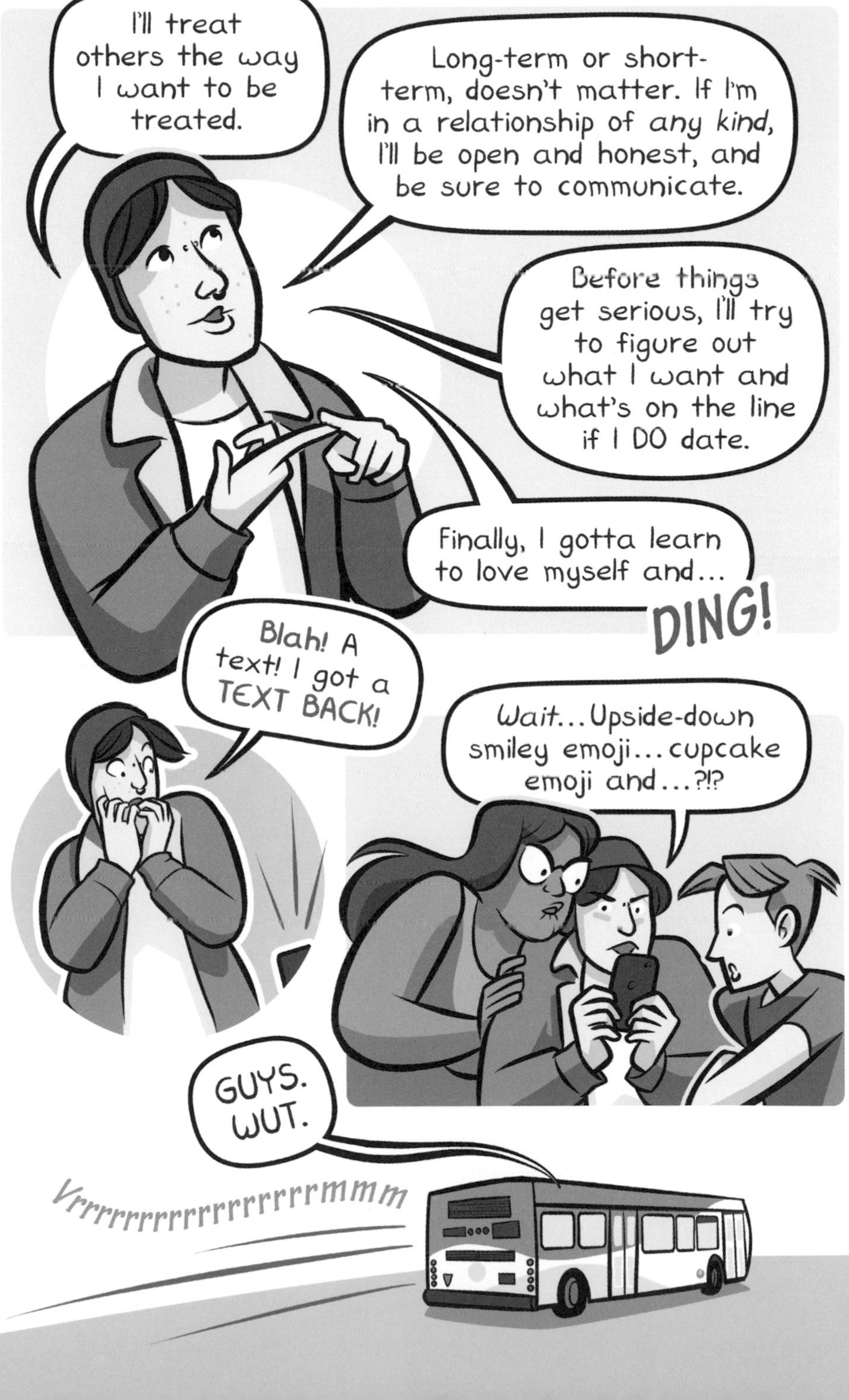
I'll treat others the way I want to be treated.
Long-term or short-term, doesn't matter. If I'm in a relationship of *any kind*, I'll be open and honest, and be sure to communicate.
Before things get serious, I'll try to figure out what I want and what's on the line if I DO date.
Finally, I gotta learn to love myself and...
DING!
Blah! A text! I got a TEXT BACK!
*Wait...*Upside-down smiley emoji...cupcake emoji and...?!?
GUYS. WUT.
Vrrrrrrrrrrrrrrrrmmm

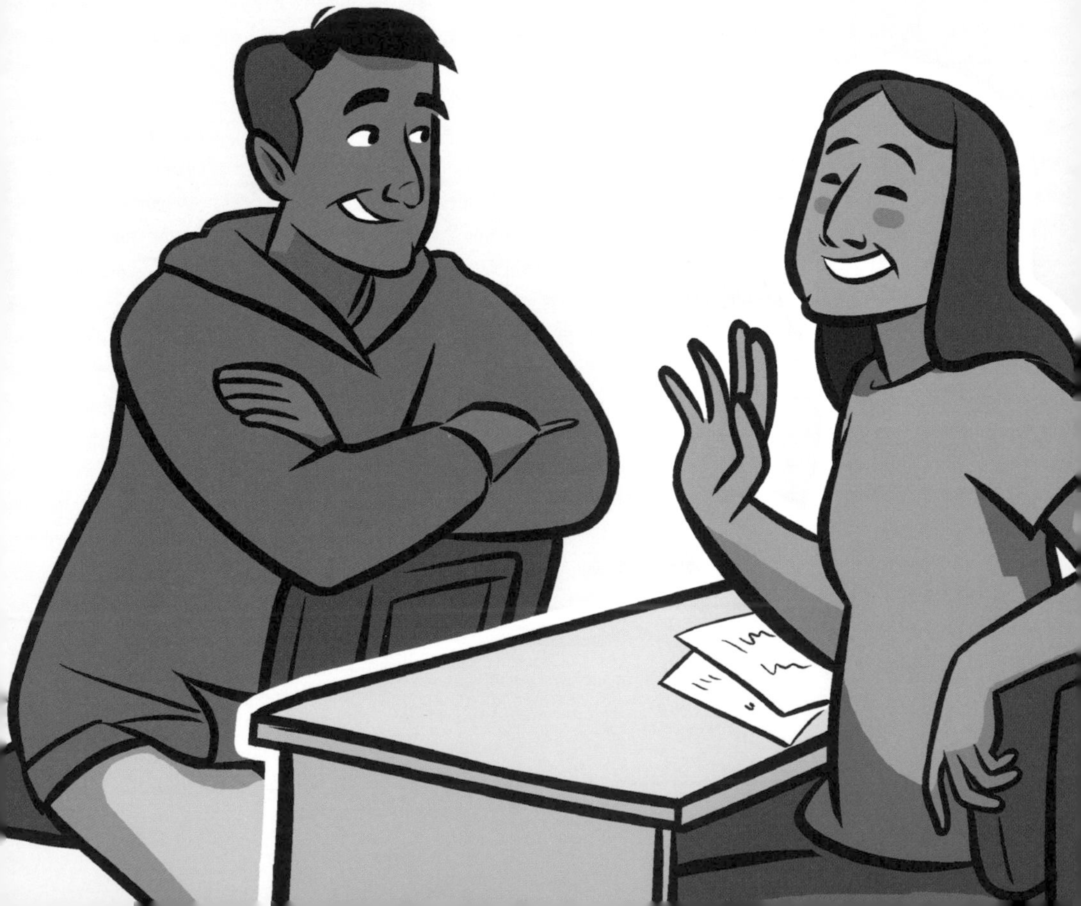

What are . . . gender and sexuality?

Why do gender and sexuality seem so complicated? How do you learn about them? How do you ask people about their gender and sexuality? Do we think about these things differently today than we did in the past? And how do pronouns work?

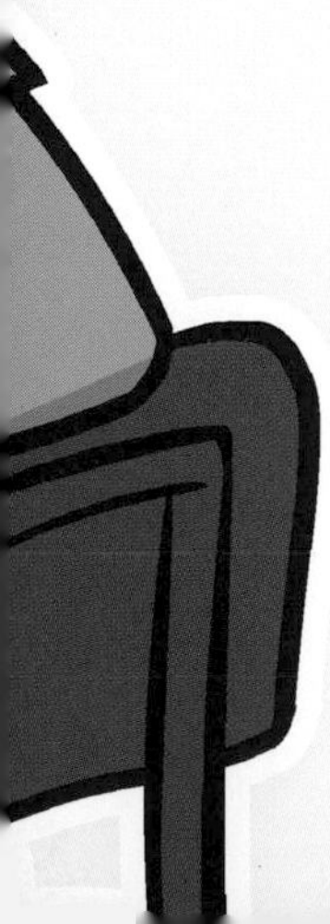

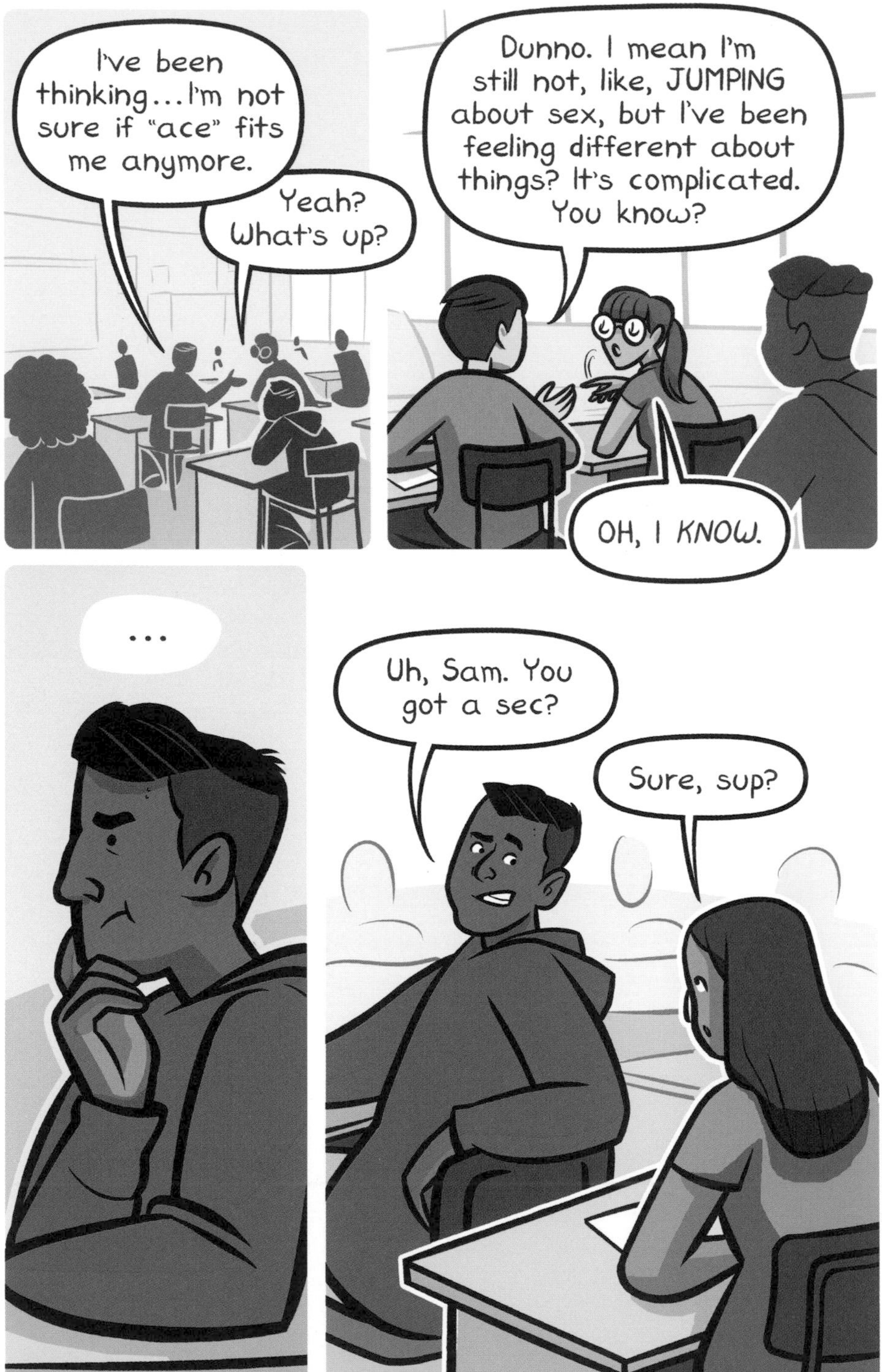
I've been thinking...I'm not sure if "ace" fits me anymore.
Yeah? What's up?
Dunno. I mean I'm still not, like, JUMPING about sex, but I've been feeling different about things? It's complicated. You know?
OH, I KNOW.
...
Uh, Sam. You got a sec?
Sure, sup?

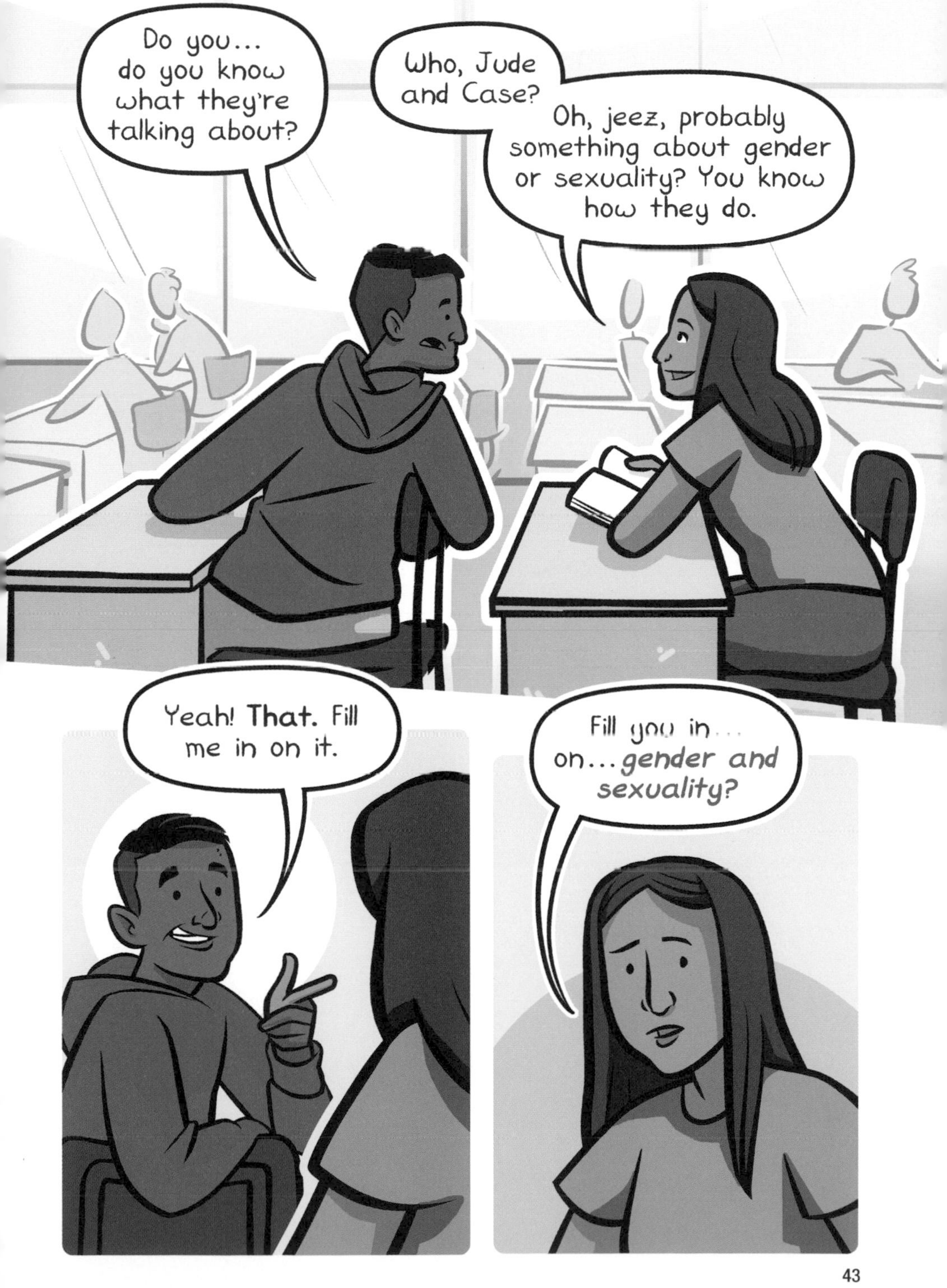
Do you... do you know what they're talking about?
Who, Jude and Case?
Oh, jeez, probably something about gender or sexuality? You know how they do.
Yeah! **That.** Fill me in on it.
Fill you in... on... *gender and sexuality?*

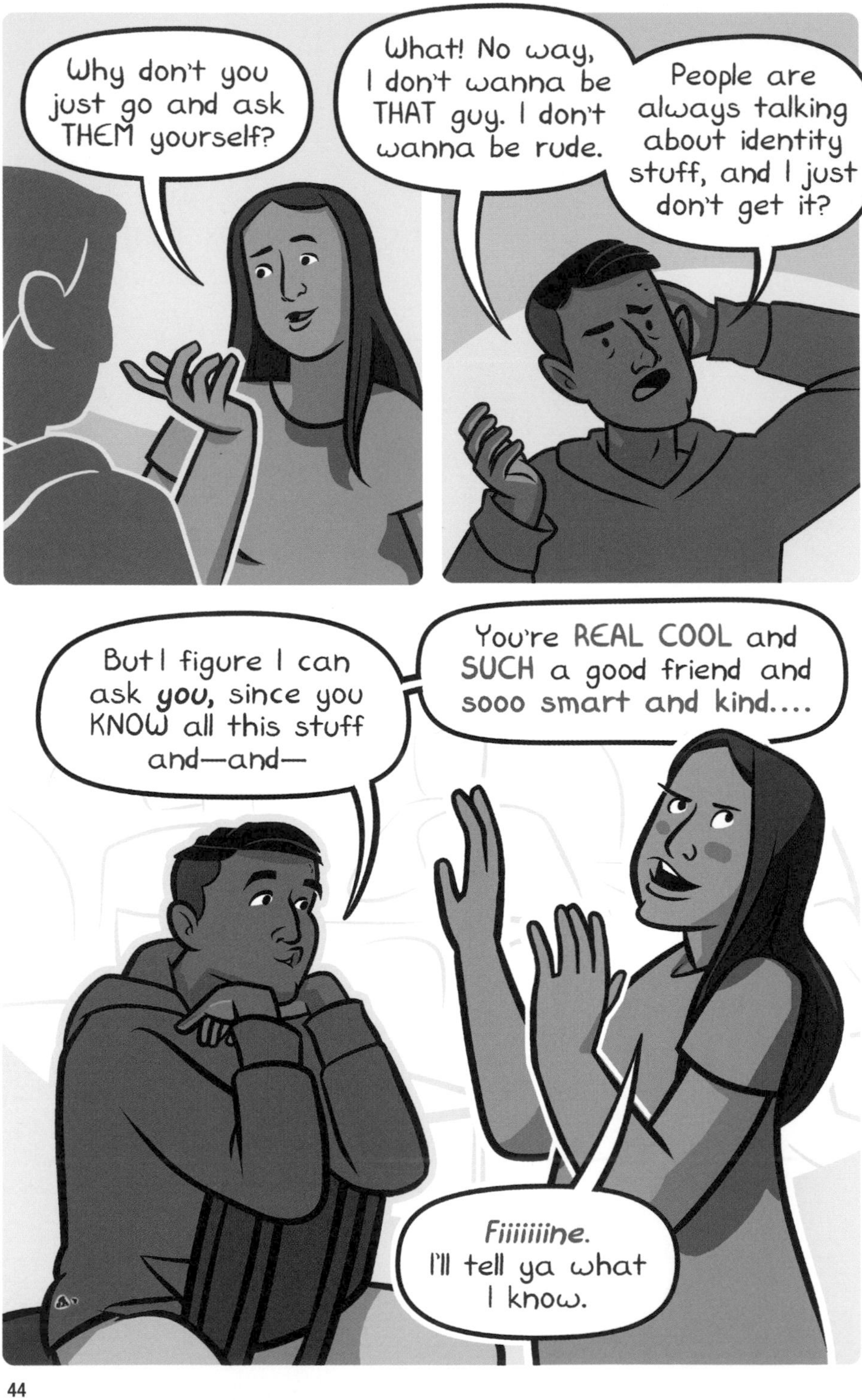
Why don't you just go and ask THEM yourself?
What! No way, I don't wanna be THAT guy. I don't wanna be rude.
People are always talking about identity stuff, and I just don't get it?
But I figure I can ask **you,** since you KNOW all this stuff and—and—
You're REAL COOL and SUCH a good friend and sooo smart and kind....
Fiiiiiiine.
I'll tell ya what I know.

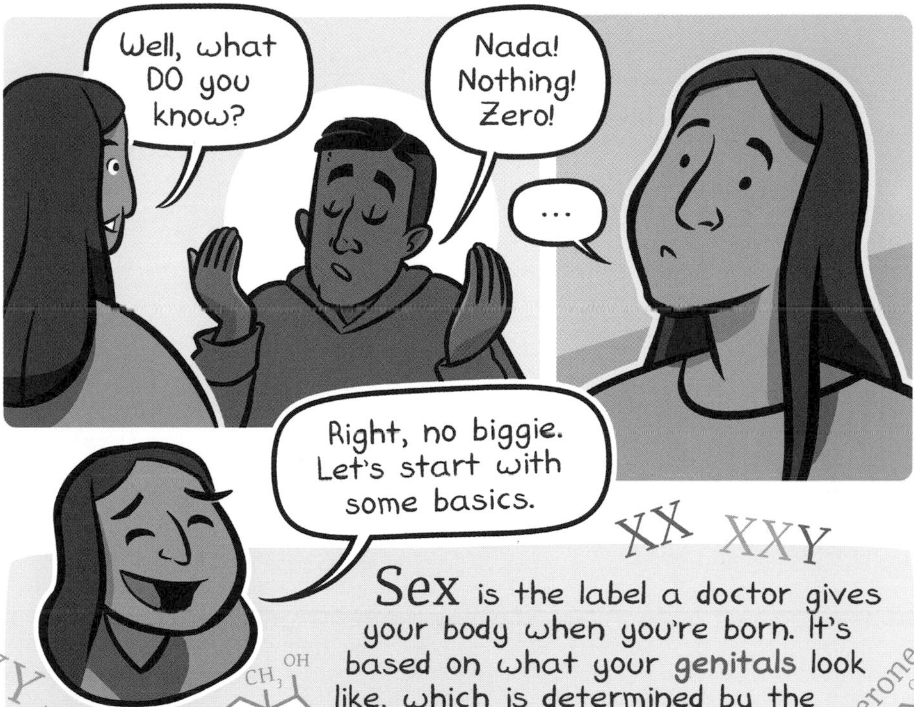
Well, what DO you know?
Nada! Nothing! Zero!
...
Right, no biggie. Let's start with some basics.
XX
XXY

Sex is the label a doctor gives your body when you're born. It's based on what your **genitals** look like, which is determined by the **chromosomes** and **hormones** you have. It's typically male, female, or intersex.

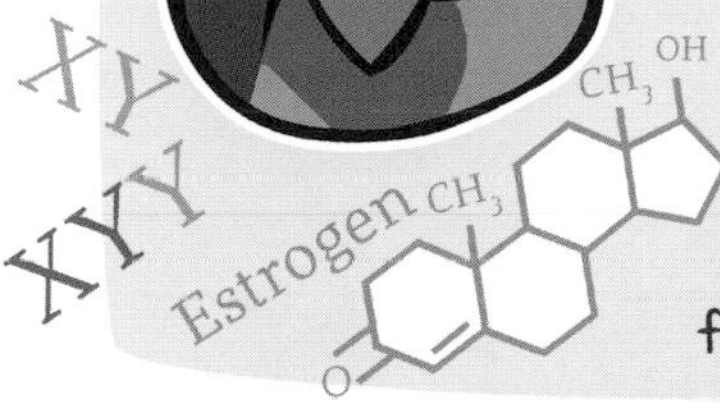
XY
XYY
Estrogen
CH3
OH
O

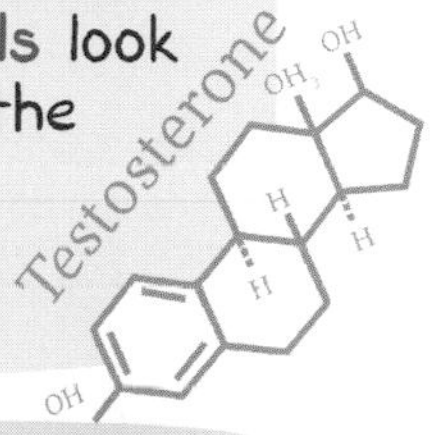
Testosterone
OH
H
OH

Gender is your **behavior, characteristics,** and the **expectations society** has of you. It's how you **identify,** how you **present** yourself, and how the world **perceives** you. Traditionally it's been seen as a binary with just two options, masculine or feminine, but it's much more like a spectrum, with **many different possibilities.**

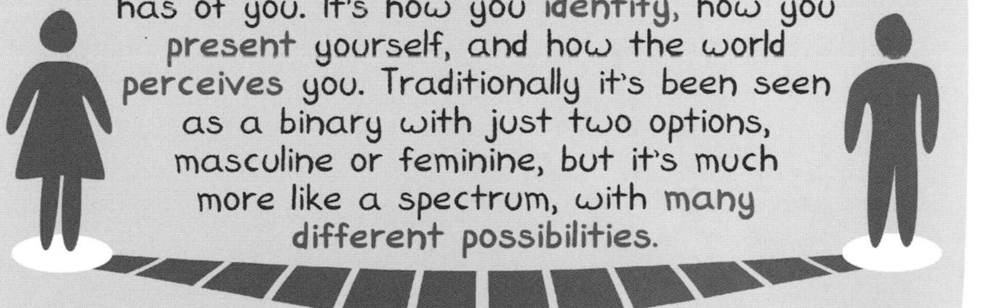

Sexuality describes your sexual orientation. It helps explain who and what you're attracted to and how you feel sexual desire.

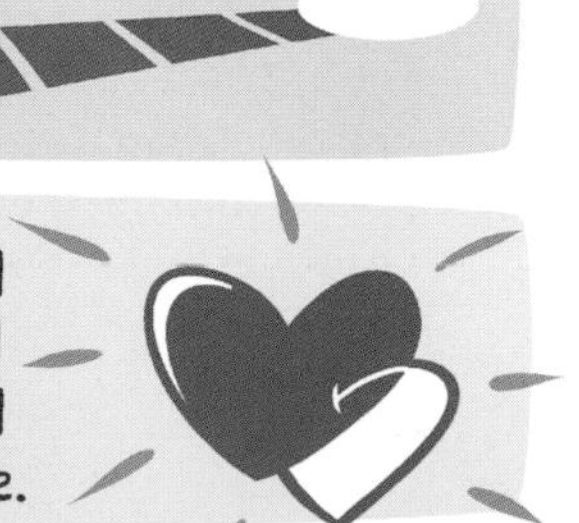

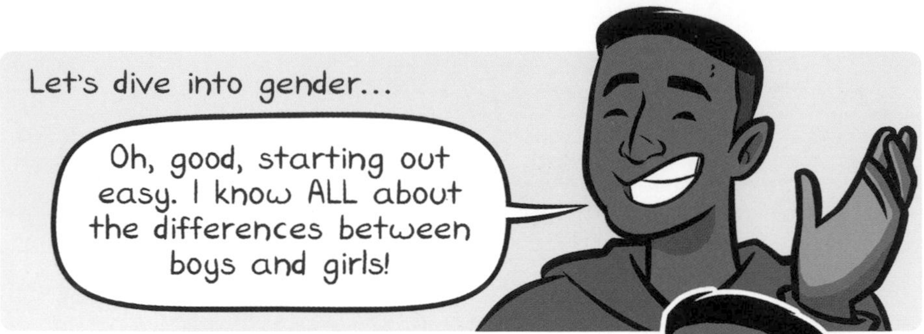
Let's dive into gender...
Oh, good, starting out easy. I know ALL about the differences between boys and girls!

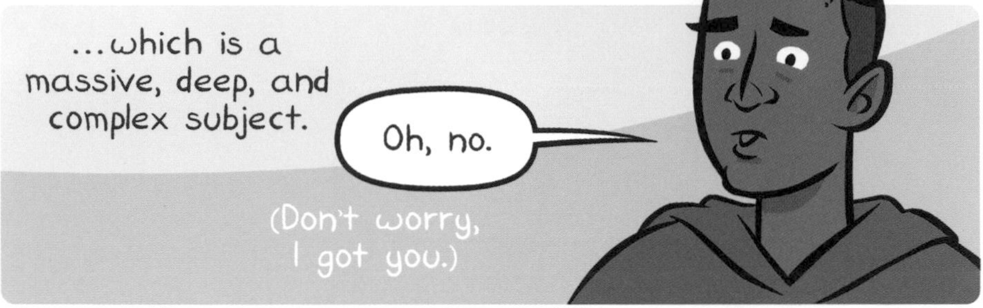
...which is a massive, deep, and complex subject.
Oh, no.
(Don't worry, I got you.)

Gender is defined by the society and the culture you live in. It's the expectations and assumptions our community has for how we are "supposed" to behave according to our perceived sex.

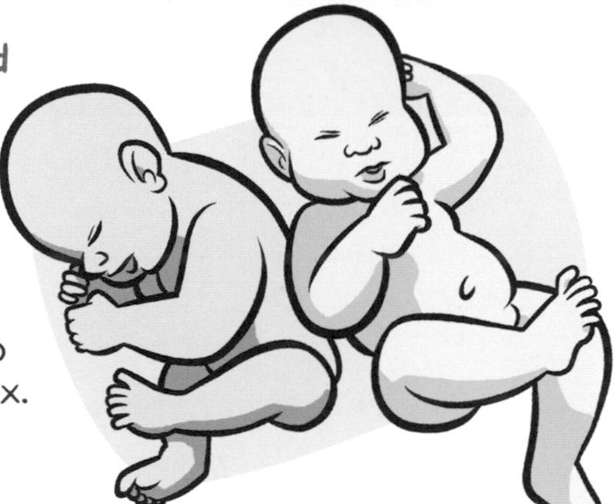

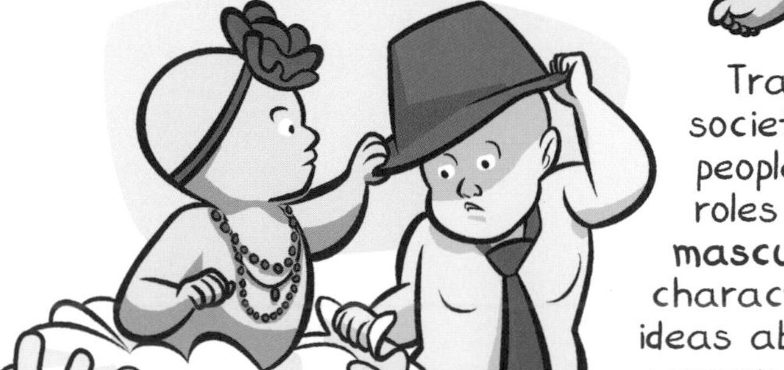

Traditionally, societies have placed people into **male** or **female** roles that are defined by **masculine** and **feminine** characteristics. These are ideas about how a man or woman should act, dress, think, and work.

This male/female gender binary works for some folks but leaves a ton of others out.

It's an obsolete viewpoint based on a lack of understanding of just how diverse and nuanced people can be.

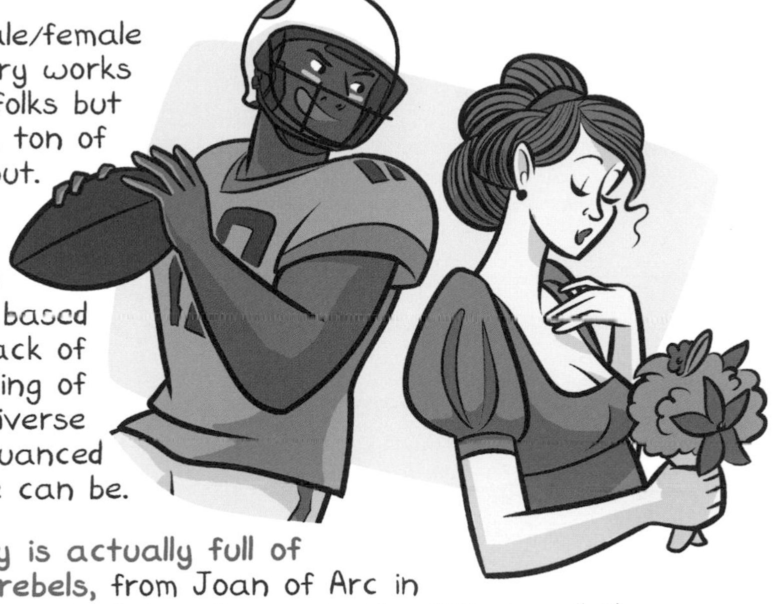

History is actually full of gender rebels, from Joan of Arc in the 1400s to Sylvia Rivera in the 1970s to all the people who are "out" today. Fortunately, stepping outside the binary is becoming better understood and respected nowadays.

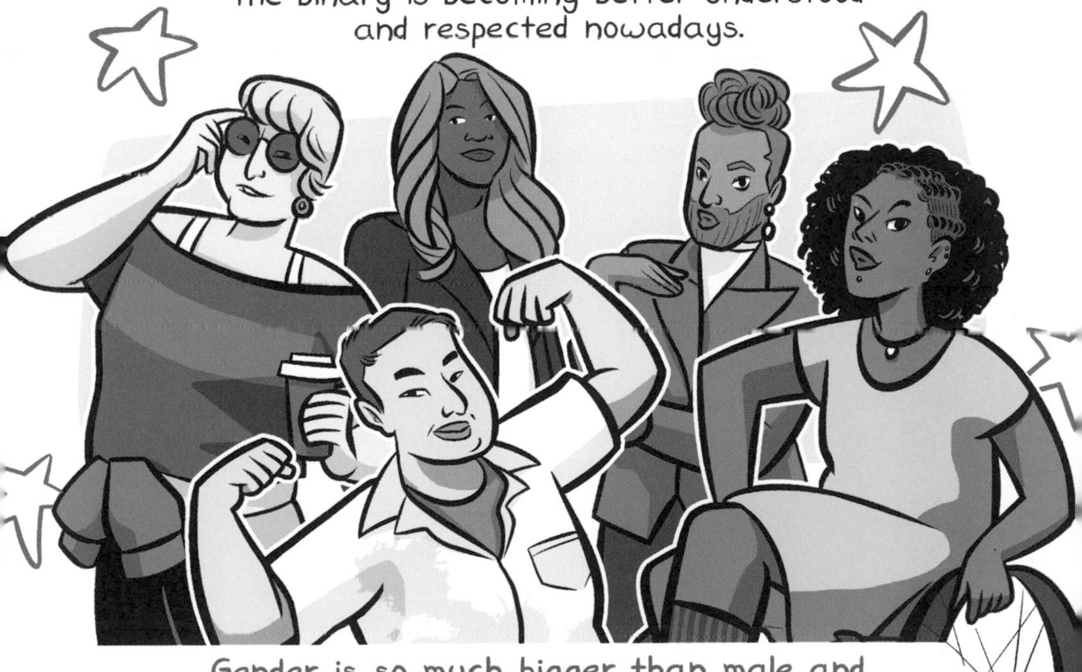

Gender is so much bigger than male and female, and thankfully our vocabulary on gender has begun to reflect that.

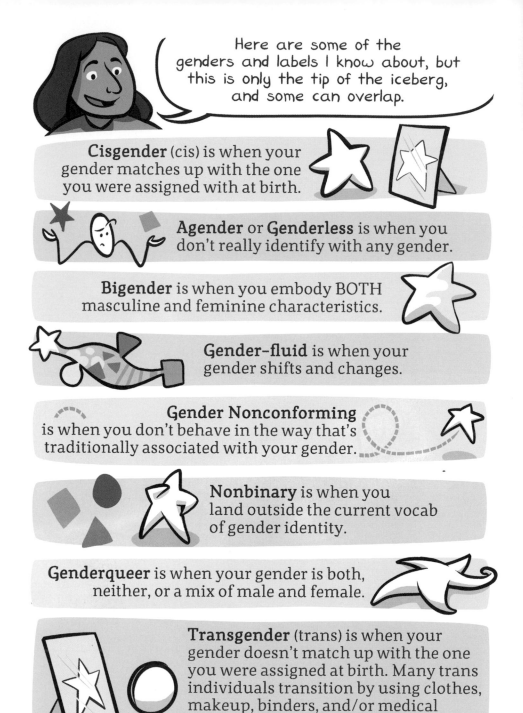

Here are some of the genders and labels I know about, but this is only the tip of the iceberg, and some can overlap.

Cisgender (cis) is when your gender matches up with the one you were assigned with at birth.

Agender or **Genderless** is when you don't really identify with any gender.

Bigender is when you embody BOTH masculine and feminine characteristics.

Gender-fluid is when your gender shifts and changes.

Gender Nonconforming is when you don't behave in the way that's traditionally associated with your gender.

Nonbinary is when you land outside the current vocab of gender identity.

Genderqueer is when your gender is both, neither, or a mix of male and female.

Transgender (trans) is when your gender doesn't match up with the one you were assigned at birth. Many trans individuals transition by using clothes, makeup, binders, and/or medical treatments to change their body to match their gender identity.

You and your gender can change as often as you want! All these labels are here to help you describe how you feel, but they aren't "RULES." The vocabulary of gender is still growing, so if you don't see something here that fits you, don't sweat it. Your identity is still real and valid.

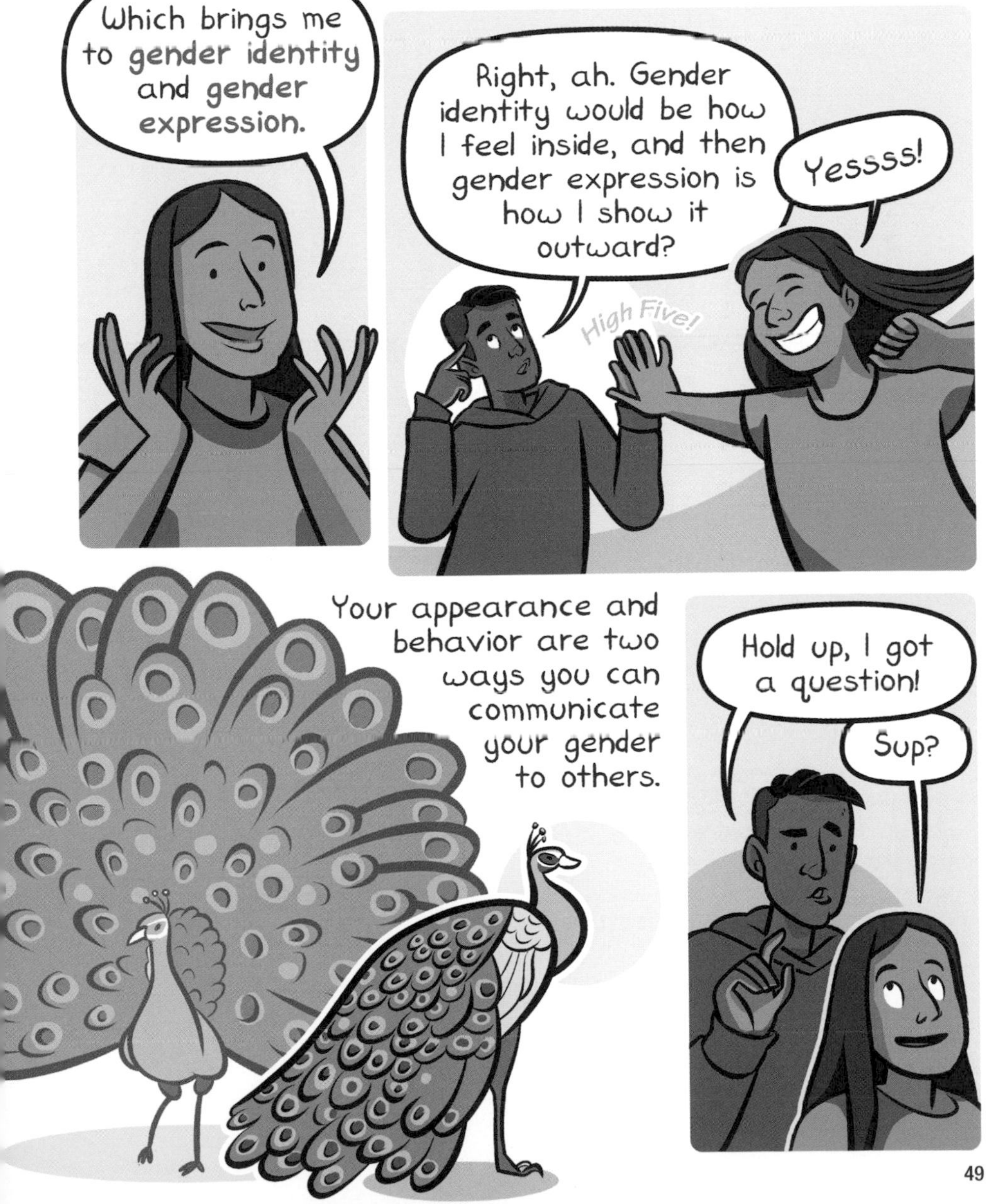

Which brings me to gender identity and gender expression.
Right, ah. Gender identity would be how I feel inside, and then gender expression is how I show it outward?
Yessss!
High Five!
Your appearance and behavior are two ways you can communicate your gender to others.
Hold up, I got a question!
Sup?

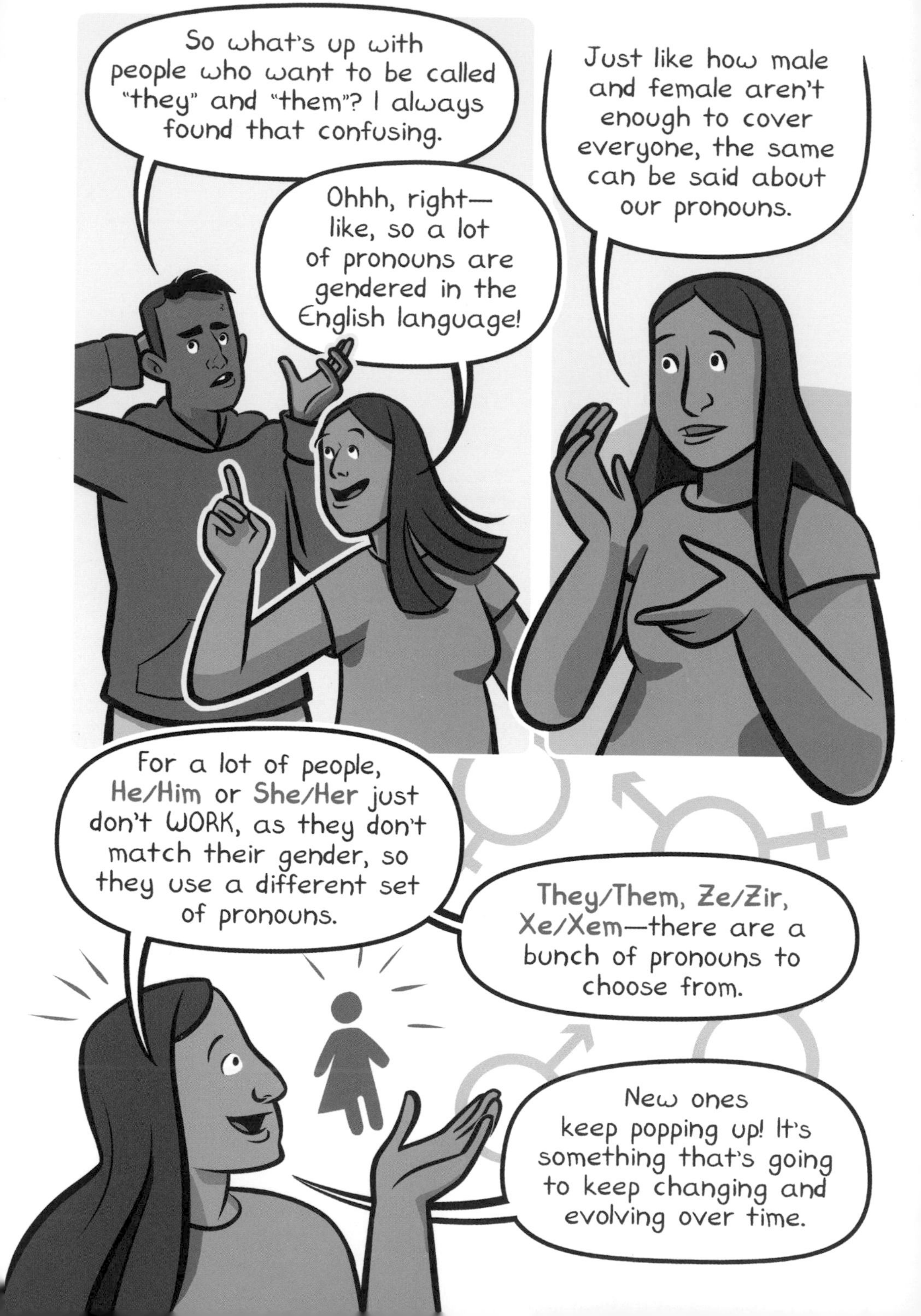

So what's up with people who want to be called "they" and "them"? I always found that confusing.
Ohhh, right—like, so a lot of pronouns are gendered in the English language!
Just like how male and female aren't enough to cover everyone, the same can be said about our pronouns.
For a lot of people, He/Him or She/Her just don't WORK, as they don't match their gender, so they use a different set of pronouns.
They/Them, Ze/Zir, Xe/Xem—there are a bunch of pronouns to choose from.
New ones keep popping up! It's something that's going to keep changing and evolving over time.

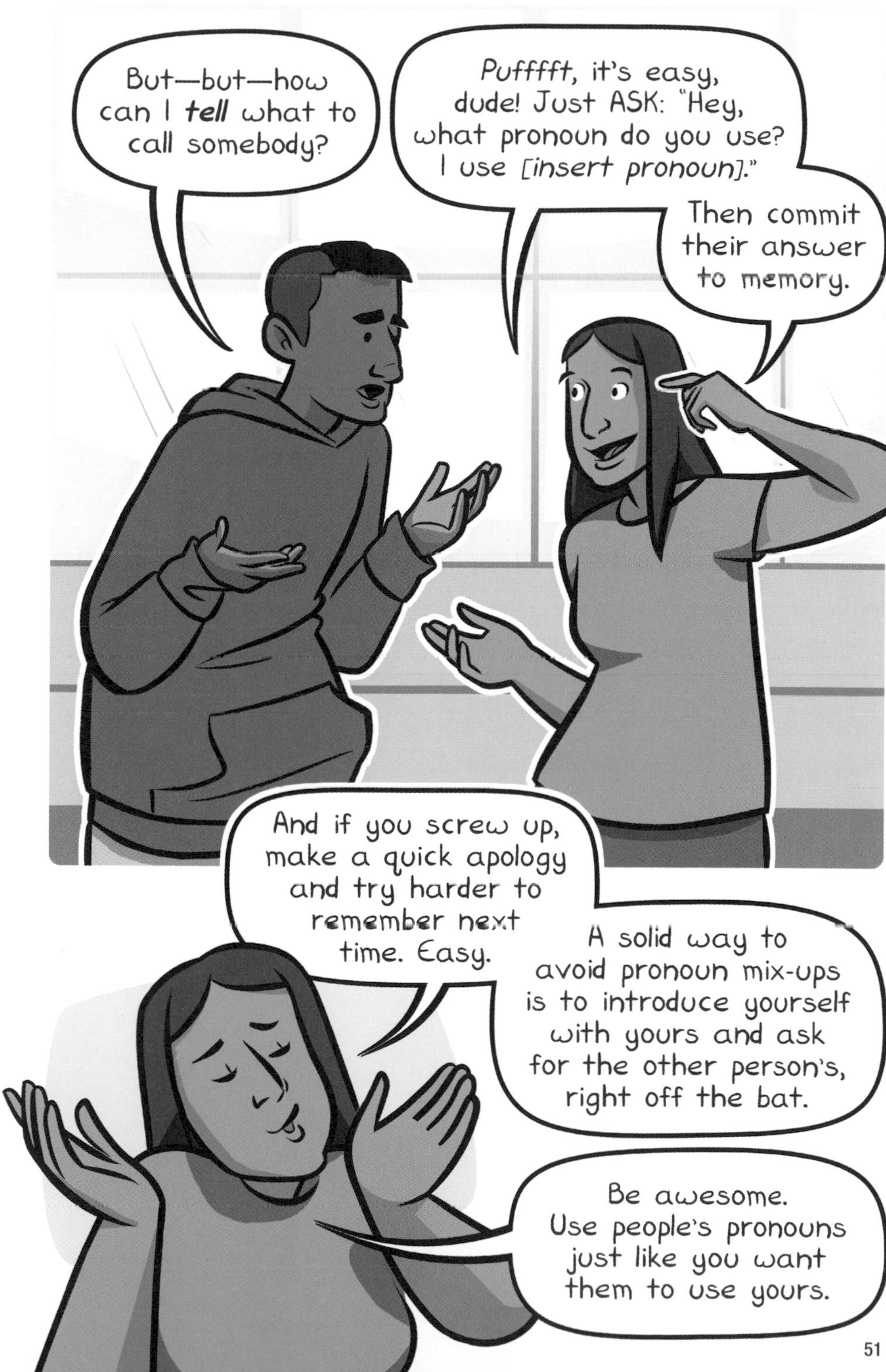

But—but—how can I ***tell*** what to call somebody?
Pufffft, it's easy, dude! Just ASK: "Hey, what pronoun do you use? I use [*insert pronoun*]."
Then commit their answer to memory.
And if you screw up, make a quick apology and try harder to remember next time. Easy.
A solid way to avoid pronoun mix-ups is to introduce yourself with yours and ask for the other person's, right off the bat.
Be awesome. Use people's pronouns just like you want them to use yours.

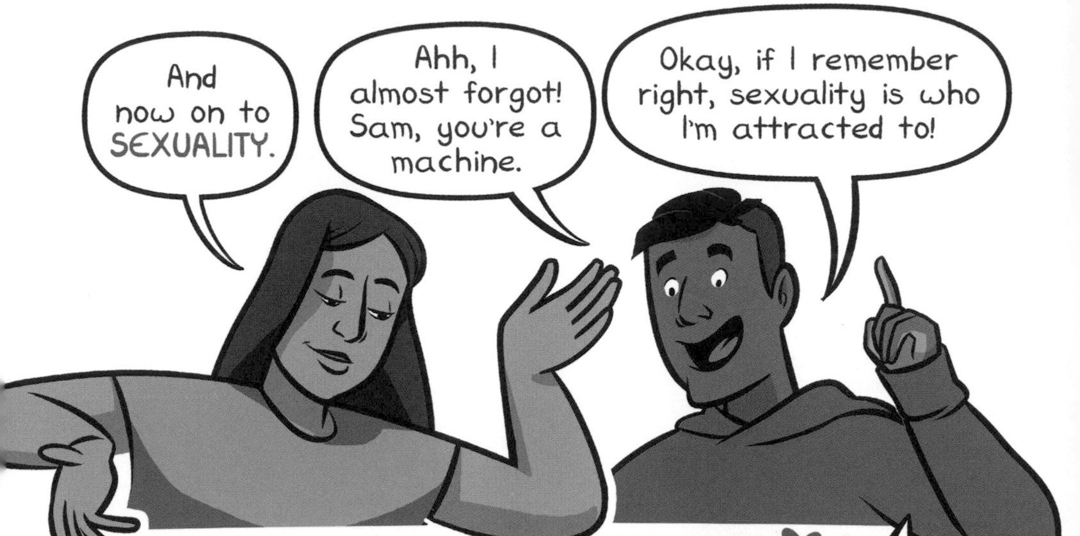

And now on to SEXUALITY.
Ahh, I almost forgot! Sam, you're a machine.
Okay, if I remember right, sexuality is who I'm attracted to!

Heterosexual is being attracted to people of a different gender.

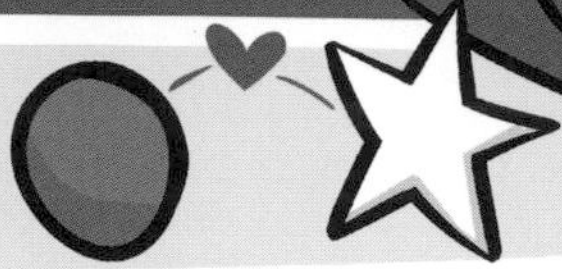

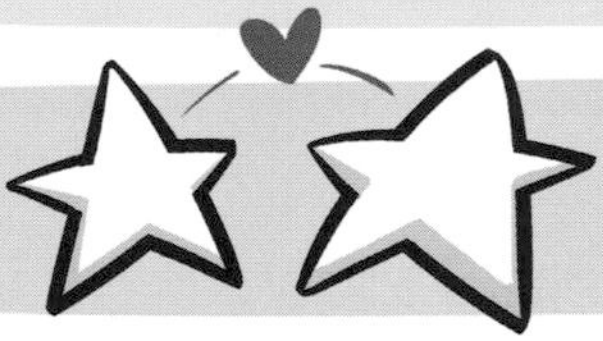

Homosexual is being attracted to the same gender.

Bisexual is being attracted to more than one gender.

Polysexual/Pansexual is being attracted to people regardless of gender or sex.

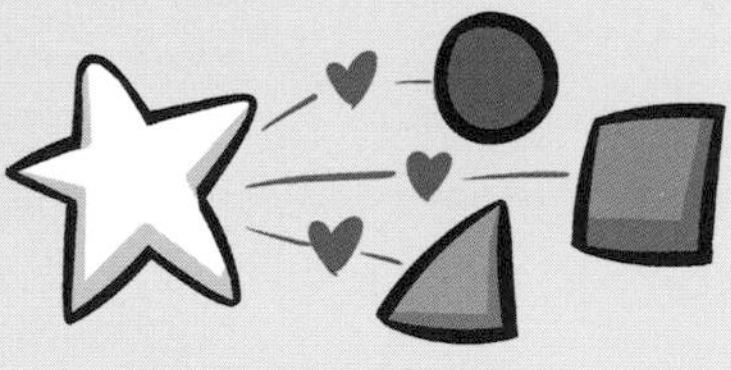

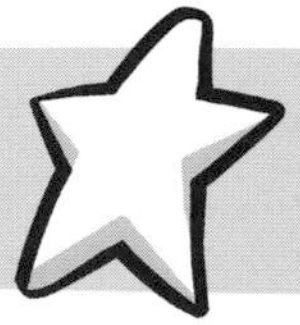

Asexual is having little to no sexual desire or attraction for others.

And **Queer** is a great catchall umbrella label that covers everything that isn't strictly heterosexual.

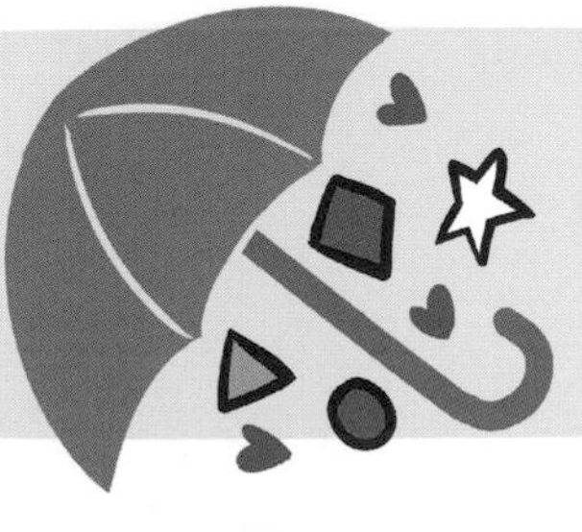

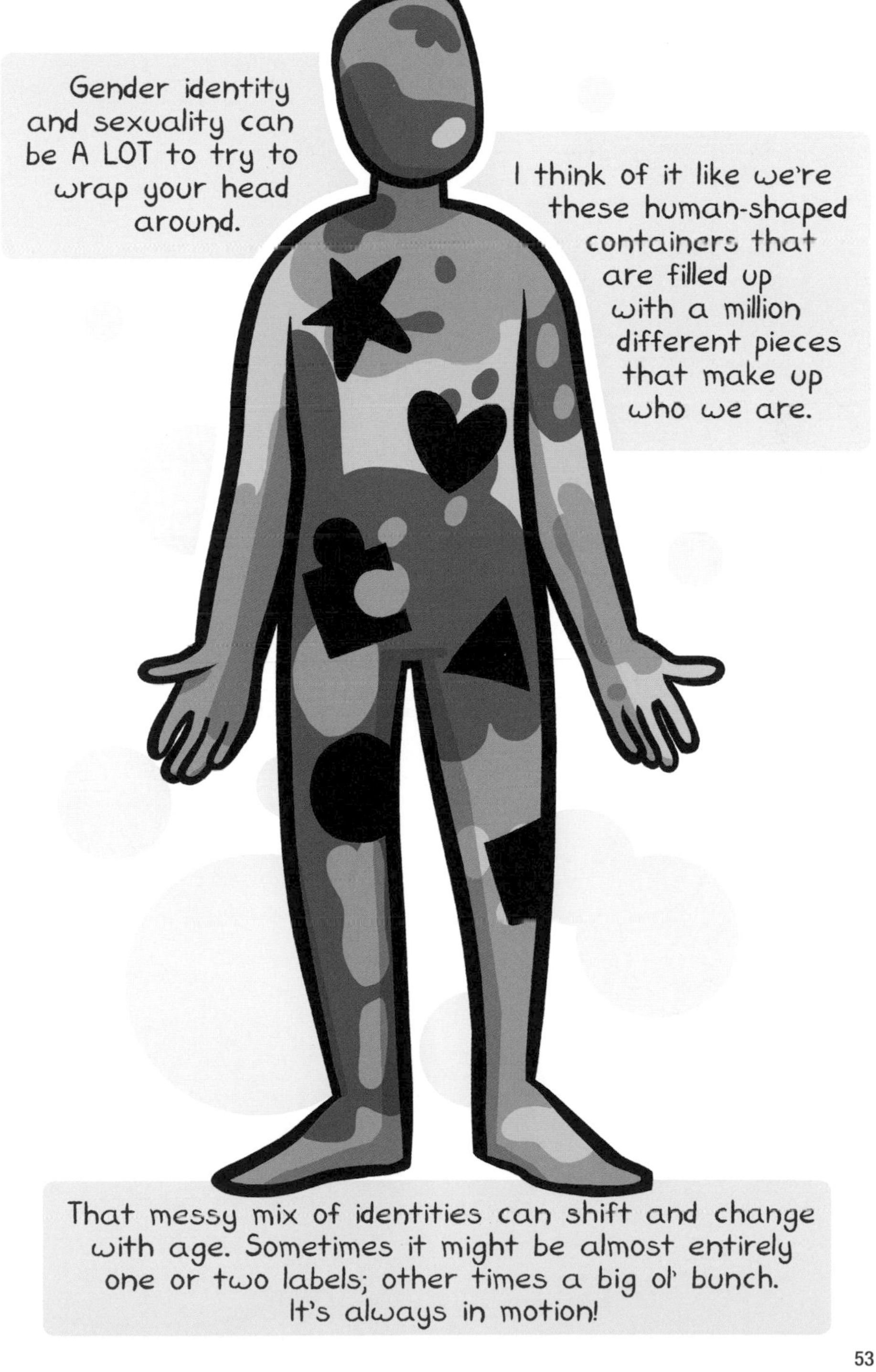
Gender identity and sexuality can be A LOT to try to wrap your head around.
I think of it like we're these human-shaped containers that are filled up with a million different pieces that make up who we are.
That messy mix of identities can shift and change with age. Sometimes it might be almost entirely one or two labels; other times a big ol' bunch. It's always in motion!

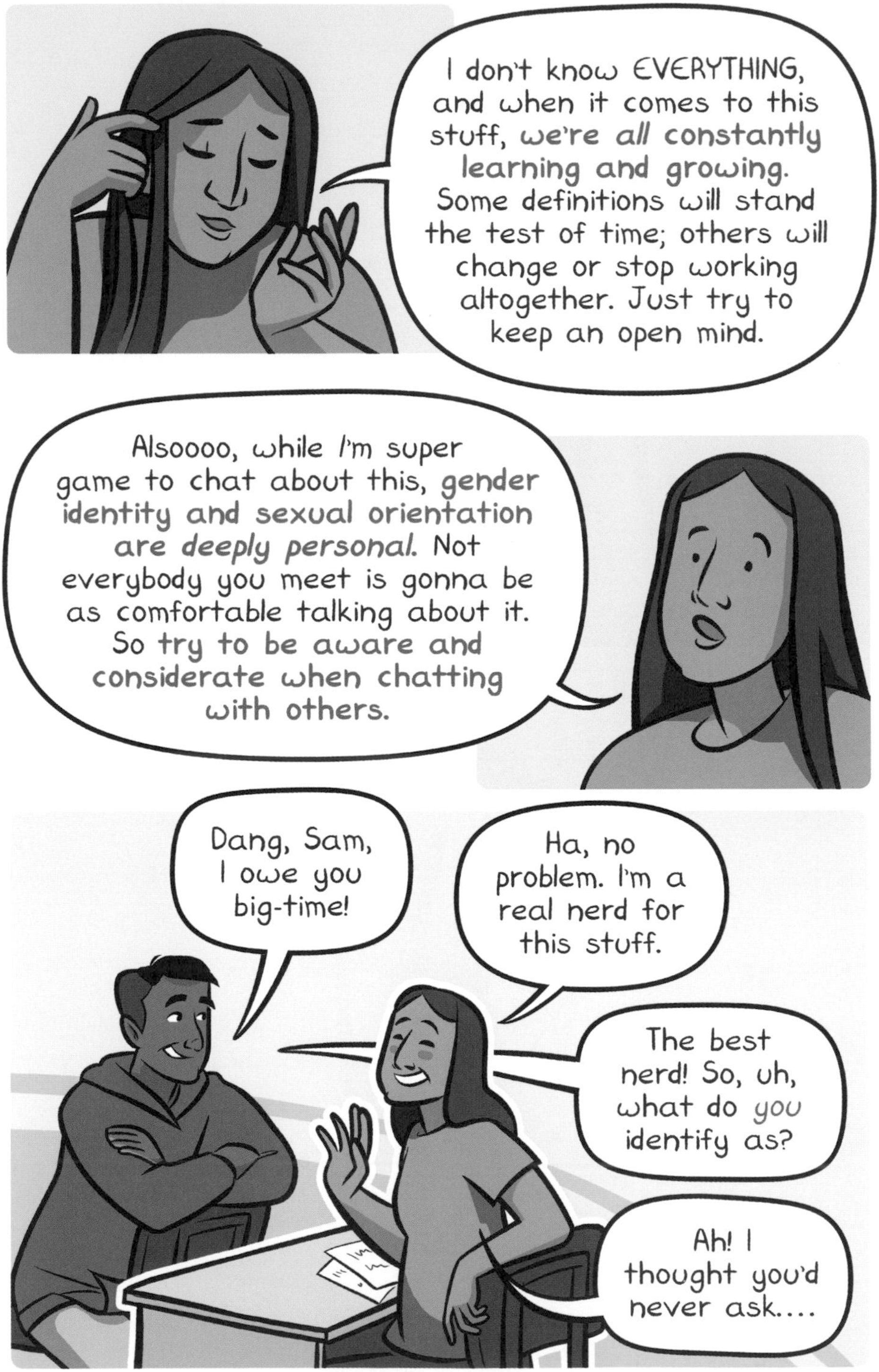
I don't know EVERYTHING, and when it comes to this stuff, we're all constantly learning and growing. Some definitions will stand the test of time; others will change or stop working altogether. Just try to keep an open mind.
Alsoooo, while I'm super game to chat about this, gender identity and sexual orientation are deeply personal. Not everybody you meet is gonna be as comfortable talking about it. So try to be aware and considerate when chatting with others.
Dang, Sam, I owe you big-time!
Ha, no problem. I'm a real nerd for this stuff.
The best nerd! So, uh, what do you identify as?
Ah! I thought you'd never ask....

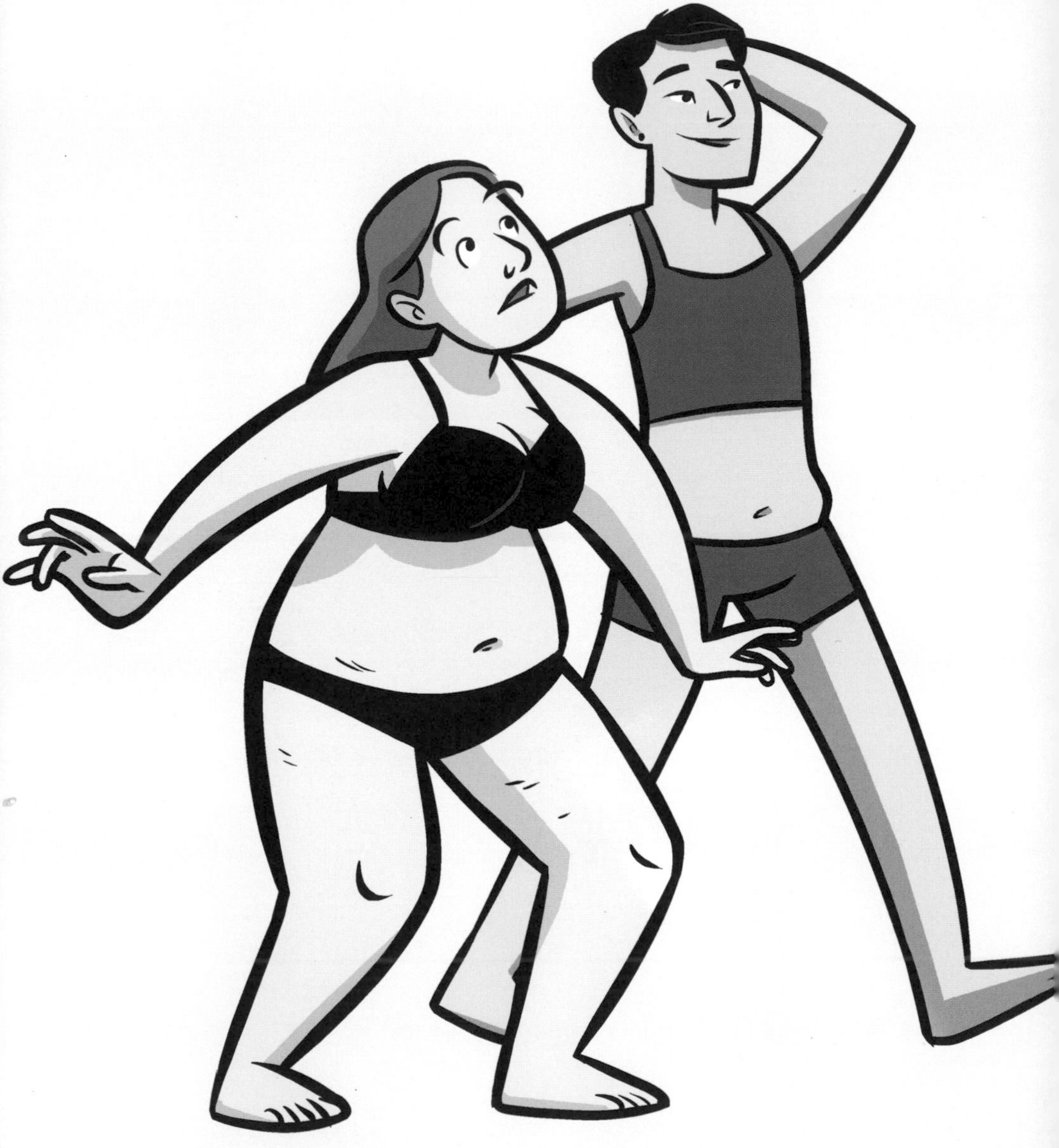

What is . . .
body image?

How do you feel about the way you look? Why do people in the movies and in media look so different from real people? Why don't you look like that? How can you feel good about your body?

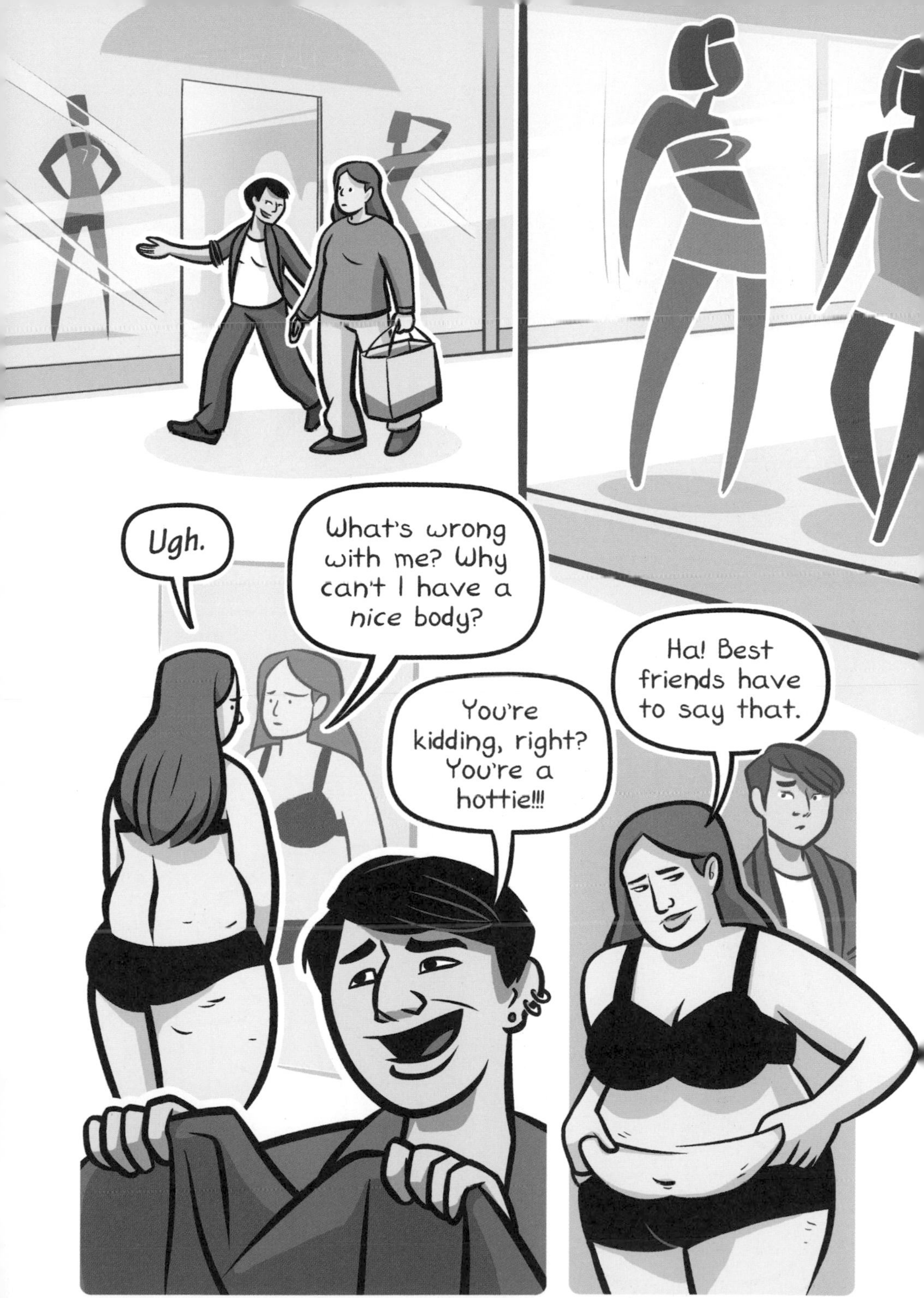
Ugh.
What's wrong with me? Why can't I have a nice body?
You're kidding, right? You're a hottie!!!
Ha! Best friends have to say that.

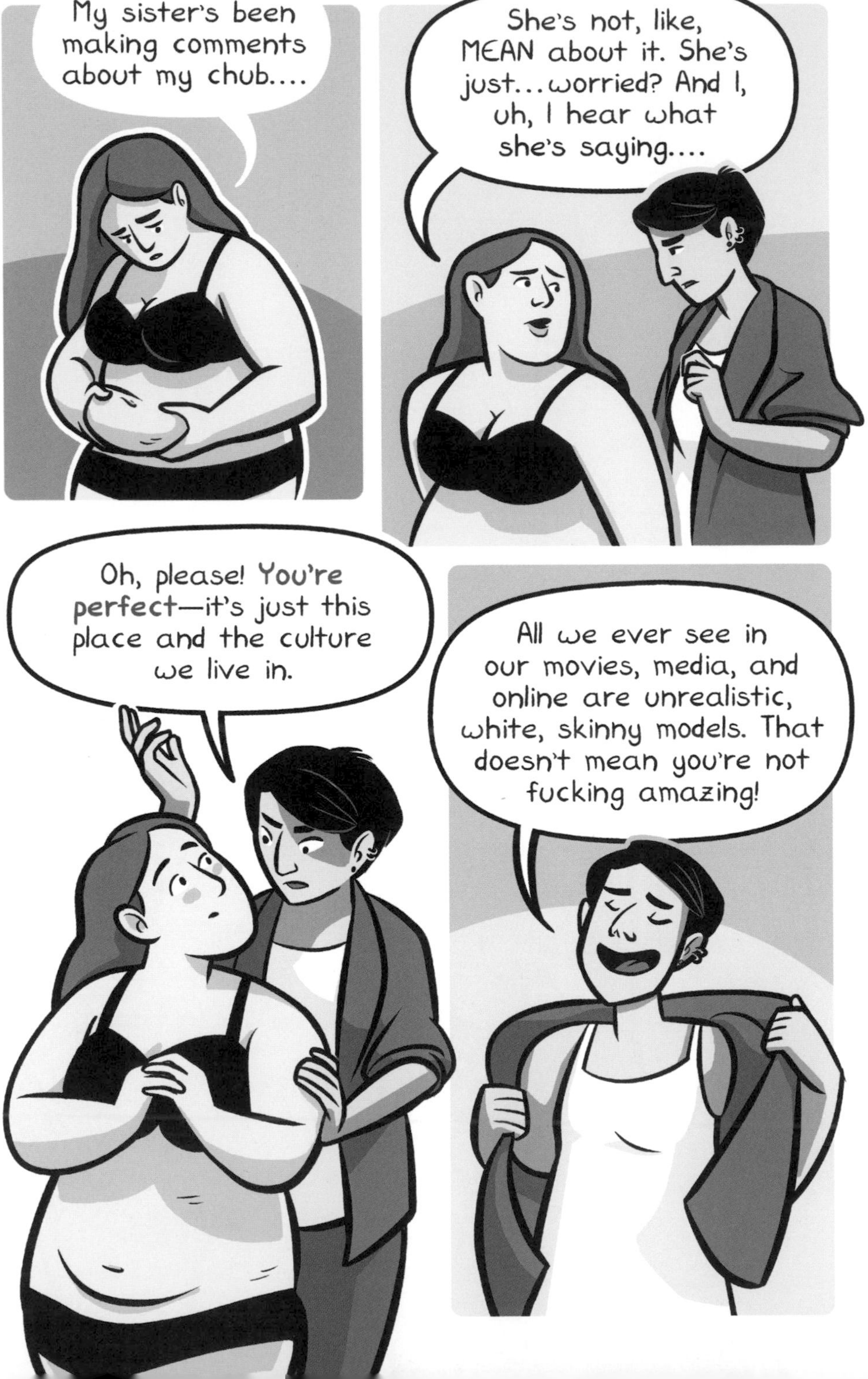
My sister's been making comments about my chub....
She's not, like, MEAN about it. She's just...worried? And I, uh, I hear what she's saying....
Oh, please! You're perfect—it's just this place and the culture we live in.
All we ever see in our movies, media, and online are unrealistic, white, skinny models. That doesn't mean you're not fucking amazing!

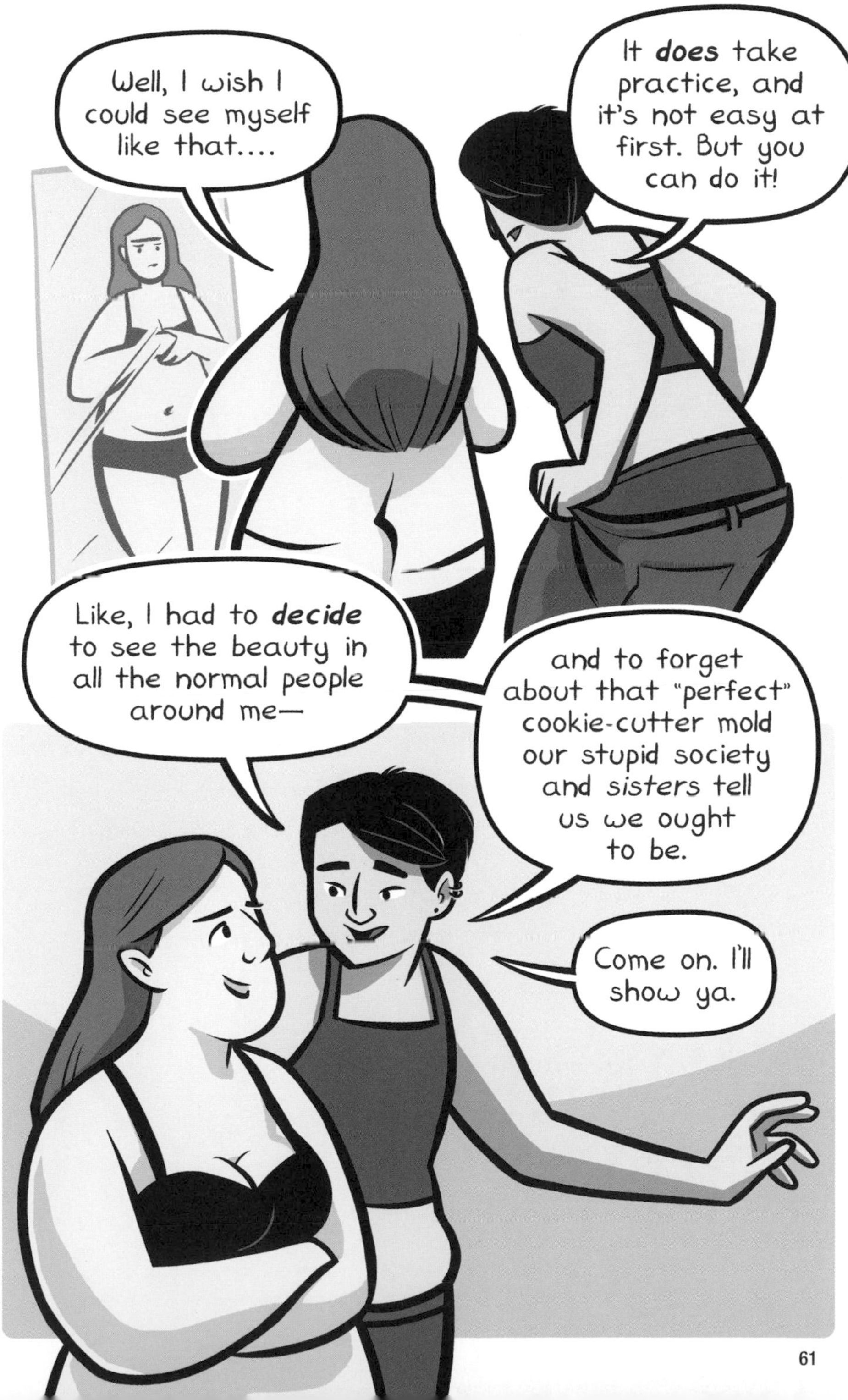

Well, I wish I could see myself like that....
It **does** take practice, and it's not easy at first. But you can do it!
Like, I had to ***decide*** to see the beauty in all the normal people around me—
and to forget about that "perfect" cookie-cutter mold our stupid society and *sisters* tell us we ought to be.
Come on. I'll show ya.

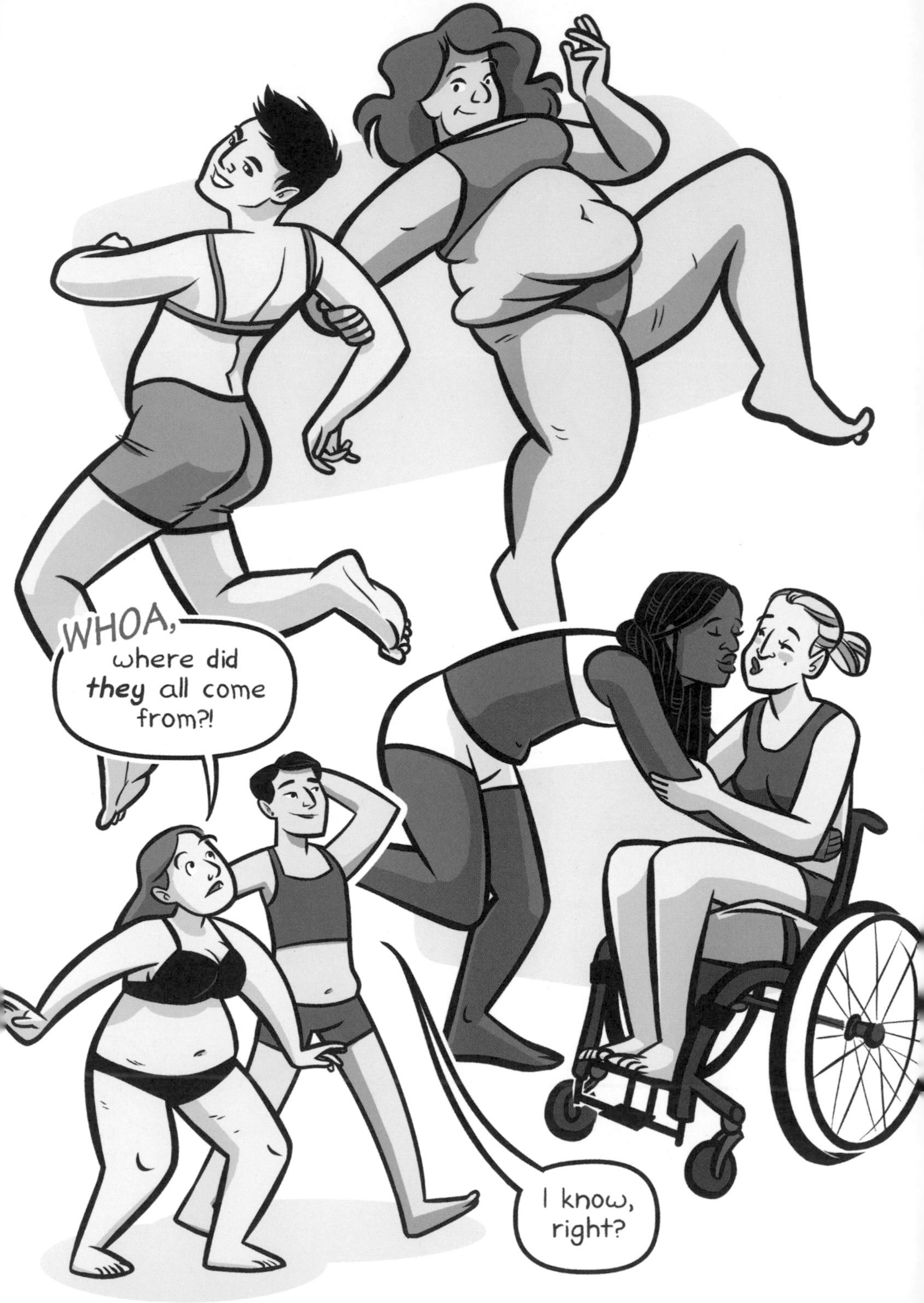
WHOA, where did *they* all come from?!
I know, right?

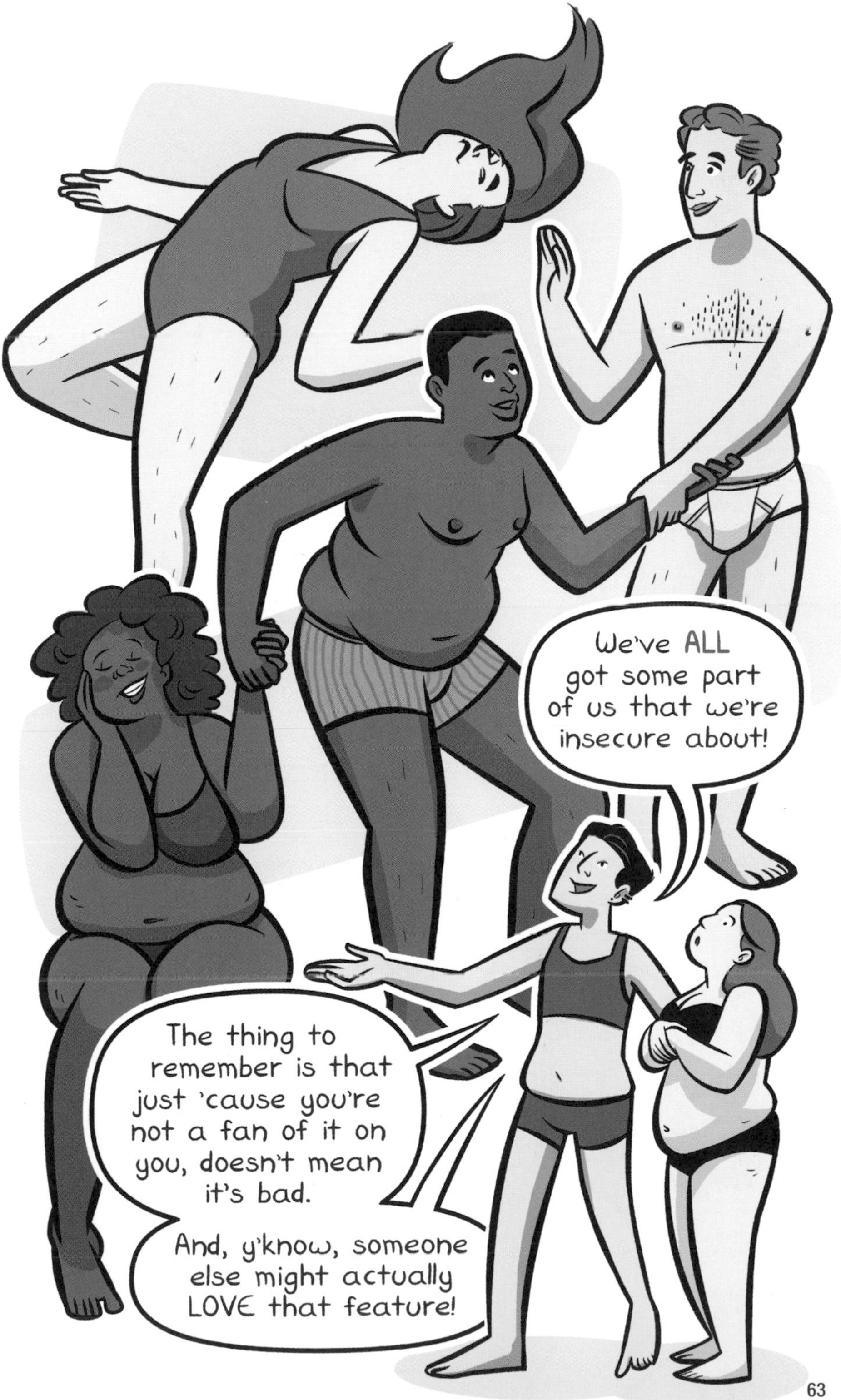
We've ALL got some part of us that we're insecure about!
The thing to remember is that just 'cause you're not a fan of it on you, doesn't mean it's bad.
And, y'know, someone else might actually LOVE that feature!

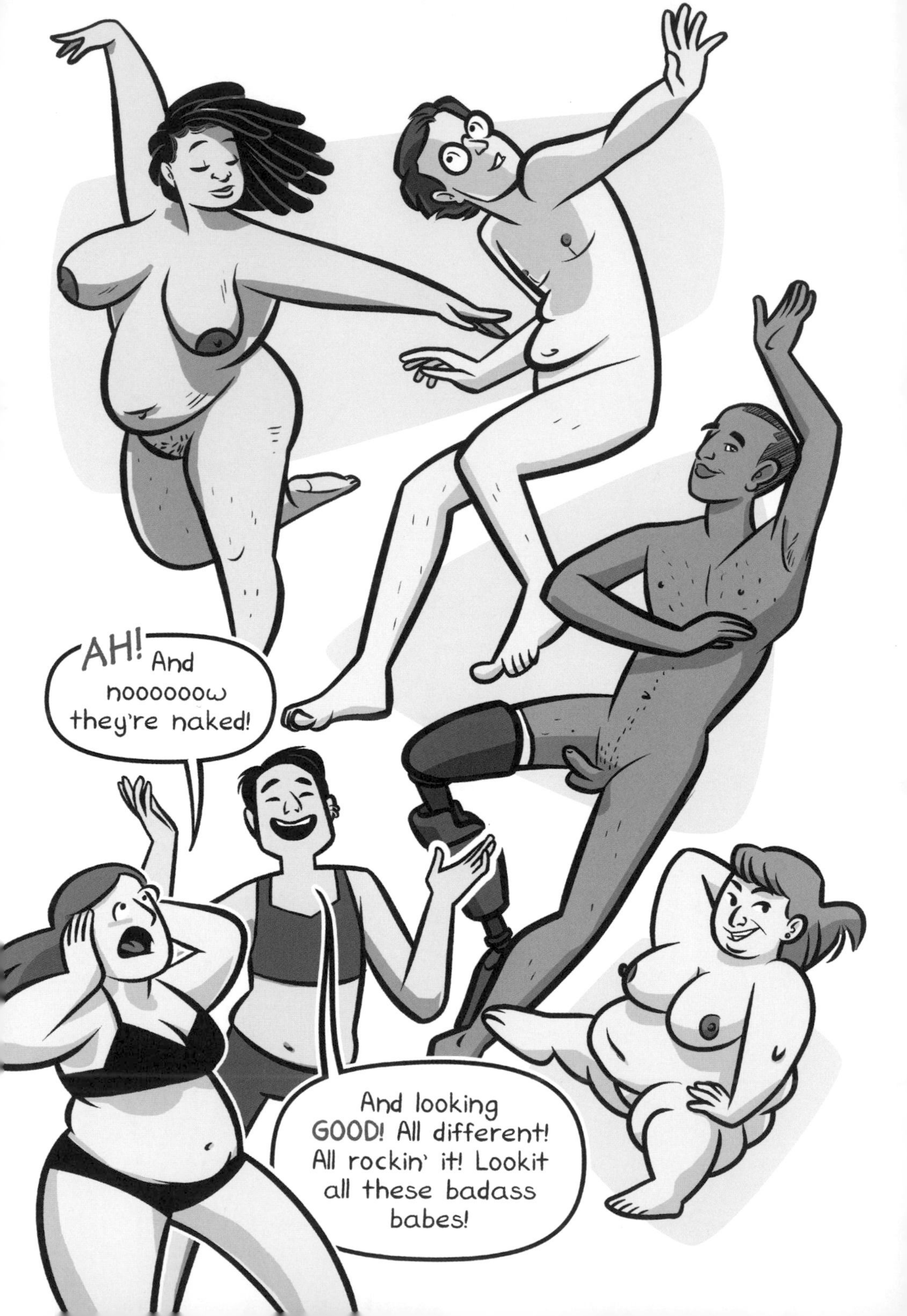
AH! And noooooow they're naked!
And looking GOOD! All different! All rockin' it! Lookit all these badass babes!

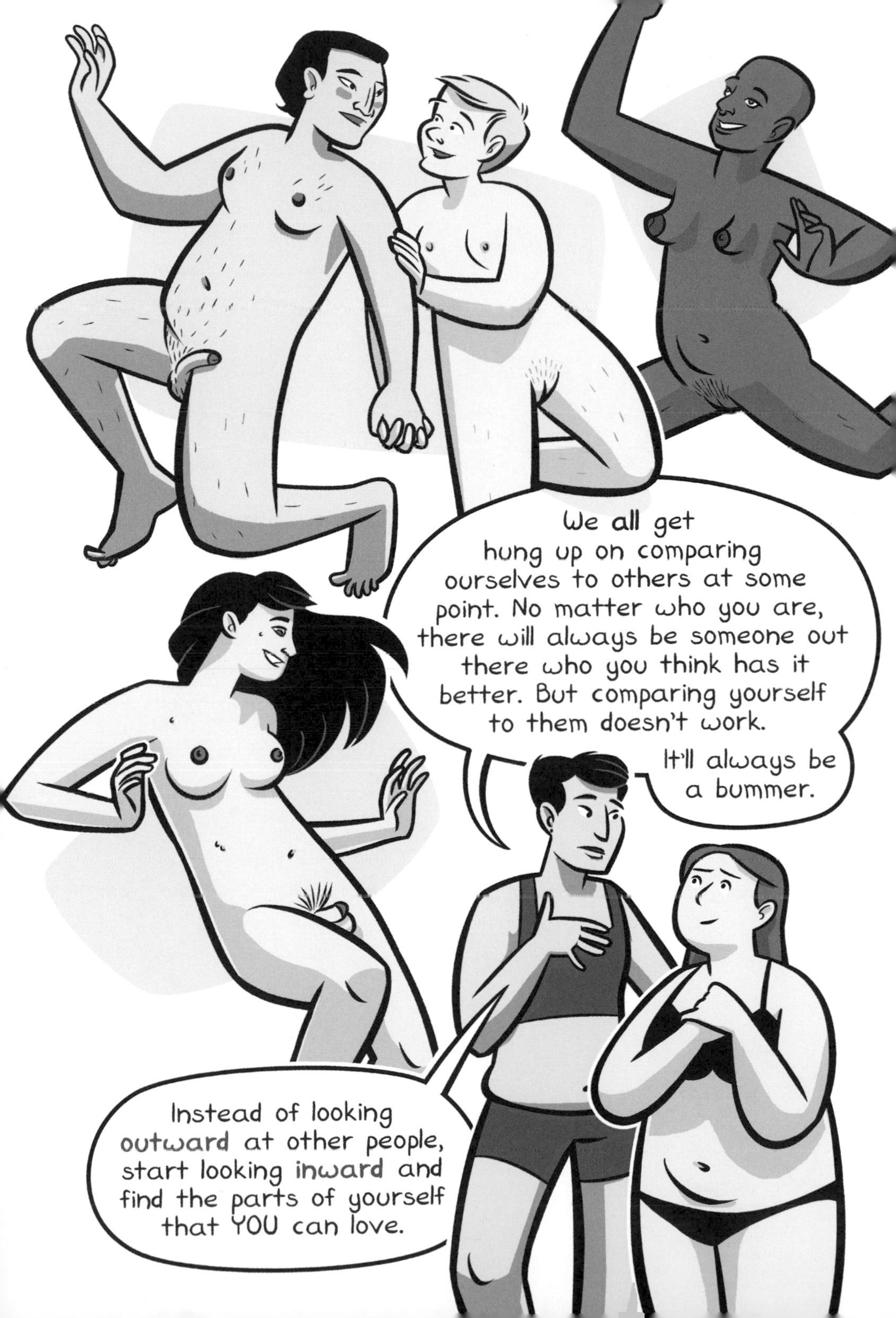
We all get hung up on comparing ourselves to others at some point. No matter who you are, there will always be someone out there who you think has it better. But comparing yourself to them doesn't work.
It'll always be a bummer.
Instead of looking outward at other people, start looking inward and find the parts of yourself that YOU can love.

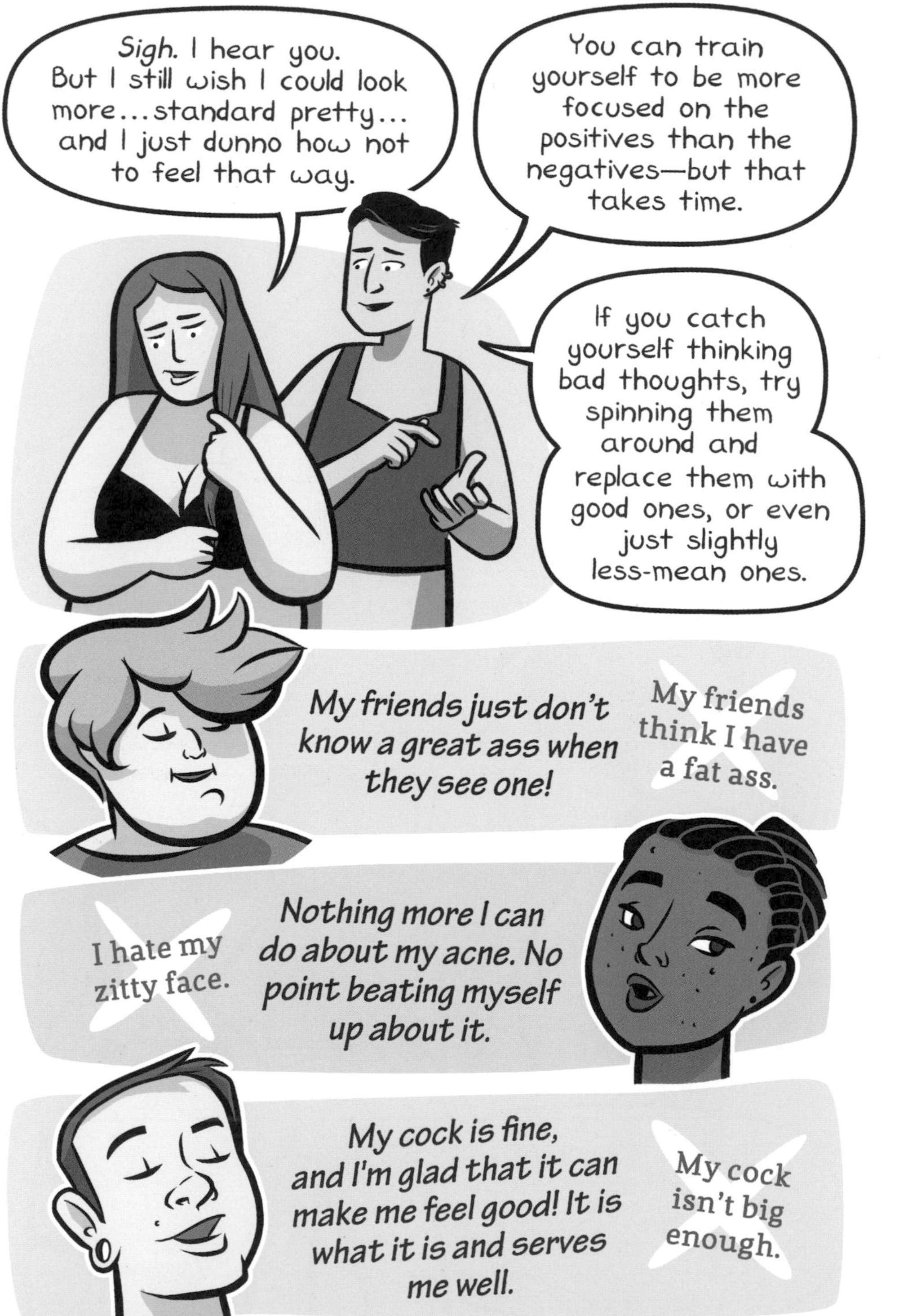

Sigh. I hear you. But I still wish I could look more...standard pretty... and I just dunno how not to feel that way.
You can train yourself to be more focused on the positives than the negatives—but that takes time.
If you catch yourself thinking bad thoughts, try spinning them around and replace them with good ones, or even just slightly less-mean ones.
My friends just don't know a great ass when they see one!
My friends think I have a fat ass.
I hate my zitty face.
Nothing more I can do about my acne. No point beating myself up about it.
My cock is fine, and I'm glad that it can make me feel good! It is what it is and serves me well.
My cock isn't big enough.

They're so fit and I'm so ... not.

Why compare myself? I'm awesome and my body lets me do great things!

Do I really NEED to, though? I don't have time for that kinda upkeep!

I'll never look like THAT....

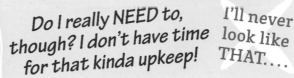

Few people truly love EVERY part of themselves, but you *can* learn to love some of you.

Remind yourself of your positive points as often as you can, say it out loud, maybe keep a journal. Keep pushing that outlook and it'll come naturally someday.

You'll have ups and downs, and loving—or even just *liking*—yourself is gonna be a lifelong journey.

On the other side of the coin, for when you DO get there: it IS okay to feel hot and attractive.

You don't have to feel guilty or bad about it. Relish that positive feeling and try to remember it next time you're not feeling it!

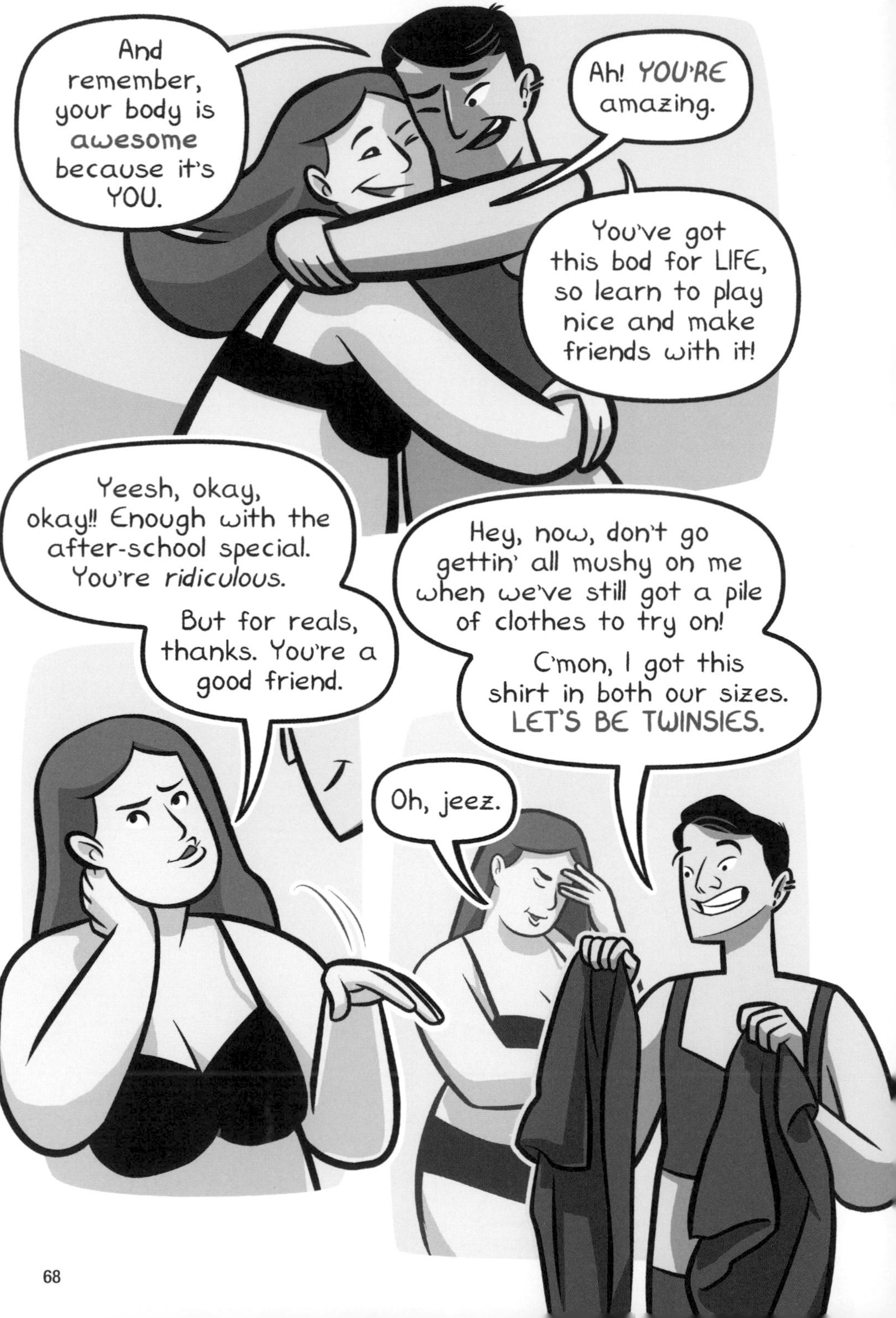
And remember, your body is awesome because it's YOU.
Ah! YOU'RE amazing.
You've got this bod for LIFE, so learn to play nice and make friends with it!
Yeesh, okay, okay!! Enough with the after-school special. You're ridiculous.
But for reals, thanks. You're a good friend.
Hey, now, don't go gettin' all mushy on me when we've still got a pile of clothes to try on!
C'mon, I got this shirt in both our sizes. LET'S BE TWINSIES.
Oh, jeez.

What is . . .
your body?

What are all the parts of your body called? How do they work? Is how they look and react normal? How are they changing now that you're getting older? Please explain all the things!

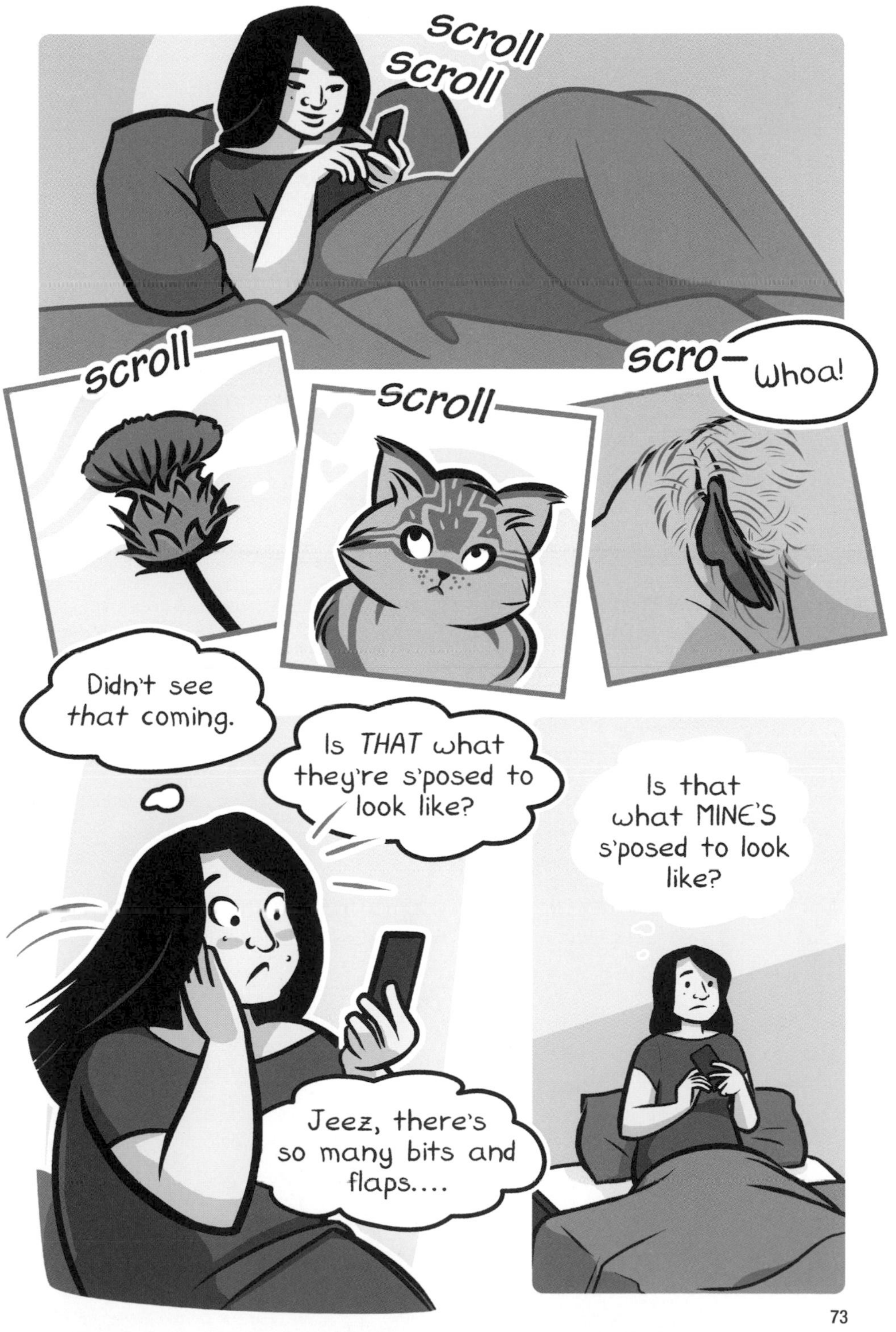
Scroll
Scroll
Scroll
Scroll
Scro–
Whoa!
Didn't see that coming.
Is THAT what they're s'posed to look like?
Jeez, there's so many bits and flaps....
Is that what MINE'S s'posed to look like?

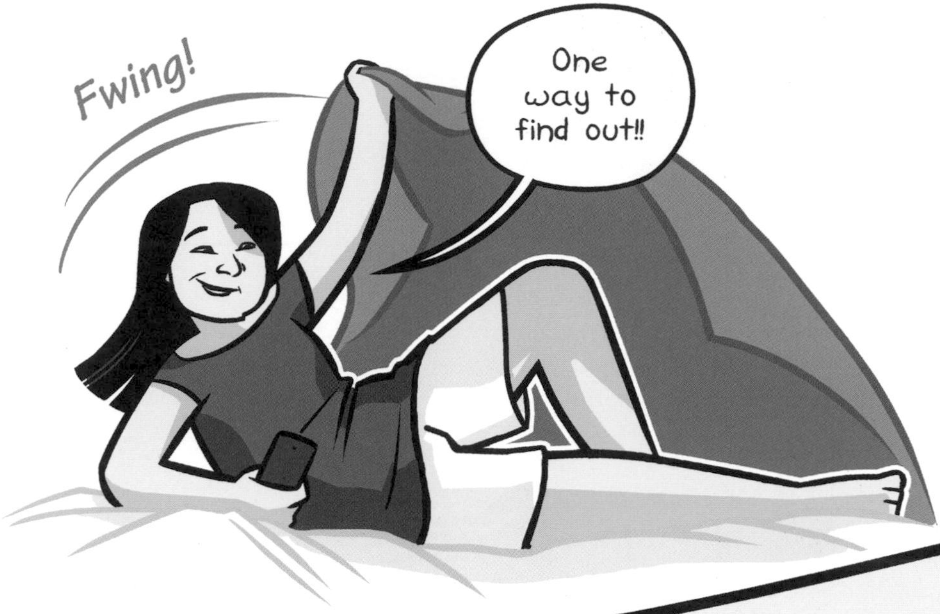
Fwing!
One way to find out!!

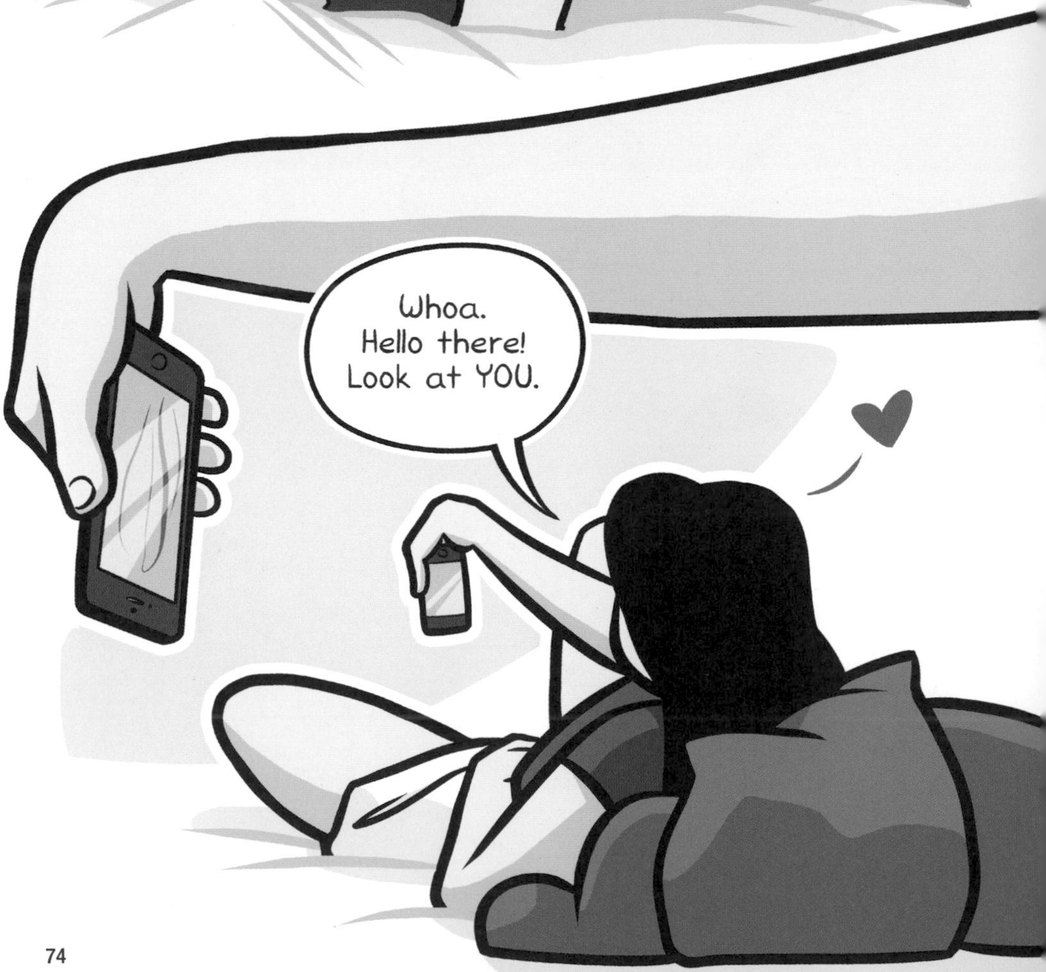
Whoa. Hello there! Look at YOU.

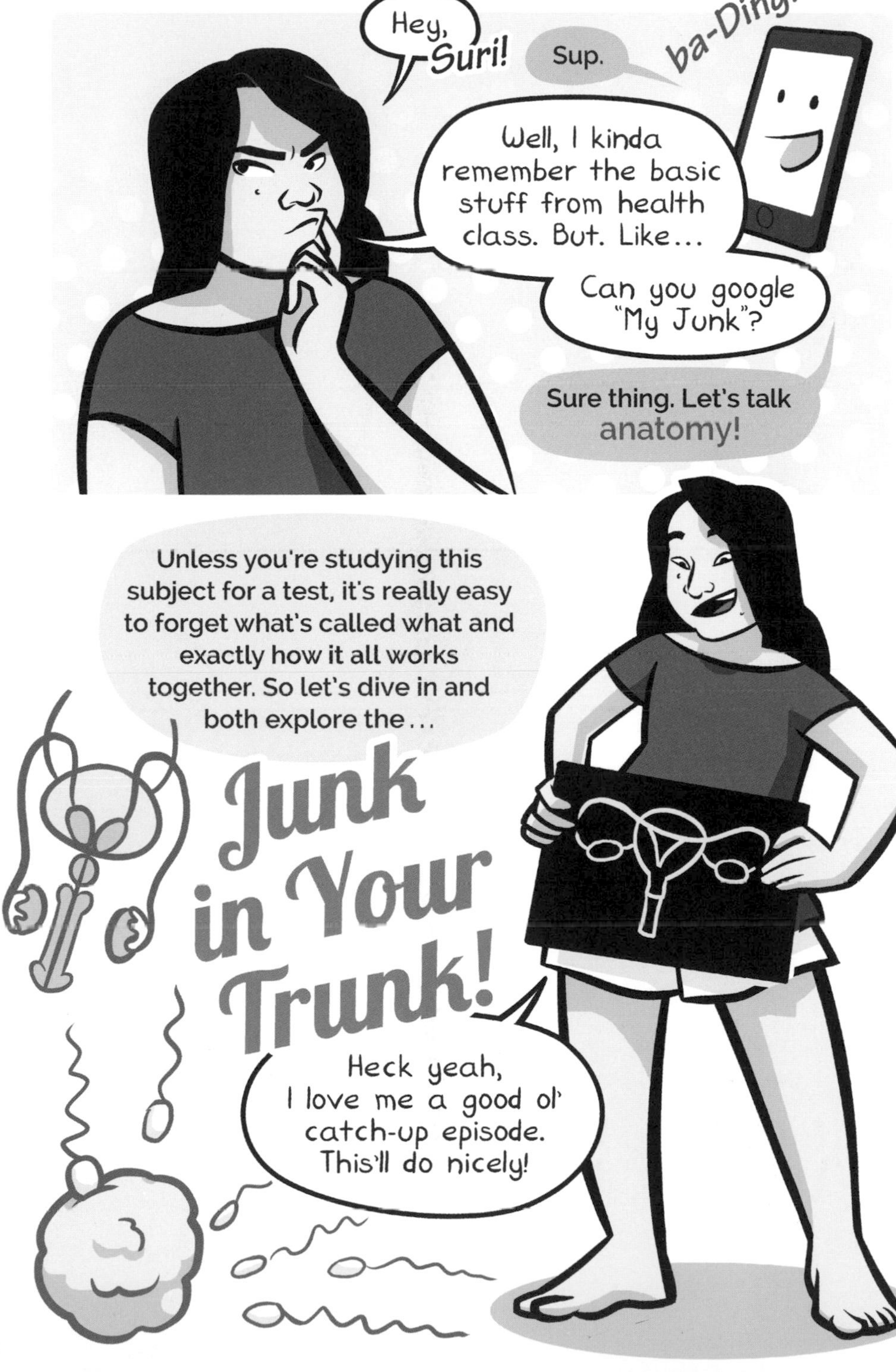

Hey, Suri!
Sup.
ba-Ding!
Well, I kinda remember the basic stuff from health class. But. Like...
Can you google "My Junk"?
Sure thing. Let's talk anatomy!
Unless you're studying this subject for a test, it's really easy to forget what's called what and exactly how it all works together. So let's dive in and both explore the...
Junk in Your Trunk!
Heck yeah, I love me a good ol' catch-up episode. This'll do nicely!

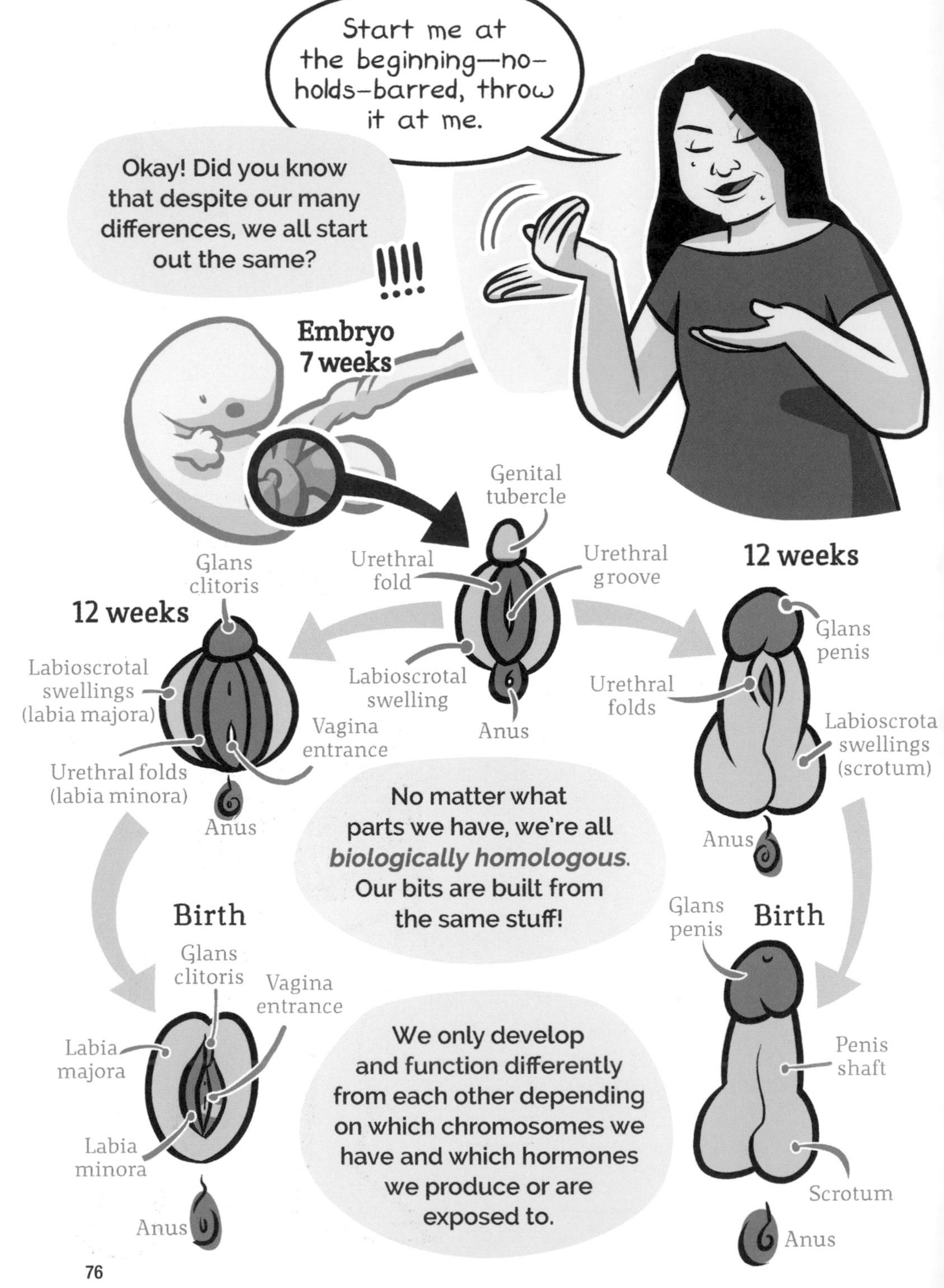

Start me at the beginning—no-holds-barred, throw it at me.
Okay! Did you know that despite our many differences, we all start out the same?
!!!!
Embryo 7 weeks
Genital tubercle
Urethral fold
Urethral groove
Labioscrotal swelling
Anus
12 weeks
Glans clitoris
Labioscrotal swellings (labia majora)
Urethral folds (labia minora)
Vagina entrance
Anus
12 weeks
Glans penis
Urethral folds
Labioscrota swellings (scrotum)
Anus
No matter what parts we have, we're all ***biologically homologous***. Our bits are built from the same stuff!
Birth
Glans clitoris
Vagina entrance
Labia majora
Labia minora
Anus
Birth
Glans penis
Penis shaft
Scrotum
Anus
We only develop and function differently from each other depending on which chromosomes we have and which hormones we produce or are exposed to.

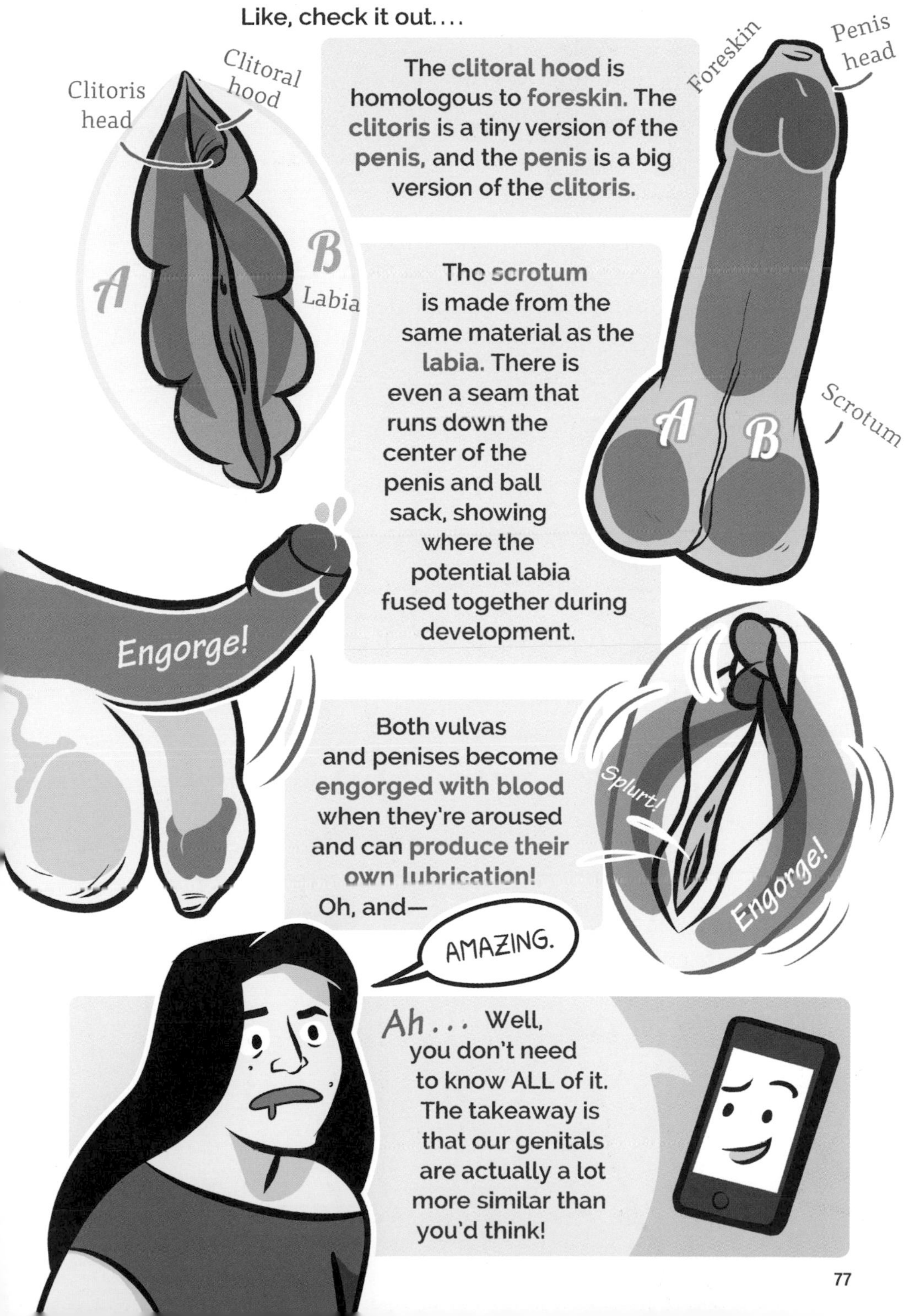

Like, check it out....
Clitoris head
Clitoral hood
The clitoral hood is homologous to foreskin. The clitoris is a tiny version of the penis, and the penis is a big version of the clitoris.
Foreskin
Penis head
A
B
Labia
The scrotum is made from the same material as the labia. There is even a seam that runs down the center of the penis and ball sack, showing where the potential labia fused together during development.
Scrotum
A
B
Engorge!
Both vulvas and penises become engorged with blood when they're aroused and can produce their own lubrication! Oh, and—
Splurt!
Engorge!
AMAZING.
Ah . . . Well, you don't need to know ALL of it. The takeaway is that our genitals are actually a lot more similar than you'd think!

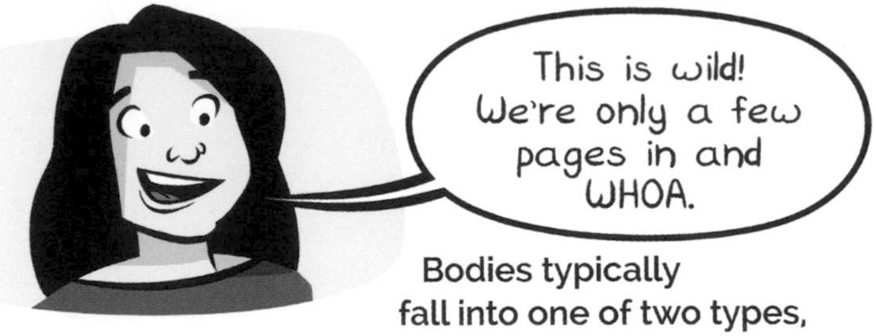
This is wild! We're only a few pages in and WHOA.

Bodies typically fall into one of two types, **depending on their anatomy, genetics, and hormones.** **Testes** historically label someone as "male," and lead to a testosterone-rich puberty. **Ovaries** historically label someone as "female," and lead to an estrogen-rich puberty. Some people have anatomy or genetics that don't exactly fit either of these two categories, which is called "intersex." Lots of people also medically change their bodies to have the traits that are right for them; this includes cisgender, transgender, and nonbinary people.

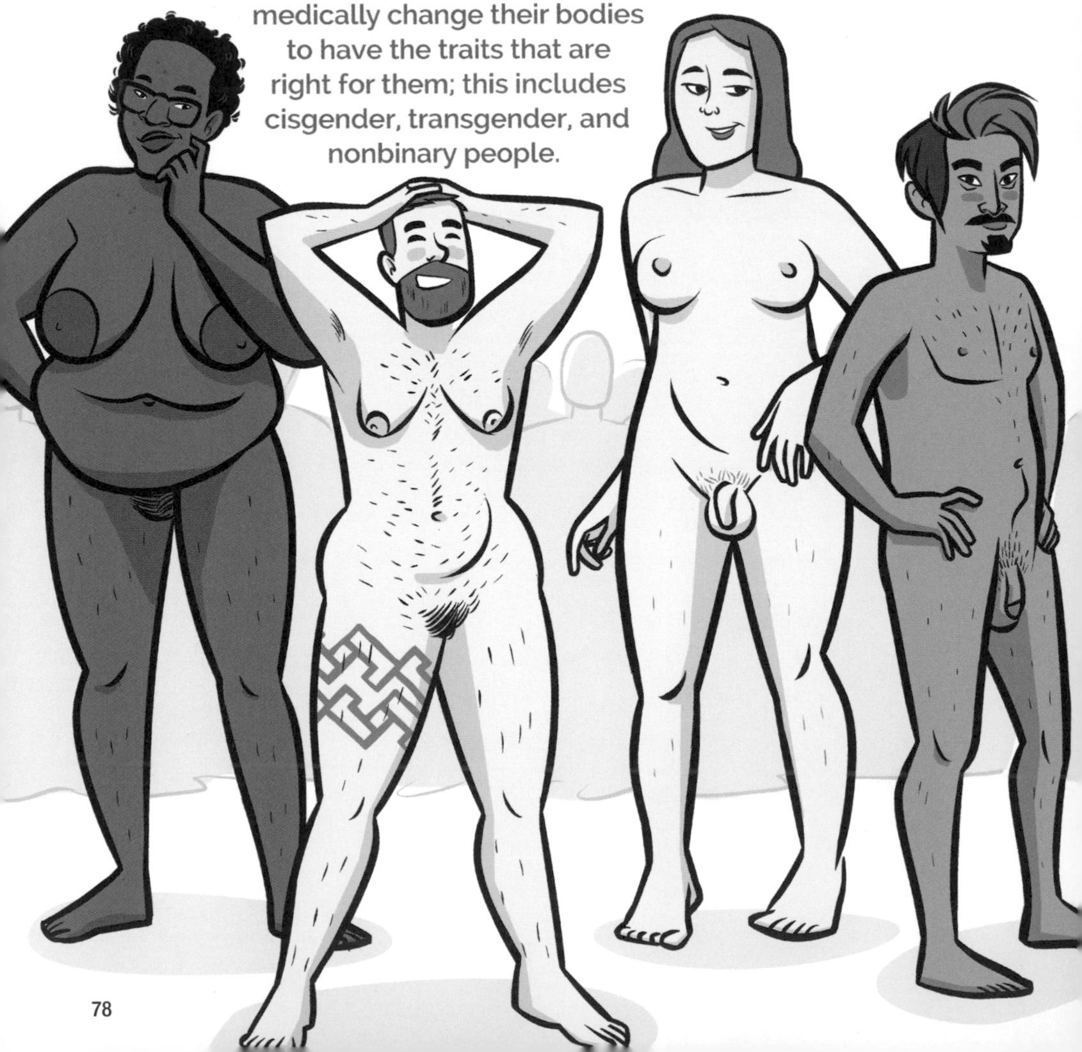

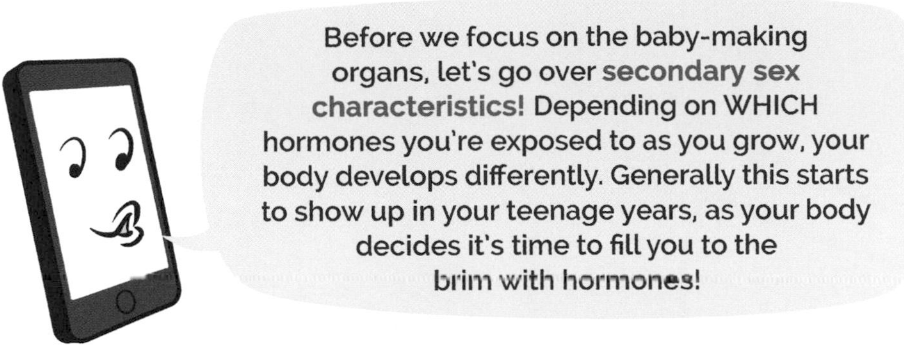
Before we focus on the baby-making organs, let's go over secondary sex characteristics! Depending on WHICH hormones you're exposed to as you grow, your body develops differently. Generally this starts to show up in your teenage years, as your body decides it's time to fill you to the brim with hormones!

Generally Testosterone-Rich Body

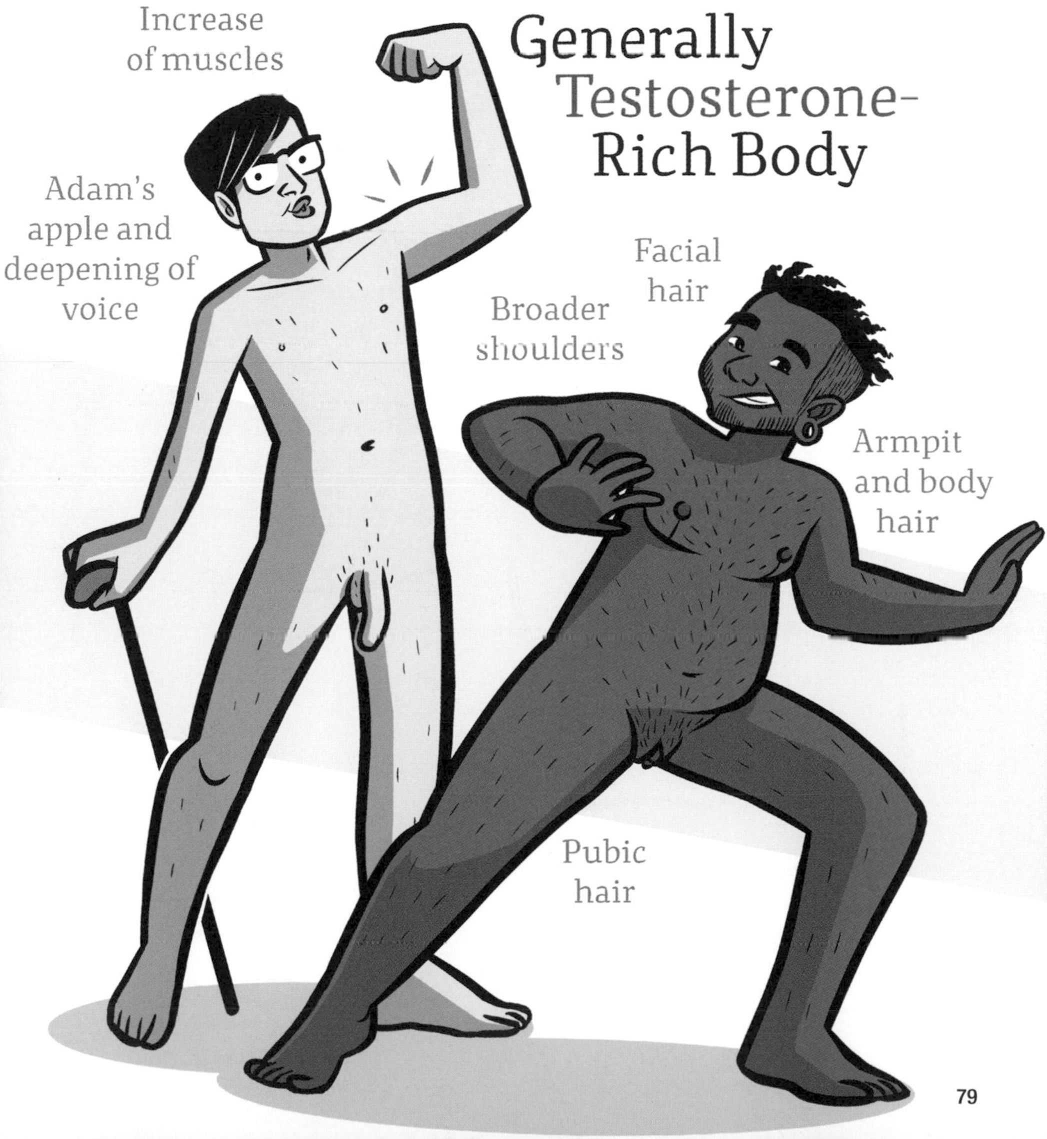
Increase of muscles
Adam's apple and deepening of voice
Facial hair
Broader shoulders
Armpit and body hair
Pubic hair

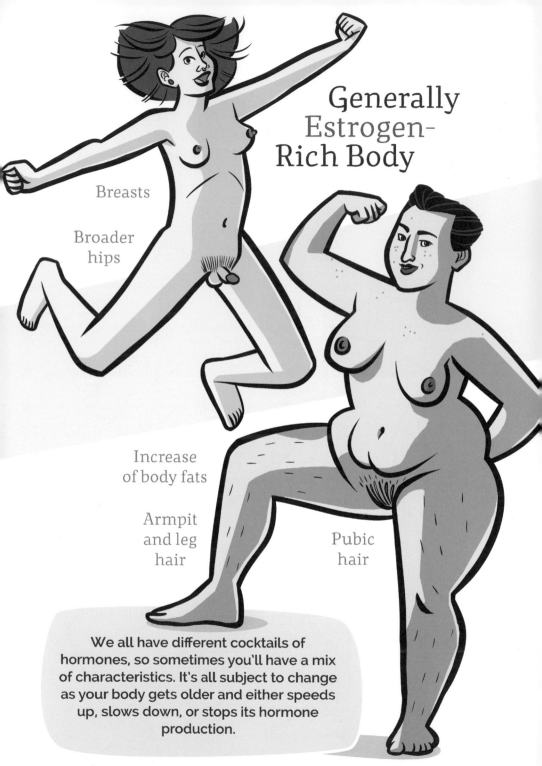

Generally Estrogen-Rich Body

Breasts

Broader hips

Increase of body fats

Armpit and leg hair

Pubic hair

We all have different cocktails of hormones, so sometimes you'll have a mix of characteristics. It's all subject to change as your body gets older and either speeds up, slows down, or stops its hormone production.

Let's take a look at some universal
zones and attributes of the body.

Brain

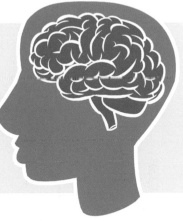

Aw yeah, the big boss,
responsible for all of your
thoughts, feelings, and
actions—which includes your
sexual functioning! Your erotic
imagination, your arousal, your
sexual response: it's all
controlled from here!

Skin

It's such a complicated and
fascinating organ that we often
overlook because it's right there in
front of us all day every day. It covers
our body from tip to toe in sensitive
nerves and feel-good zones. It
responds to touches, stroking, holding,
and other forms of contact—soft, hard,
and everything in between.

Mouth

One of the most
versatile things on
your face! It takes in
nourishment, spits
out language, and is
another sensitive spot.

Chests, Breasts, and Nipples

We're all born with a chest that sports a set of nipples, which can feel very sensitive for some people or like nothing at all for others. Some folks develop visible breasts if their body gets the right combination of hormones and/or fatty tissue. The fun thing about boobs is that they're all unique: some are responsive and soft, others indifferent and rugged. No two are alike, and every pair is asymmetrical. Some people love to have theirs touched; others hate it!

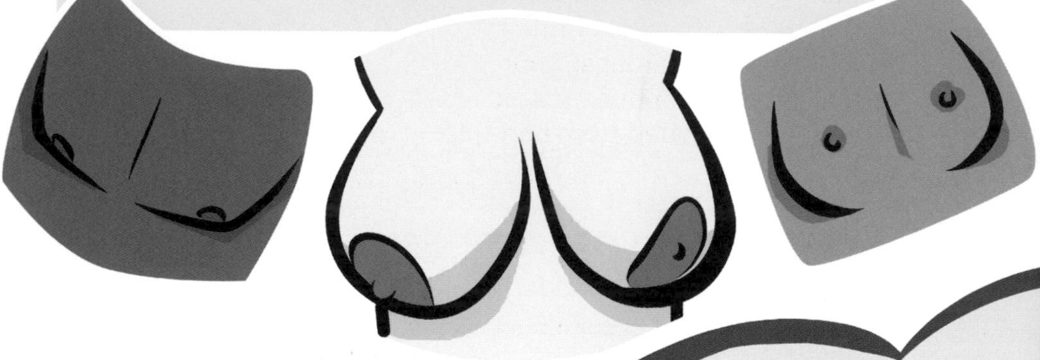

Anus

Both practical and pleasurable, this tight, flexible hole serves two purposes! This is the entrance to your bowels, the passageway for getting food waste (poop) outta your body. The opening is ALSO chock-full of sensitive nerves, making it a primo erogenous zone for touching and penetrating.

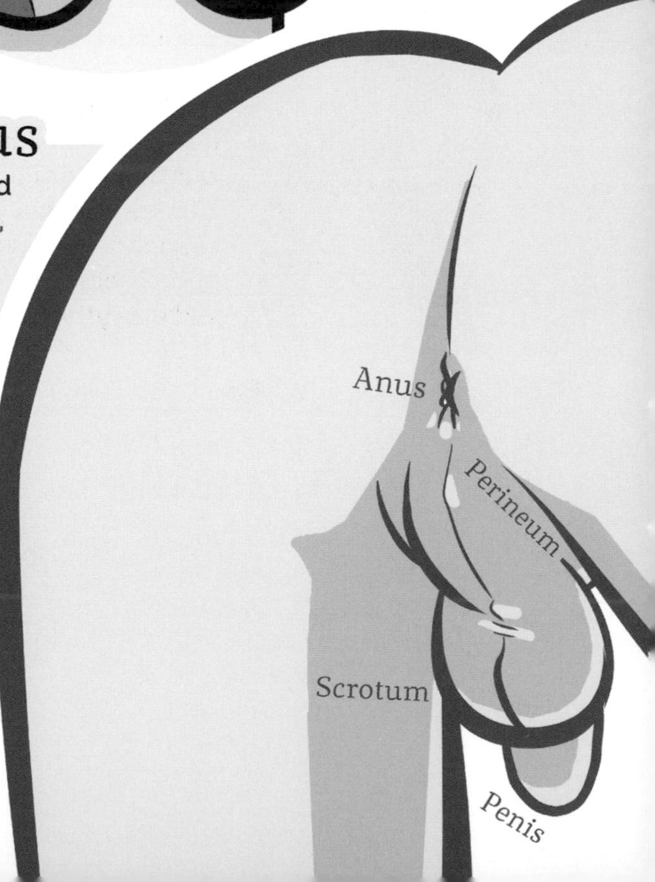
Anus
Perineum
Scrotum
Penis

Time to talk genitals!
Let's start with . . .

The Vulva (and friends)

The vulva, vagina, uterus, and all its accompanying parts are a deeply entwined and complex system—pretty much what you'd expect from the organs that are designed to make brand-new human beings! So let's work our way in from the outside.

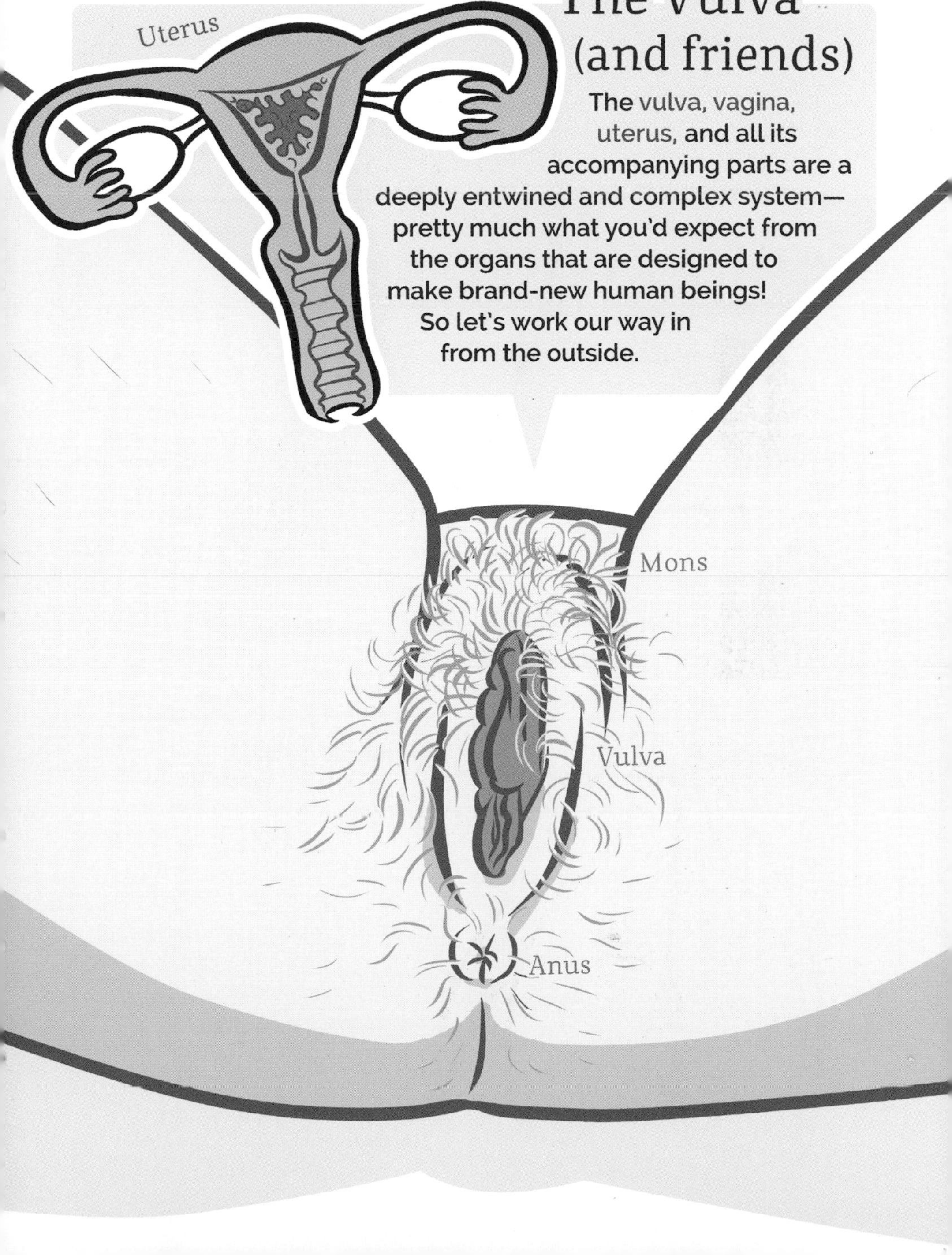

Uterus
Mons
Vulva
Anus

Labia

These are the cushions and outside protection a happy vulva needs! There are two sets: the fatter, outside labia majora, and the thinner, inner labia minora!

They come in ALL sizes and give your vulva its shape and appearance.

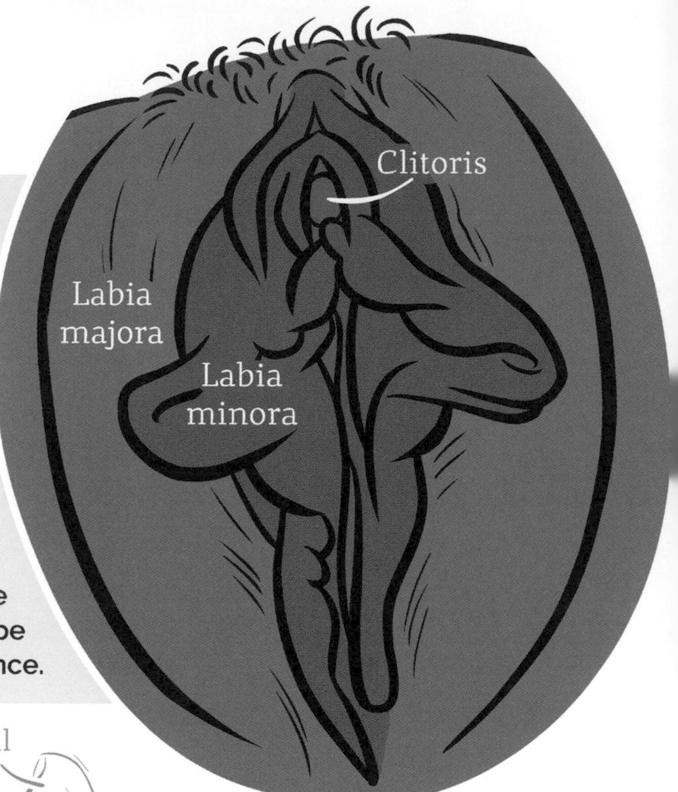

Clitoris

Labia majora

Labia minora

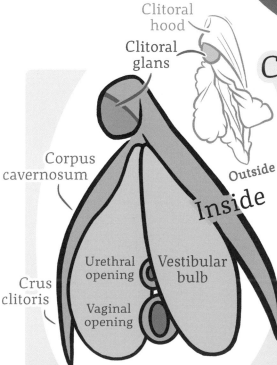

Clitoral hood

Clitoral glans

Corpus cavernosum

Outside

Inside

Crus clitoris

Urethral opening

Vestibular bulb

Vaginal opening

Clitoris

The labia minora meets up with your clitoris, which has its own hood for further protection from the outside world. This is the tip of the iceberg with the rest of the clitoral body hidden underneath; filled with THOUSANDS of nerves, its only purpose is to give the body pleasure. When aroused, it swells up with blood, getting larger, harder, and more sensitive!

From the outside you can also see the entrances to the...

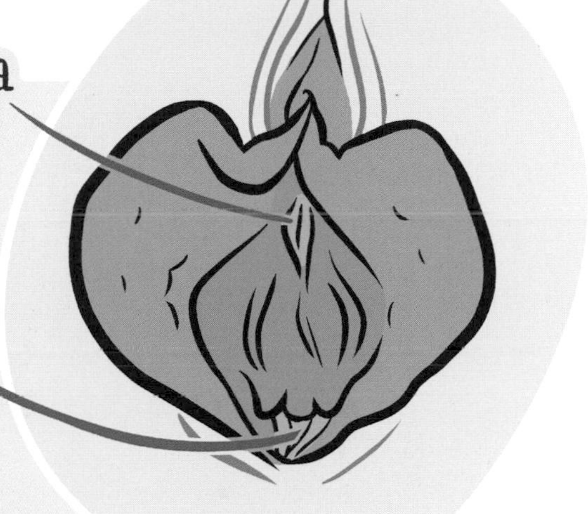

Urethra

This is where pee comes out! It travels inward and connects up to the bladder.

Vagina

This is the self-cleaning and regulating tunnel that leads to the cervix and uterus! It can take IN fingers, penises, sperm, sex toys, and period products, and lets OUT discharge, menstrual blood, and babies.

Just inside, you can find the...

G-spot

A sensitive area that can trigger an ejaculation of fluid when pressed.

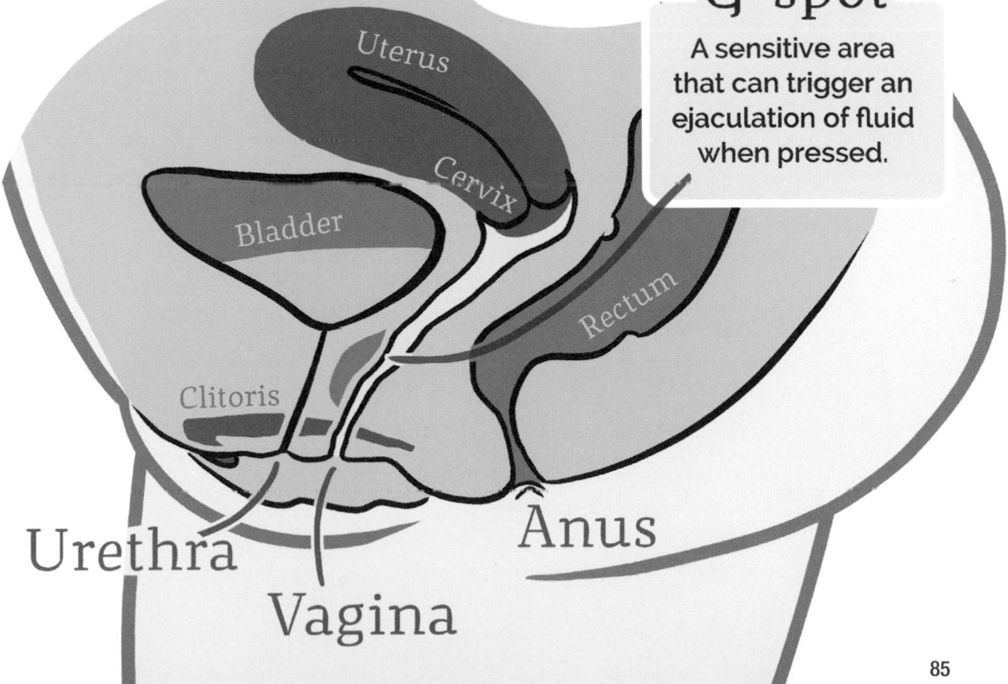
Uterus
Cervix
Bladder
Rectum
Clitoris
Urethra
Vagina
Anus

Normally, the vagina is deflated like an empty balloon. But when aroused, it opens up and expands deeper into you as your uterus and cervix shift to make more space.

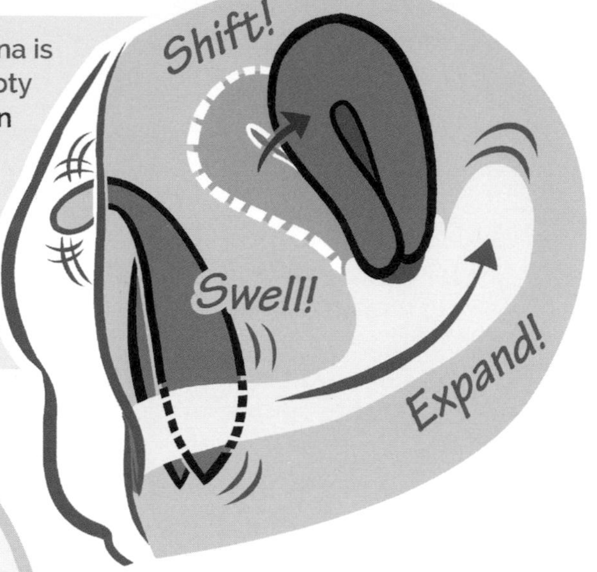
Shift!
Swell!
Expand!

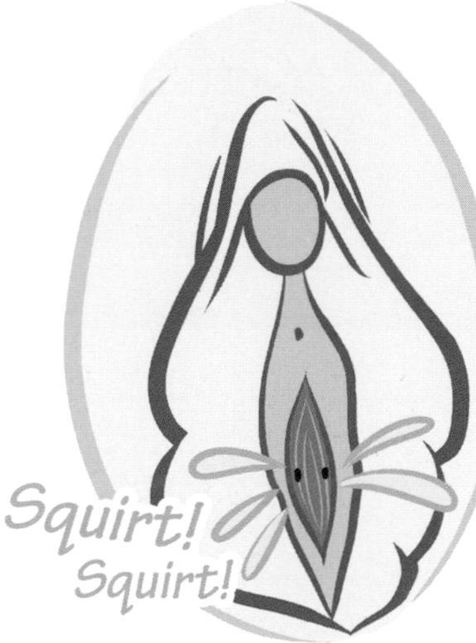
Squirt!
Squirt!

As if **that** wasn't cool enough, it self-lubricates when aroused with the help of the two Bartholin's glands that sit at the opening and add their slippery fluid.

Vaginas can also come with a hymen near the entrance; it's a thin, perforated tissue that partially covers the opening. It's hole-y and not always very apparent. Sometimes it'll tear when a person first puts something inside themself—ESPECIALLY if the vagina isn't already aroused and lubed up. Most will eventually wear away entirely.

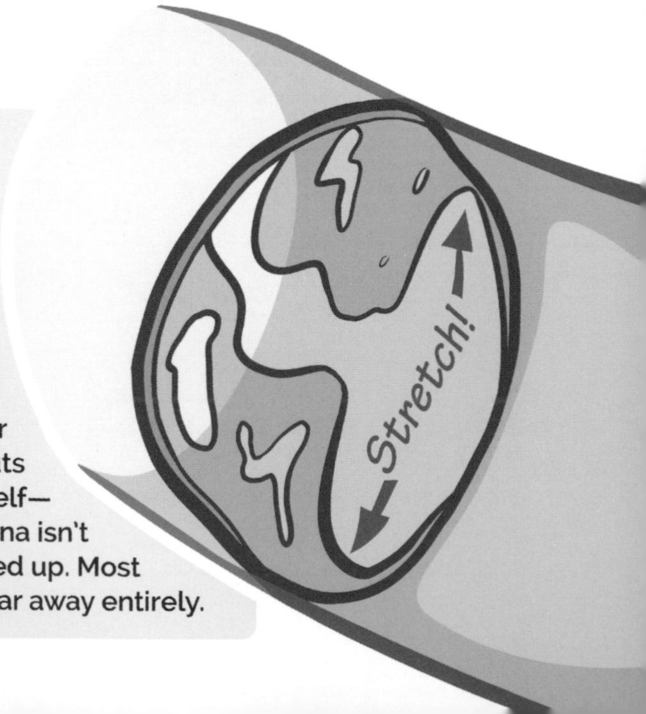
Stretch!

Cervix

The gatekeeper to your uterus! This fleshy little doughnut changes its hardness, mucous viscosity, and position in the vagina throughout the menstrual cycle. During the primo baby-making days, it allows easy access for sperm, while during the less fertile days it becomes harder to bypass, although not impossible for the wiliest swimmers.

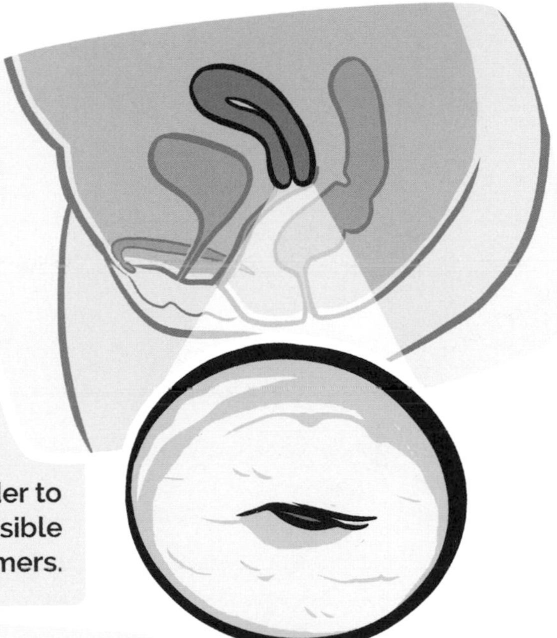

The cervix is also the lowest part of the…

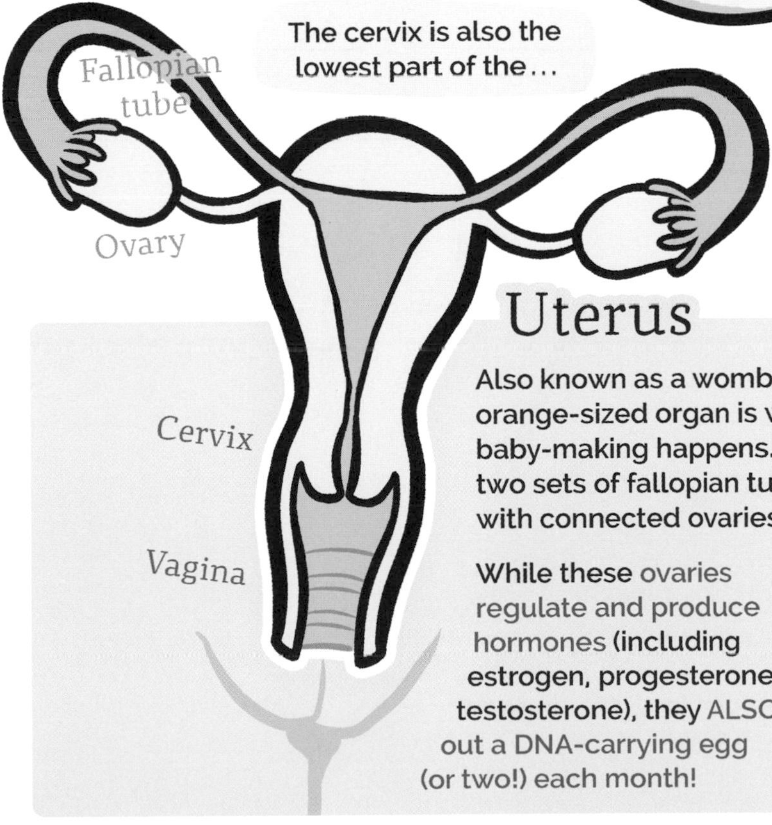
Fallopian tube
Ovary
Cervix
Vagina

Uterus

Also known as a womb, this orange-sized organ is where the baby-making happens. It has two sets of fallopian tubes with connected ovaries.

While these ovaries regulate and produce hormones (including estrogen, progesterone, and testosterone), they ALSO pop out a DNA-carrying egg (or two!) each month!

This little egg slides into its fallopian tube, where it hangs out waiting for a single sperm to find and fertilize it.

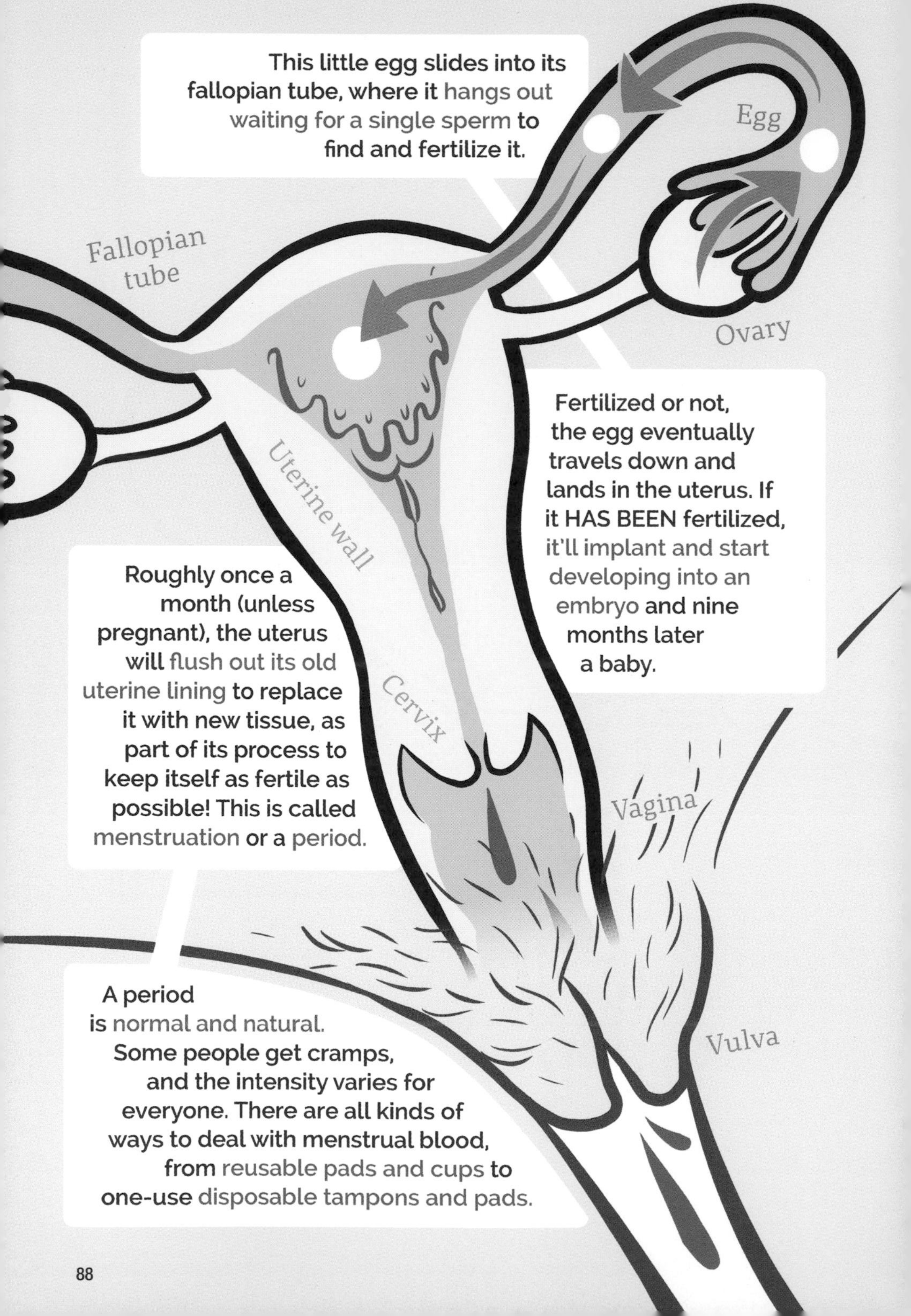
Egg
Fallopian tube
Ovary
Uterine wall
Cervix
Vagina
Vulva

Fertilized or not, the egg eventually travels down and lands in the uterus. If it HAS BEEN fertilized, it'll implant and start developing into an embryo and nine months later a baby.

Roughly once a month (unless pregnant), the uterus will flush out its old uterine lining to replace it with new tissue, as part of its process to keep itself as fertile as possible! This is called menstruation or a period.

A period is normal and natural. Some people get cramps, and the intensity varies for everyone. There are all kinds of ways to deal with menstrual blood, from reusable pads and cups to one-use disposable tampons and pads.

You'd think this would be a case of what-you-see-is-what-you-get, but the penis, scrotum, and all that pipework are just as complicated and interesting as their counterparts from the previous pages. Check it out. . . .

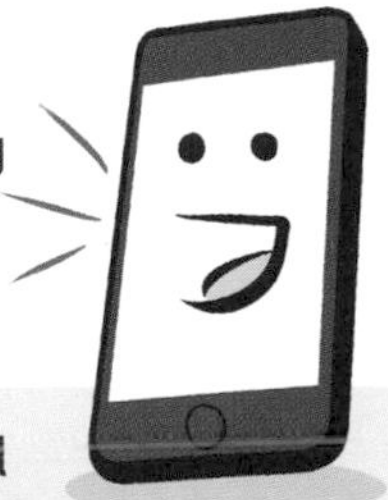

Penis

Penises start INSIDE the body, and then extrude outward. They come in ALL sorts of shapes and sizes and are naturally topped by a foreskin (a protective layer of movable skin, which is sometimes surgically removed). They start out soft and flaccid, but when aroused, fill up with blood to become larger and harder.

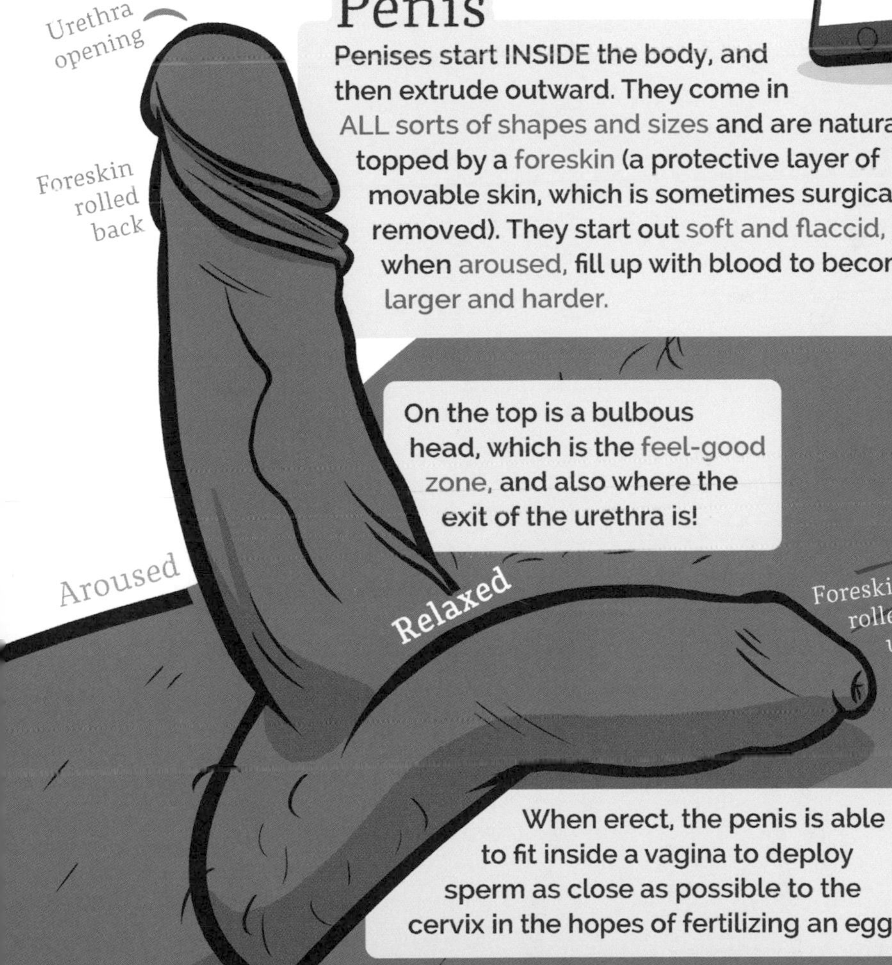

Urethra opening
Foreskin rolled back
Aroused
Relaxed
Foreskin rolled up

On the top is a bulbous head, which is the feel-good zone, and also where the exit of the urethra is!

When erect, the penis is able to fit inside a vagina to deploy sperm as close as possible to the cervix in the hopes of fertilizing an egg.

Urethra

This tube travels down the underside of the penis and eventually connects to the bladder and prostate. It's doubly useful, because it carries both pee AND semen out of the body.

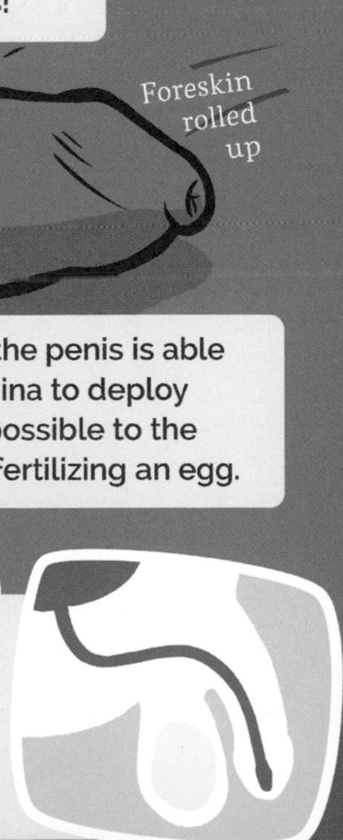

Here's where things get wild. Before the urethra meets up with the bladder, it runs into a junction of tubes that are surrounded by a walnut-shaped organ: the prostate! This hunk of muscle is here to add protective juices to the sperm and to help push out ejaculate during an orgasm. Some people like it stimulated by putting a finger in the bum and doing a come-hither motion toward the belly.

Prostate

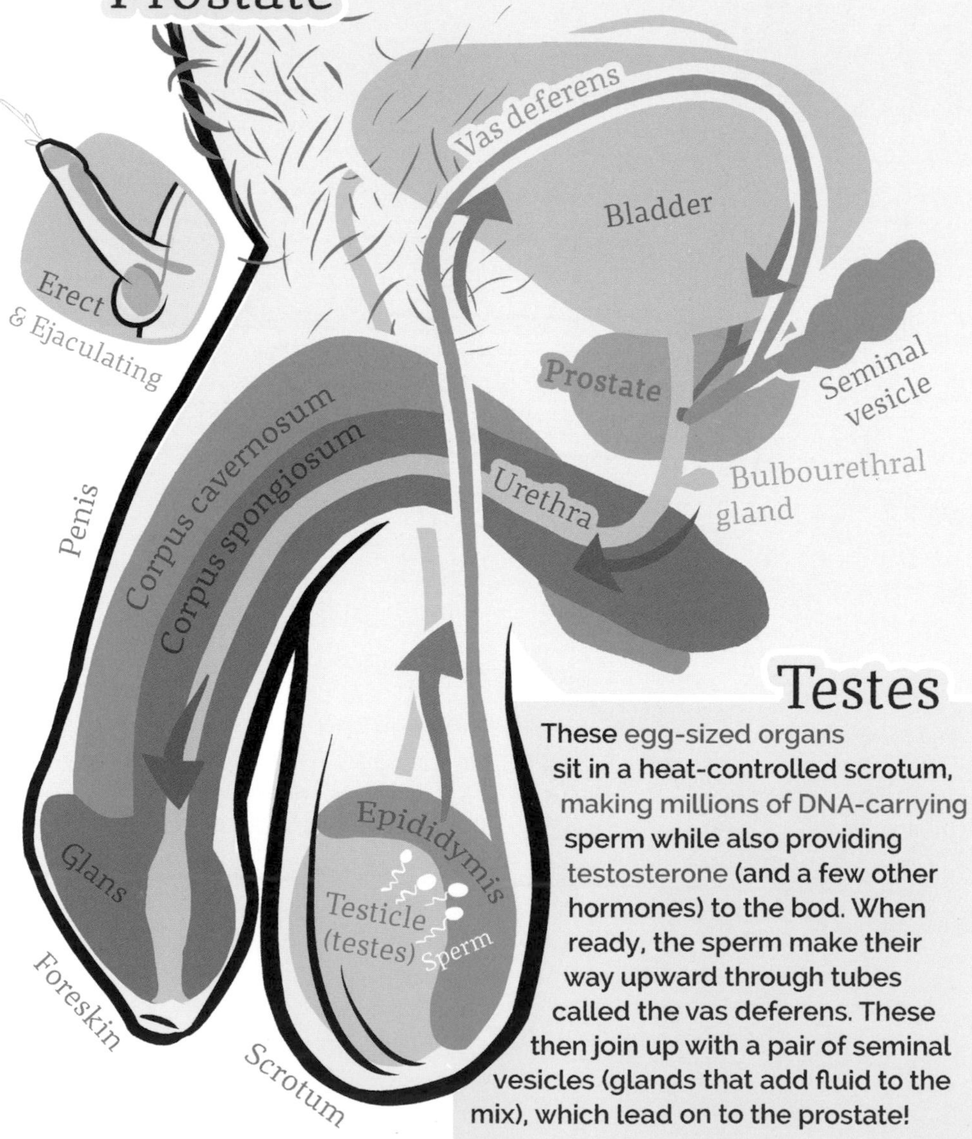

Erect
& Ejaculating
Vas deferens
Bladder
Prostate
Seminal vesicle
Bulbourethral gland
Urethra
Corpus cavernosum
Corpus spongiosum
Penis
Glans
Foreskin
Epididymis
Testicle (testes)
Sperm
Scrotum

Testes

These egg-sized organs sit in a heat-controlled scrotum, making millions of DNA-carrying sperm while also providing testosterone (and a few other hormones) to the bod. When ready, the sperm make their way upward through tubes called the vas deferens. These then join up with a pair of seminal vesicles (glands that add fluid to the mix), which lead on to the prostate!

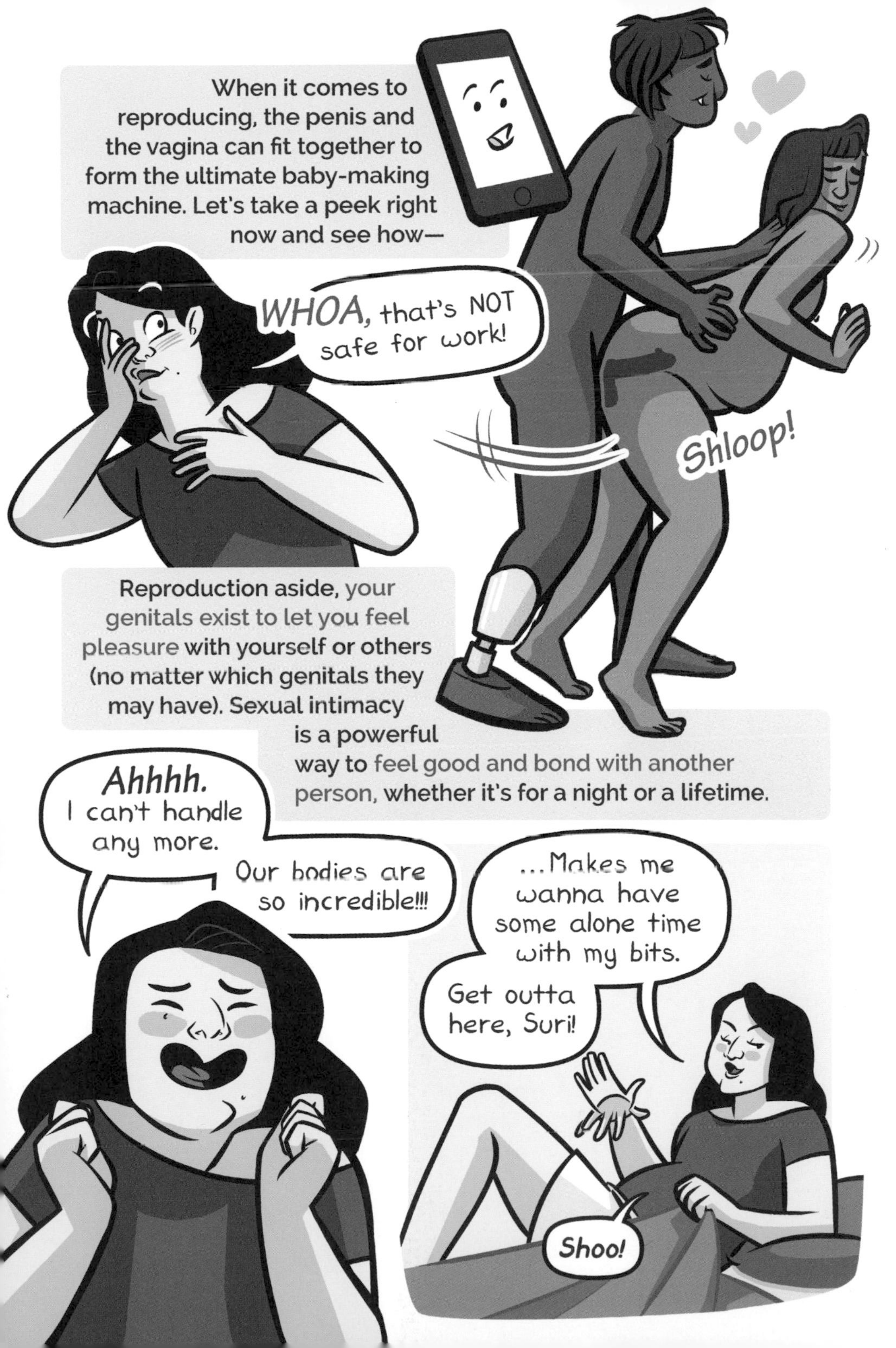

When it comes to reproducing, the penis and the vagina can fit together to form the ultimate baby-making machine. Let's take a peek right now and see how—
WHOA, that's NOT safe for work!
Shloop!
Reproduction aside, your genitals exist to let you feel pleasure with yourself or others (no matter which genitals they may have). Sexual intimacy is a powerful way to feel good and bond with another person, whether it's for a night or a lifetime.
Ahhhh. I can't handle any more.
Our bodies are so incredible!!!
...Makes me wanna have some alone time with my bits.
Get outta here, Suri!
Shoo!

Where do you . . . start?

Are you thinking about relationships?
Are you thinking about . . . sex? What
do you do? What do you DO? How do
you know you're ready? When will you
know you're ready? What does it even
feel like to be ready? Why is this so
stressful and complicated?

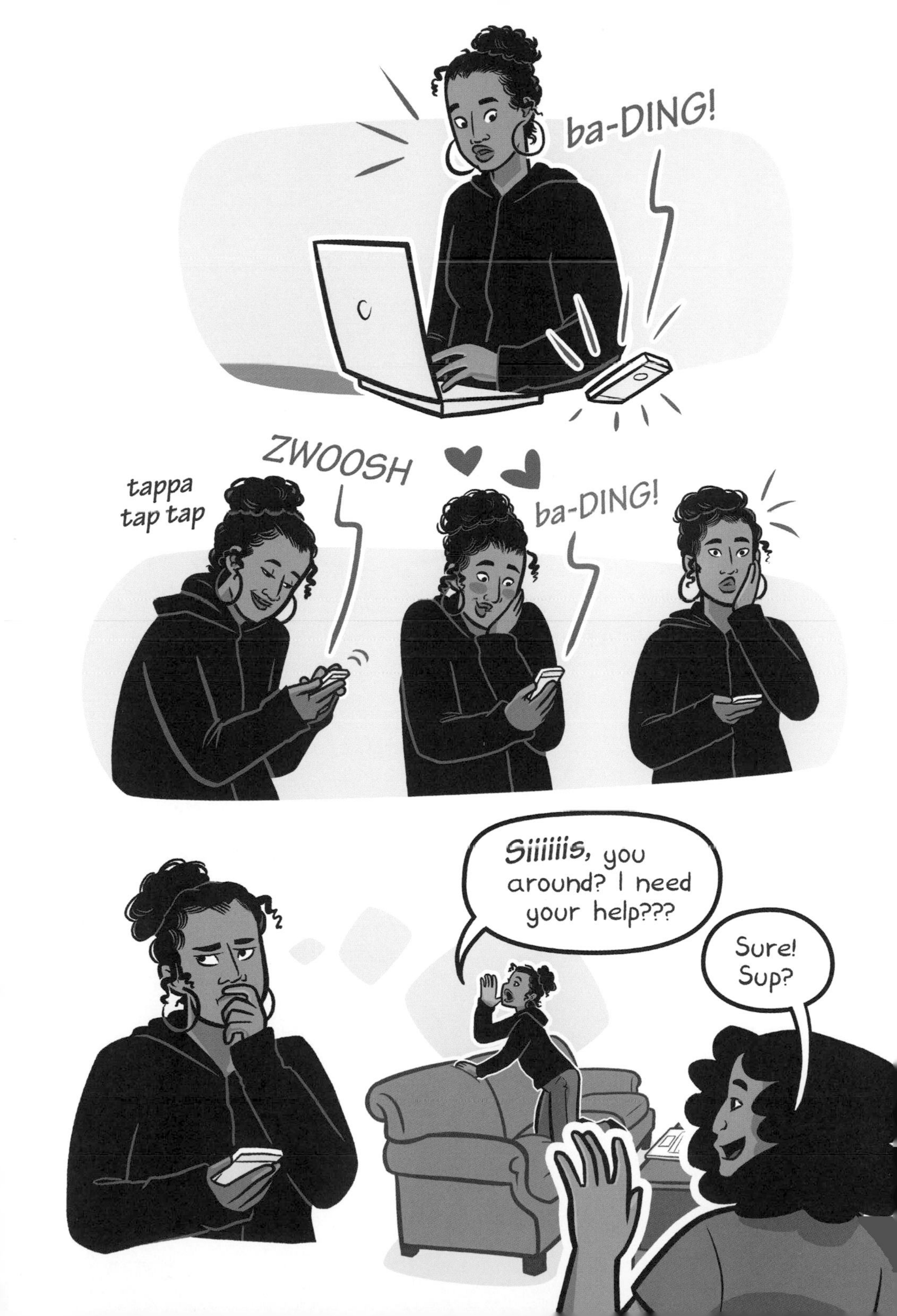
ba-DING!
tappa tap tap
ZWOOSH
ba-DING!
Siiiiiis, you around? I need your help???
Sure! Sup?

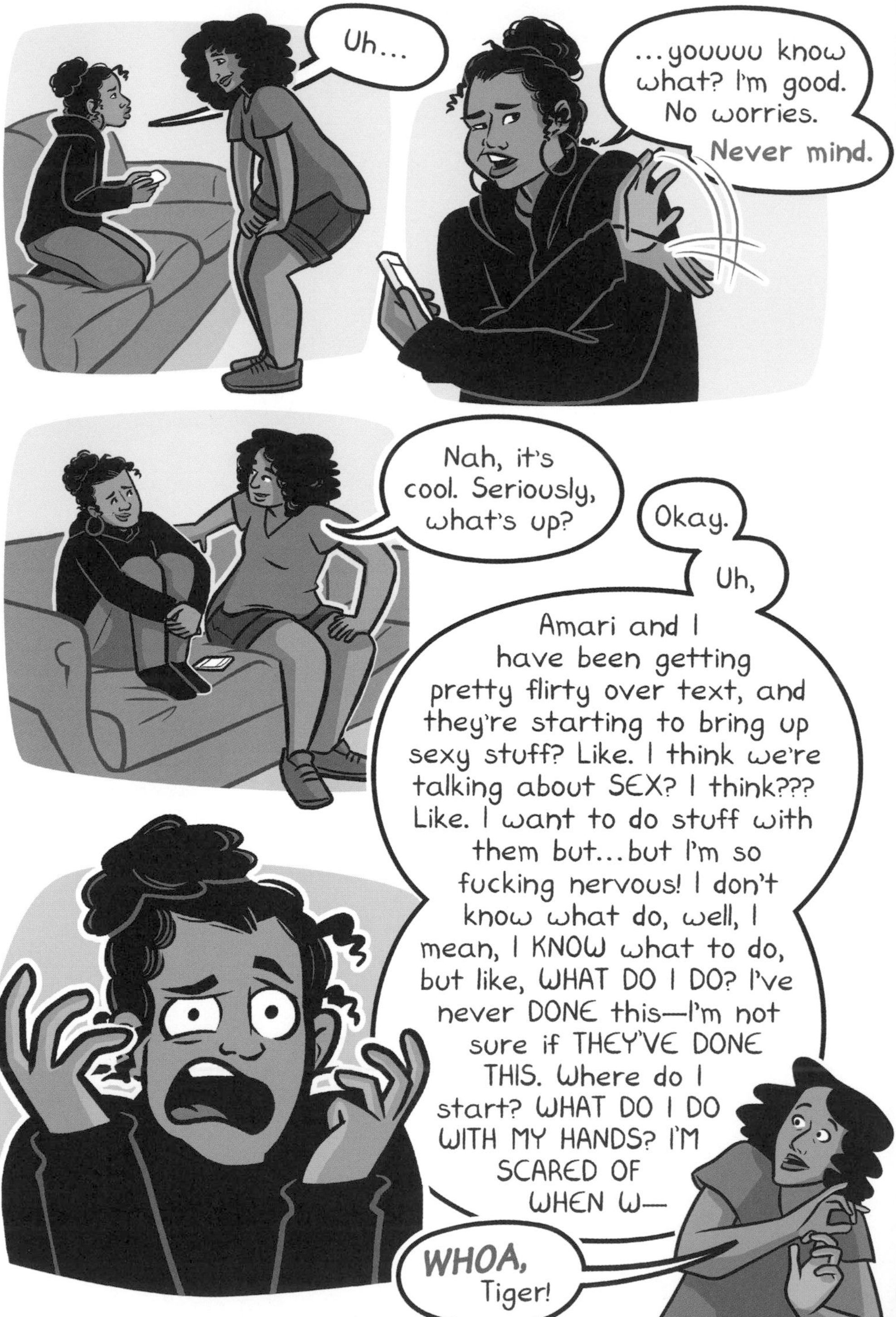
Uh...
...youuuu know what? I'm good. No worries.
Never mind.
Nah, it's cool. Seriously, what's up?
Okay.
Uh,
Amari and I have been getting pretty flirty over text, and they're starting to bring up sexy stuff? Like. I think we're talking about SEX? I think??? Like. I want to do stuff with them but...but I'm so fucking nervous! I don't know what do, well, I mean, I KNOW what to do, but like, WHAT DO I DO? I've never DONE this—I'm not sure if THEY'VE DONE THIS. Where do I start? WHAT DO I DO WITH MY HANDS? I'M SCARED OF WHEN W—
WHOA, Tiger!

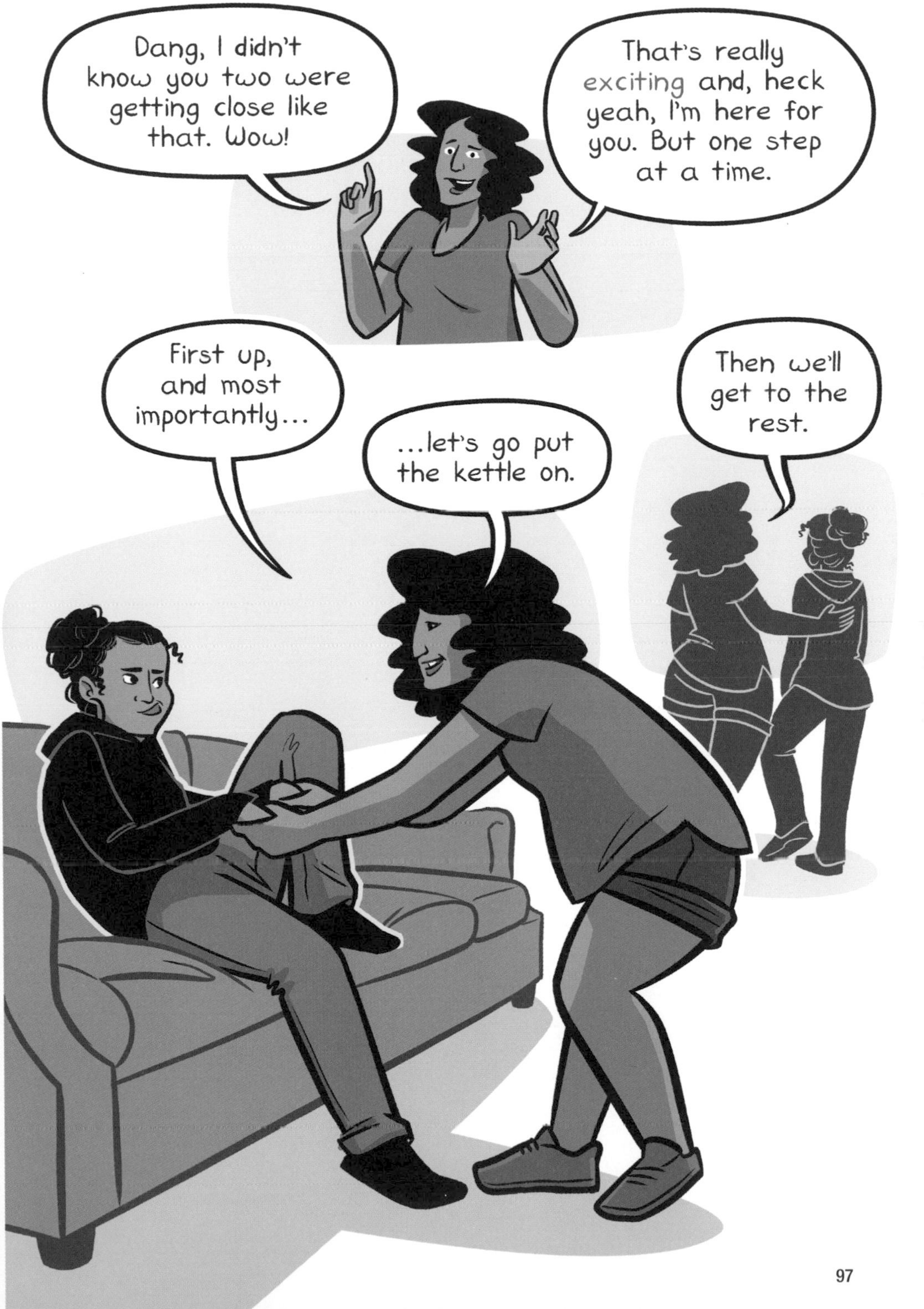
Dang, I didn't know you two were getting close like that. Wow!
That's really exciting and, heck yeah, I'm here for you. But one step at a time.
First up, and most importantly...
...let's go put the kettle on.
Then we'll get to the rest.

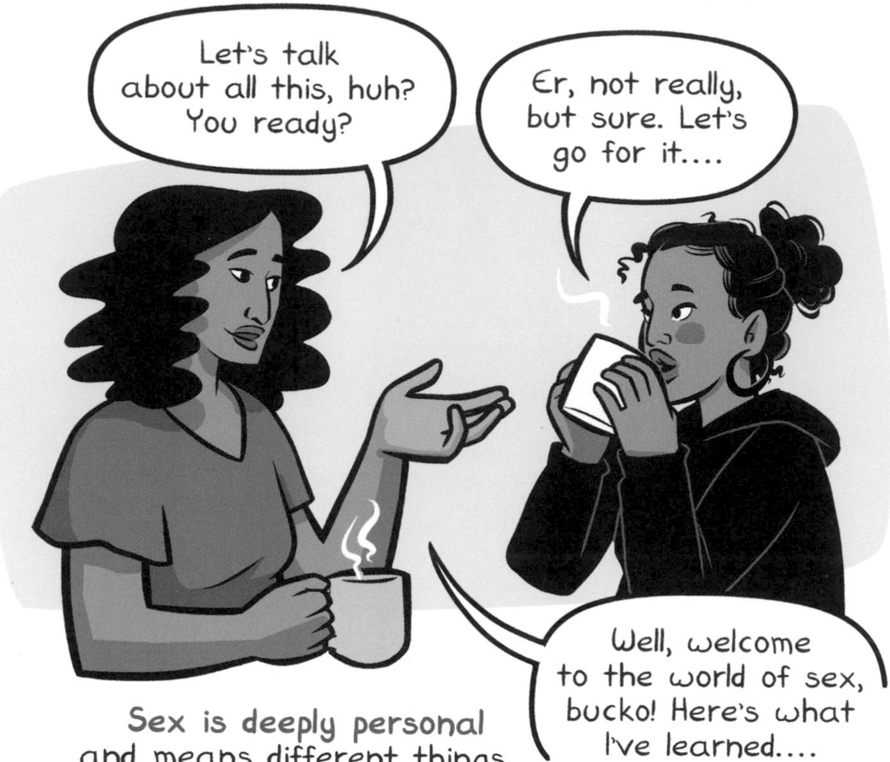
Let's talk about all this, huh? You ready?
Er, not really, but sure. Let's go for it....
Well, welcome to the world of sex, bucko! Here's what I've learned....

Sex is deeply personal and means different things to different people. It may seem daunting, but as you start to learn about this stuff, you're gonna see just how fascinating it can be.

There's no one correct way you're supposed to feel about it.

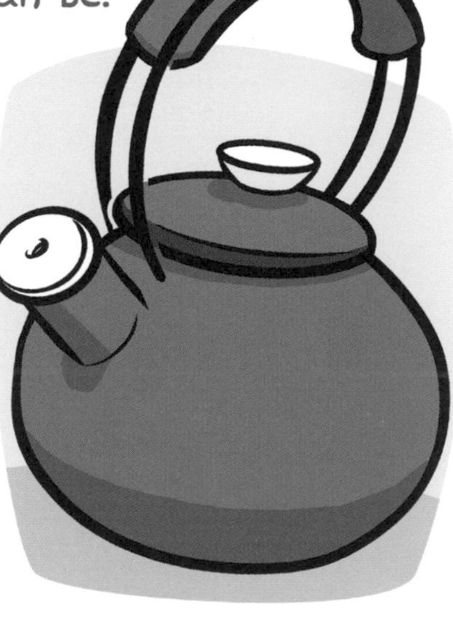

Sex can be a space for personal growth and exploration, a world of connection, intimacy, and fun. It's an interesting part of being human, though it's not for everyone. Some folks have little or no interest in it, which is perfectly normal too.

It probably seems like everyone you know and the world itself is telling you to dive on in, but take a breath and pause for a bit!

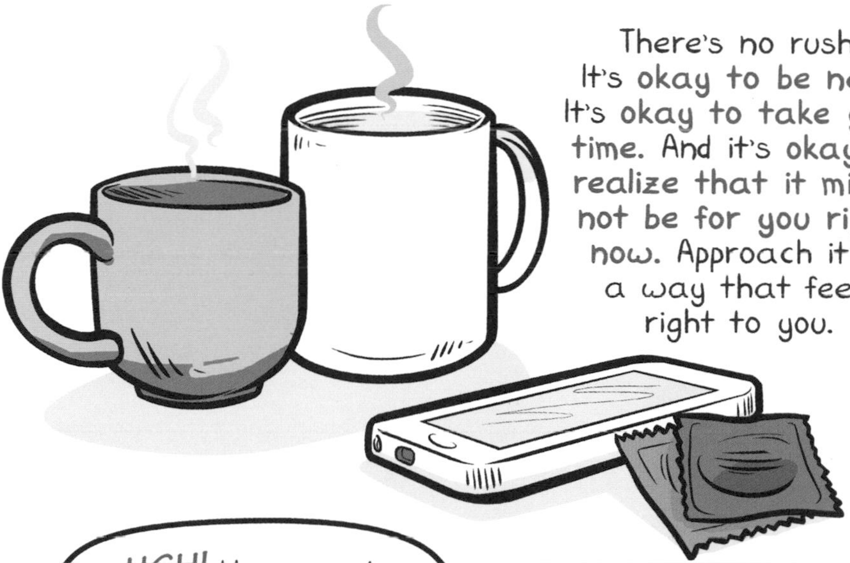

There's no rush. It's okay to be new. It's okay to take your time. And it's okay to realize that it might not be for you right now. Approach it in a way that feels right to you.

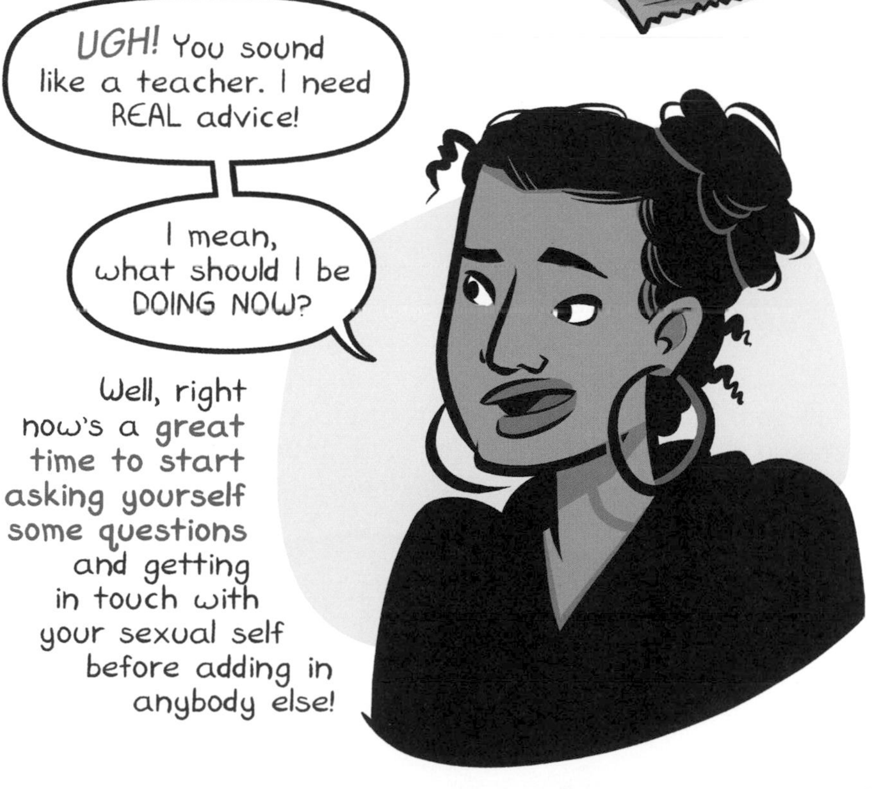
UGH! You sound like a teacher. I need REAL advice!
I mean, what should I be DOING NOW?

Well, right now's a great time to start asking yourself some questions and getting in touch with your sexual self before adding in anybody else!

Begin with some of these questions and see where they take you. There are no wrong answers: it's all an exercise in exploration!

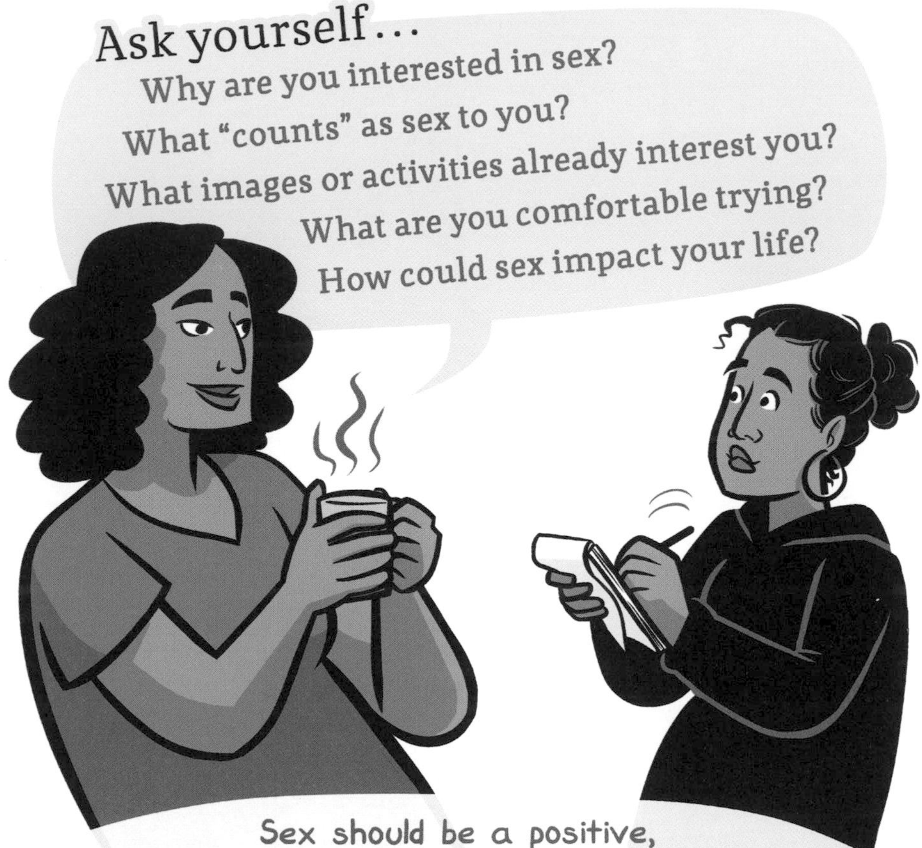
Ask yourself...
Why are you interested in sex?
What "counts" as sex to you?
What images or activities already interest you?
What are you comfortable trying?
How could sex impact your life?

Sex should be a positive, pleasurable activity for all participants. If you feel like any of your answers don't reflect that kind of an experience, give yourself some more time to think about it. Remember, there's no rush.

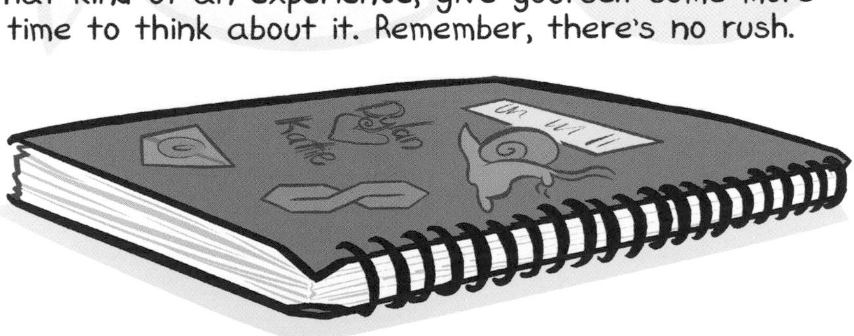

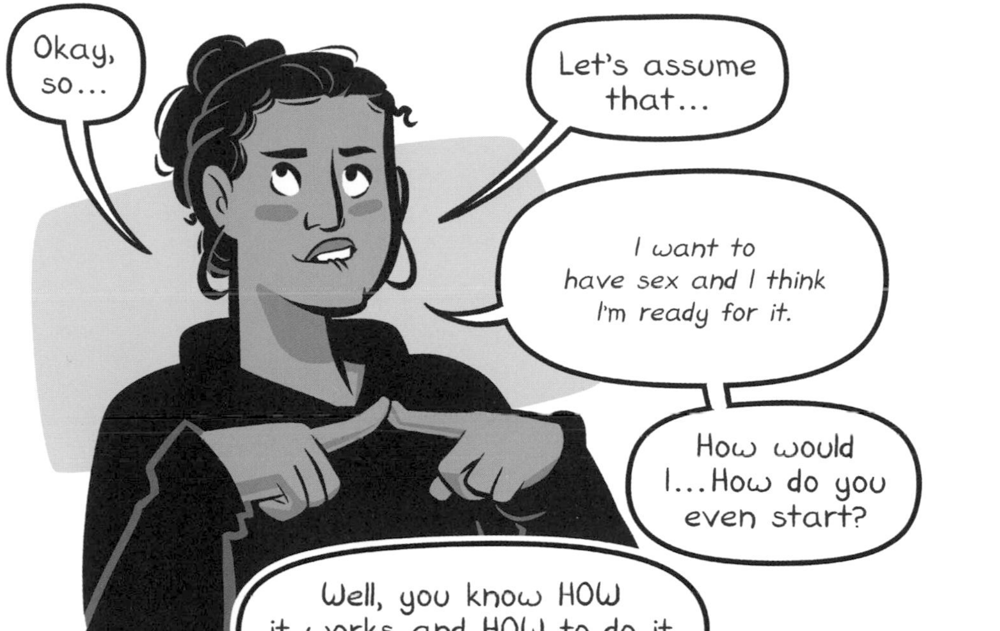
Okay, so...
Let's assume that...
I want to have sex and I think I'm ready for it.
How would I...How do you even start?
Well, you know HOW it works and HOW to do it with protection, right?
Ah, yeah. I did my research. We have... condoms.
Then it's just a matter of talking it up with your would-be partner!

Whether you're having a one-night fling or you're in a long-term relationship, you want to be on the same page with your partner, so make sure to talk about sex ahead of time.

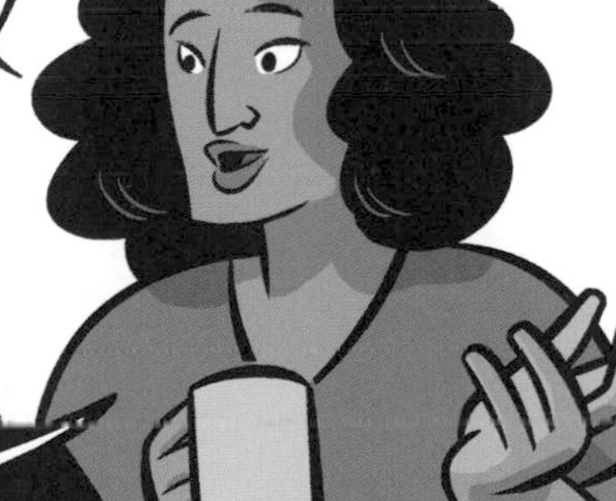

It can be a long chat way in advance, or something shorter right before you hook up. It all counts as long as you're talking!

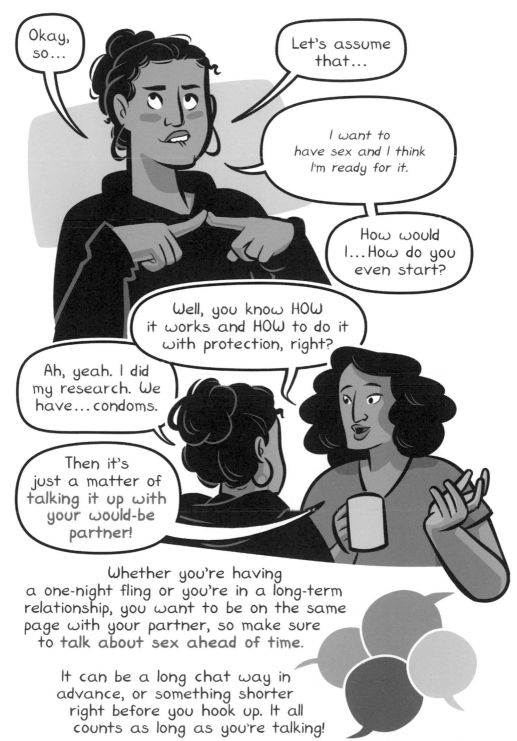

Ask your partners…

What would YOU like to do and try?

Here is what I'm interested in doing with you….

This is what I'm thinking. What are YOUR thoughts?

Here's where and how I want to be touched.

How do you like to be touched?

Here's what's off-limits for me….

What do you want to avoid?

If you run into a disagreement, talk it out. You want the experience to be good and fun for BOTH of you. So don't do anything either of you are uncomfortable with. Respect each other's wishes.

Sometimes you might not be able to find a good middle ground when you're having the sexy talk, and that's okay too. We're all super different in our wants and needs! If that happens, just don't go forward. Forcing things leads to bad experiences.

Broaching the topic of sex can be super scary and sort of the last thing you might want to do, buuuut it's a necessary step. Talking about sex with the person you're thinking of doing it with can be a relief and actually... *kinda* sexy.

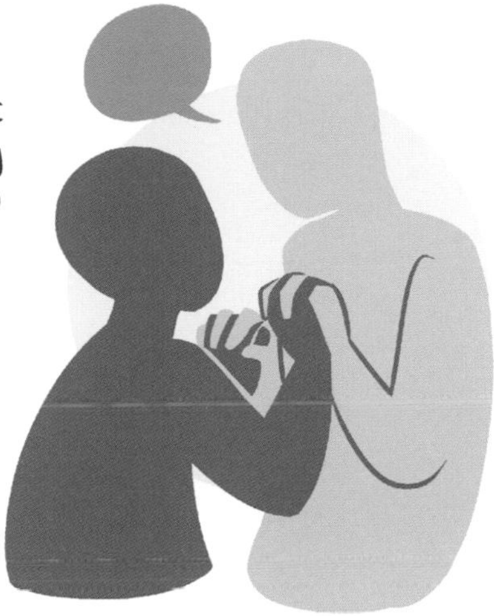

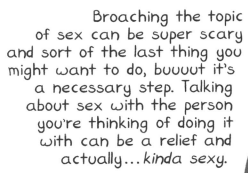

You're planning to get *intimate with their intimates*, so **be brave, be bold, and bring it up before you bone!** If your partner's too shy to talk with you about sex right now, give them space and try again another time.

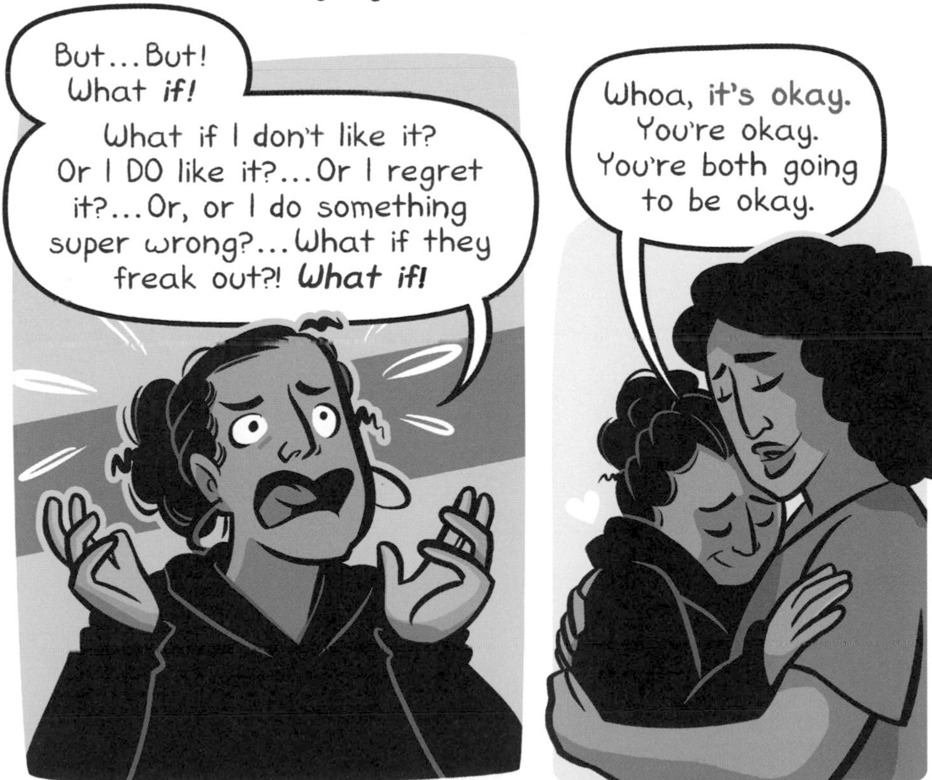
But... But! What *if!*
What if I don't like it? Or I DO like it?... Or I regret it?... Or, or I do something super wrong?... What if they freak out?! ***What if!***
Whoa, it's okay. You're okay. You're both going to be okay.

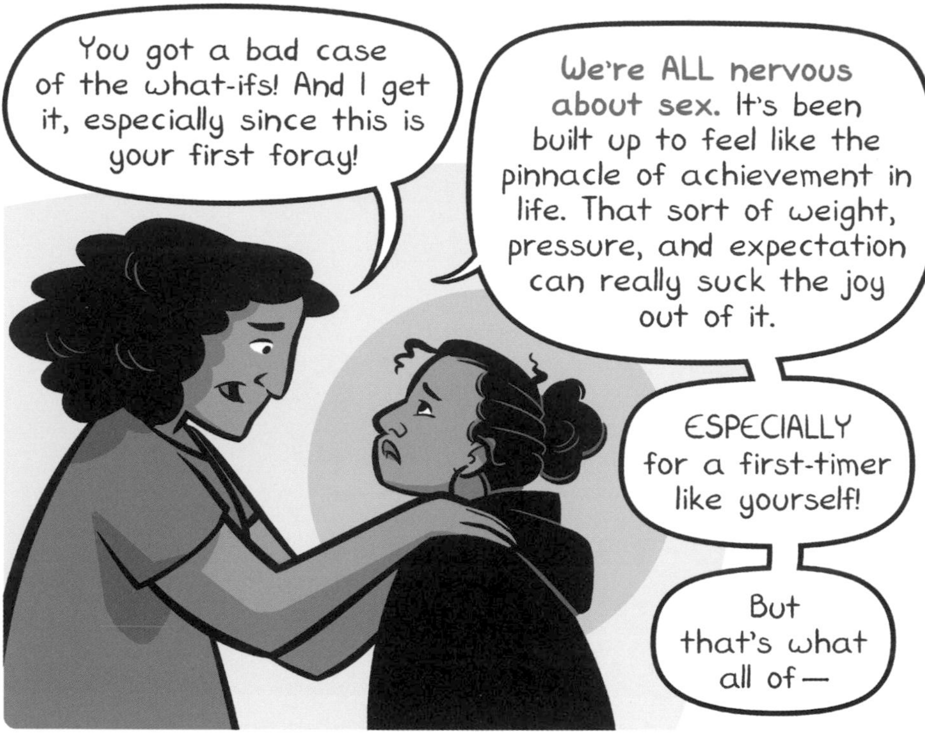
You got a bad case of the what-ifs! And I get it, especially since this is your first foray!
We're ALL nervous about sex. It's been built up to feel like the pinnacle of achievement in life. That sort of weight, pressure, and expectation can really suck the joy out of it.
ESPECIALLY for a first-timer like yourself!
But that's what all of—

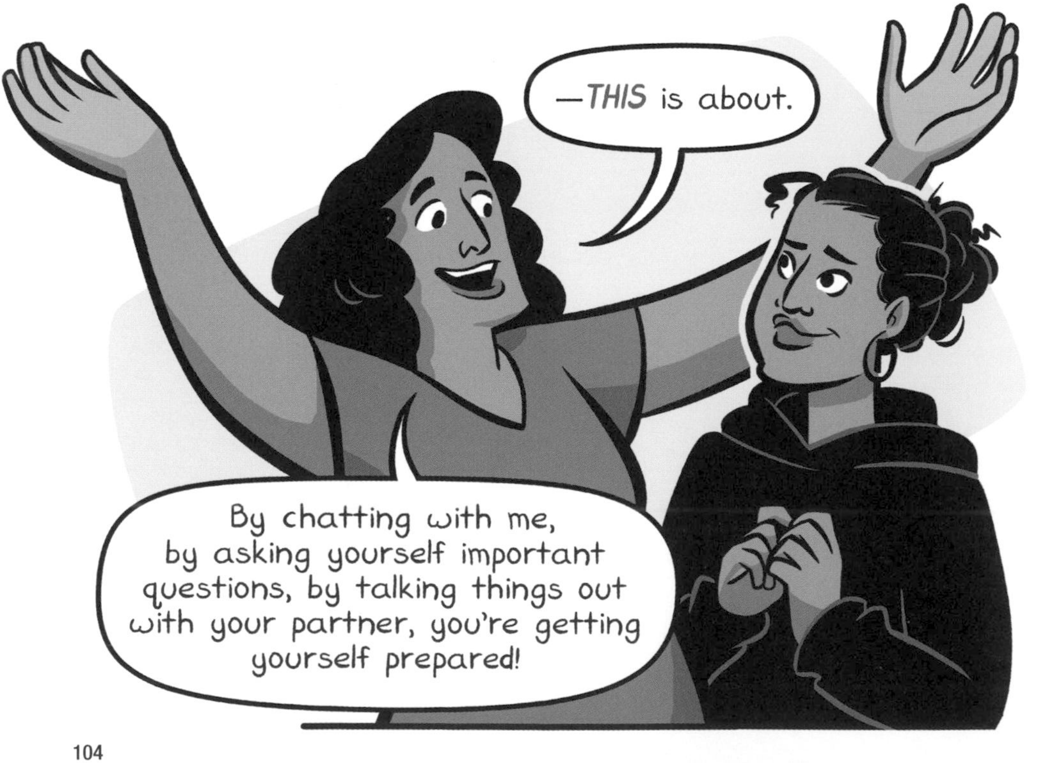
—*THIS* is about.
By chatting with me, by asking yourself important questions, by talking things out with your partner, you're getting yourself prepared!

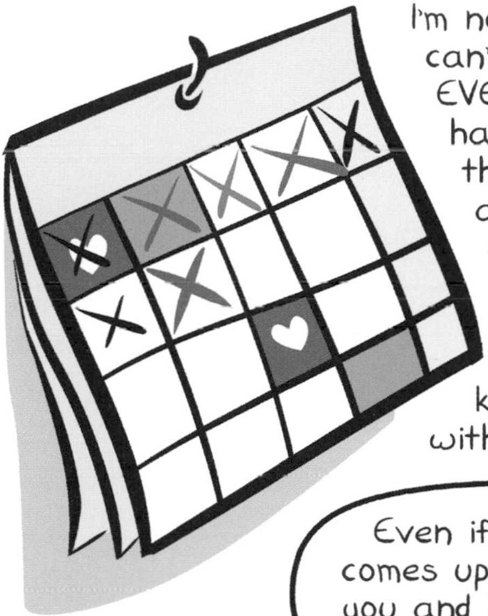

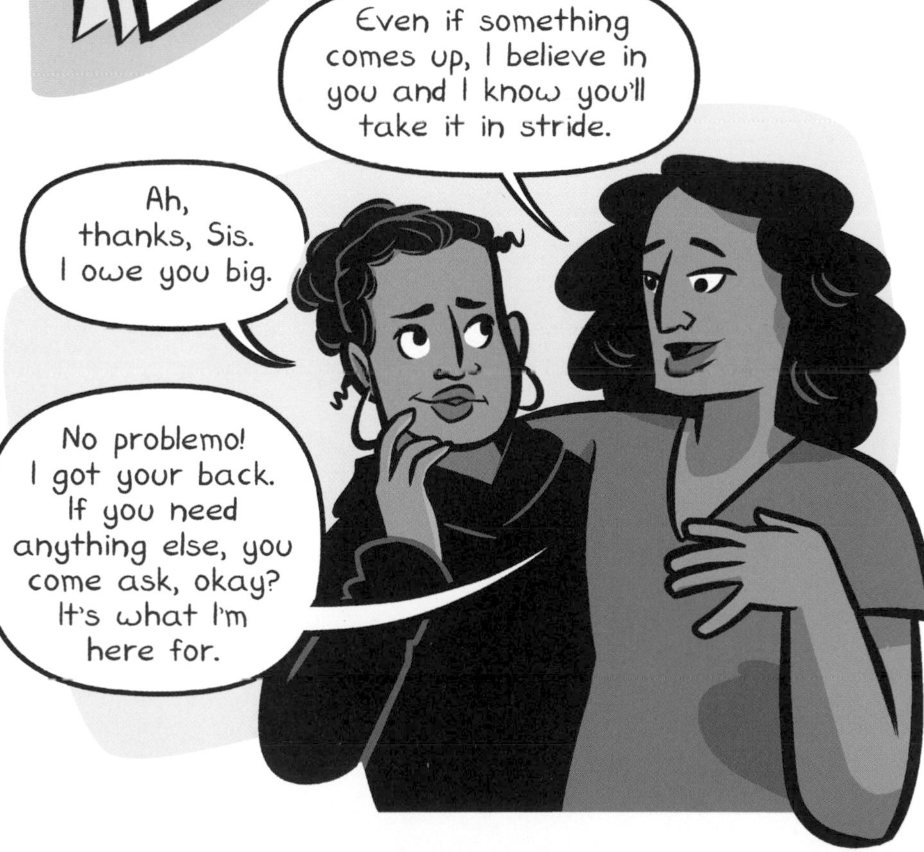

What is . . .
masturbation?

Why would you want to masturbate?
Is masturbation . . . okay? How do
you do it? How do you get good at it?

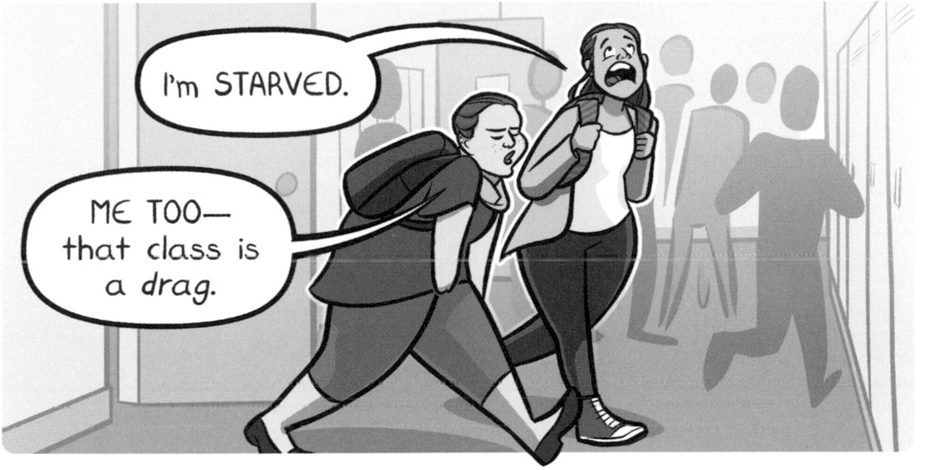
I'm STARVED.
ME TOO— that class is a *drag*.
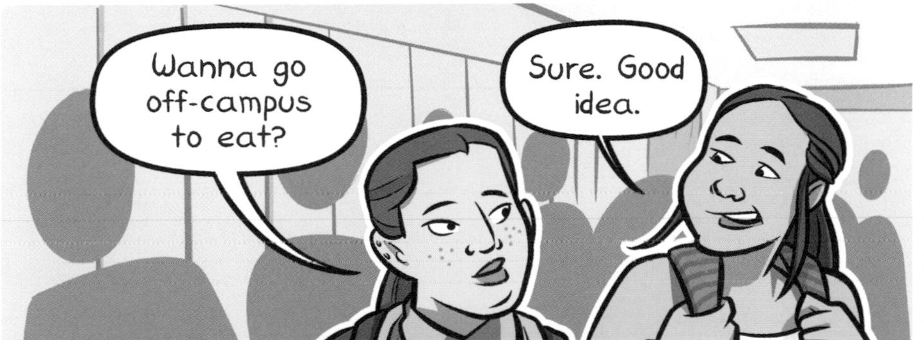
Wanna go off-campus to eat?
Sure. Good idea.
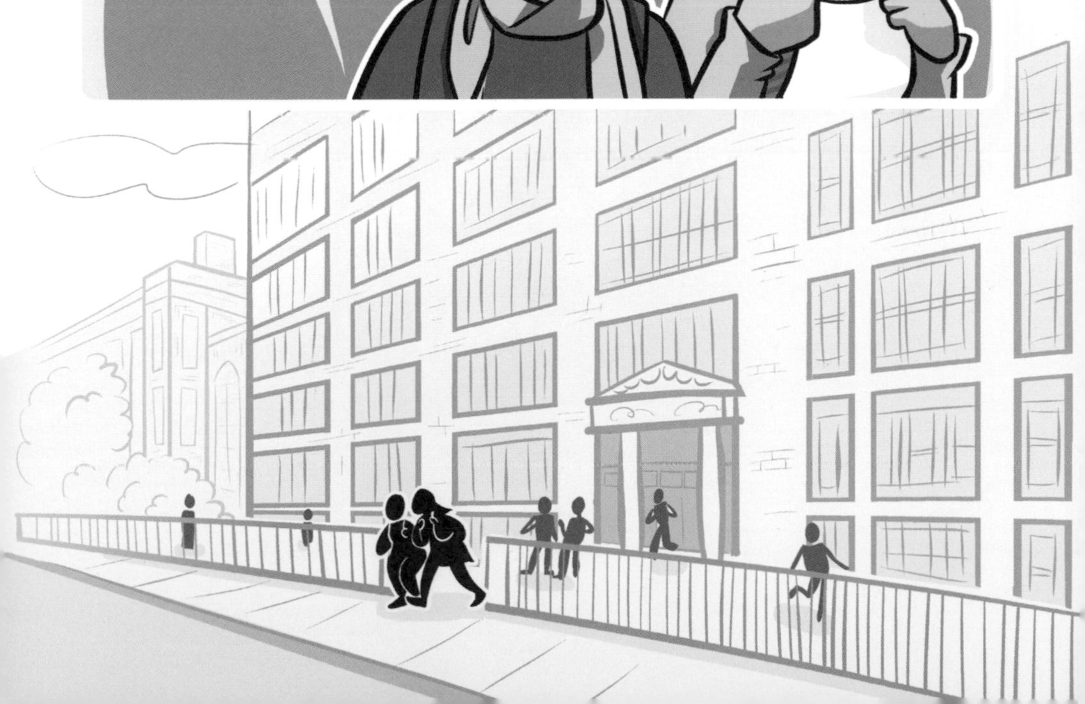

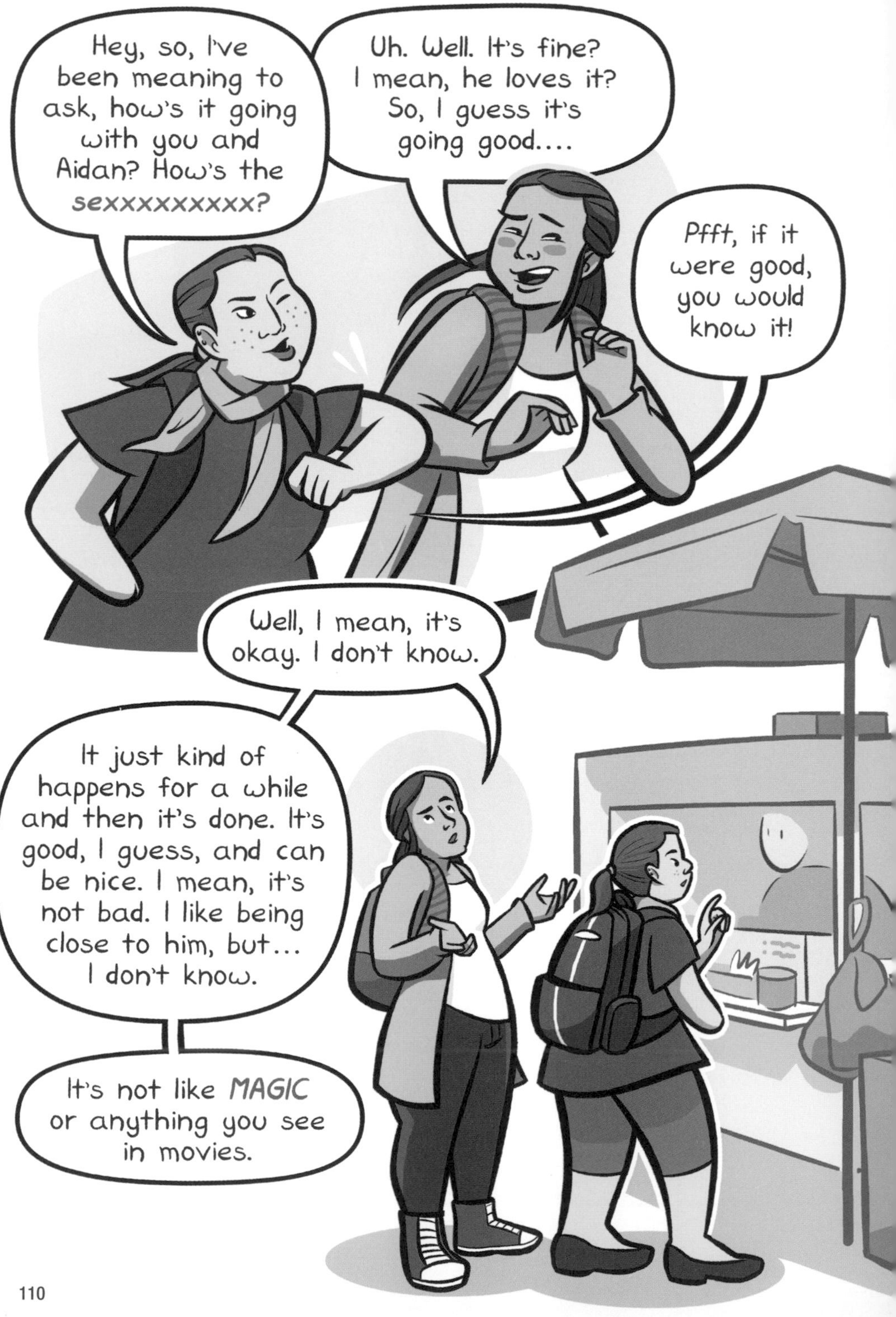
Hey, so, I've been meaning to ask, how's it going with you and Aidan? How's the *sexxxxxxxxx*?
Uh. Well. It's fine? I mean, he loves it? So, I guess it's going good....
Pfft, if it were good, you would know it!
Well, I mean, it's okay. I don't know.
It just kind of happens for a while and then it's done. It's good, I guess, and can be nice. I mean, it's not bad. I like being close to him, but... I don't know.
It's not like *MAGIC* or anything you see in movies.

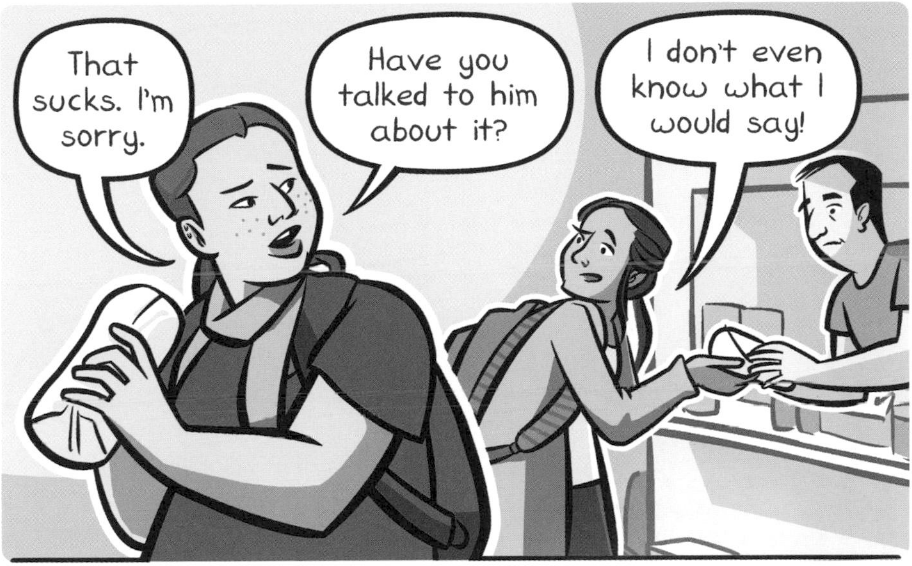
That sucks. I'm sorry.
Have you talked to him about it?
I don't even know what I would say!

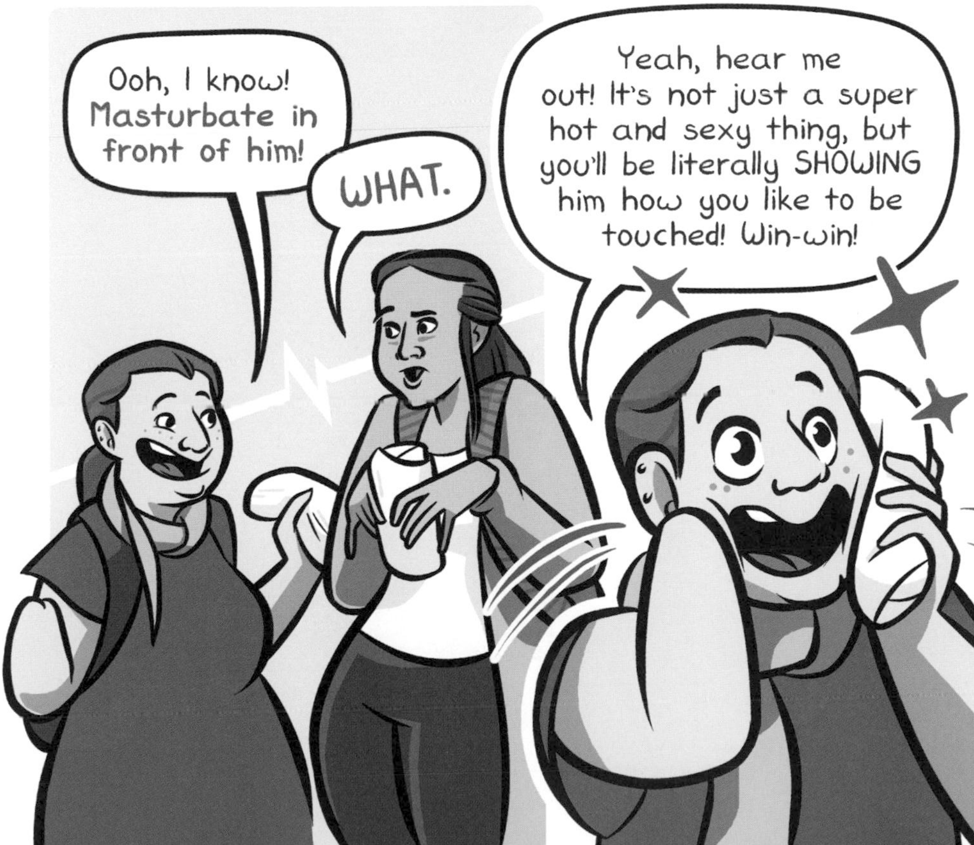
Ooh, I know! Masturbate in front of him!
WHAT.
Yeah, hear me out! It's not just a super hot and sexy thing, but you'll be literally SHOWING him how you like to be touched! Win-win!

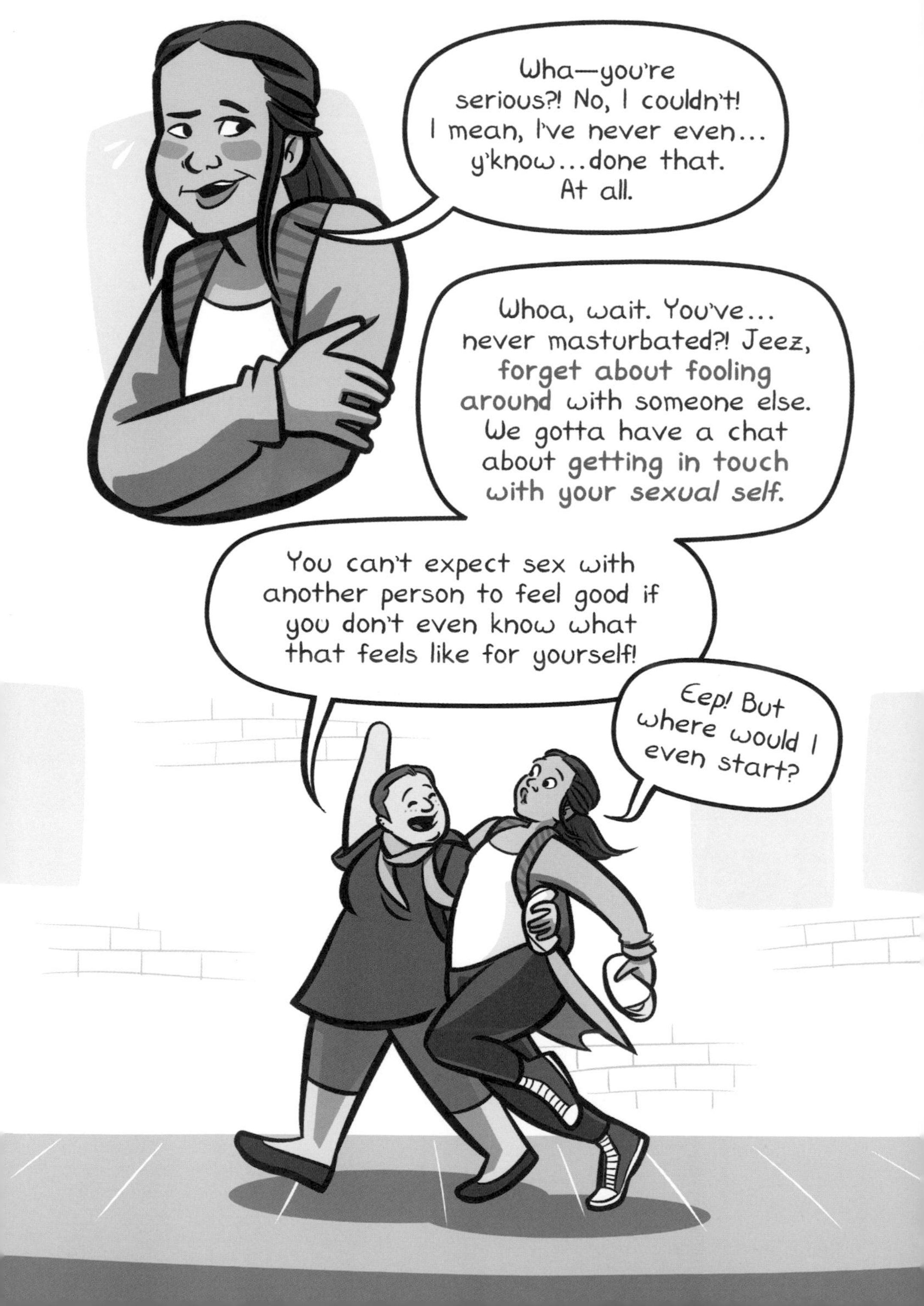
Wha—you're serious?! No, I couldn't! I mean, I've never even... y'know...done that. At all.
Whoa, wait. You've... never masturbated?! Jeez, forget about fooling around with someone else. We gotta have a chat about getting in touch with your *sexual self*.
You can't expect sex with another person to feel good if you don't even know what that feels like for yourself!
Eep! But where would I even start?

Start wherever it feels right for you! It's *super normal* for someone to have never played with themself before! There's a lot of negative messages out here telling us that it's no good.
It's ridiculous how society has made rubbing one out seem so shameful!
Masturbation is the safest sex a person can have! There's no risk of pregnancy or STI transfer or personal boundary violations; it's a one-stop shop for getting your sexual needs met.
It's never too late to start!
Sexual... self?
Oh, yeah! The SEXUAL YOU. The part of you that is a sexual being.

Your sexual self is this constantly evolving piece of you. Sometimes it's a huge and important part of your life and other times it's teeny tiny. Wherever you're at, it's a part of you worth understanding.

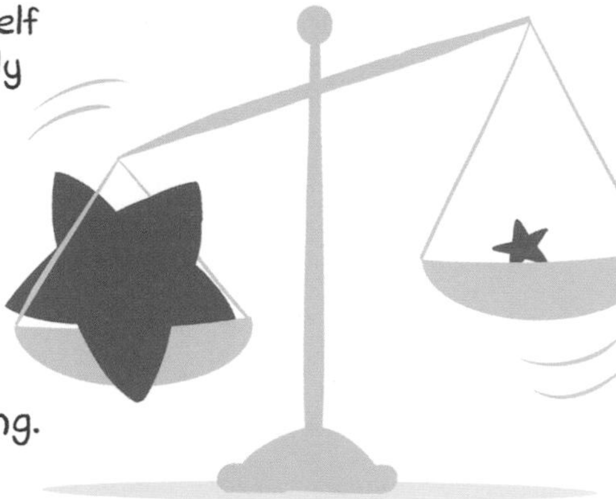

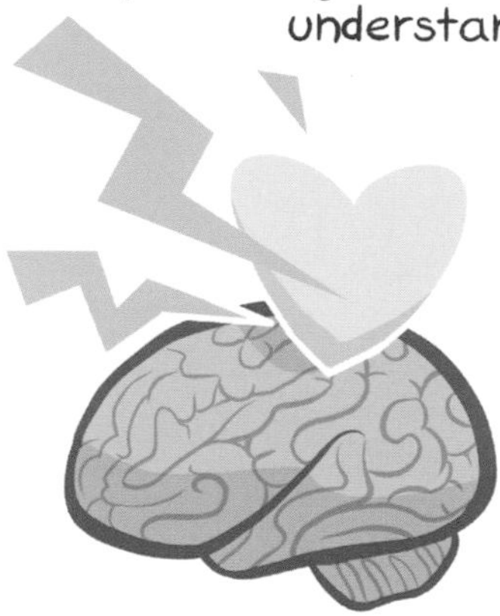

For a lot of us, feeling sexual starts around our teens when our hormones kick into high gear. You end up getting crushes, fantasizing, masturbating, orgasming, and experimenting with others. All of it's SUPER normal.

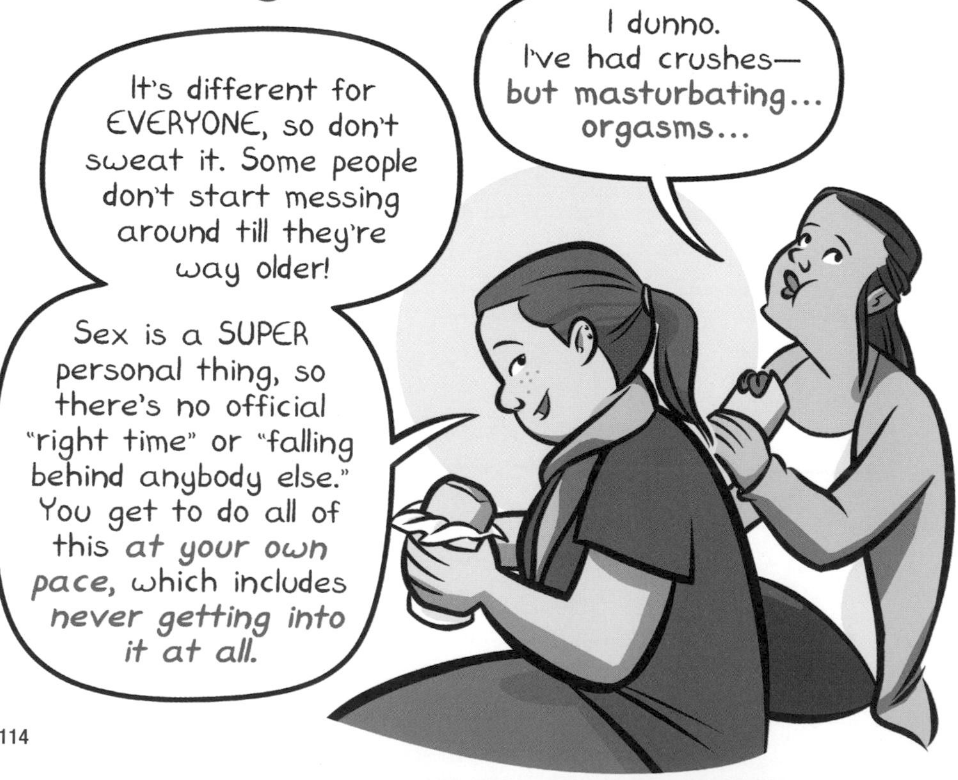
I dunno. I've had crushes— **but masturbating... orgasms...**
It's different for EVERYONE, so don't sweat it. Some people don't start messing around till they're way older!
Sex is a SUPER personal thing, so there's no official "right time" or "falling behind anybody else." You get to do all of this *at your own pace,* which includes *never getting into it at all.*

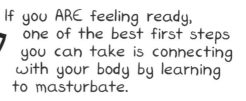

If you ARE feeling ready, one of the best first steps you can take is connecting with your body by learning to masturbate.

When you're safe and alone, give yourself permission to touch and explore your bod.

Relax, let your mind wander, and let your hands roam. There's no *perfect* way to touch yourself.

Try running the palms of your hands up and down your body. Touch ALL the different parts of you and not just the "naughty bits."

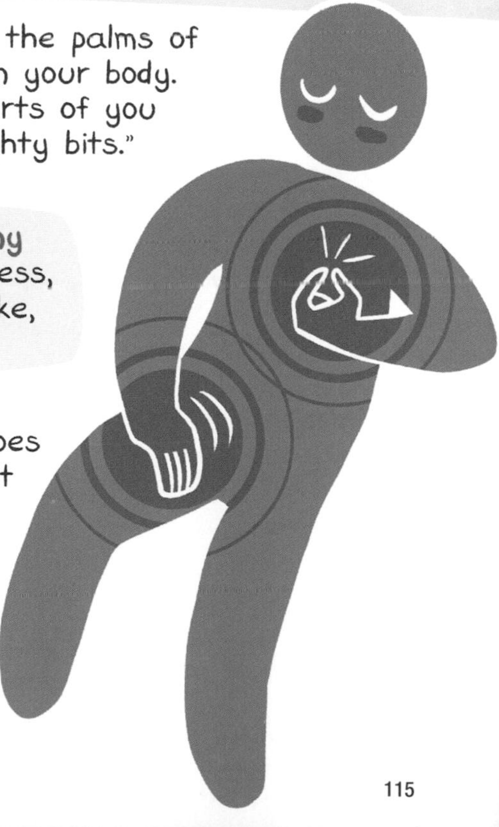

Your hands can do so many different things; they can press, massage, squeeze, pat, stroke, lightly pinch, and flick.

What kind of touch does your thigh like? Does your butt like being squeezed? What happens when you gently pat yourself? Does your nipple like to be pinched? Start light and apply more pressure. Discover what makes *you* feel good.

When you're ready to play with your body, there are a few things to try. But the first thing to learn is that a HAPPY vulva or penis is a WET vulva or penis.

Use lots of lube!

Lube (or "lubricant") is a liquid designed to make your sensitive zones slippery, which not only makes contact feel better but also reduces your chance of chafing or tearing your softest, most delicate bits.

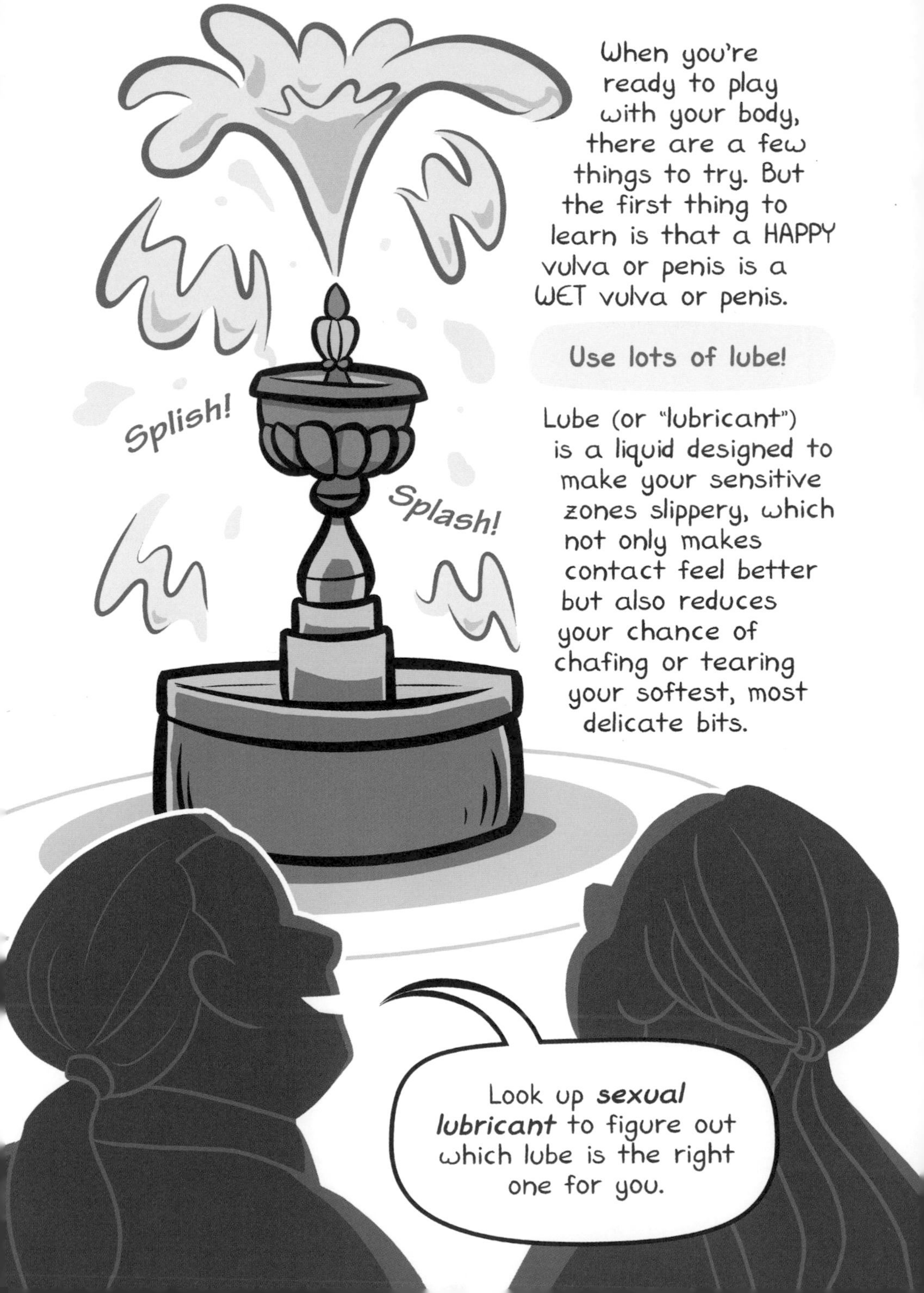
Splish!
Splash!
Look up *sexual lubricant* to figure out which lube is the right one for you.

Things to Try!

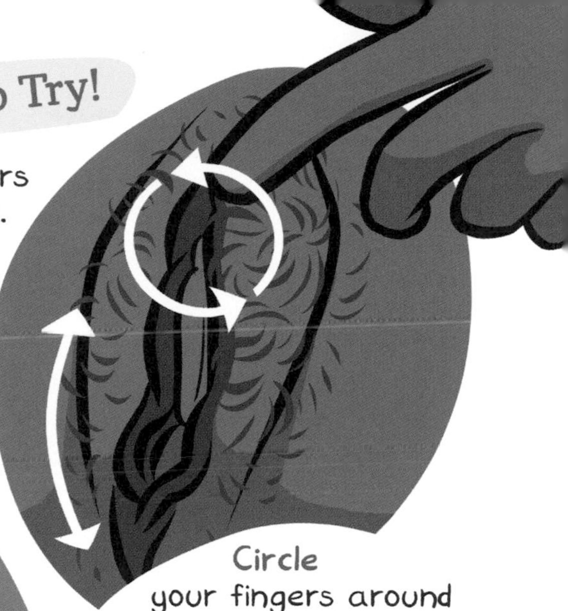

Trail your fingers around and over your vulva. Flutter your fingers lightly from place to place.

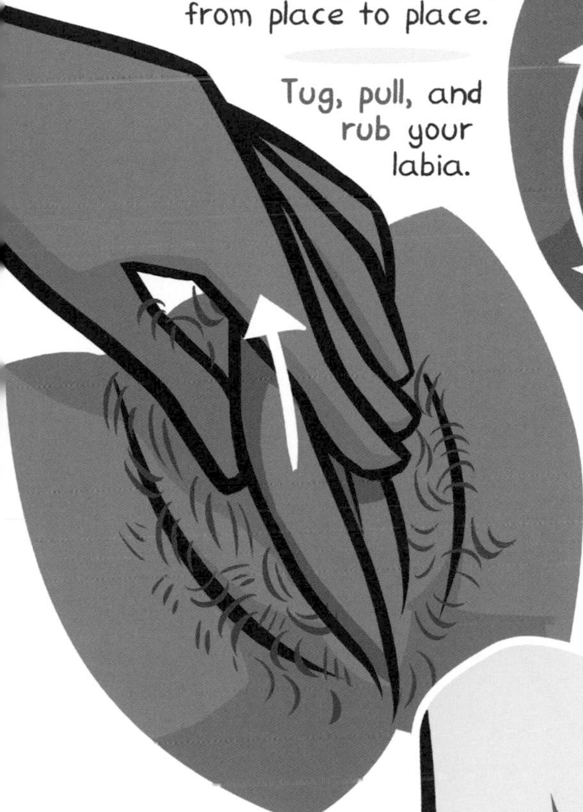

Tug, pull, and rub your labia.

Circle your fingers around and over your clit. Give it a couple quick pats!

Press and pull on the skin around your vulva to make it taut.

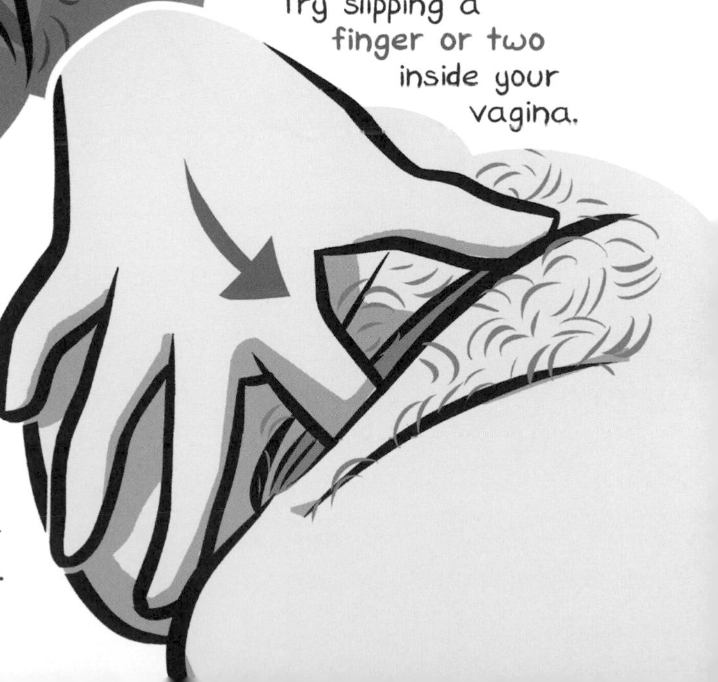

Try slipping a finger or two inside your vagina.

Later on, try adding a sex toy to your masturbation! They can bring a completely new sensation that you can't experience with just your hands.

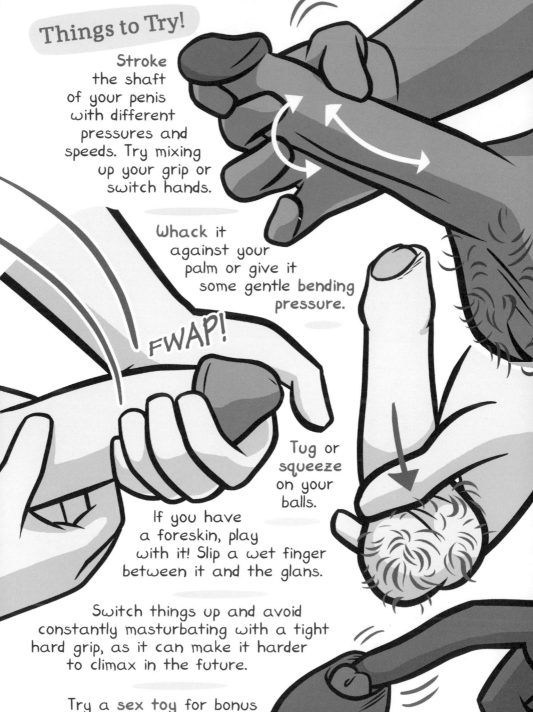

Things to Try!

Stroke the shaft of your penis with different pressures and speeds. Try mixing up your grip or switch hands.

Whack it against your palm or give it some gentle bending pressure.

FWAP!

Tug or **squeeze** on your balls.

If you have a foreskin, play with it! Slip a wet finger between it and the glans.

Switch things up and avoid constantly masturbating with a tight hard grip, as it can make it harder to climax in the future.

Try a **sex toy** for bonus fun. Vibes and strokers are awesome!

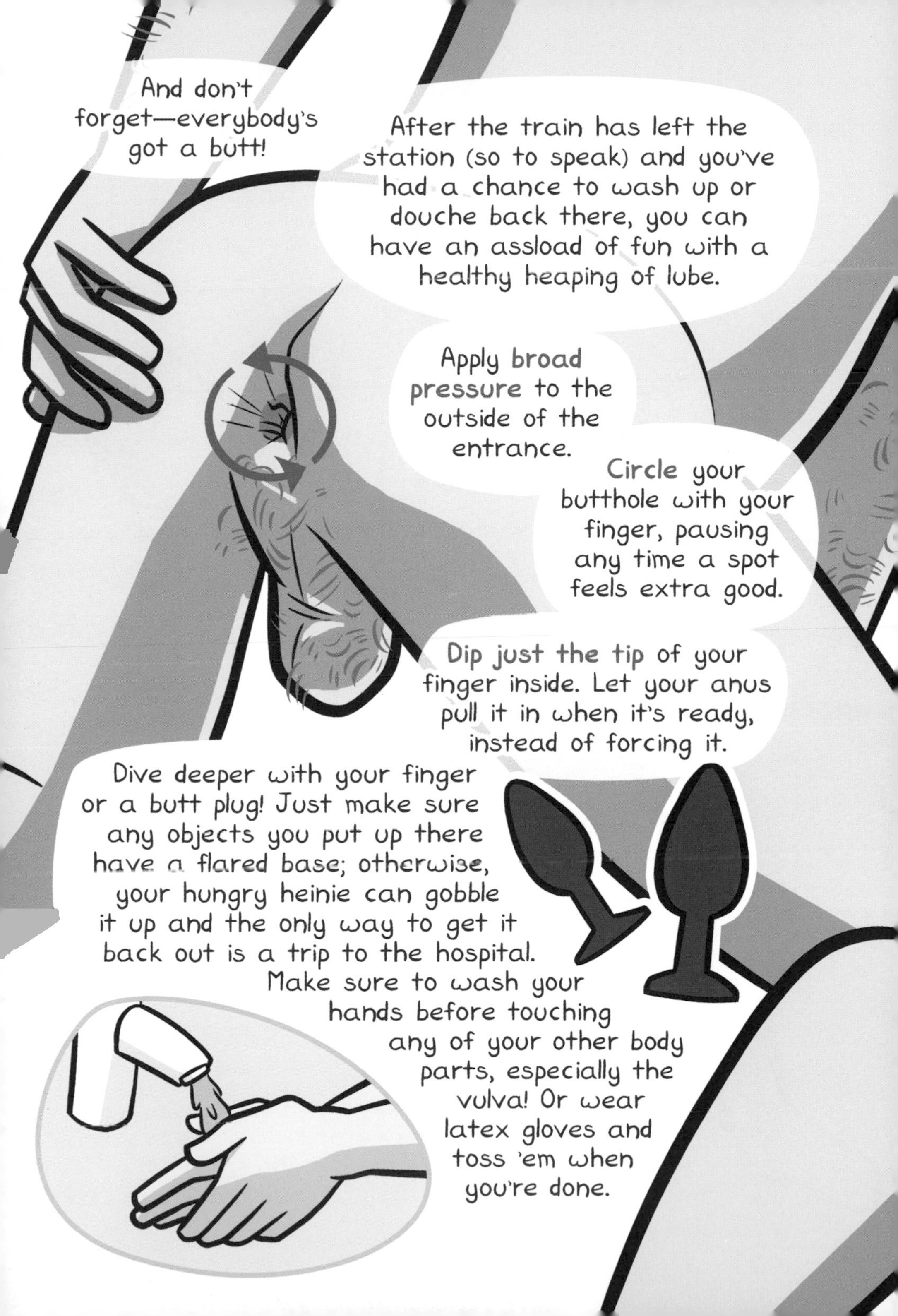

And don't forget—everybody's got a butt!
After the train has left the station (so to speak) and you've had a chance to wash up or douche back there, you can have an assload of fun with a healthy heaping of lube.
Apply broad pressure to the outside of the entrance.
Circle your butthole with your finger, pausing any time a spot feels extra good.
Dip just the tip of your finger inside. Let your anus pull it in when it's ready, instead of forcing it.
Dive deeper with your finger or a butt plug! Just make sure any objects you put up there have a flared base; otherwise, your hungry heinie can gobble it up and the only way to get it back out is a trip to the hospital.
Make sure to wash your hands before touching any of your other body parts, especially the vulva! Or wear latex gloves and toss 'em when you're done.

The point of playing with yourself is to feel good. Some people can bring themselves to orgasm, but it's not the aim of the game. Touching your body can be relaxing and fun, a way to relieve tension and feel *pleasure*—with or without an orgasm.

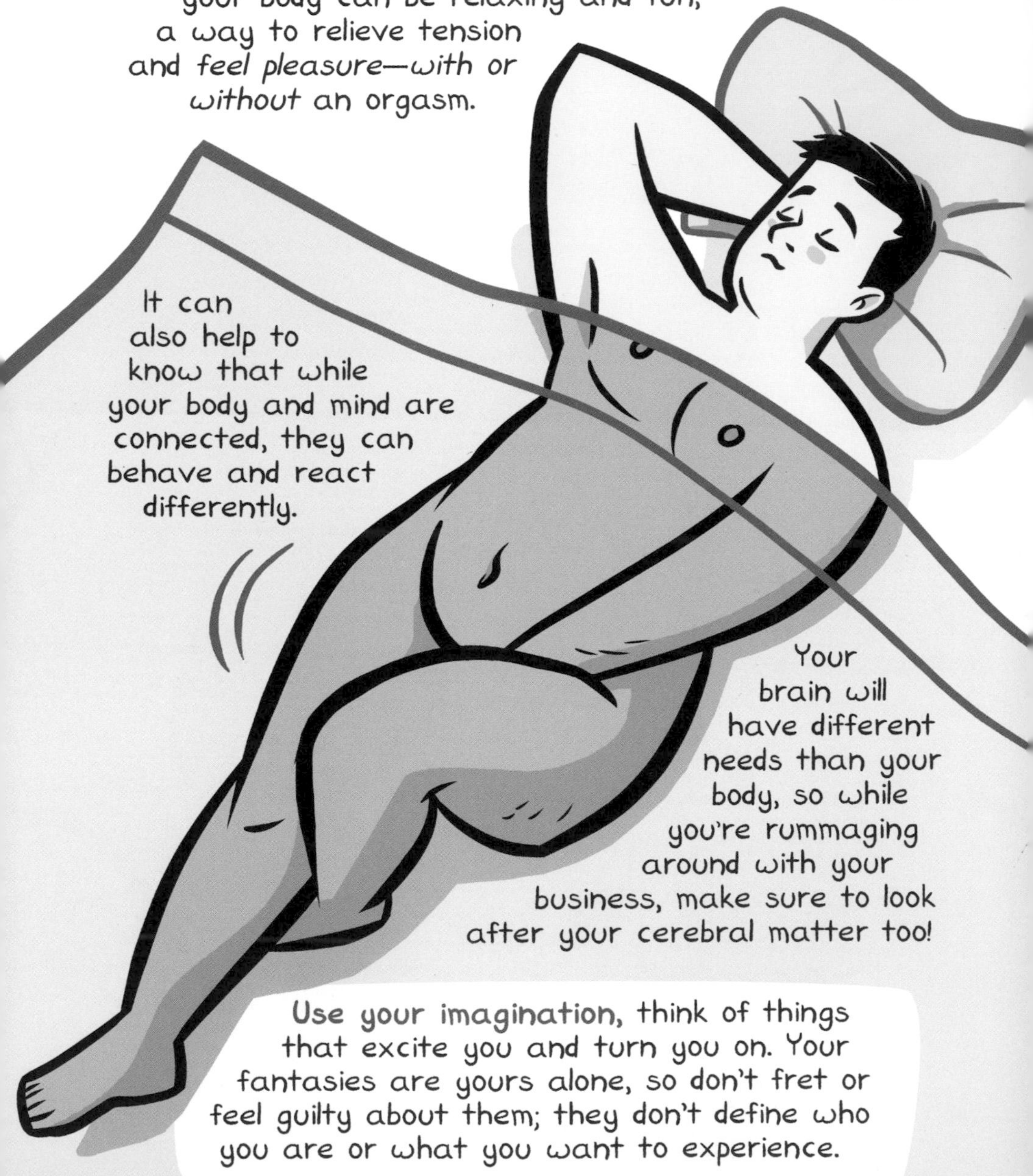

It can also help to know that while your body and mind are connected, they can behave and react differently.

Your brain will have different needs than your body, so while you're rummaging around with your business, make sure to look after your cerebral matter too!

Use your imagination, think of things that excite you and turn you on. Your fantasies are yours alone, so don't fret or feel guilty about them; they don't define who you are or what you want to experience.

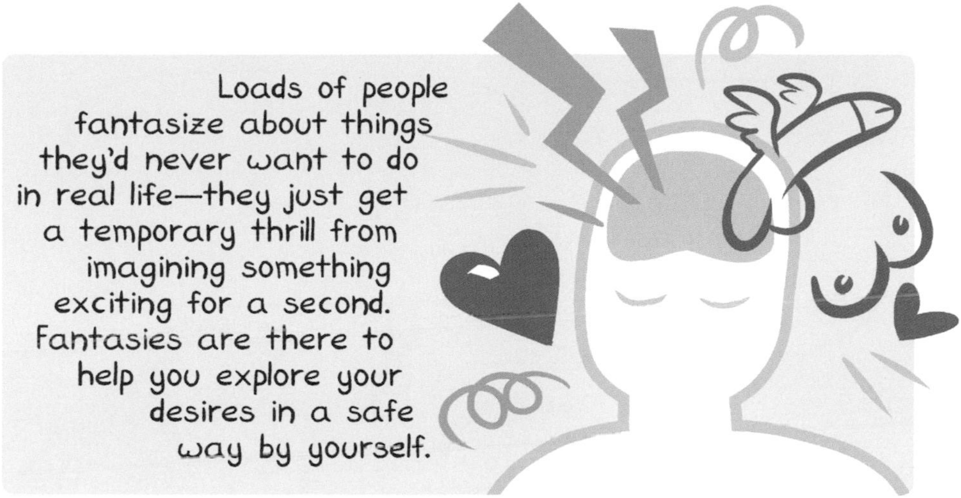
Loads of people fantasize about things they'd never want to do in real life—they just get a temporary thrill from imagining something exciting for a second. Fantasies are there to help you explore your desires in a safe way by yourself.

Sometimes your brain and body can fall out of sync too!

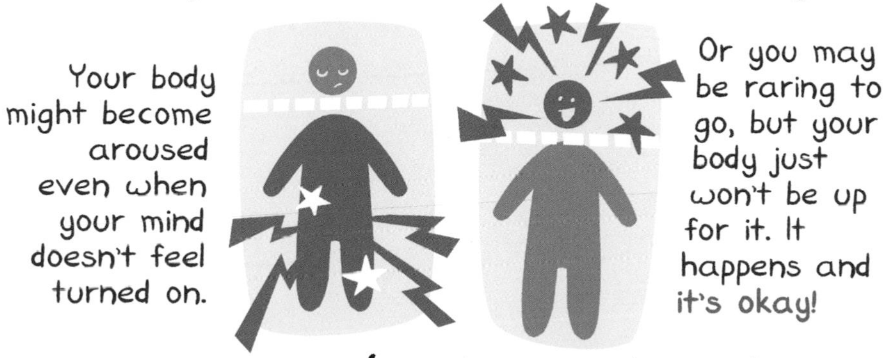
Your body might become aroused even when your mind doesn't feel turned on.
Or you may be raring to go, but your body just won't be up for it. It happens and it's okay!

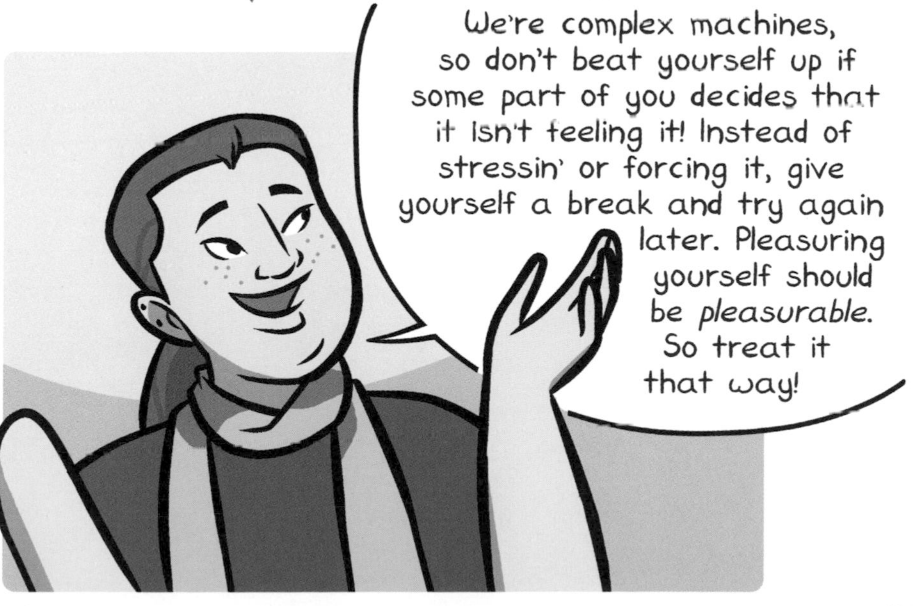
We're complex machines, so don't beat yourself up if some part of you decides that it isn't feeling it! Instead of stressin' or forcing it, give yourself a break and try again later. Pleasuring yourself should be *pleasurable.* So treat it that way!

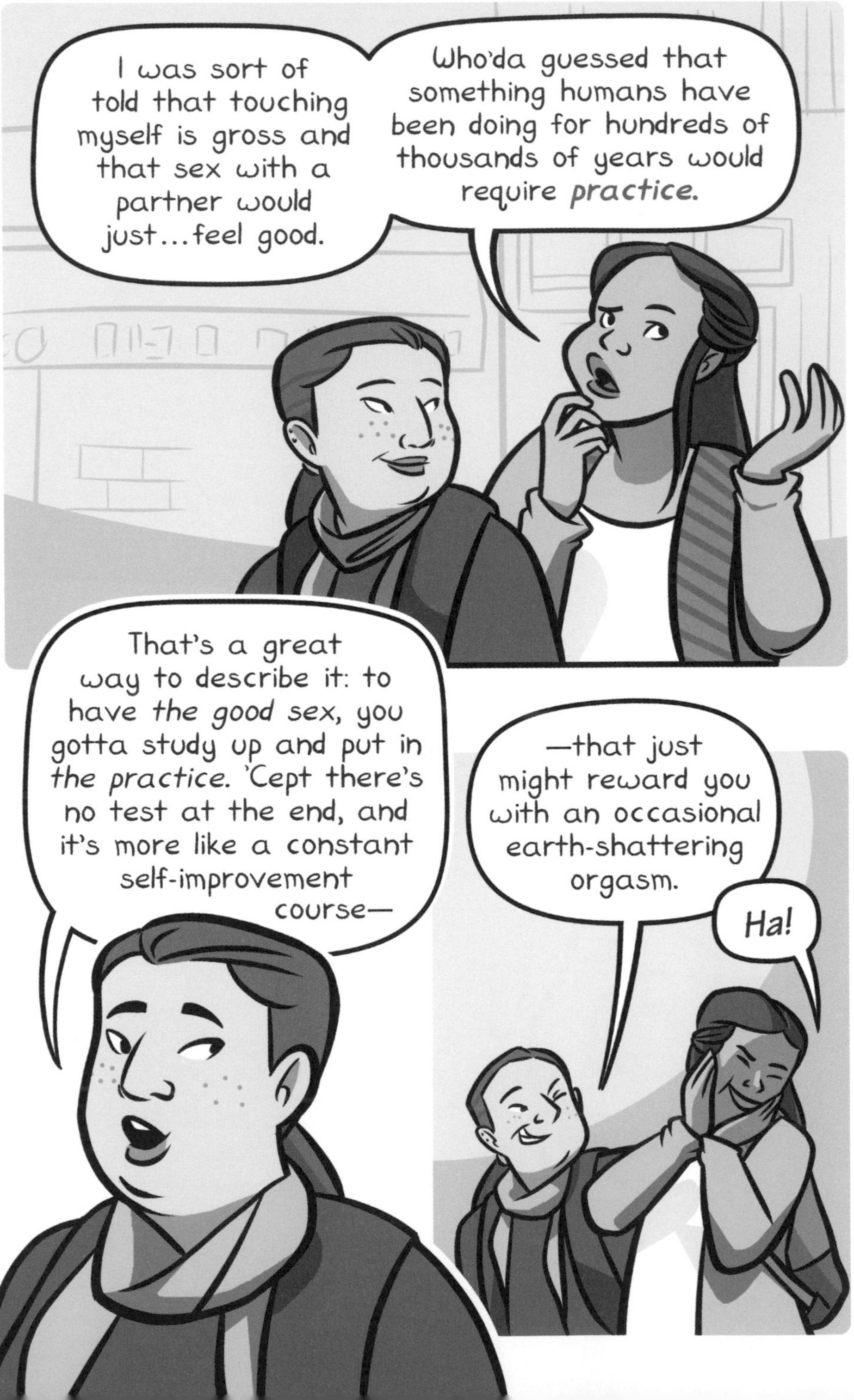
I was sort of told that touching myself is gross and that sex with a partner would just...feel good.
Who'da guessed that something humans have been doing for hundreds of thousands of years would require *practice.*
That's a great way to describe it: to have *the good sex,* you gotta study up and put in *the practice.* 'Cept there's no test at the end, and it's more like a constant self-improvement course—
—that just might reward you with an occasional earth-shattering orgasm.
Ha!

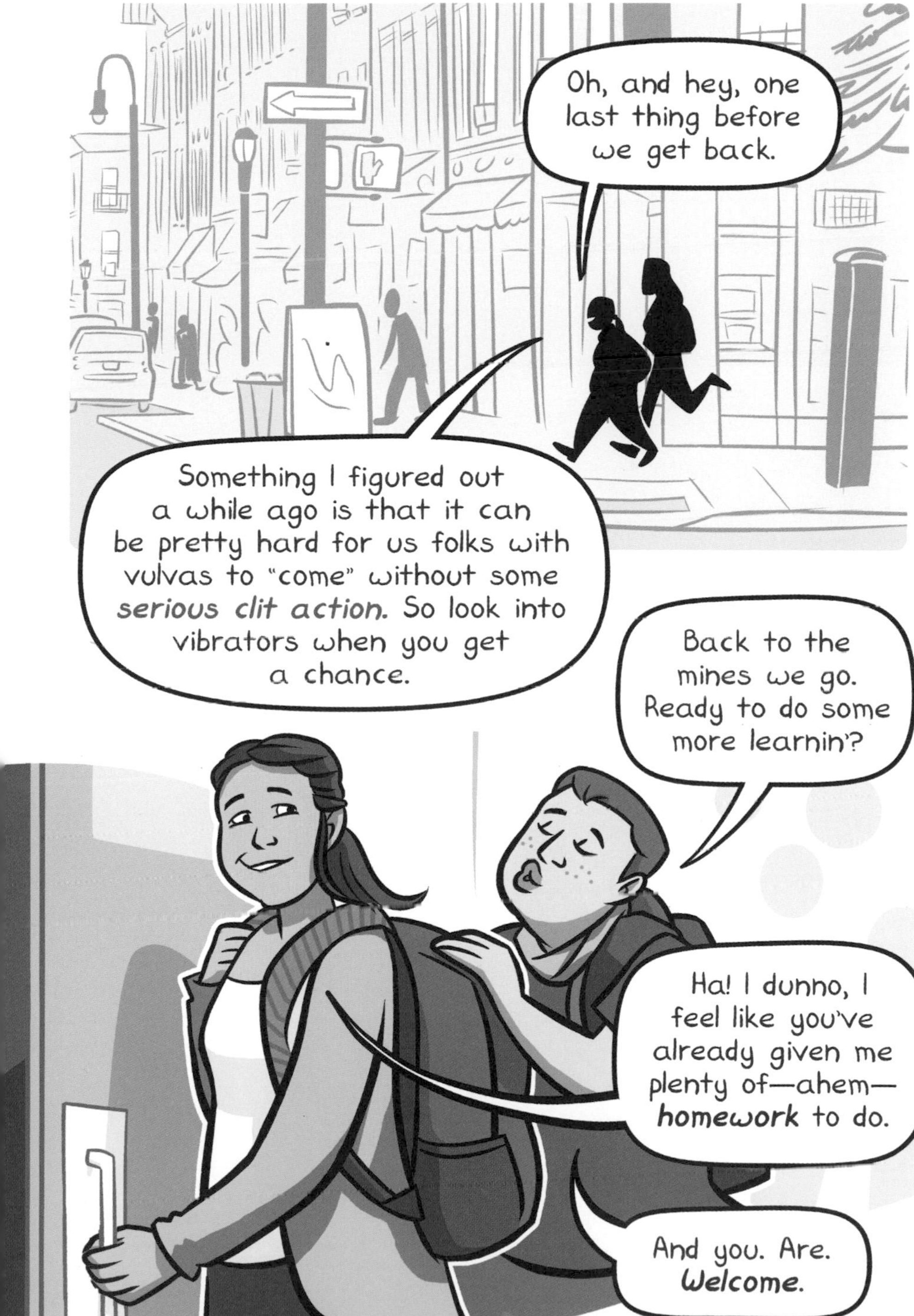
Oh, and hey, one last thing before we get back.
Something I figured out a while ago is that it can be pretty hard for us folks with vulvas to "come" without some *serious clit action.* So look into vibrators when you get a chance.
Back to the mines we go. Ready to do some more learnin'?
Ha! I dunno, I feel like you've already given me plenty of—ahem—**homework** to do.
And you. Are. ***Welcome***.

What is . . .
safe sex?

Is sex ever really safe? How do you avoid getting pregnant? How do you avoid getting an STI? How do you talk about any of this with your partner? How do you talk about any of this with your doctor?

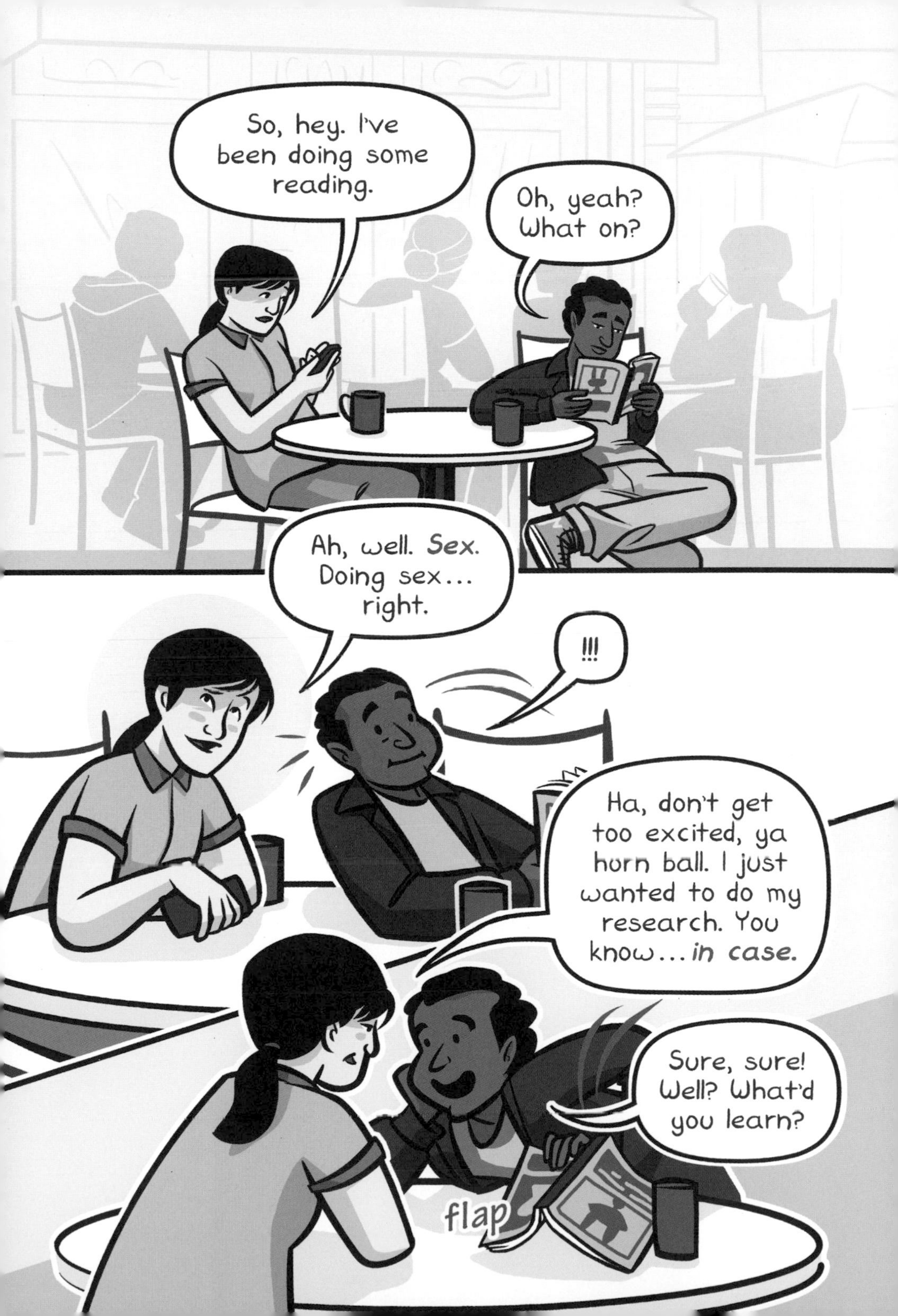
So, hey. I've been doing some reading.
Oh, yeah? What on?
Ah, well. Sex. Doing sex... right.
!!!
Ha, don't get too excited, ya horn ball. I just wanted to do my research. You know... *in case.*
Sure, sure! Well? What'd you learn?
flap

All right. Lemme see. **Safer sex.**
Pfft, *sure.* I mean, I already know how to roll a rubber on. What else is there?
Oh ho ho, SO MUCH.

Like any other fun physical activity, there's some risk that goes with sex. Whether you're trying to avoid pregnancy or sexually transmitted infections (STIs), there are a bunch of helpful things to learn beyond how a condom works.

STIs are **super common** and you can be exposed to them even when you aren't being sexually active. Sometimes all it takes is a bit of fluid exchange.

But that doesn't mean you shouldn't be careful and practice safer sex. It still massively reduces your chances of picking up something nasty.

So don't wait until the last minute to talk with your partner about the protection you'll use. Have an open and frank chat early on, before you get hot and horny!

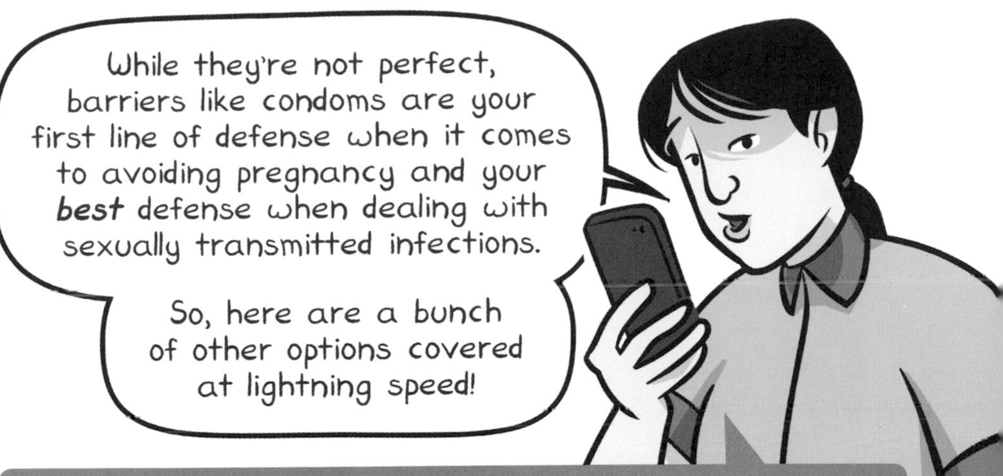
While they're not perfect, barriers like condoms are your first line of defense when it comes to avoiding pregnancy and your ***best*** defense when dealing with sexually transmitted infections.
So, here are a bunch of other options covered at lightning speed!

♥ Barriers that prevent babies and STIs ♥

These are all single-use items; make sure to use a fresh one every time!

Condom

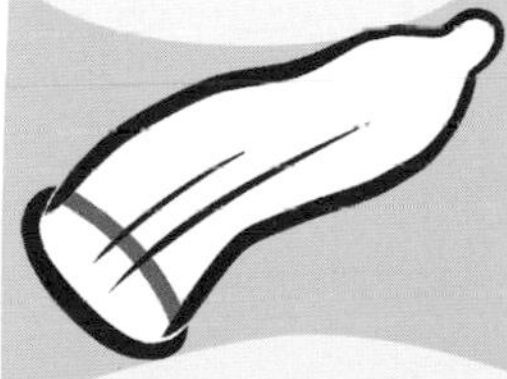

85% effective as birth control

●

Roll onto an erect penis.

Latex or Nitrile Gloves

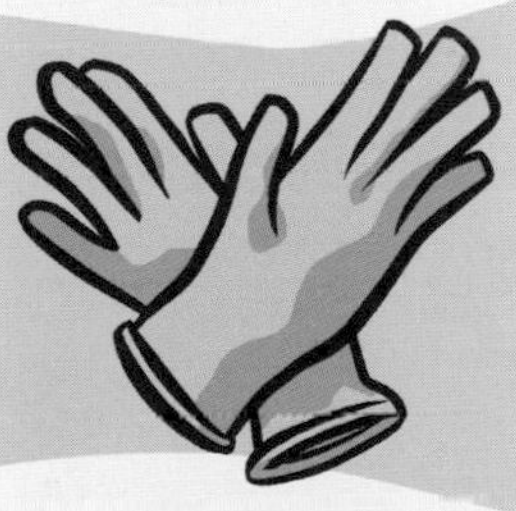

Use for hand safety.

Internal Condom

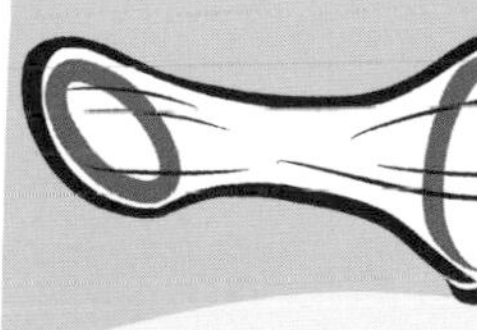

79% effective as birth control

●

Slide it into a wet vagina or anus.

Dental Dam

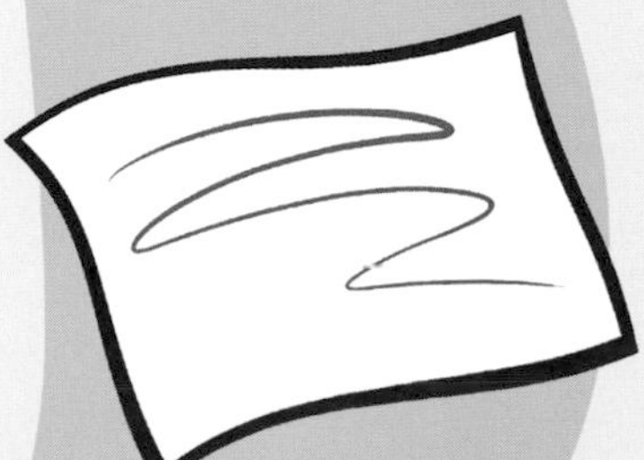

Use one for oral protection.

●

Lay onto a vulva or anus with a dab of lube.

●

Pro tip: cut a condom vertically to make one!

♥ Birth control that just prevents pregnancy ♥

None of these stop STI transmission!

Vaginal Ring

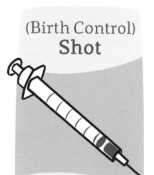

91% effective
•
Replace monthly.
•
Rests inside the vagina and releases contraceptive hormones.

IUD

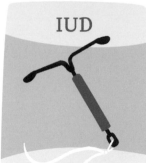

99% effective
•
Lasts 3–12 years.
•
Sits in the uterus and either releases hormones or kills sperm.

(Birth Control) Implant

99% effective
•
Lasts up to 5 years.
•
Inserted in the arm. It releases contraceptive hormones.

(Birth Control) Shot

94% effective
•
Contraceptive hormones injected every 3 months.

Diaphragm

88% effective
•
Use every time with spermicide.
•
A soft cup that you slide into the vagina, covering the cervix and blocking sperm.

(Birth Control) Sponge

76–88% effective
•
Use every time.
•
Slide into the vagina. It covers the cervix, blocking and killing sperm with spermicide.

Patch

91% effective
•
Replace weekly.
•
Placed onto the skin and releases contraceptive hormones.

(Birth Control) Pill

91% effective
•
Taken daily.
•
Oral pill that releases contraceptive hormones.

Spermicide

71% effective
•
Use every time.
•
Sperm-killing jelly that's inserted into the vagina.

Cervical Cap

71–86% effective
•
Use every time with spermicide.
•
A little cup that slides into the vagina to cover the cervix, blocking sperm.

Some use lots of hormones, some don't use any. Some take a while to become effective, and some are immediate.

There are side effects, best practices, more deets...

AND this isn't even a full list!

Whoa...

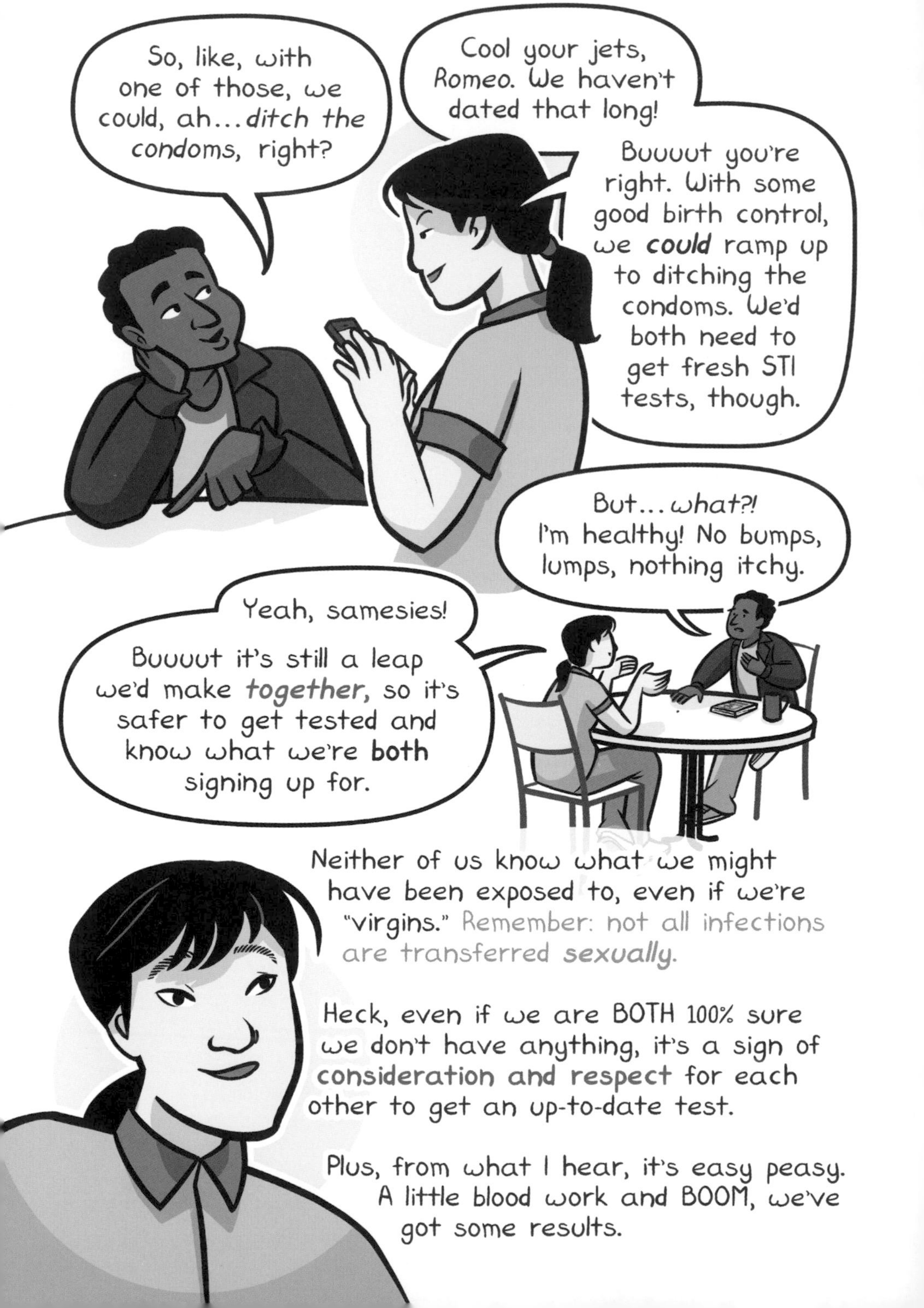

So, like, with one of those, we could, ah...*ditch the condoms,* right?
Cool your jets, Romeo. We haven't dated that long!
Buuuut you're right. With some good birth control, we **could** ramp up to ditching the condoms. We'd both need to get fresh STI tests, though.
But...*what?!* I'm healthy! No bumps, lumps, nothing itchy.
Yeah, samesies!
Buuuut it's still a leap we'd make ***together,*** so it's safer to get tested and know what we're **both** signing up for.
Neither of us know what we might have been exposed to, even if we're "virgins." Remember: not all infections are transferred ***sexually***.
Heck, even if we are BOTH 100% sure we don't have anything, it's a sign of **consideration and respect** for each other to get an up-to-date test.
Plus, from what I hear, it's easy peasy. A little blood work and BOOM, we've got some results.

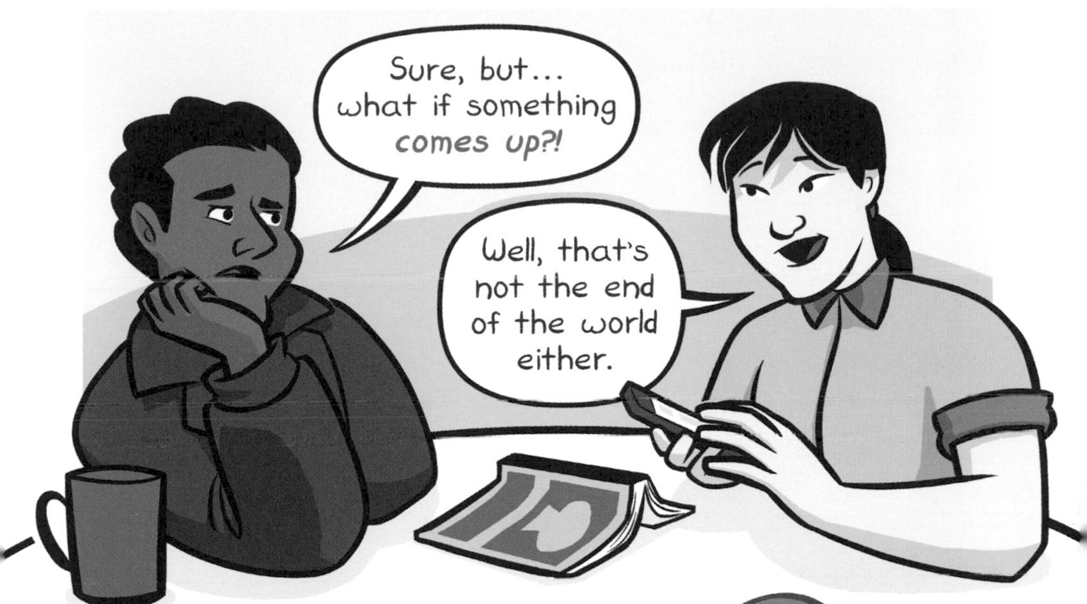
Sure, but... what if something comes up?!
Well, that's not the end of the world either.

Turns out, the majority of STIs are treatable and, if caught early, no biggie. There are some that are untreatable like HPV and herpes (both of which the majority of people have, even if they're symptomless). But even those aren't worth fretting over beyond keeping some good practices (like pap smears for HPV and avoiding contact when having a herpes outbreak).

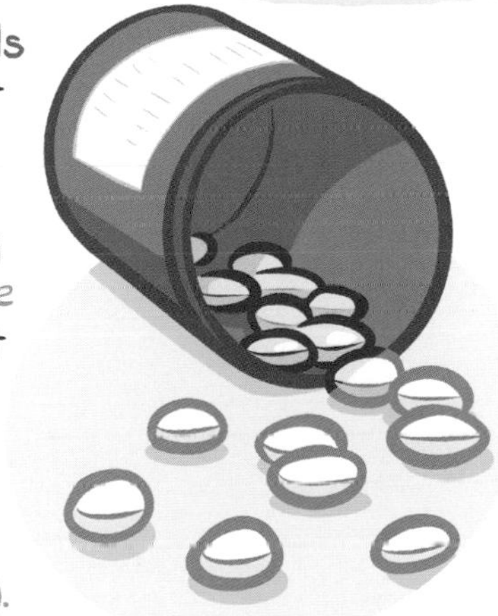

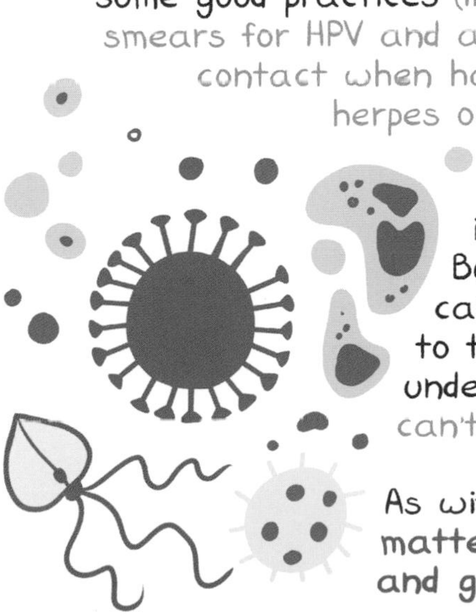

There ARE some scary infections out there, like HIV. But you know what? Even that can be treated with antivirals to the point where it becomes undetectable (which means it can't be passed to someone else).

As with all STIs, it's just a matter of catching them early and getting treatment.

STIs aren't as big of a deal as a lot of people make them out to be. That's not to say you should go around having unsafe sex, but it does mean that you shouldn't kick yourself if you DO get one.

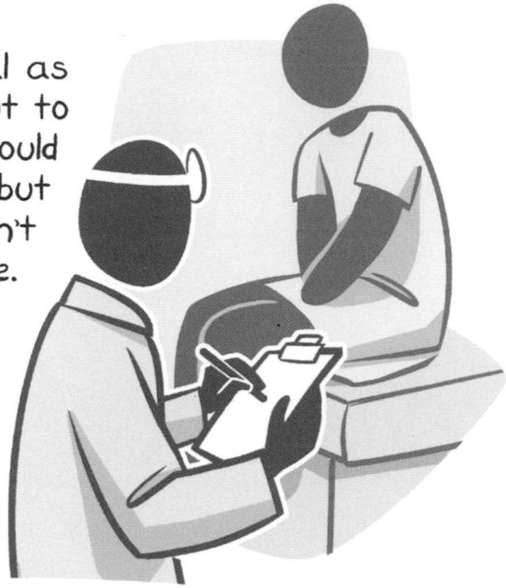

The key is to get tested regularly. A great way to do that is to go with your boo to the doc's when you're ready to swap fluids.

Here are some good general practices that take a tiny amount of effort and can help you avoid a ton of trouble.

Avoid tears and abrasions in your delicate areas by using **lots of lube!**

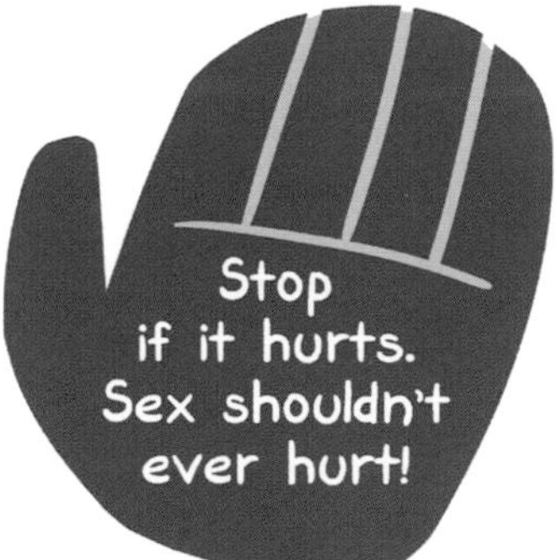
Stop
if it hurts.
Sex shouldn't
ever hurt!

If you have a vagina, pee after sex to clean out your urethra to avoid a potential urinary tract infection.

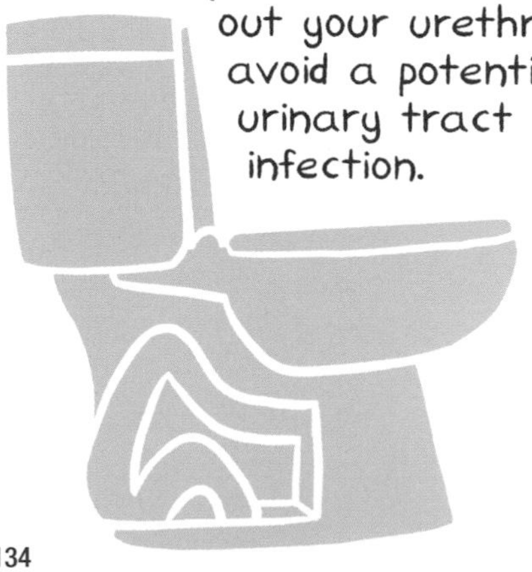

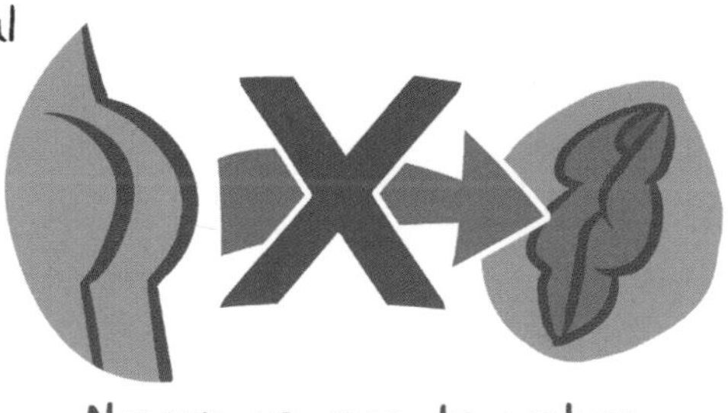

Never go ass to vulva. Butt germs can really screw up a vulva.

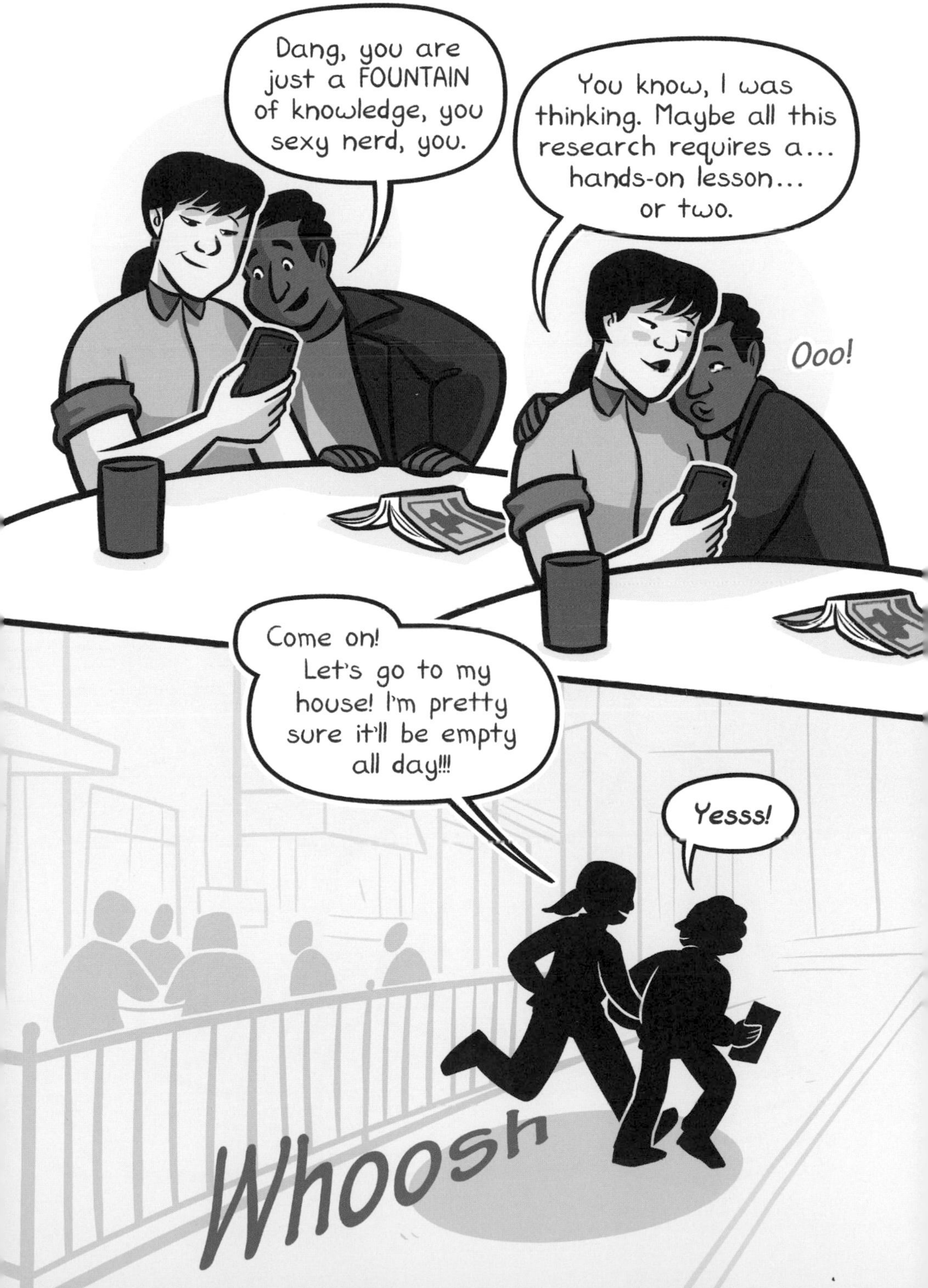
Dang, you are just a FOUNTAIN of knowledge, you sexy nerd, you.
You know, I was thinking. Maybe all this research requires a... hands-on lesson... or two.
Ooo!
Come on! Let's go to my house! I'm pretty sure it'll be empty all day!!!
Yesss!
Whoosh

What is . . .
climax?

What are orgasms? How do they
even work? Can sex still be good if
orgasms don't happen? How do you
deal with performance anxiety?

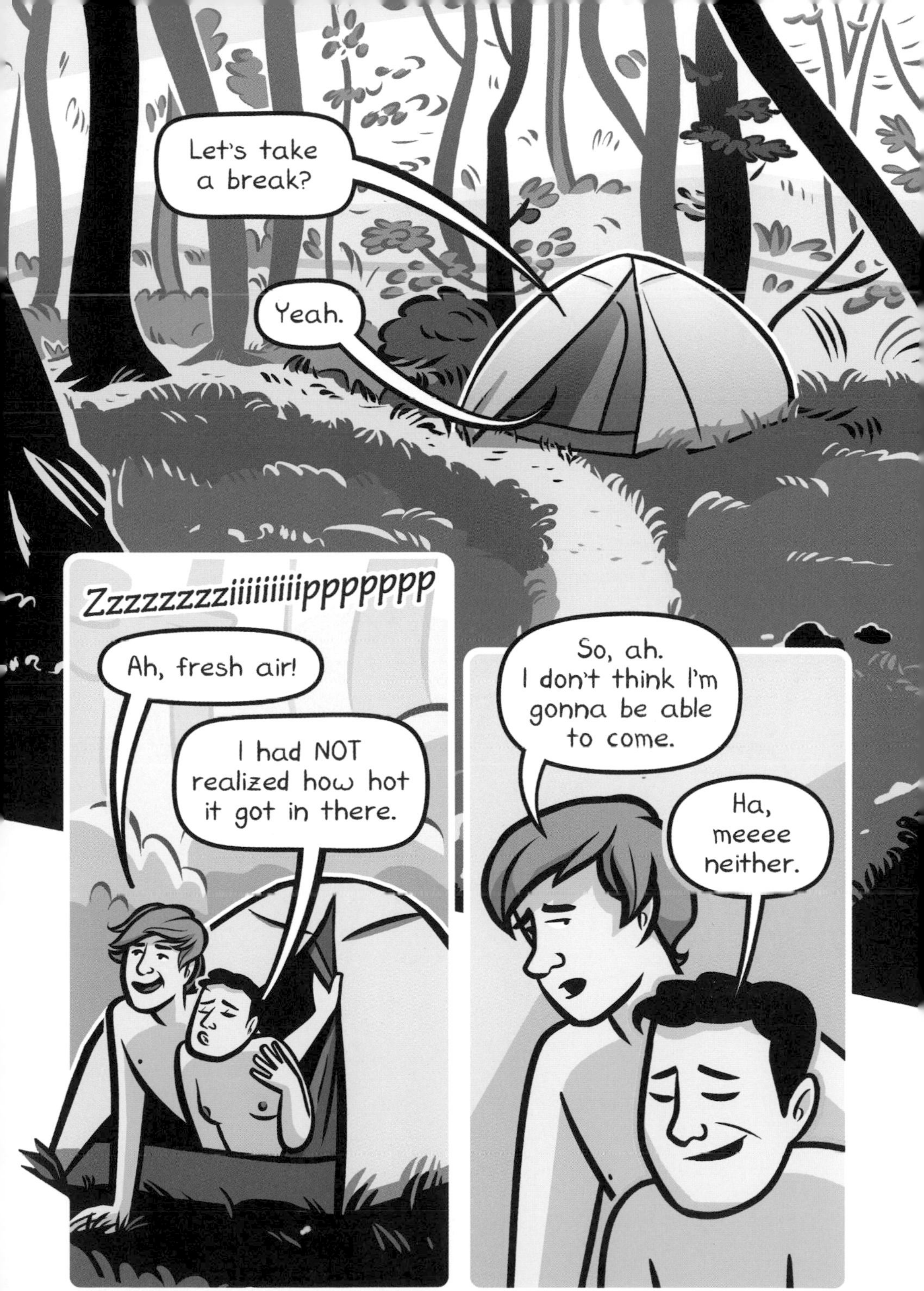
Let's take a break?
Yeah.
Zzzzzzzziiiiiiiipppppp
Ah, fresh air!
I had NOT realized how hot it got in there.
So, ah. I don't think I'm gonna be able to come.
Ha, meeee neither.

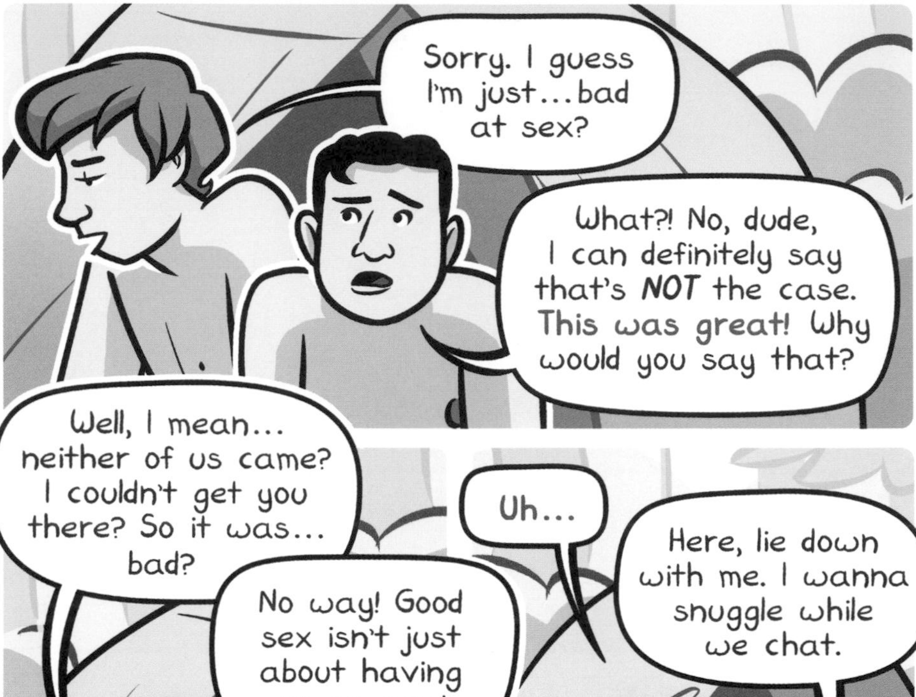
Sorry. I guess I'm just... bad at sex?
What?! No, dude, I can definitely say that's **NOT** the case. This was great! Why would you say that?
Well, I mean... neither of us came? I couldn't get you there? So it was... bad?
No way! Good sex isn't just about having an orgasm!
Uh...
Here, lie down with me. I wanna snuggle while we chat.

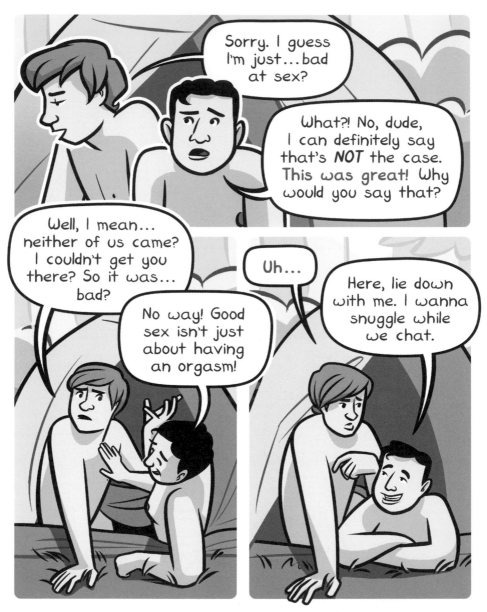

I know it's easy to get hung up on *coming*. But an orgasm is like getting a fancy dessert at the end of dinner. While it's fun, it doesn't MAKE the meal.

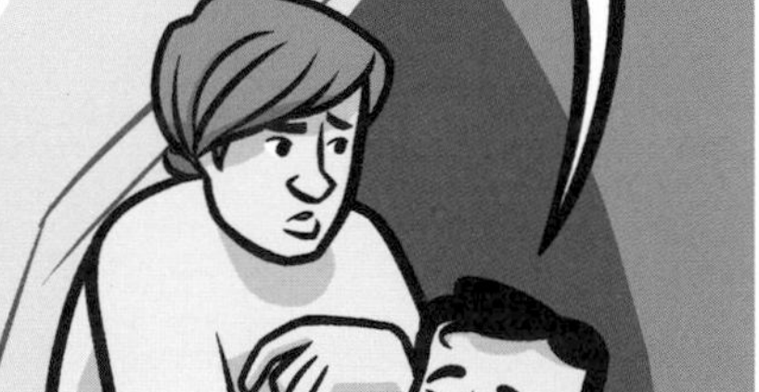

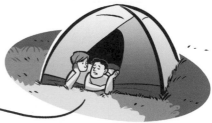

Good sex and bad sex are subjective and depend on A LOT of things.

Whether or not you and your partner *climax* isn't the most important detail.

What matters is the in-the-moment sexual chemistry, the communication between everyone, and how enjoyable things are.

Climaxing, coming, or orgasming is the sudden release of all the sexual tension and excitement built up during whatever sexy times you're having.

It can look many different ways.

Some people ejaculate fluid (whether they have a penis or a vulva), tremble, shout out, or moan. Others may not show any outward signs at all.

The intensity also varies wildly, from an explosion...

...to a tickle.

141

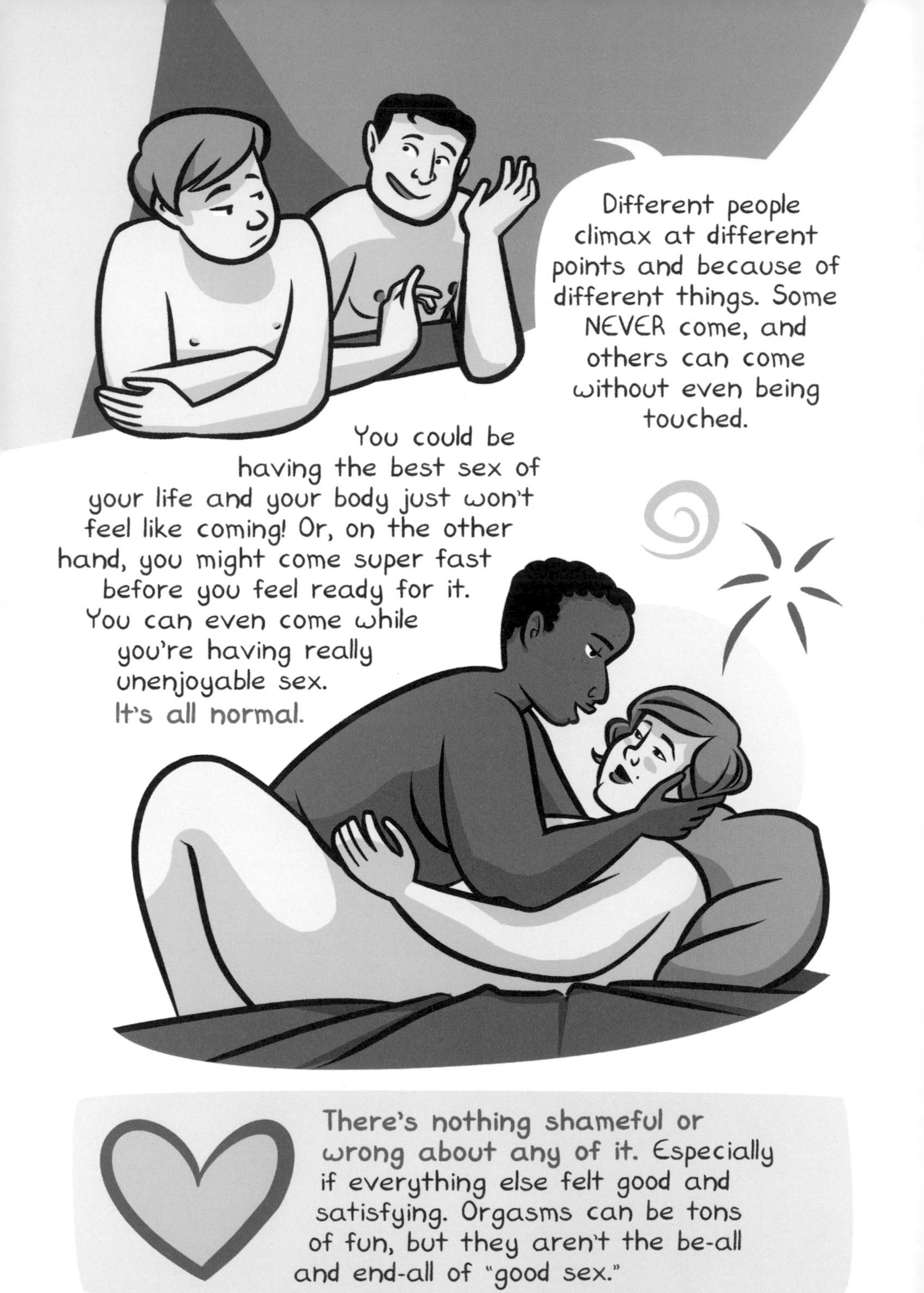
Different people climax at different points and because of different things. Some NEVER come, and others can come without even being touched.
You could be having the best sex of your life and your body just won't feel like coming! Or, on the other hand, you might come super fast before you feel ready for it. You can even come while you're having really unenjoyable sex.
It's all normal.
There's nothing shameful or wrong about any of it. Especially if everything else felt good and satisfying. Orgasms can be tons of fun, but they aren't the be-all and end-all of "good sex."

Instead of chasing the orgasm, focus on the moment and your partner. If you want to judge the success of the sex you're having, do it by how much fun you're both having.

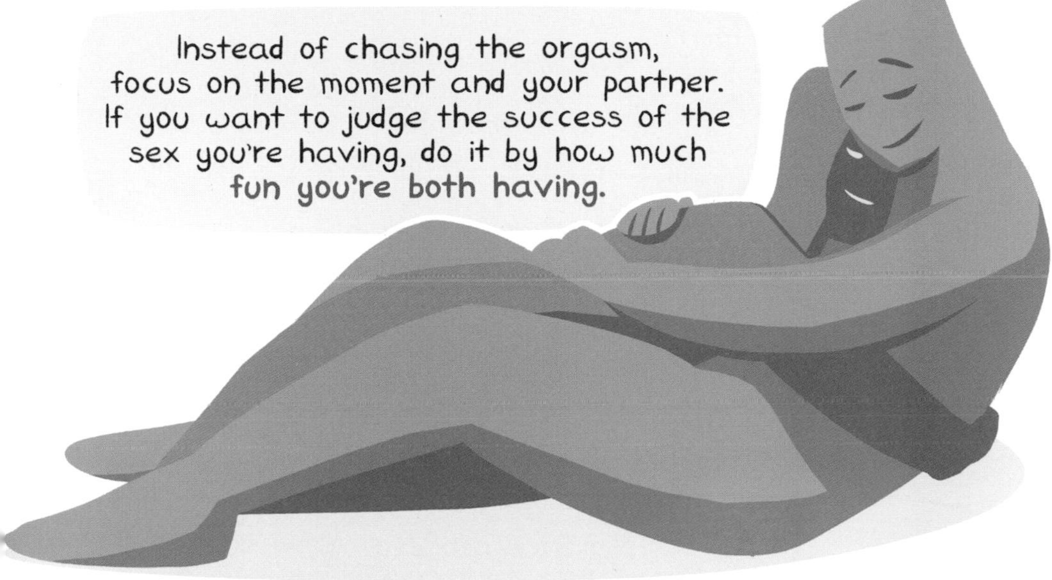

Good sex is consensual, communicative, fun, and enjoyable. None of those things really have anything to do with an orgasm.

Figuring out how to make sex feel good for you and your partner takes time and practice! Find out what works for both of you through trial and error and lots and lots of chitchat.

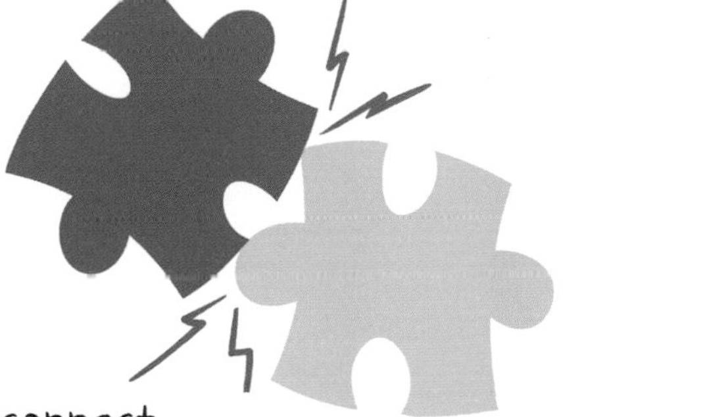

Sometimes people never connect physically with each other, and that's okay too. Some folks just aren't a good sexual match, while others might be a perfect fit.

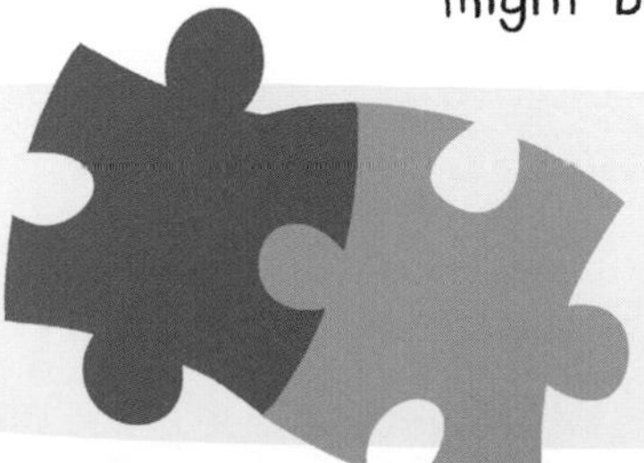

It's OKAY to take your time exploring. The adventure of sex is going to be different for everyone.

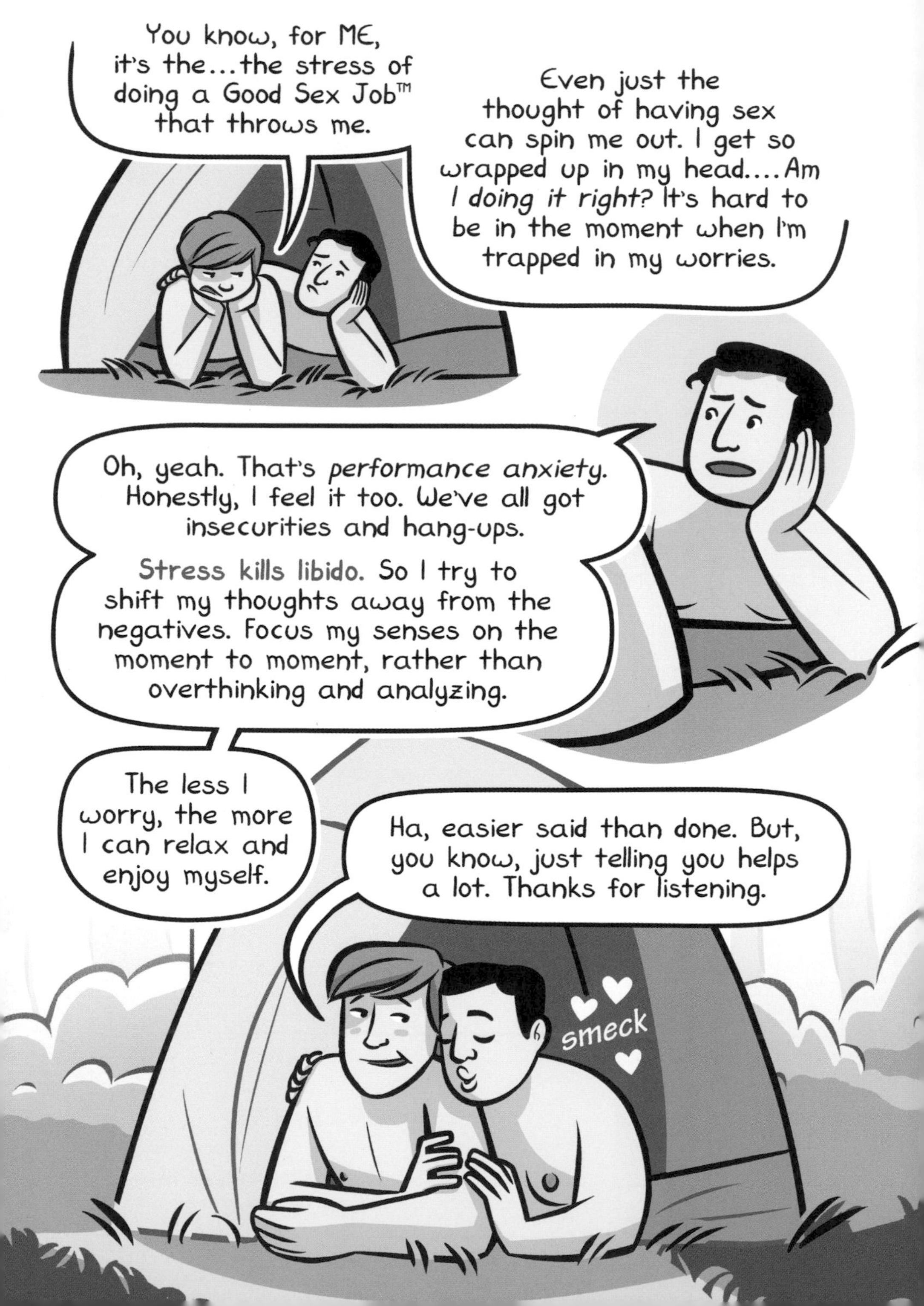
You know, for ME, it's the...the stress of doing a Good Sex Job™ that throws me.
Even just the thought of having sex can spin me out. I get so wrapped up in my head.... Am *I doing it right?* It's hard to be in the moment when I'm trapped in my worries.
Oh, yeah. That's *performance anxiety.* Honestly, I feel it too. We've all got insecurities and hang-ups.
Stress kills libido. So I try to shift my thoughts away from the negatives. Focus my senses on the moment to moment, rather than overthinking and analyzing.
The less I worry, the more I can relax and enjoy myself.
Ha, easier said than done. But, you know, just telling you helps a lot. Thanks for listening.
smeck

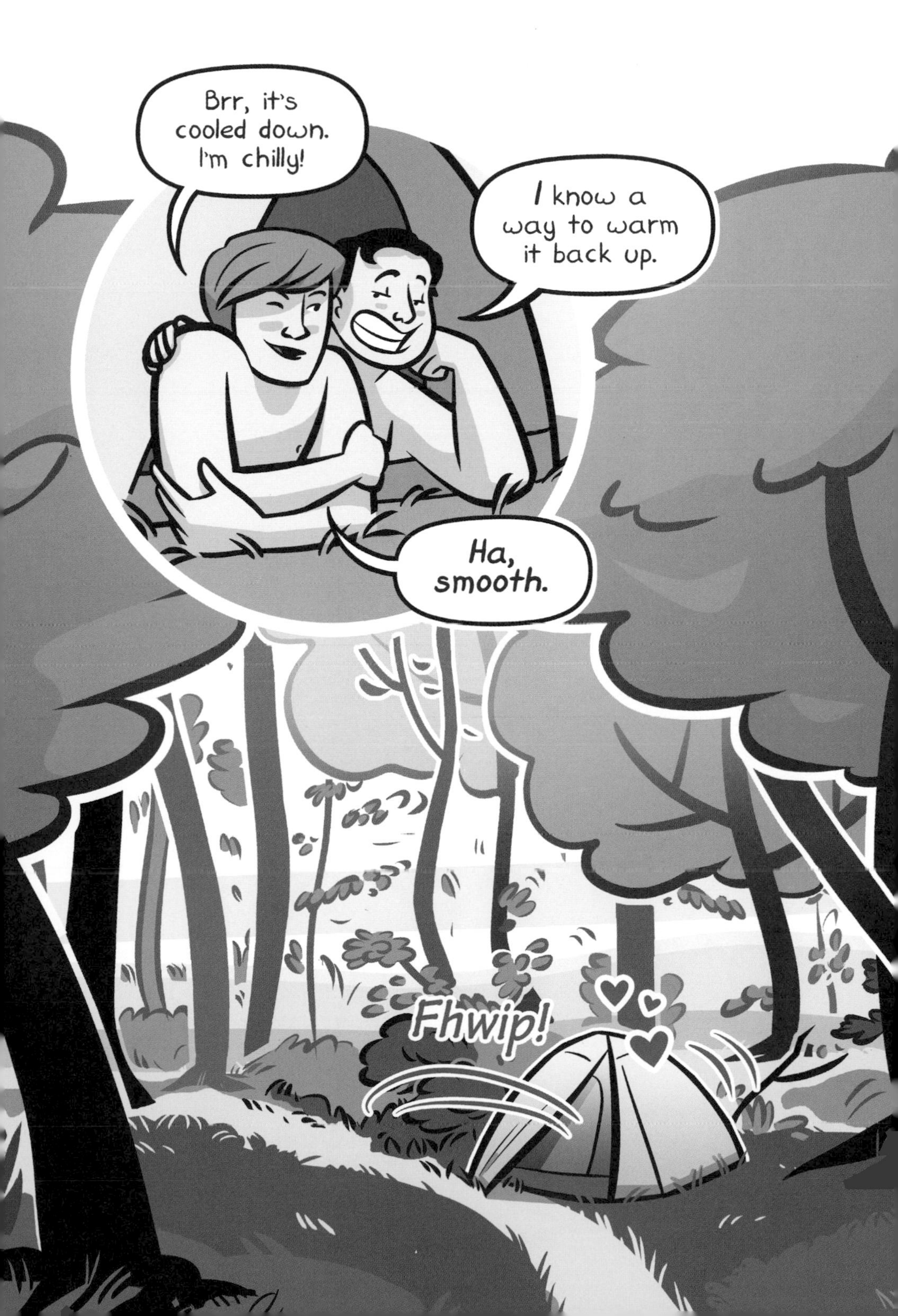
Brr, it's cooled down. I'm chilly!
I know a way to warm it back up.
Ha, smooth.
Fhwip!

What is . . .
sexting?

Do you just . . . send someone a photo? Do you ask first? How do you ask? What sort of ground rules do you establish? How do you deal with your photos potentially being shared?

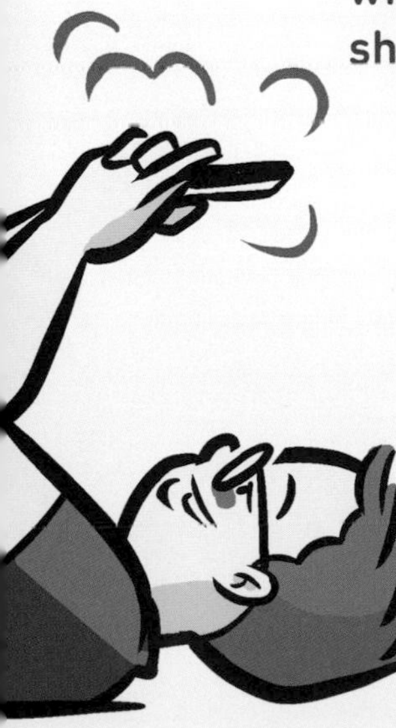

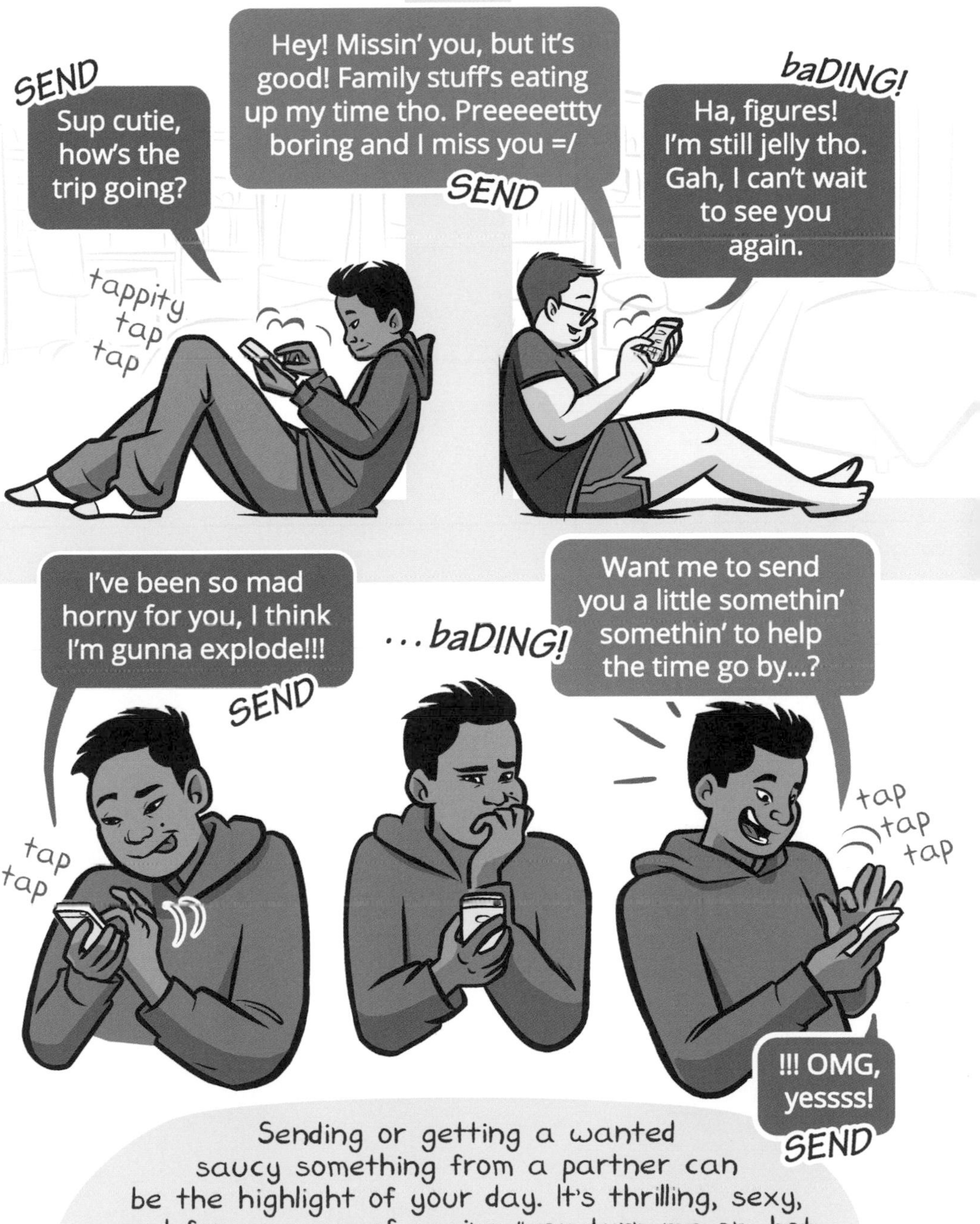
SEND
Sup cutie, how's the trip going?
tappity tap tap
Hey! Missin' you, but it's good! Family stuff's eating up my time tho. Preeeeettty boring and I miss you =/
SEND
baDING!
Ha, figures! I'm still jelly tho. Gah, I can't wait to see you again.
I've been so mad horny for you, I think I'm gunna explode!!!
tap tap
SEND
...baDING!
Want me to send you a little somethin' somethin' to help the time go by...?
tap tap tap
!!! OMG, yessss!
SEND

Sending or getting a wanted saucy something from a partner can be the highlight of your day. It's thrilling, sexy, and fun—a way of saying "you turn me on, hot stuff" or "let's get turned on together." It's a long-distance act of intimacy and trust.

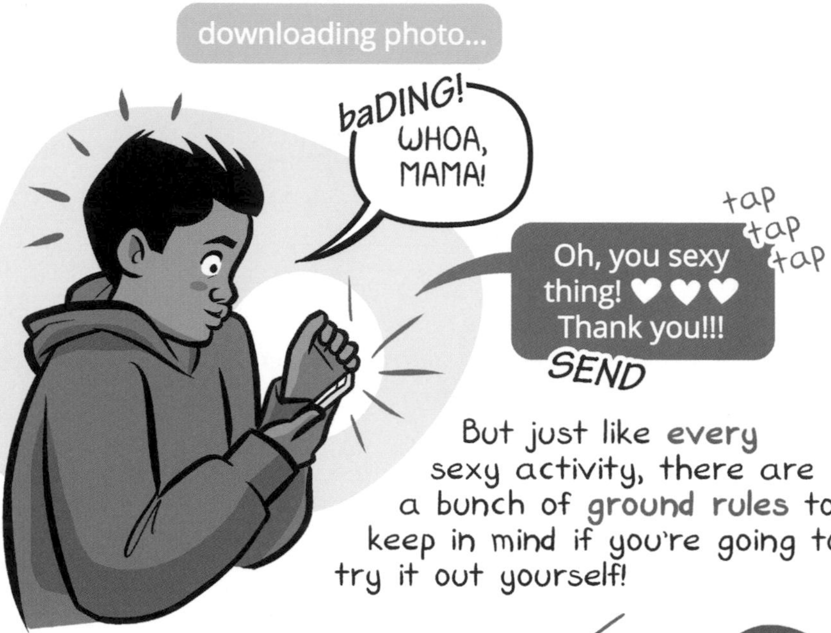
downloading photo...
baDING!
WHOA, MAMA!
Oh, you sexy thing! ♥♥♥ Thank you!!!
tap tap tap
SEND

But just like every sexy activity, there are a bunch of ground rules to keep in mind if you're going to try it out yourself!

First up, you need PLENTY of prior consent from everyone involved. Nobody wants an unsolicited picture of your junk, no matter how epic or luscious it might look. Plus, ya know, it's not only rude, but it can be harassment and illegal to send that stuff willy-nilly.

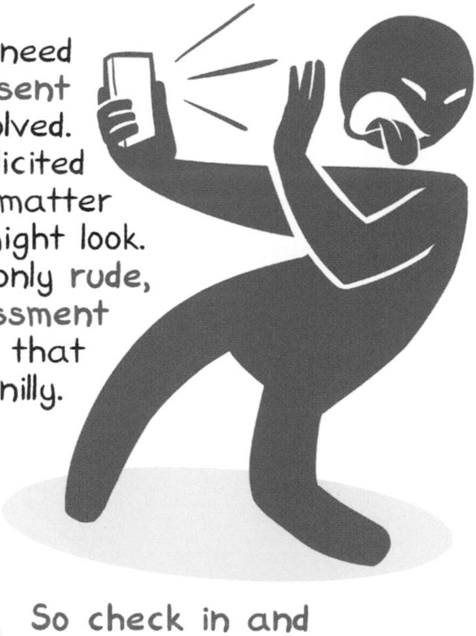

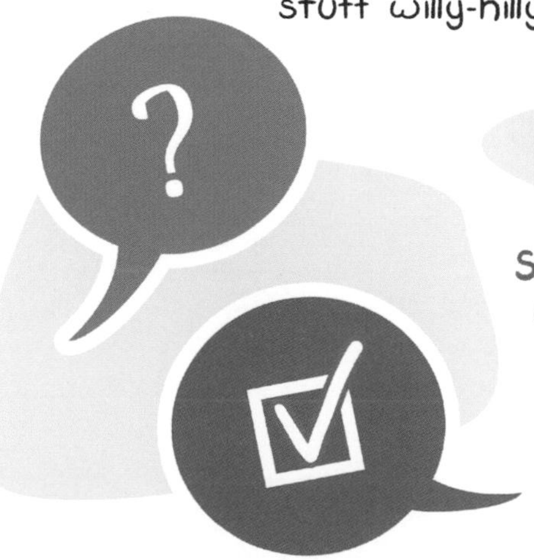
?

So check in and ask permission first! Make sure you set some ground rules about deleting this stuff at a later date, too.

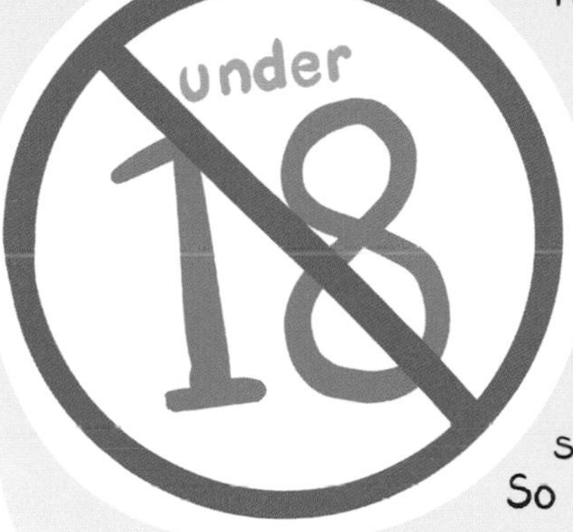
under
18

It's also really important to be aware of age laws where you live. As exciting as sexting is, there are **serious legal consequences** for sharing naked photos of folks under eighteen, even if the photos are of you and you're sharing them with someone who's the same age! So no matter how hot-to-trot you are right now, **wait till you're a legal adult**, ya horn ball!

If you're lucky enough to be on the receiving end of a requested dirty picture, **don't go sharing or spreading that photo** without permission!

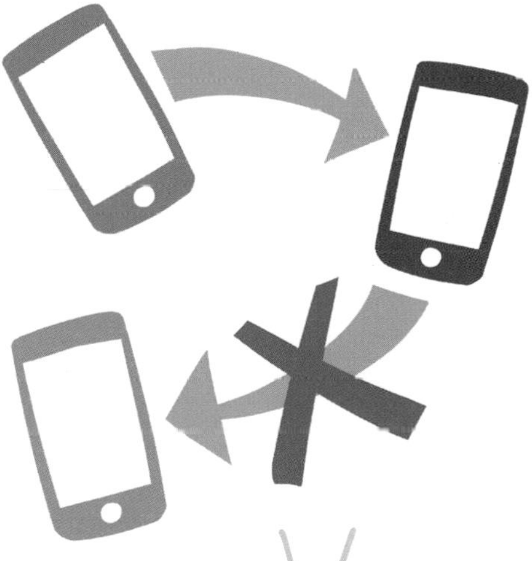

Respect your picture provider! Keep your sexy activities fun, intimate, and consensual!

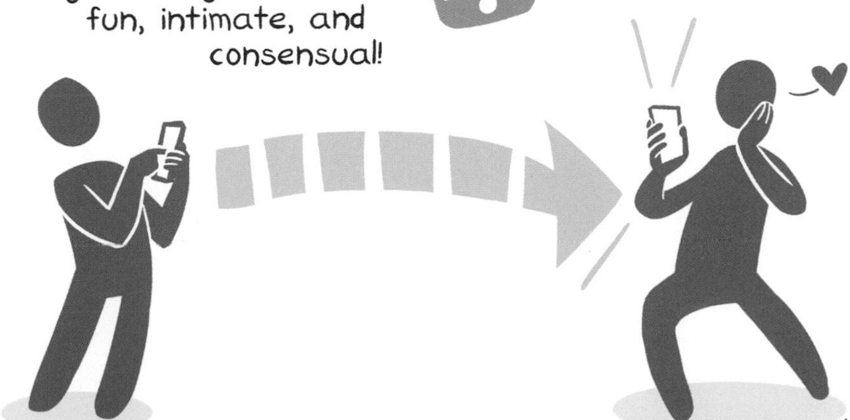

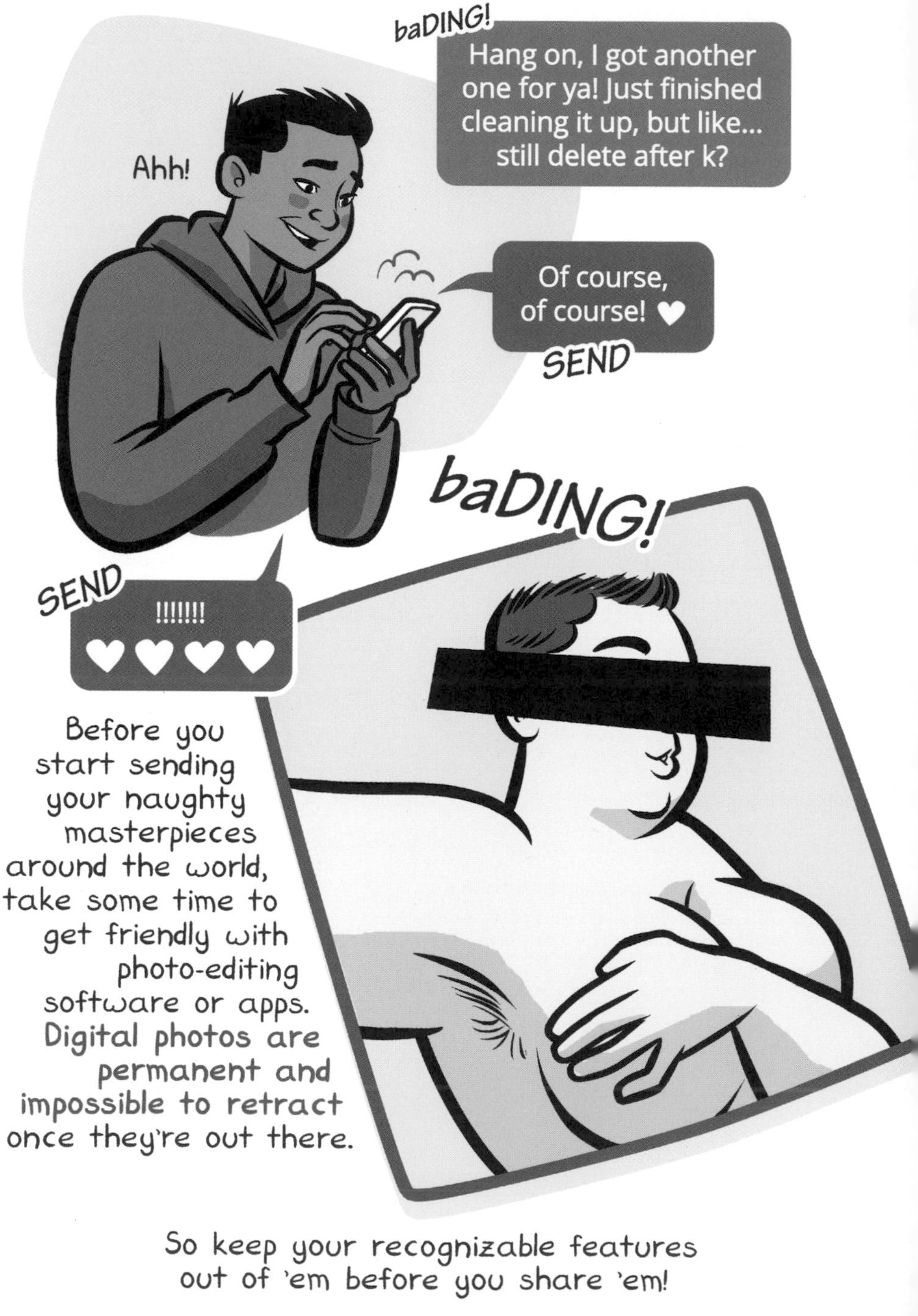
baDING!
Hang on, I got another one for ya! Just finished cleaning it up, but like... still delete after k?
Ahh!
Of course, of course! ♥
SEND
baDING!
SEND
!!!!!!! ♥♥♥♥
Before you start sending your naughty masterpieces around the world, take some time to get friendly with photo-editing software or apps. Digital photos are permanent and impossible to retract once they're out there.
So keep your recognizable features out of 'em before you share 'em!

Play safe.
Just like you use protection when you have sex in person, use protection when you sext!

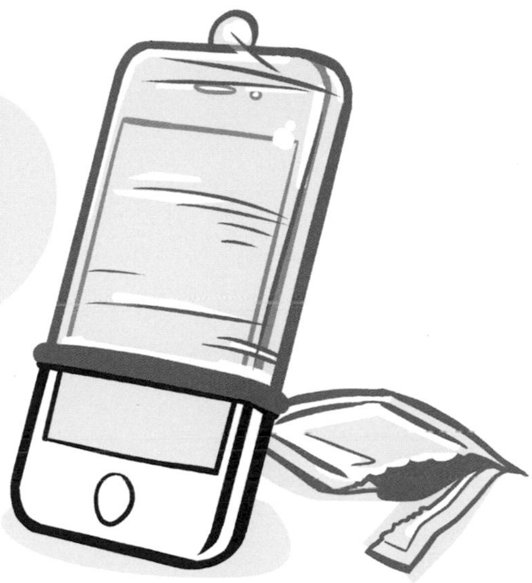

Crop out your face, hide your birthmarks and scars, and edit out your piercings and tattoos.

And don't forget to tell your sweetie how hot they look. Let 'em know you appreciate the little gift they've sent you, you lucky devil, you.

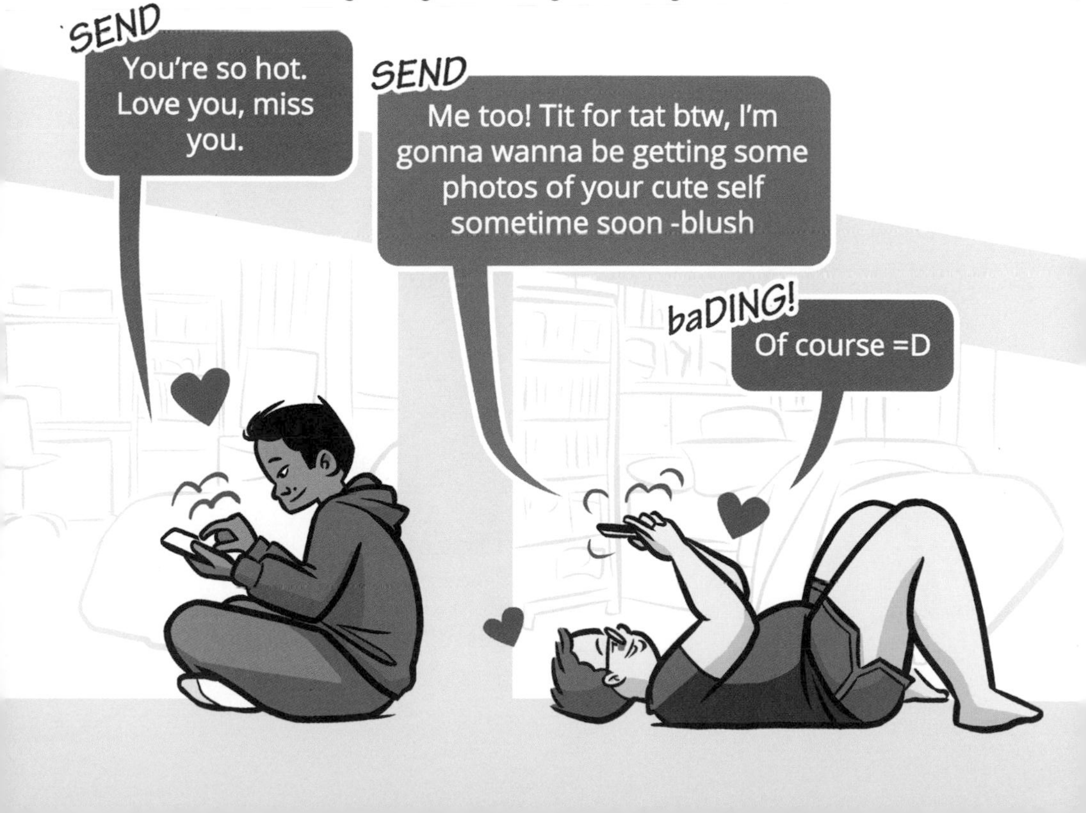
SEND
You're so hot. Love you, miss you.
SEND
Me too! Tit for tat btw, I'm gonna wanna be getting some photos of your cute self sometime soon -blush
baDING!
Of course =D

What are . . .
kinks, fantasies, and porn?

What even are these things? Why does your brain come up with kinks and fantasies? Why can't you avoid thinking about any of this altogether?

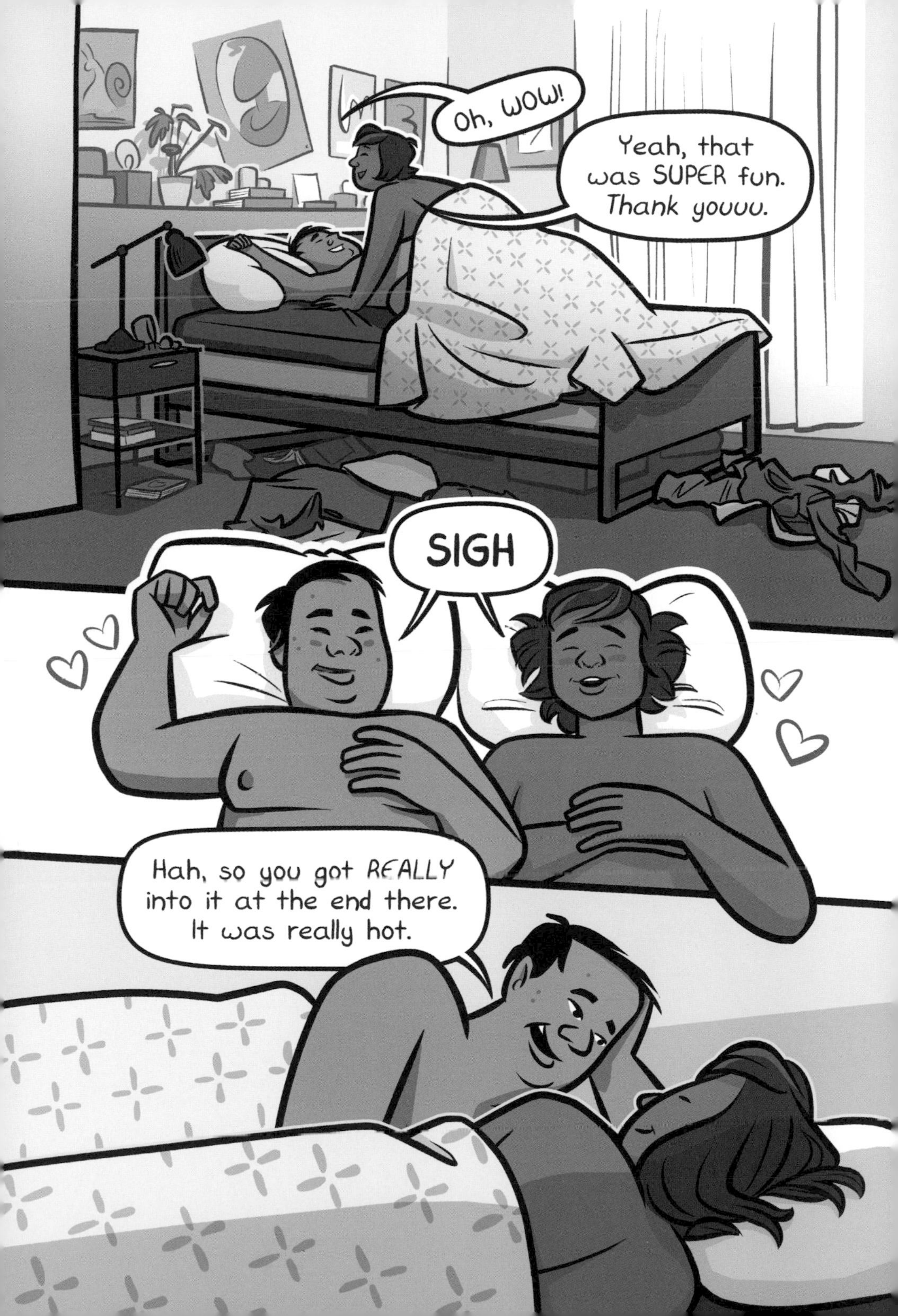
Oh, WOW!
Yeah, that was SUPER fun. Thank youuu.
SIGH
Hah, so you got REALLY into it at the end there. It was really hot.

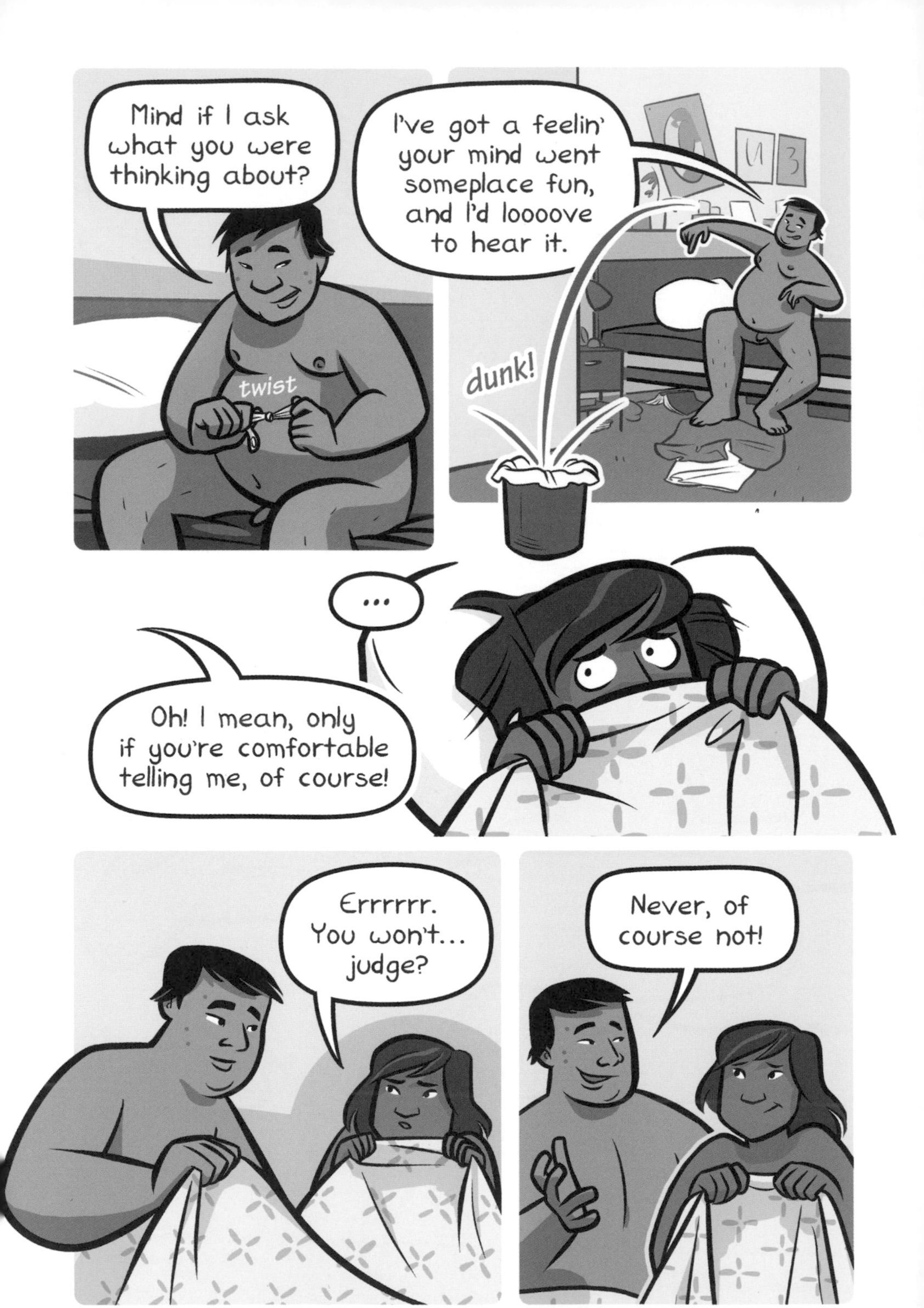
Mind if I ask what you were thinking about?
twist
I've got a feelin' your mind went someplace fun, and I'd loooove to hear it.
dunk!
...
Oh! I mean, only if you're comfortable telling me, of course!
Errrrrr. You won't... judge?
Never, of course not!

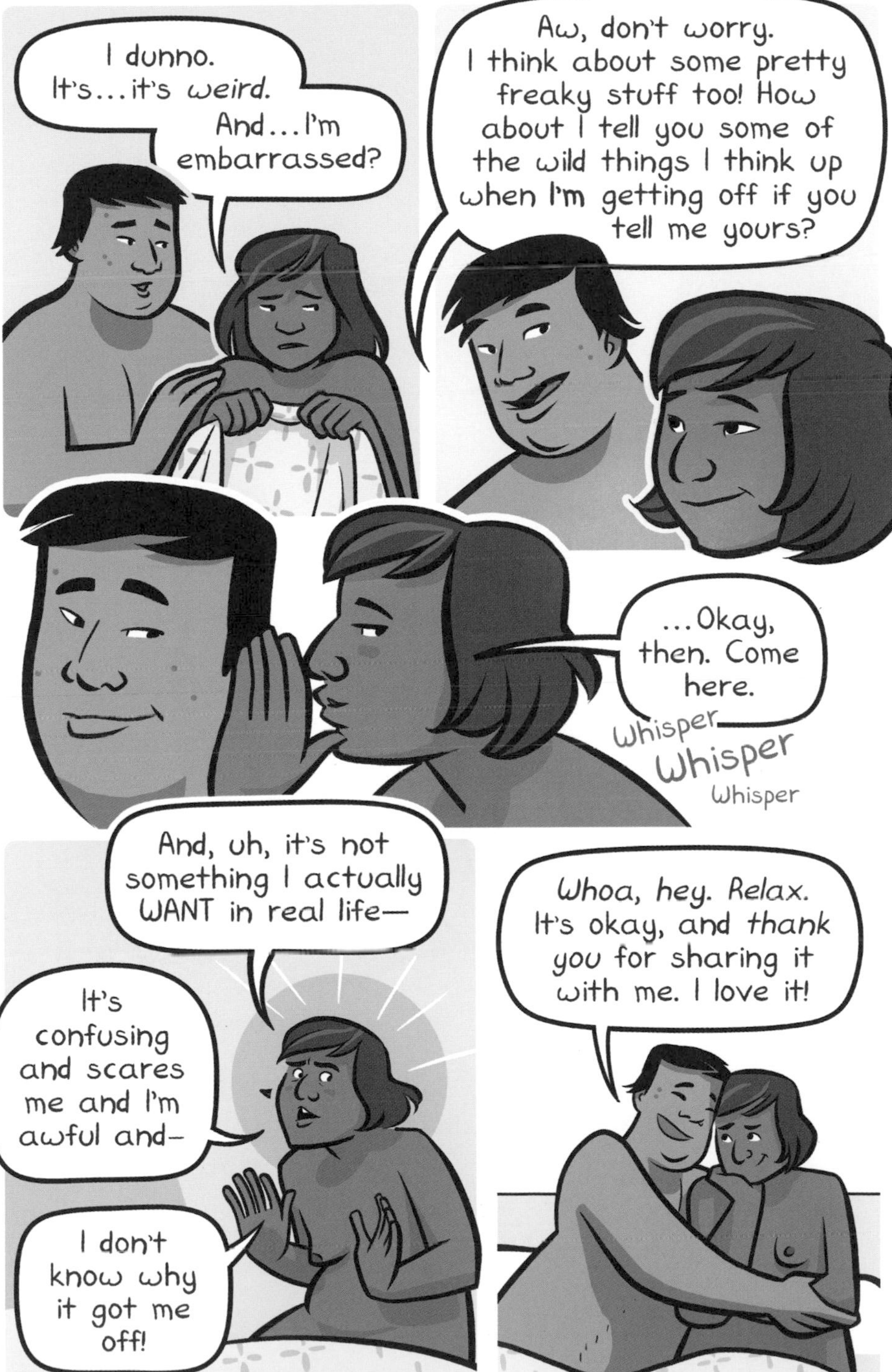
I dunno. It's...it's weird. And...I'm embarrassed?
Aw, don't worry. I think about some pretty freaky stuff too! How about I tell you some of the wild things I think up when I'm getting off if you tell me yours?
...Okay, then. Come here.
Whisper Whisper Whisper
And, uh, it's not something I actually WANT in real life—
It's confusing and scares me and I'm awful and—
I don't know why it got me off!
Whoa, hey. Relax. It's okay, and thank you for sharing it with me. I love it!

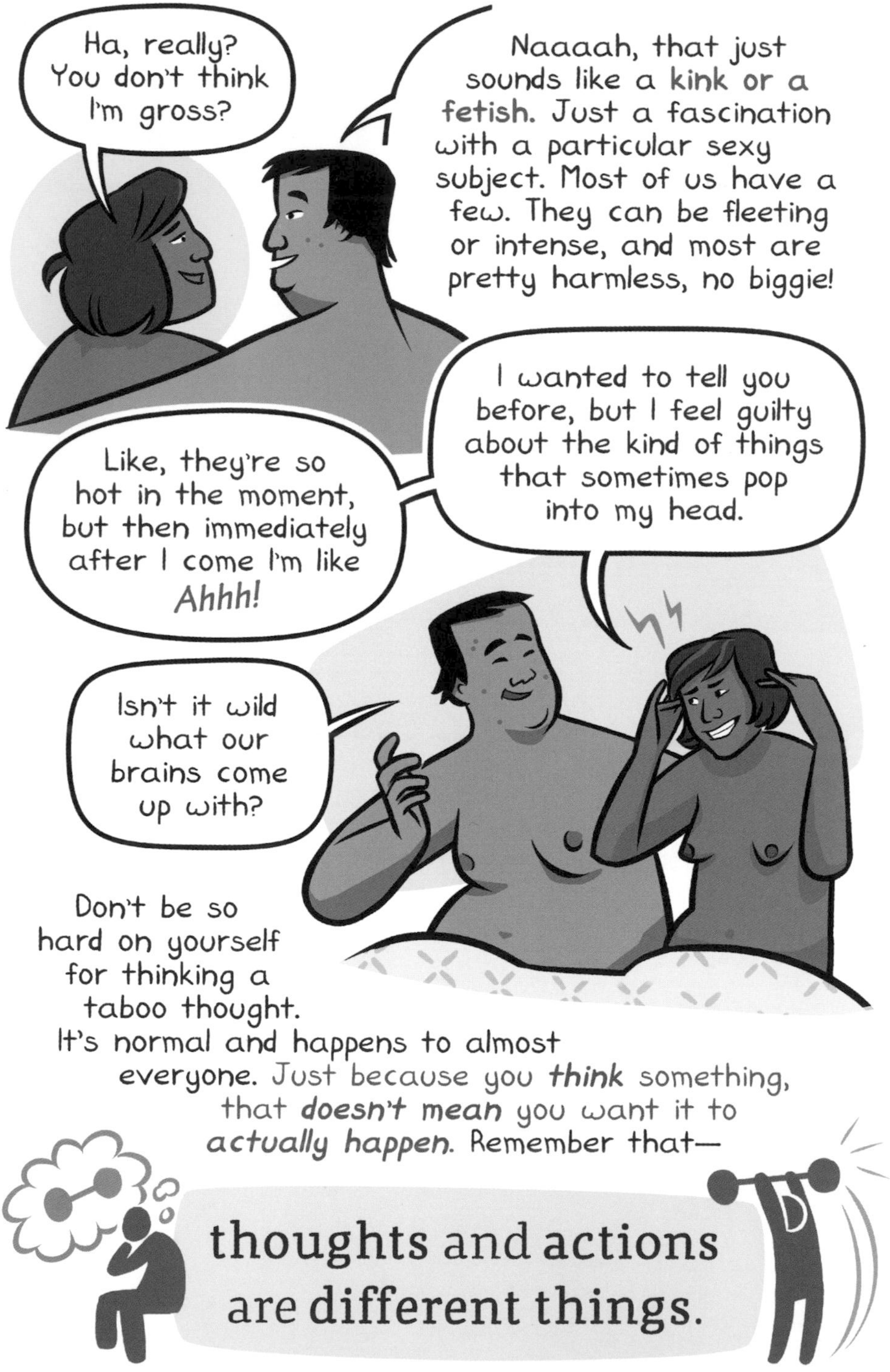

Ha, really? You don't think I'm gross?
Naaaah, that just sounds like a kink or a fetish. Just a fascination with a particular sexy subject. Most of us have a few. They can be fleeting or intense, and most are pretty harmless, no biggie!
I wanted to tell you before, but I feel guilty about the kind of things that sometimes pop into my head.
Like, they're so hot in the moment, but then immediately after I come I'm like *Ahhh!*
Isn't it wild what our brains come up with?
Don't be so hard on yourself for thinking a taboo thought. It's normal and happens to almost everyone. Just because you ***think*** something, that ***doesn't mean*** you want it to ***actually happen***. Remember that—
thoughts and actions are different things.

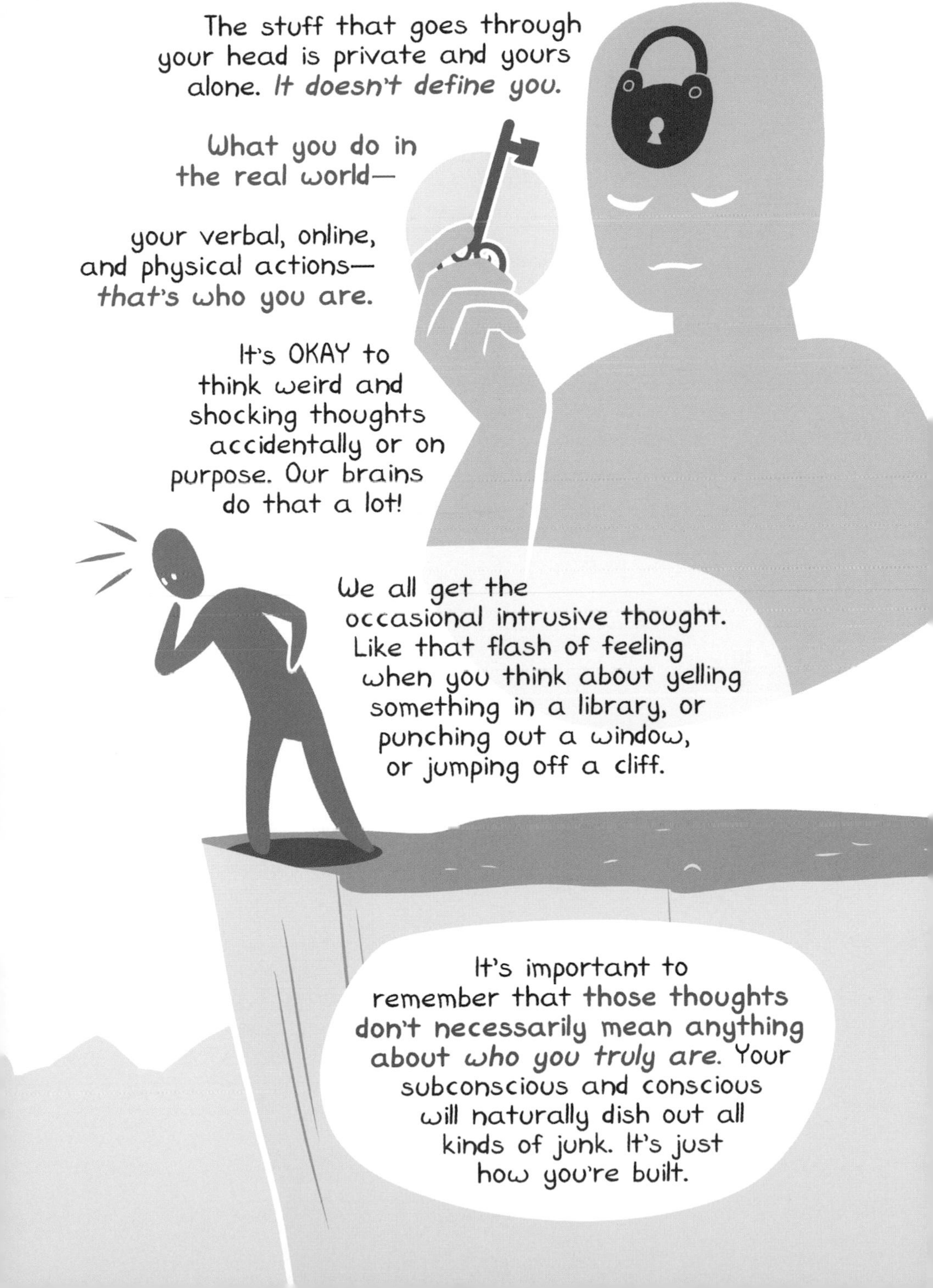
The stuff that goes through your head is private and yours alone. It doesn't define you.
What you do in the real world—
your verbal, online, and physical actions— that's who you are.
It's OKAY to think weird and shocking thoughts accidentally or on purpose. Our brains do that a lot!
We all get the occasional intrusive thought. Like that flash of feeling when you think about yelling something in a library, or punching out a window, or jumping off a cliff.
It's important to remember that those thoughts don't necessarily mean anything about who you truly are. Your subconscious and conscious will naturally dish out all kinds of junk. It's just how you're built.

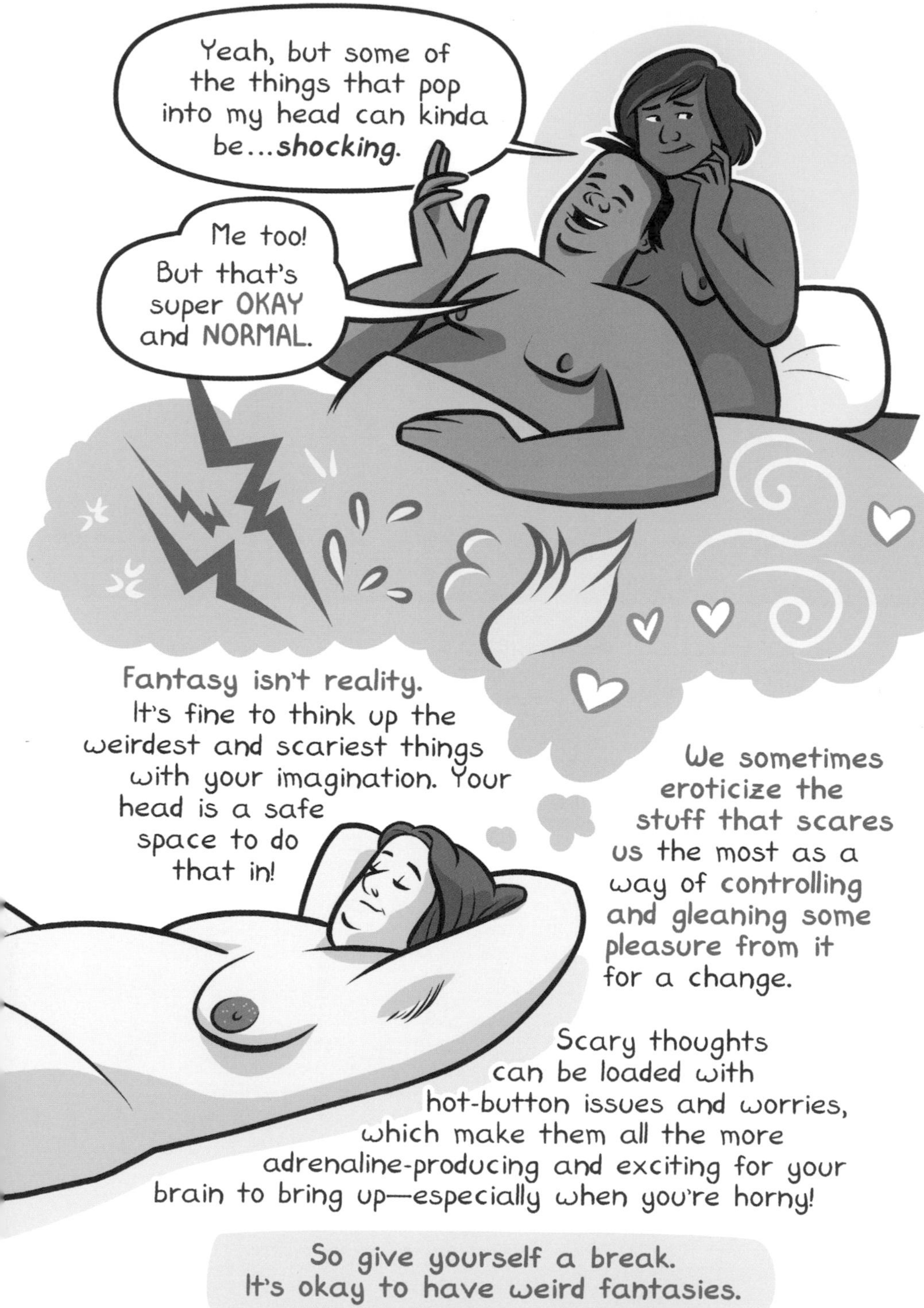
Yeah, but some of the things that pop into my head can kinda be...*shocking*.
Me too! But that's super OKAY and NORMAL.
Fantasy isn't reality. It's fine to think up the weirdest and scariest things with your imagination. Your head is a safe space to do that in!
We sometimes eroticize the stuff that scares us the most as a way of controlling and gleaning some pleasure from it for a change.
Scary thoughts can be loaded with hot-button issues and worries, which make them all the more adrenaline-producing and exciting for your brain to bring up—especially when you're horny!
So give yourself a break. It's okay to have weird fantasies.

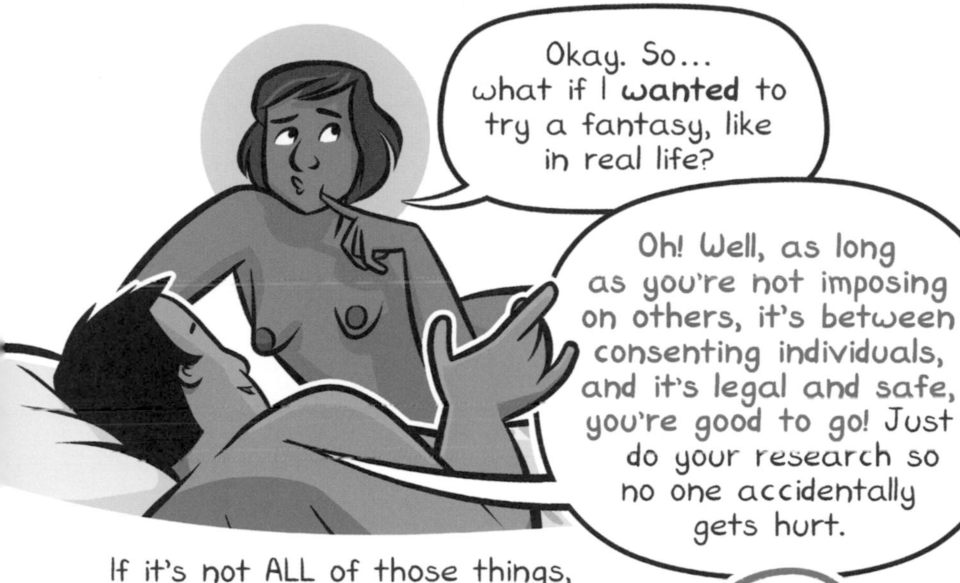
Okay. So... what if I **wanted** to try a fantasy, like in real life?
Oh! Well, as long as you're not imposing on others, it's between consenting individuals, and it's legal and safe, you're good to go! Just do your research so no one accidentally gets hurt.

If it's not ALL of those things, then acting on a fantasy becomes **unethical, harmful, and possibly illegal!**

If you're thinking of making a dangerous fantasy into reality, or if your fantasies are upsetting you, stop and go find a sex-positive therapist to help you work things out.

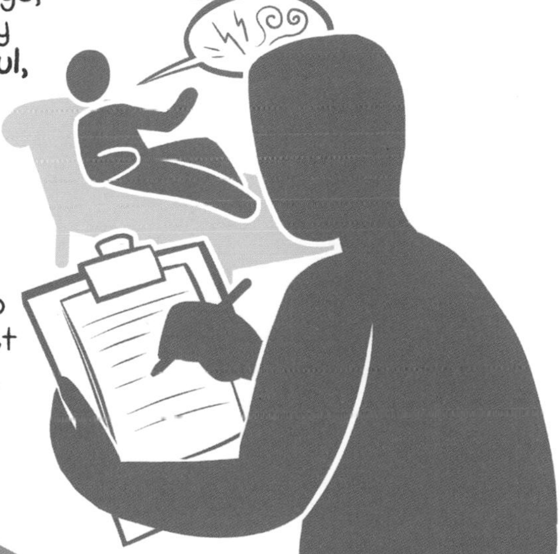

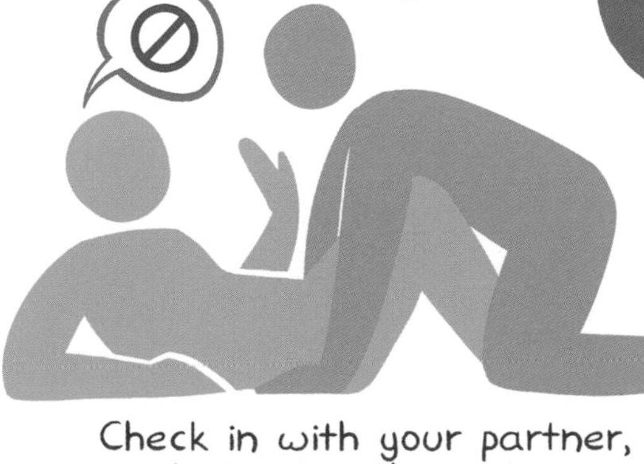

And if you do try something, it's okay to change your mind as you go.

Check in with your partner, be verbal, use safe words to stop the action, and don't do anything you're uncomfortable with.

A great place to research fantasies and kinks safely is on the internet!

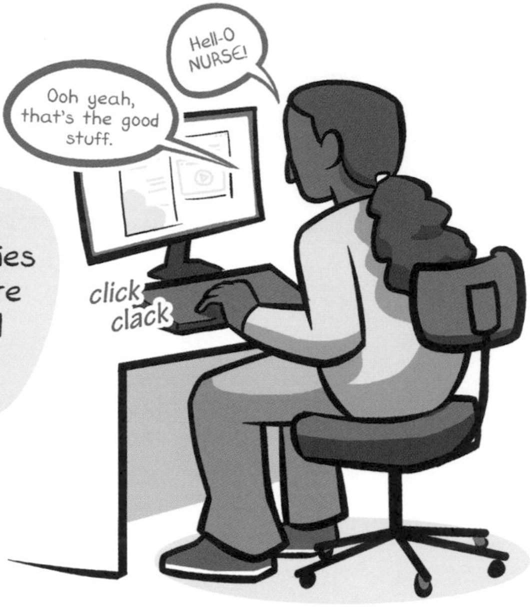
Ooh yeah, that's the good stuff.
Hell-O NURSE!
click
clack

There are tons of people and communities out there who share your interests and have all kinds of advice.

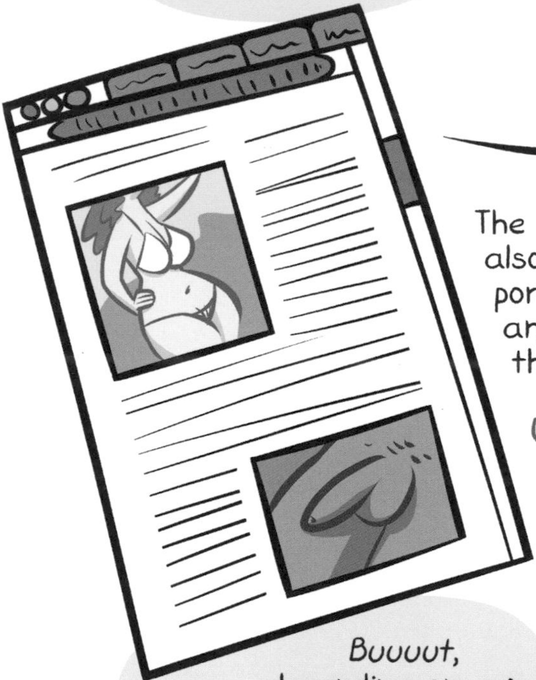

The online world is also chockablock full of pornography: professionals and amateurs alike sharing their sexy adventures online.

When consumed right, porn can help you discover new aspects of your sexuality, and help you safely explore kinks and fantasies.

Buuuut, depending on your age and where you found it, porn can also be unethical or illegal to watch. **So do your research!** Look up interviews with your fave porn performers, go to the sites they recommend, and pay for your porn.

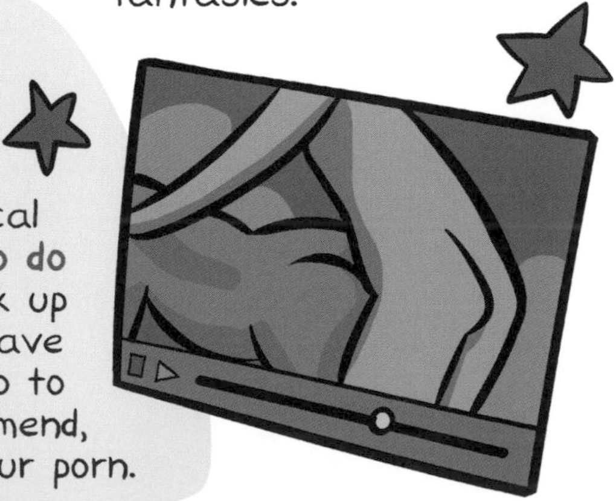

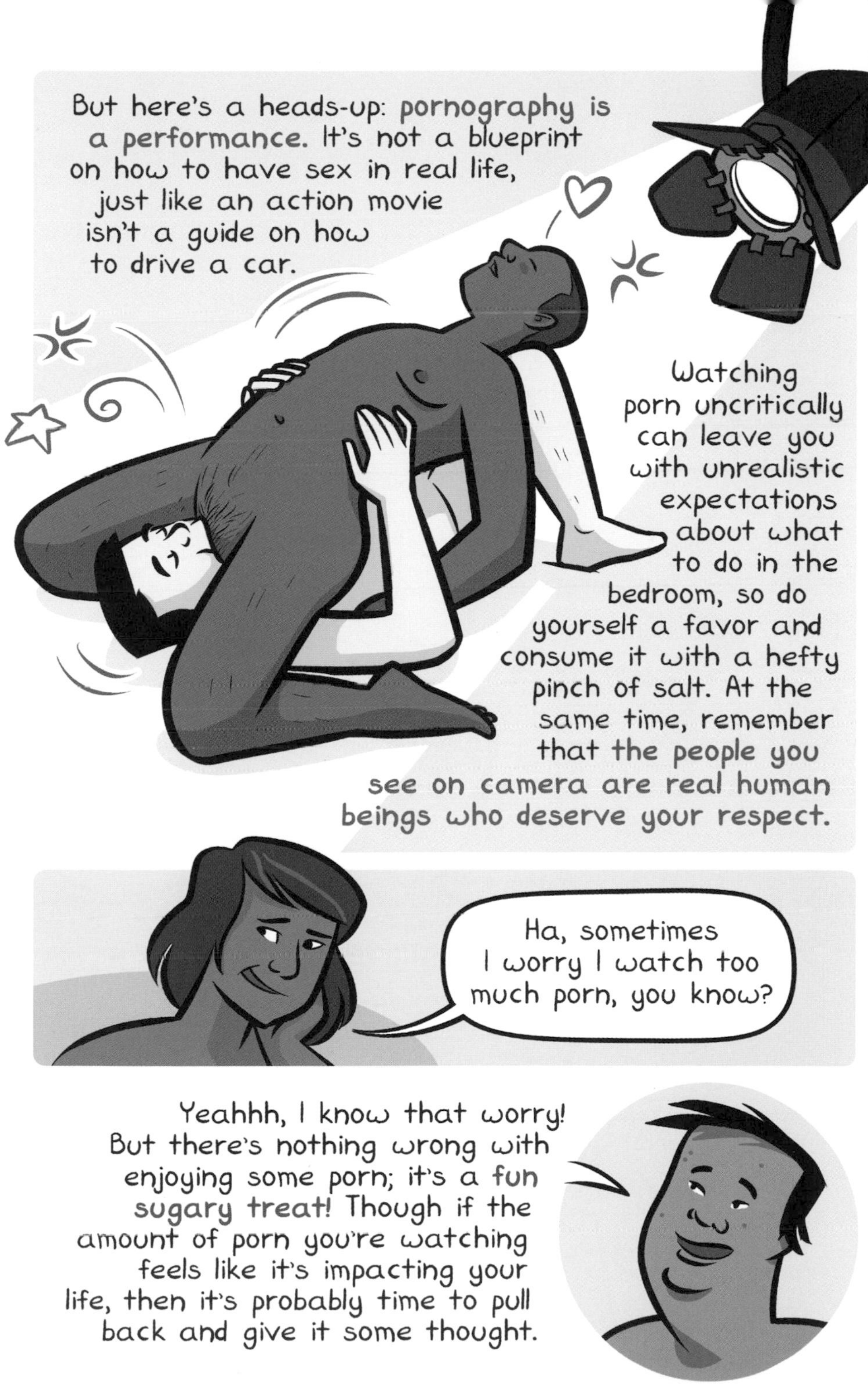
But here's a heads-up: pornography is a performance. It's not a blueprint on how to have sex in real life, just like an action movie isn't a guide on how to drive a car.
Watching porn uncritically can leave you with unrealistic expectations about what to do in the bedroom, so do yourself a favor and consume it with a hefty pinch of salt. At the same time, remember that the people you see on camera are real human beings who deserve your respect.
Ha, sometimes I worry I watch too much porn, you know?
Yeahhh, I know that worry! But there's nothing wrong with enjoying some porn; it's a fun sugary treat! Though if the amount of porn you're watching feels like it's impacting your life, then it's probably time to pull back and give it some thought.

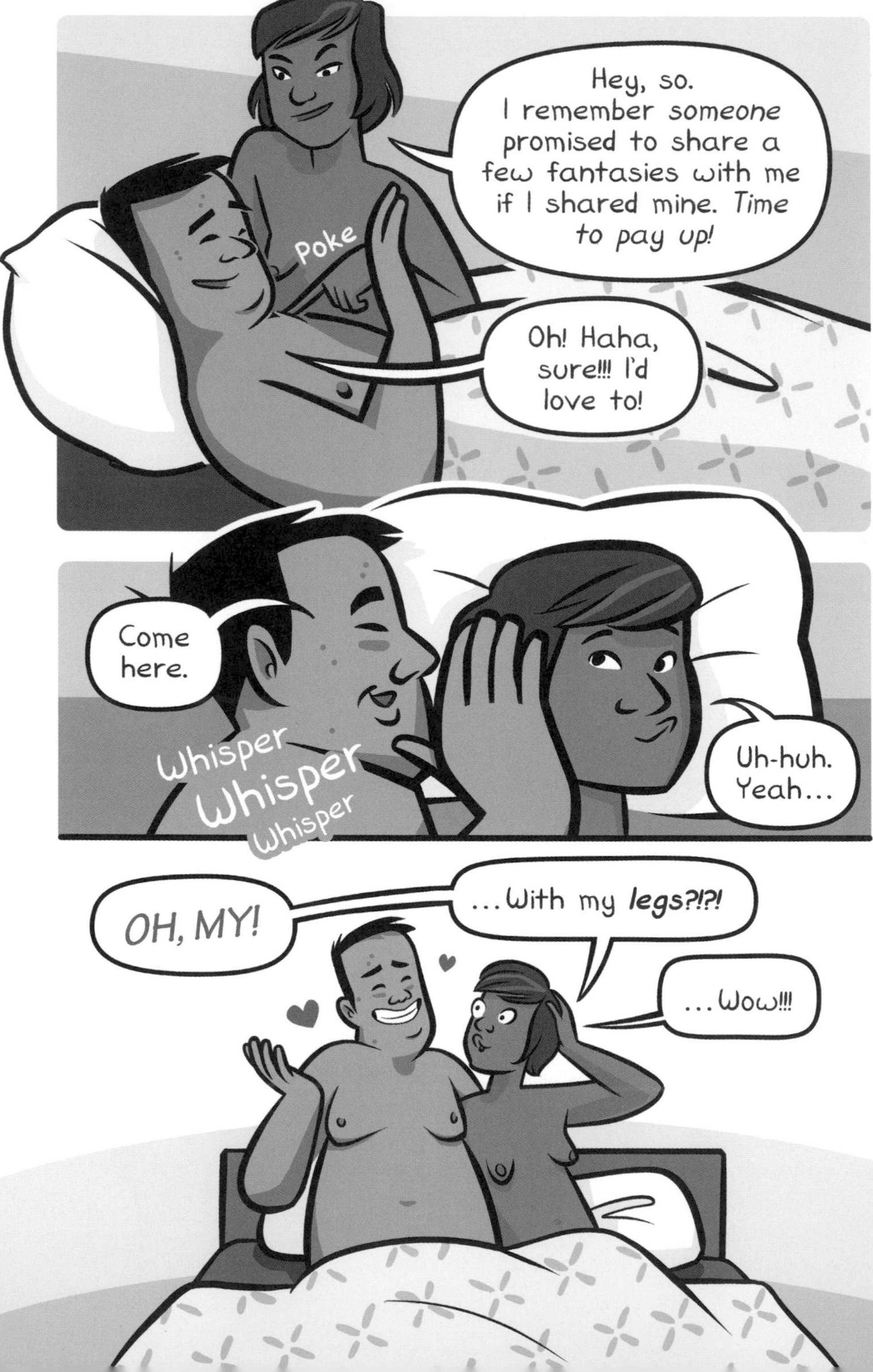
Hey, so.
I remember someone promised to share a few fantasies with me if I shared mine. Time to *pay up!*
Poke
Oh! Haha, sure!!! I'd love to!
Come here.
Whisper
Whisper
Whisper
Uh-huh. Yeah...
OH, MY!
...With my **legs?!?!**
...Wow!!!

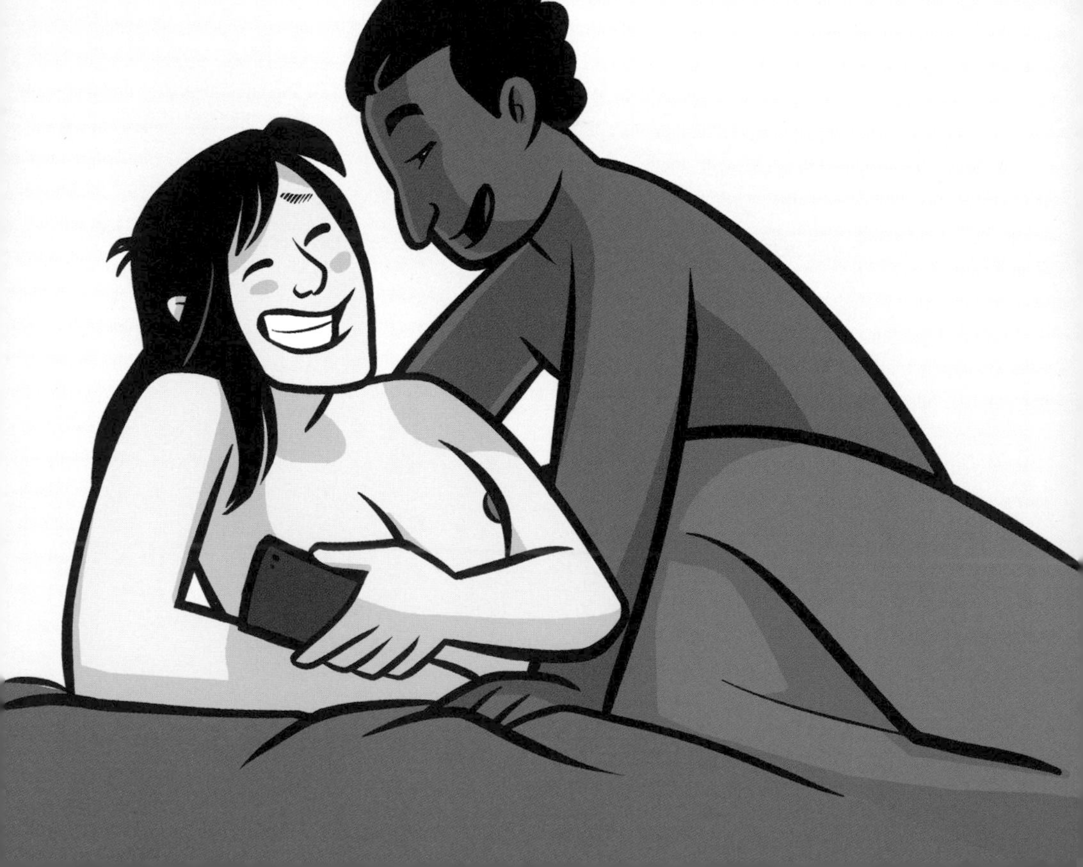

What is . . .
aftercare?

What happens to your mind and your body after sex? Is there anything special you need to do for yourself? How do you take care of your partner?

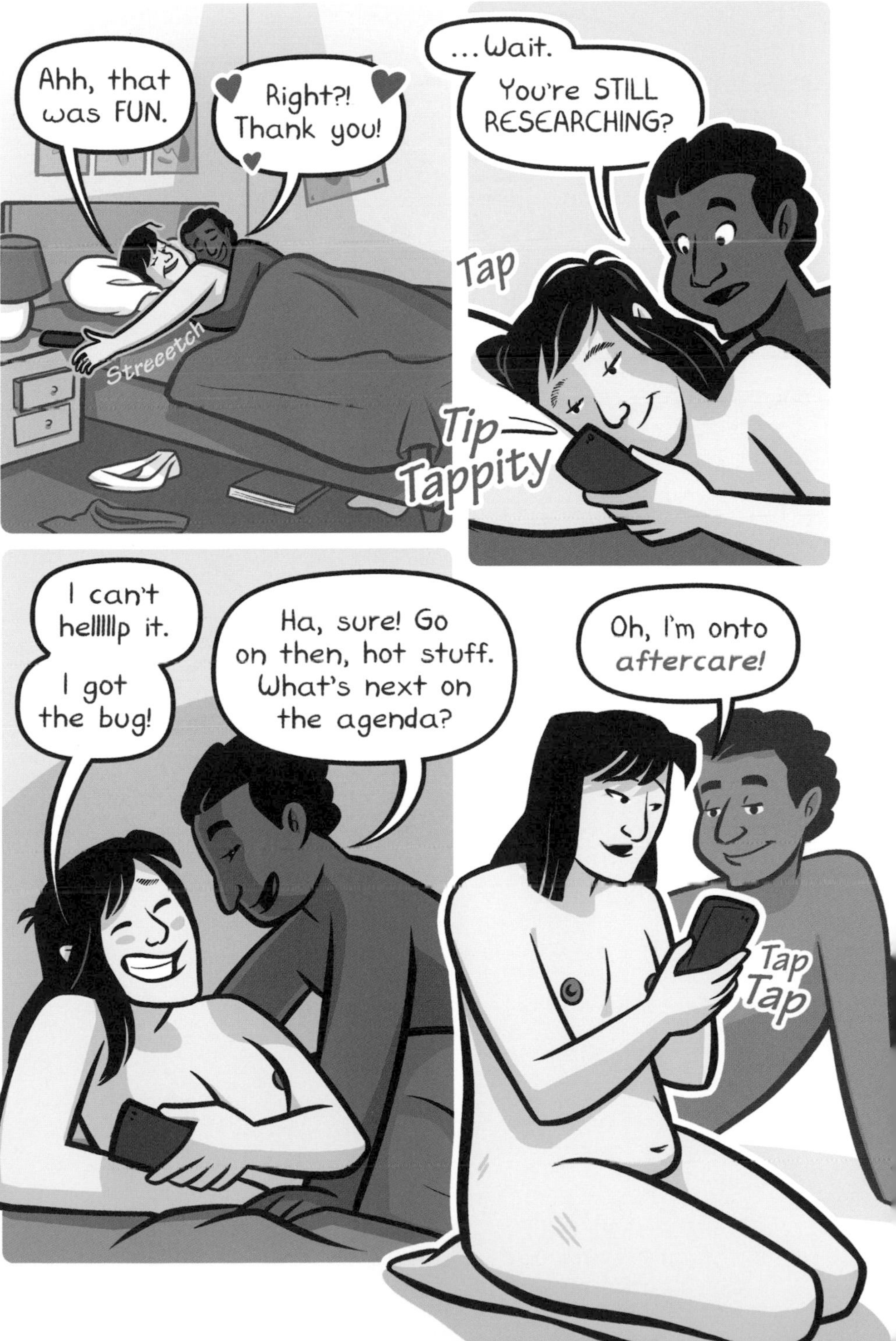
Ahh, that was FUN.
Right?! Thank you!
Streeetch
...Wait.
You're STILL RESEARCHING?
Tap
Tip-Tappity
I can't helllllp it.
I got the bug!
Ha, sure! Go on then, hot stuff. What's next on the agenda?
Oh, I'm onto aftercare!
Tap Tap

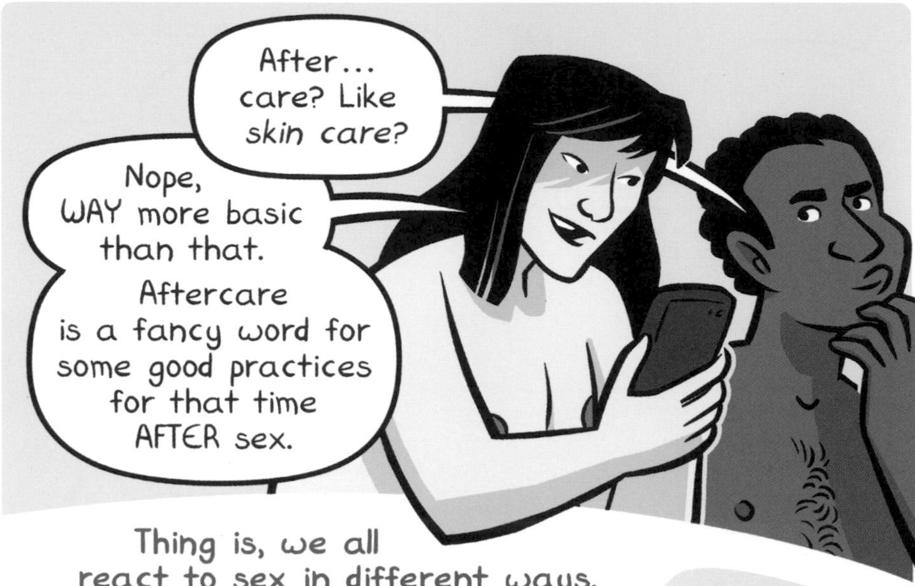
After... care? Like skin care?
Nope, WAY more basic than that.
Aftercare is a fancy word for some good practices for that time AFTER sex.

Thing is, we all react to sex in different ways. The moment right after can leave folks on a mental and physical high that they slowly come down to earth from.

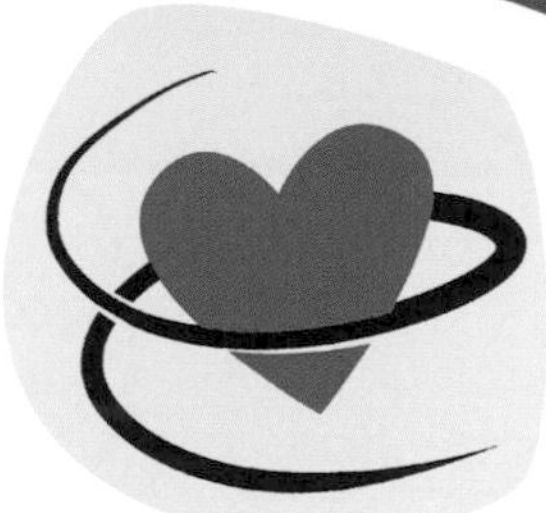

No matter what fun activity you've been enjoying, the time after affects each of us differently. It's hard to say how we might feel as the horny chemicals drain away.

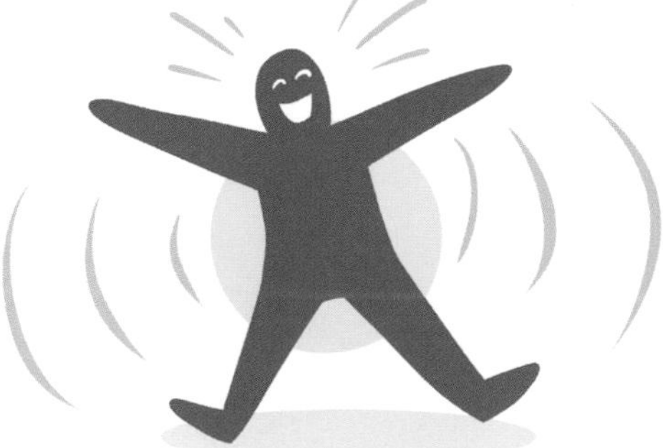

Some people might feel positive, warm, or proud.

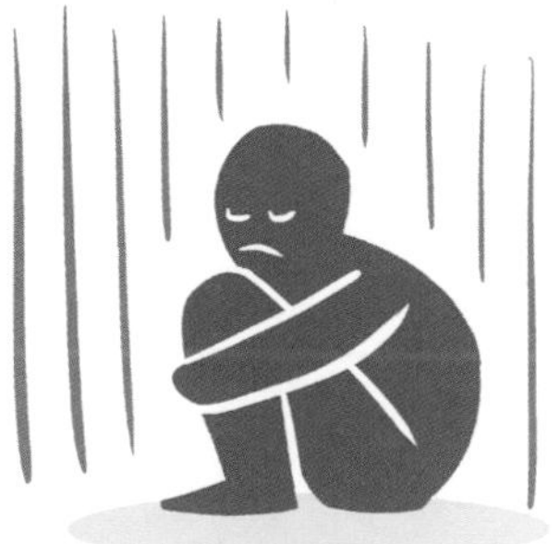

Some people might feel negative, cold, or ashamed.

Now's the perfect time to practice aftercare!

If you're feeling down...

Remind yourself that it's okay to feel this way.

Be kind to yourself.

Take your time, slow down, and try to relax as your body rebalances.

If you're feeling shaky...

Take a breath, drink some water, and eat something sweet.

Check in with your partner and ask them how they're feeling. Put something warm around them and hold them.

All of this applies whether you're in a long-term relationship or having a quickie. Sex can be a BIG deal for our bodies and brains—so be good and considerate to yourself and those you fool around with!

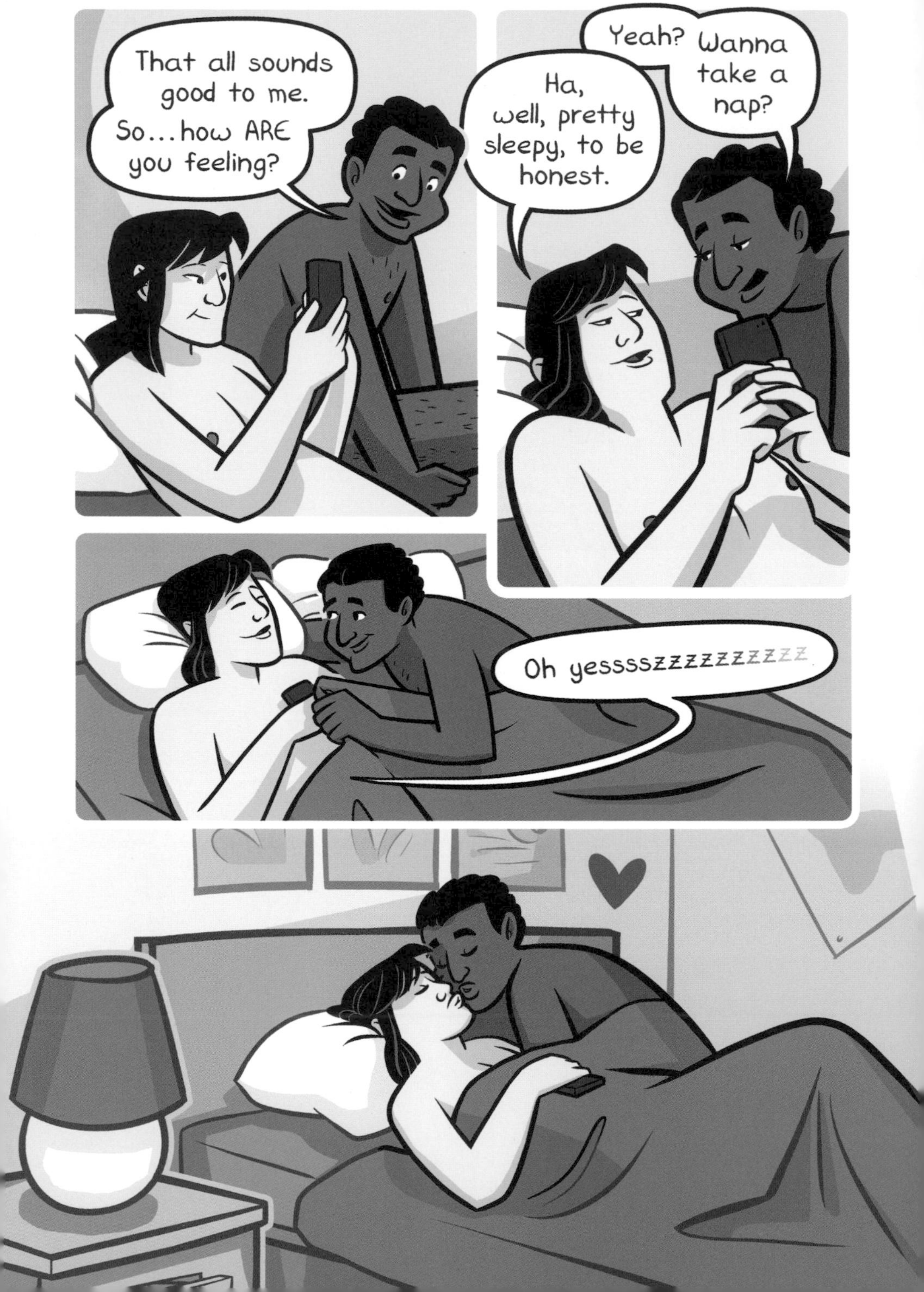
That all sounds good to me.
So... how ARE you feeling?
Ha, well, pretty sleepy, to be honest.
Yeah? Wanna take a nap?
Oh yessssZZZZZZZZZZ

Where are . . . friends in all this?

How do you balance being in a relationship and having other friends? How do you talk to your friends in relationships about not forgetting that they should take time to be friends too?

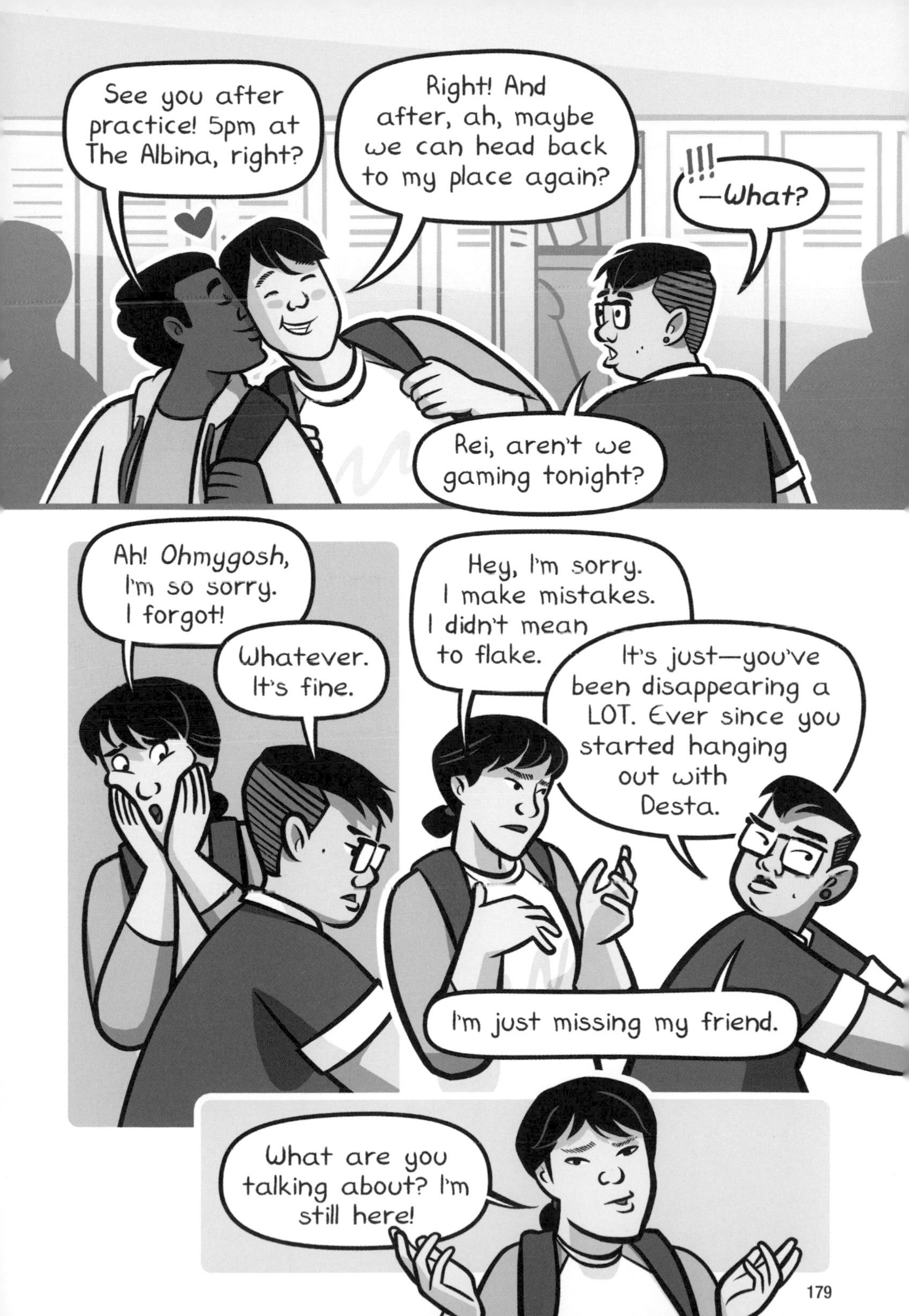

See you after practice! 5pm at The Albina, right?
Right! And after, ah, maybe we can head back to my place again?
!!!
—What?
Rei, aren't we gaming tonight?
Ah! Ohmygosh, I'm so sorry. I forgot!
Whatever. It's fine.
Hey, I'm sorry. I make mistakes. I didn't mean to flake.
It's just—you've been disappearing a LOT. Ever since you started hanging out with Desta.
I'm just missing my friend.
What are you talking about? I'm still here!

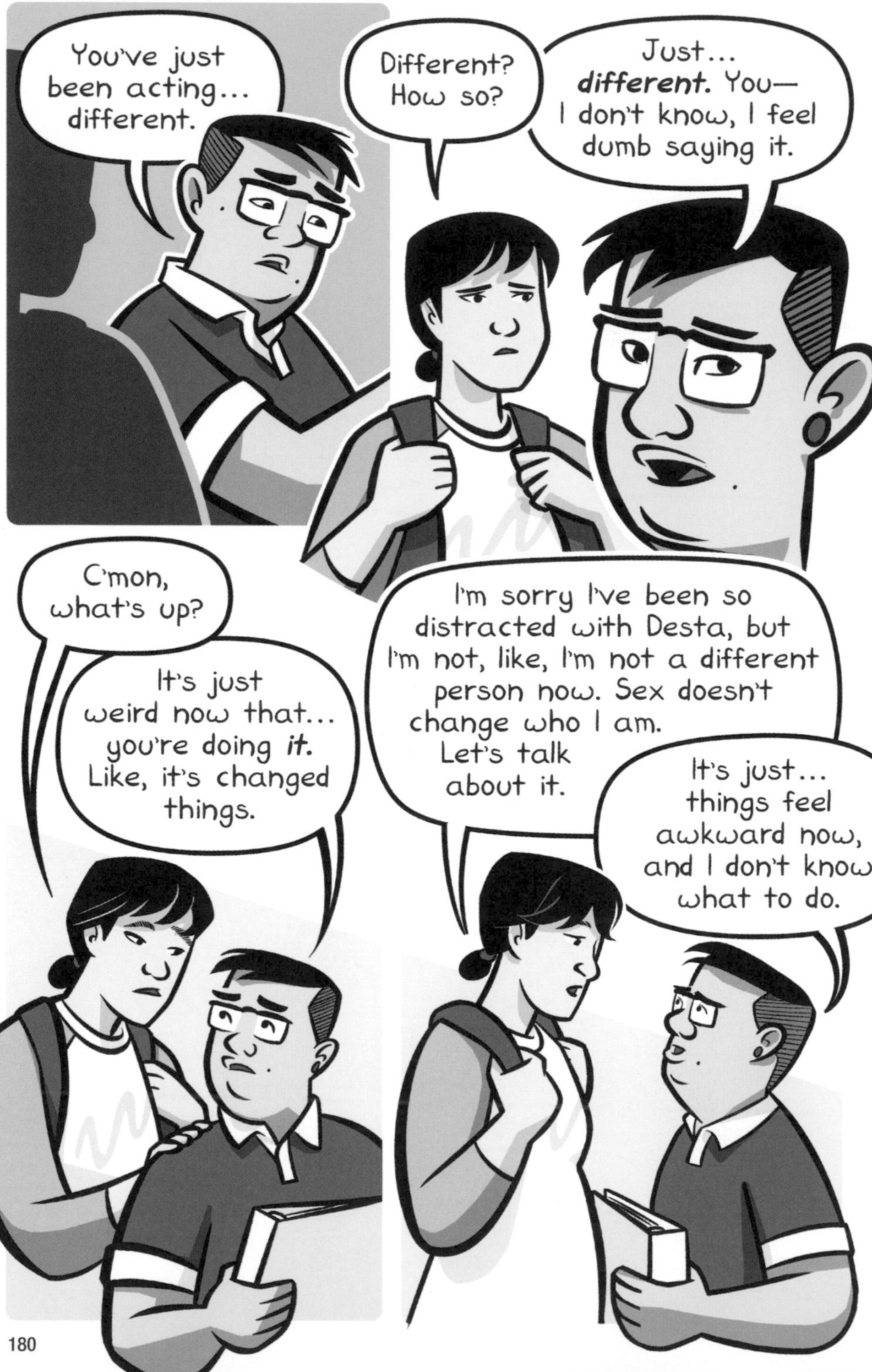
You've just been acting... different.
Different? How so?
Just... **different.** You— I don't know, I feel dumb saying it.
C'mon, what's up?
It's just weird now that... you're doing *it.* Like, it's changed things.
I'm sorry I've been so distracted with Desta, but I'm not, like, I'm not a different person now. Sex doesn't change who I am. Let's talk about it.
It's just... things feel awkward now, and I don't know what to do.

When sex starts to come into the lives of you and your friends, it can be a pretty jarring time. With something so intimate, exciting, and intense, it may be difficult to figure out how to balance that with being a good friend.

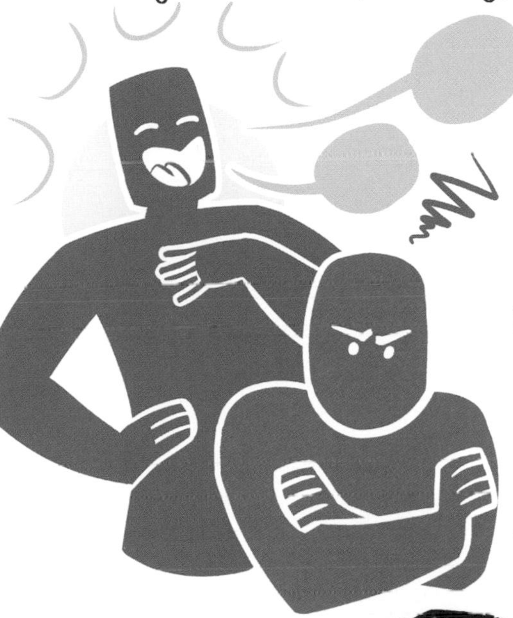

It's easy to unintentionally boast, and just generally be inconsiderate to people you care about.

Dealing with a sudden change in a friendship can be challenging. Keep talking about stuff as it comes up instead of clamming up!

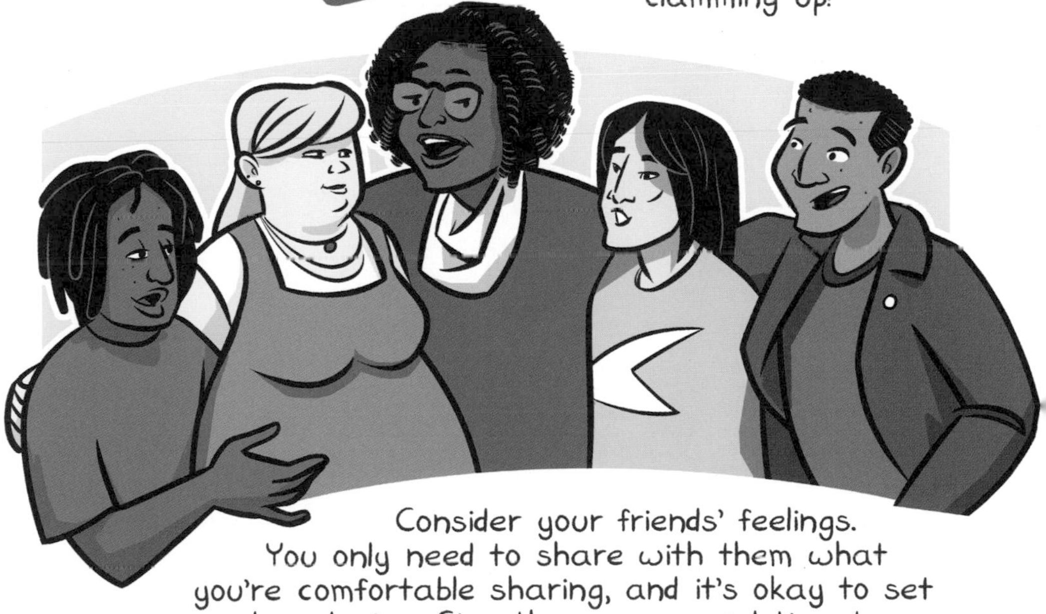

Consider your friends' feelings. You only need to share with them what you're comfortable sharing, and it's okay to set your own boundaries. Give them space and time to talk to you—both about the changes in your life and about what's happening in theirs.

If you're not sexually active, it can feel like everyone else **is.** There can be real pressure to "keep up," and that can suck. But it's totally okay and normal not to be having sex or even be interested in it.

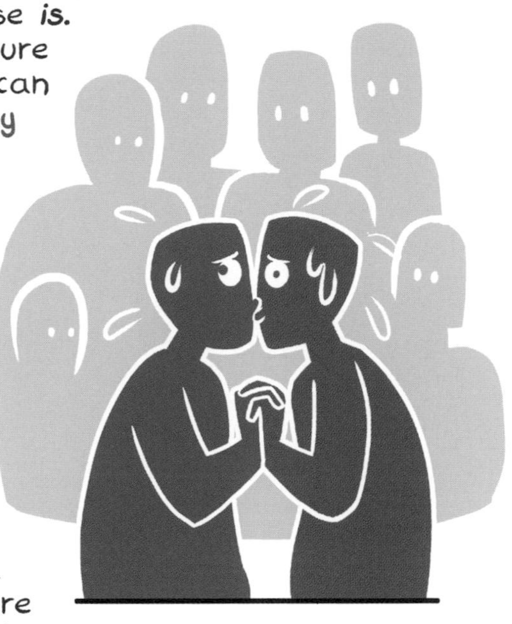

When a friend starts to explore this new part of their life, there can be a period of adjustment for everyone, including you, as they shuffle their priorities and time. Try to be patient, but also speak up when you need more just-friends-hang-out time.

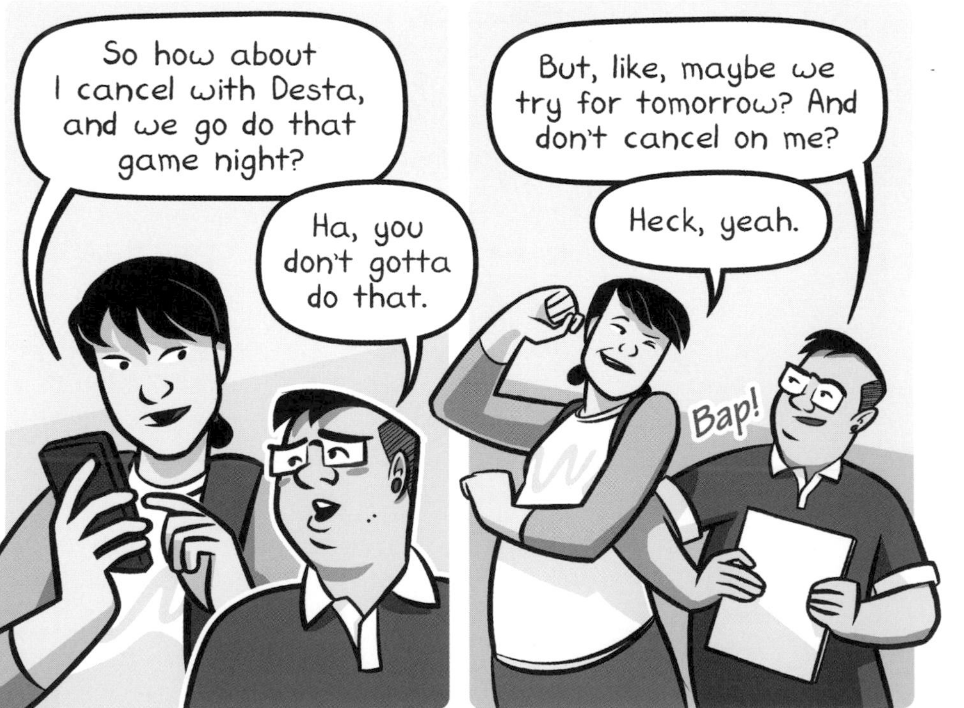
So how about I cancel with Desta, and we go do that game night?
Ha, you don't gotta do that.
But, like, maybe we try for tomorrow? And don't cancel on me?
Heck, yeah.
Bap!

What is . . . jealousy?

Why do you get jealous? What do you do when you get jealous? Should you even be jealous?

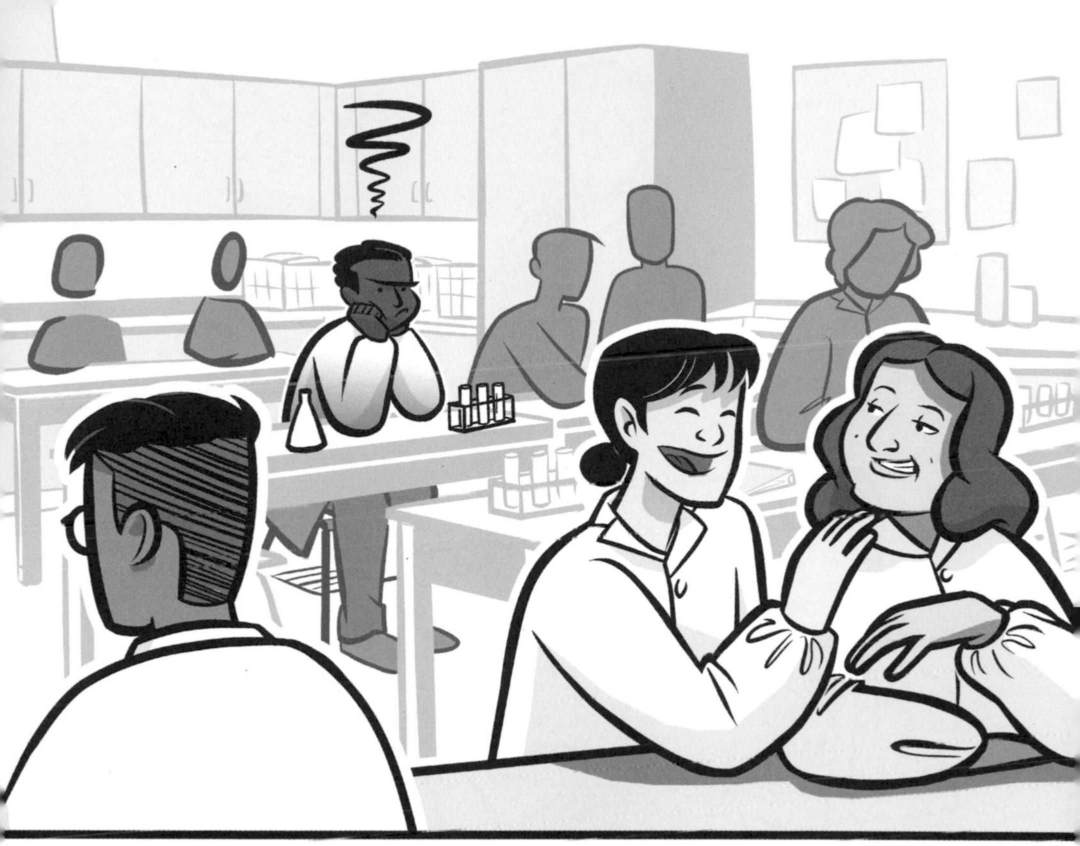

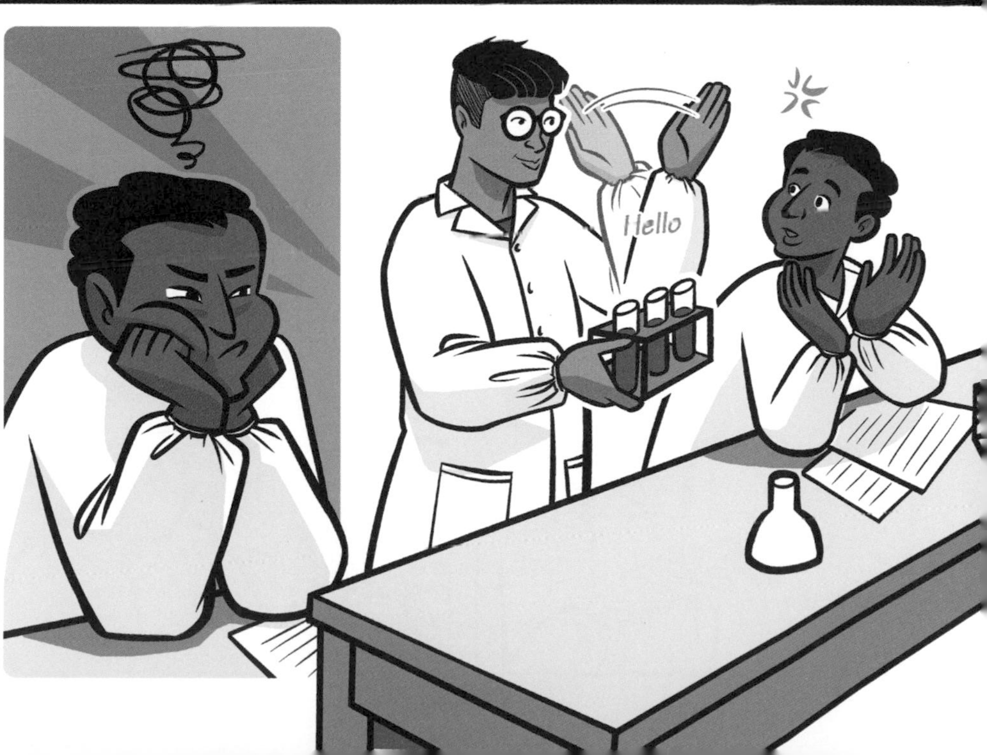
Hello

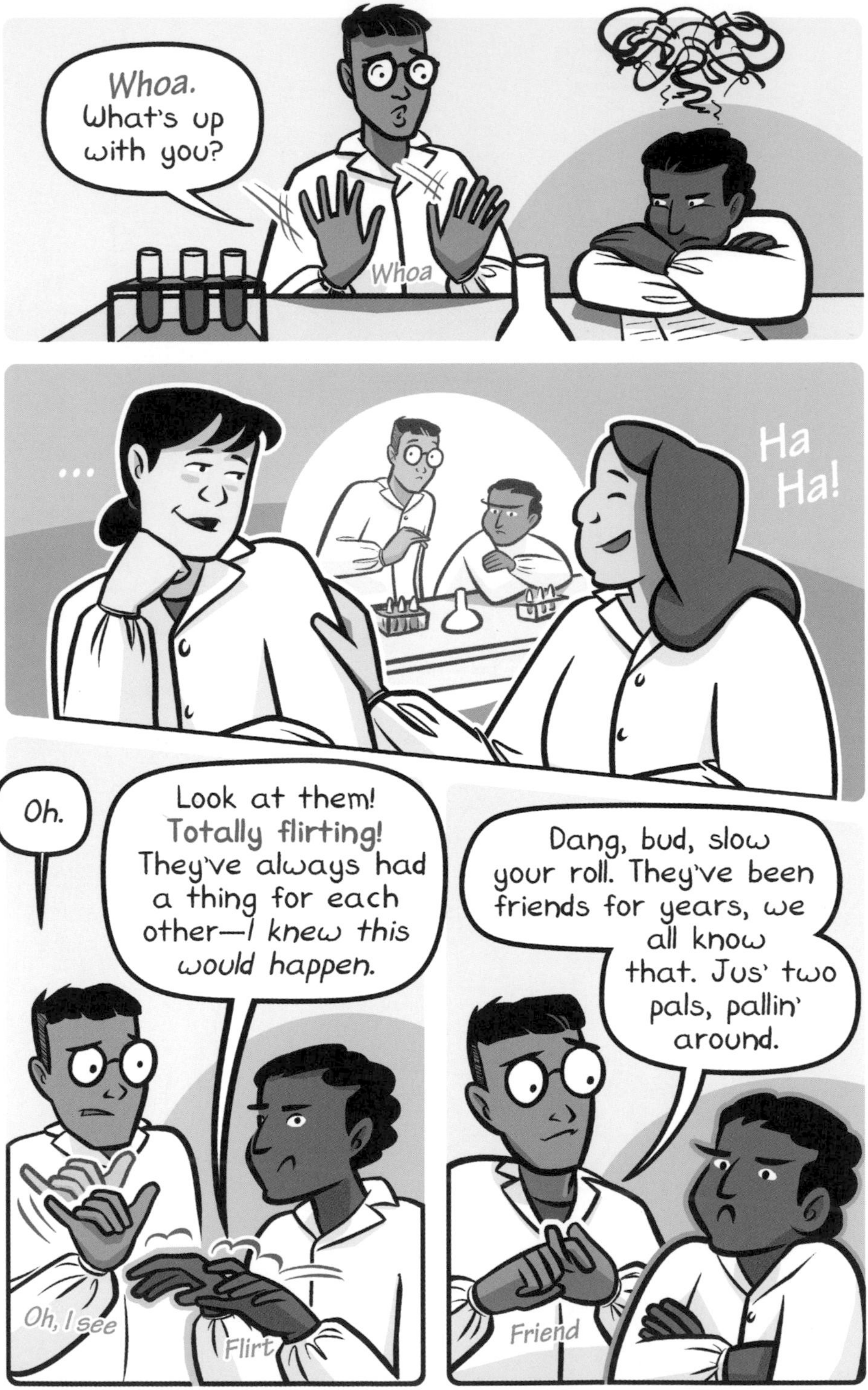
Whoa.
What's up with you?
Whoa
...
Ha Ha!
Oh.
Look at them! Totally flirting! They've always had a thing for each other—I knew this would happen.
Oh, I see
Flirt
Dang, bud, slow your roll. They've been friends for years, we all know that. Jus' two pals, pallin' around.
Friend

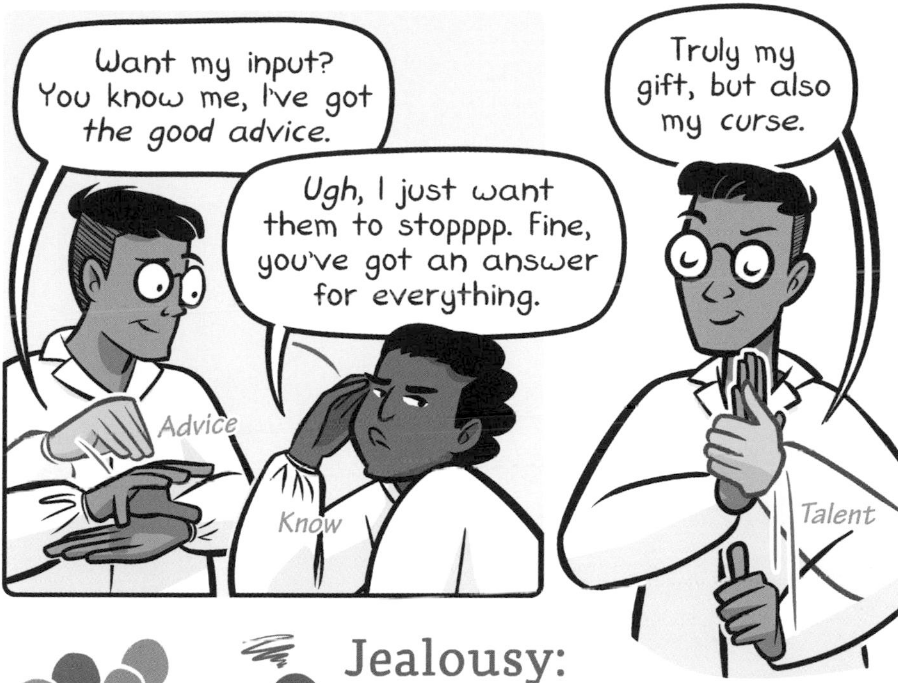
Want my input? You know me, I've got the *good* advice.
Ugh, I just want them to stopppp. Fine, you've got an answer for everything.
Truly my gift, but also my curse.
Advice
Know
Talent

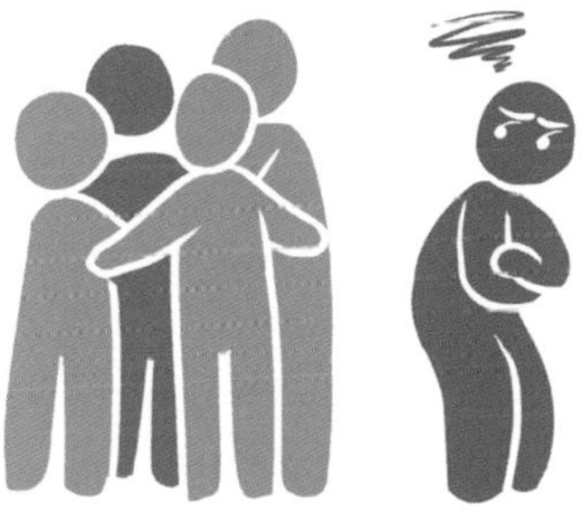

Jealousy:

It's all the feelings that come over you when you think you're being overlooked by others. It comes from inside, from your insecurities and fears—fear of loss, fear of betrayal, and fear of hurt.

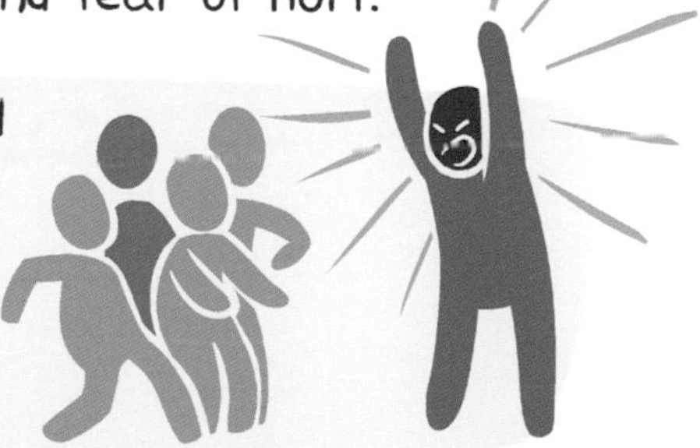

Jealousy is natural and normal, but that doesn't mean that it's right or useful. A lot of the time it can even be destructive and can lead to really shitty behavior.

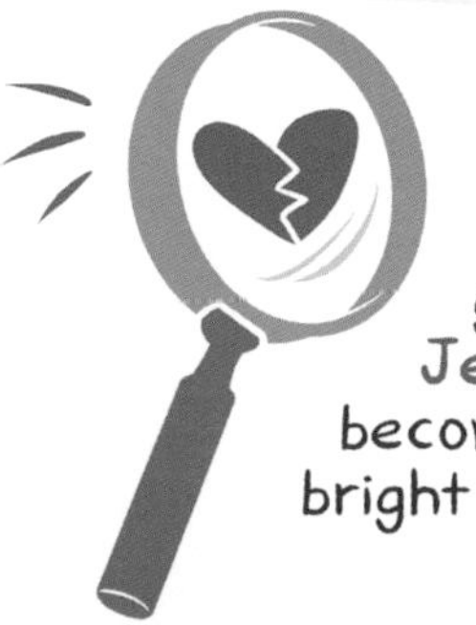

Recognizing jealousy for what it is and trying to deal with it is *way better* than bottling it up. But to do that, you gotta look at the fear ***inside yourself.*** Jealousy usually goes away, or at least becomes more manageable, when you shine a bright light on the source of your fears.

Jealousy always comes from within.
It happens when an outside event triggers a deep dark fear inside you and makes that fear feel real and validated.

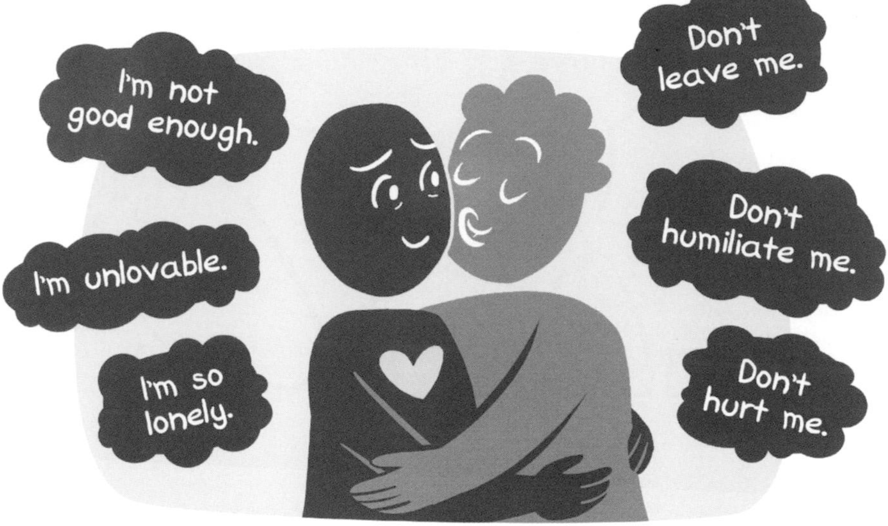
I'm not good enough.
I'm unlovable.
I'm so lonely.
Don't leave me.
Don't humiliate me.
Don't hurt me.

In reality, brains go overboard with this sort of fear validation. They love any chance to prove a fear is valid while ignoring all the reasons it's not.

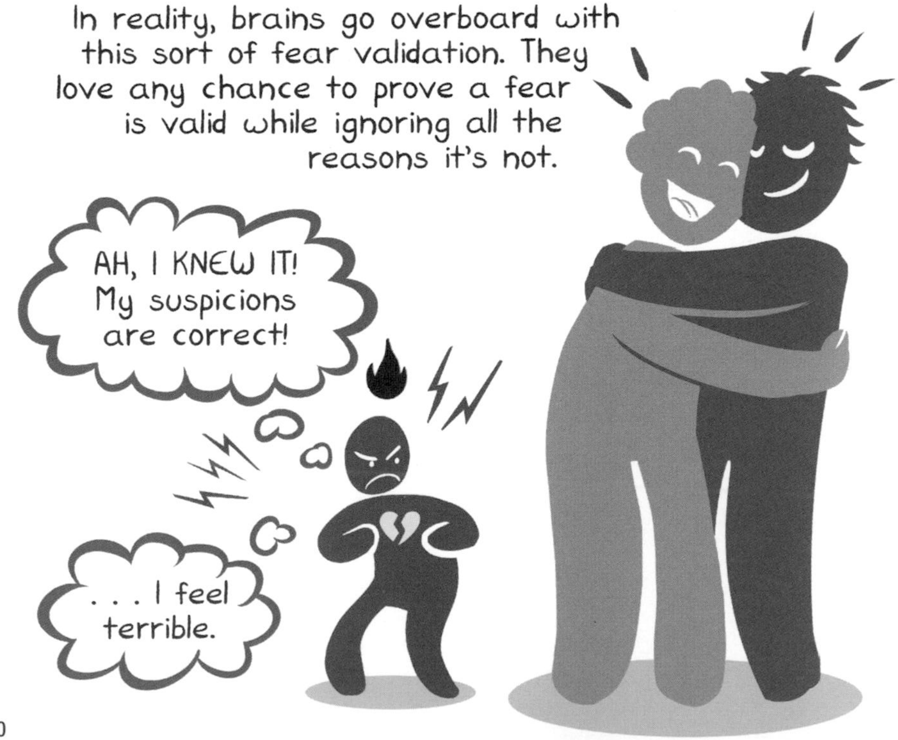
AH, I KNEW IT! My suspicions are correct!
. . . I feel terrible.

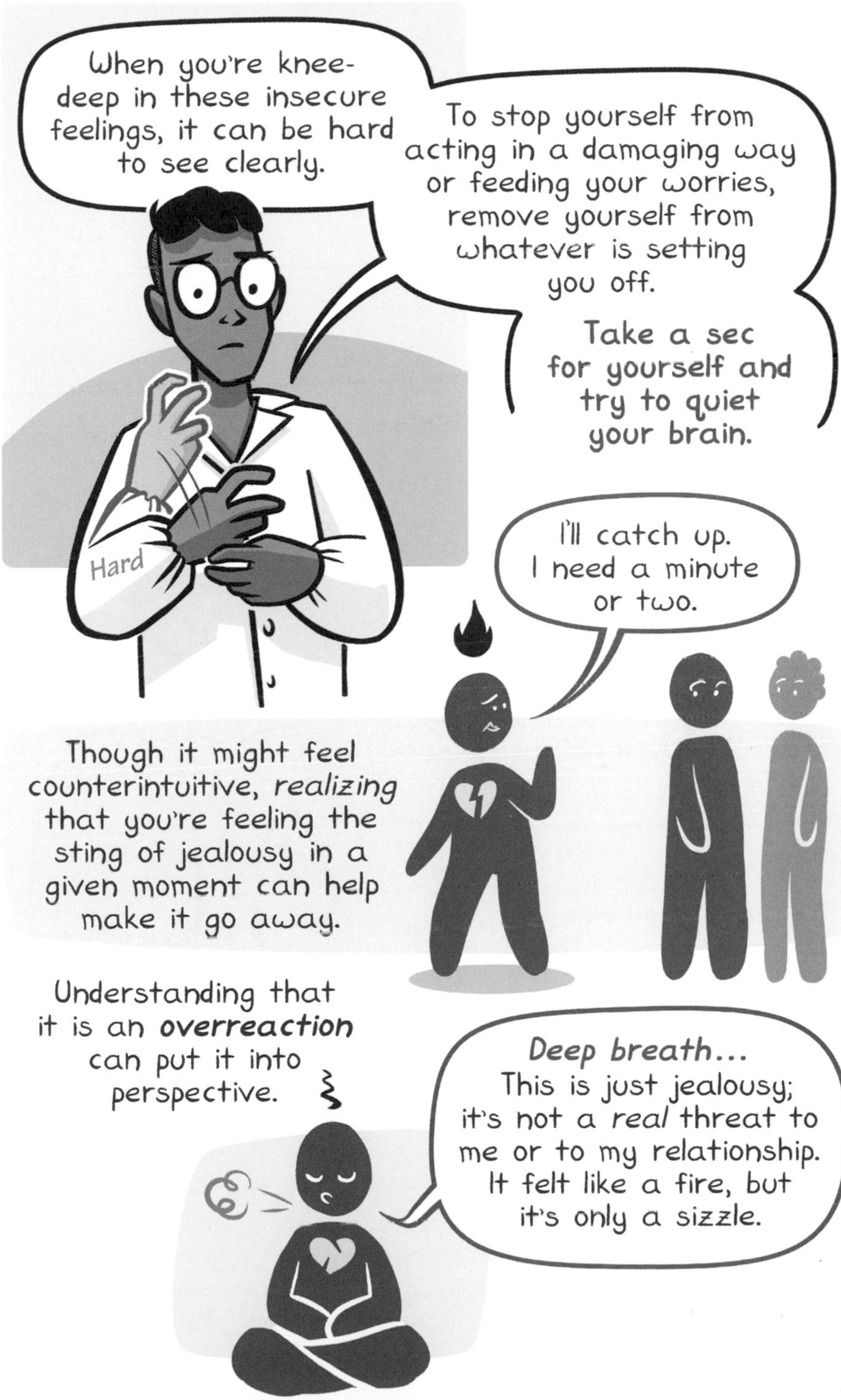
When you're knee-deep in these insecure feelings, it can be hard to see clearly.
To stop yourself from acting in a damaging way or feeding your worries, remove yourself from whatever is setting you off.
Take a sec for yourself and try to quiet your brain.
Hard
I'll catch up. I need a minute or two.
Though it might feel counterintuitive, *realizing* that you're feeling the sting of jealousy in a given moment can help make it go away.
Understanding that it is an ***overreaction*** can put it into perspective.
Deep breath... This is just jealousy; it's not a *real* threat to me or to my relationship. It felt like a fire, but it's only a sizzle.

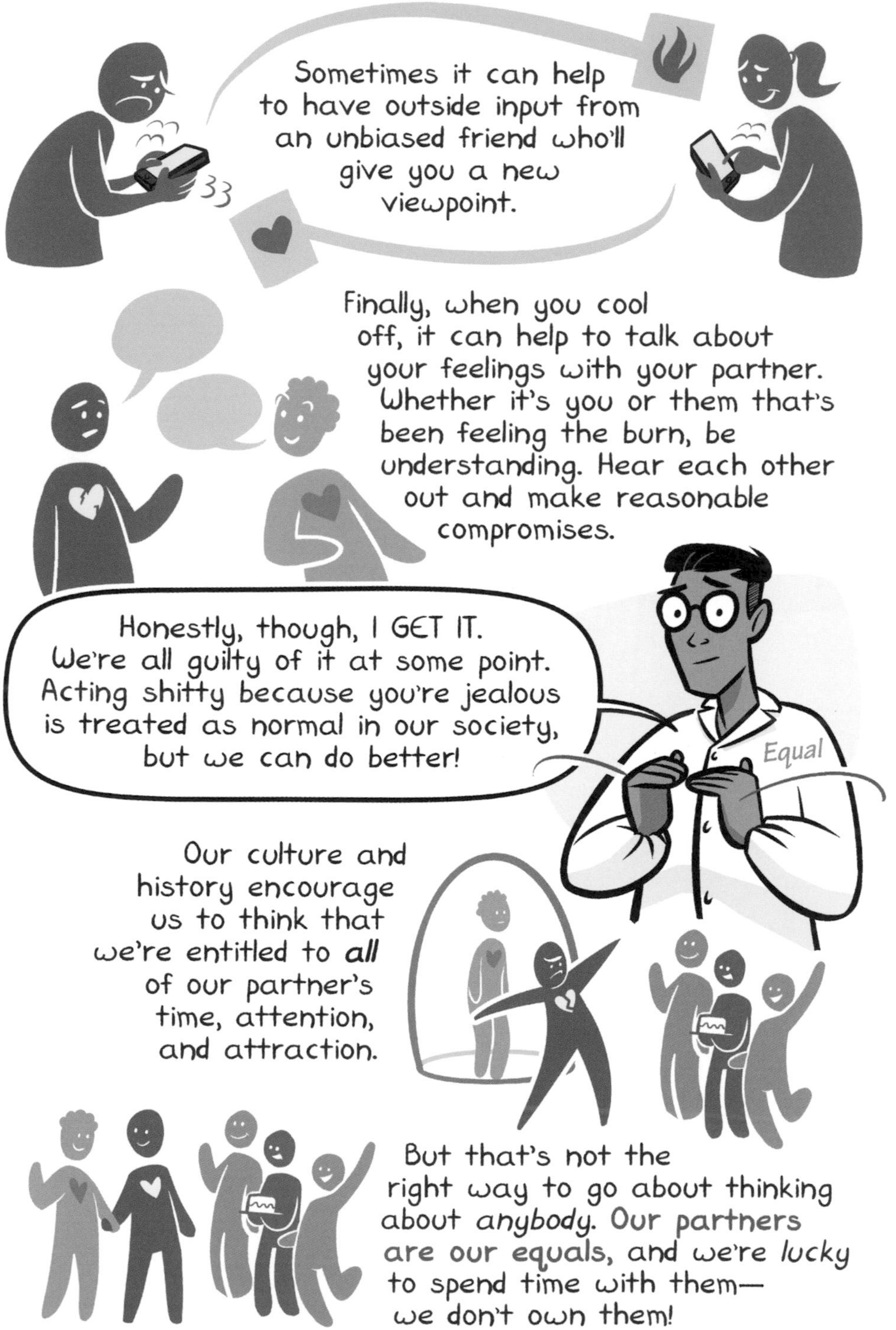
Sometimes it can help to have outside input from an unbiased friend who'll give you a new viewpoint.
Finally, when you cool off, it can help to talk about your feelings with your partner. Whether it's you or them that's been feeling the burn, be understanding. Hear each other out and make reasonable compromises.
Honestly, though, I GET IT. We're all guilty of it at some point. Acting shitty because you're jealous is treated as normal in our society, but we can do better!
Equal
Our culture and history encourage us to think that we're entitled to *all* of our partner's time, attention, and attraction.
But that's not the right way to go about thinking about *anybody*. Our partners are our equals, and we're *lucky* to spend time with them—we don't own them!

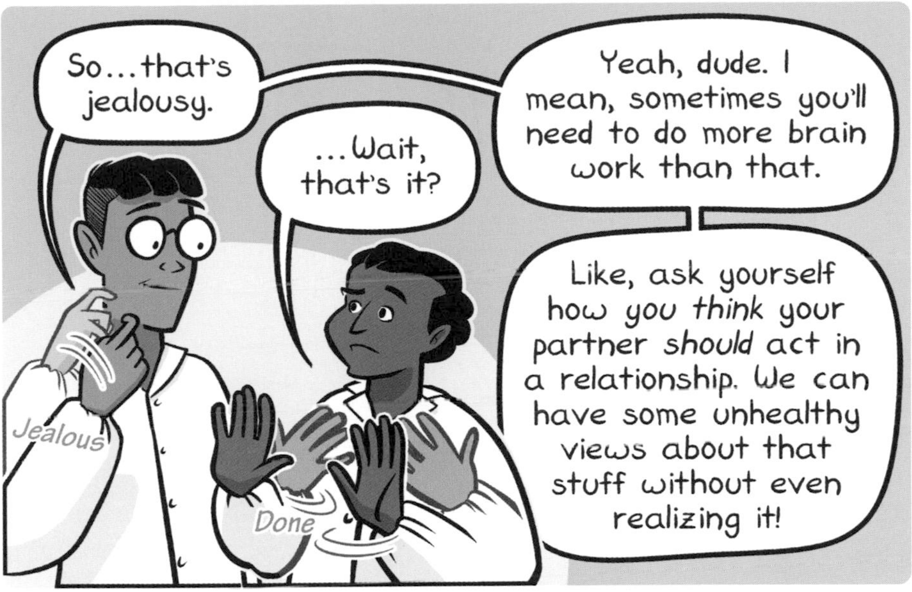
So...that's jealousy.
...Wait, that's it?
Yeah, dude. I mean, sometimes you'll need to do more brain work than that.
Like, ask yourself how *you think* your partner *should* act in a relationship. We can have some unhealthy views about that stuff without even realizing it!
Jealous
Done

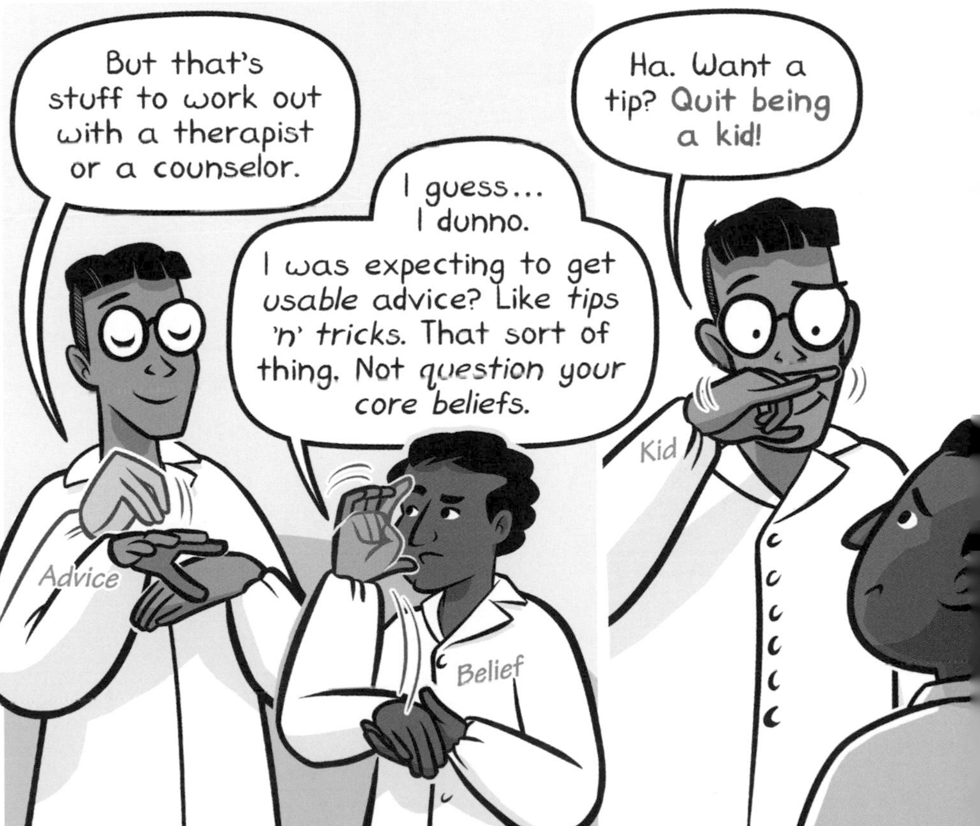
But that's stuff to work out with a therapist or a counselor.
I guess... I dunno.
I was expecting to get *usable* advice? Like *tips 'n' tricks*. That sort of thing. Not *question* your core beliefs.
Ha. Want a tip? Quit being a kid!
Advice
Belief
Kid

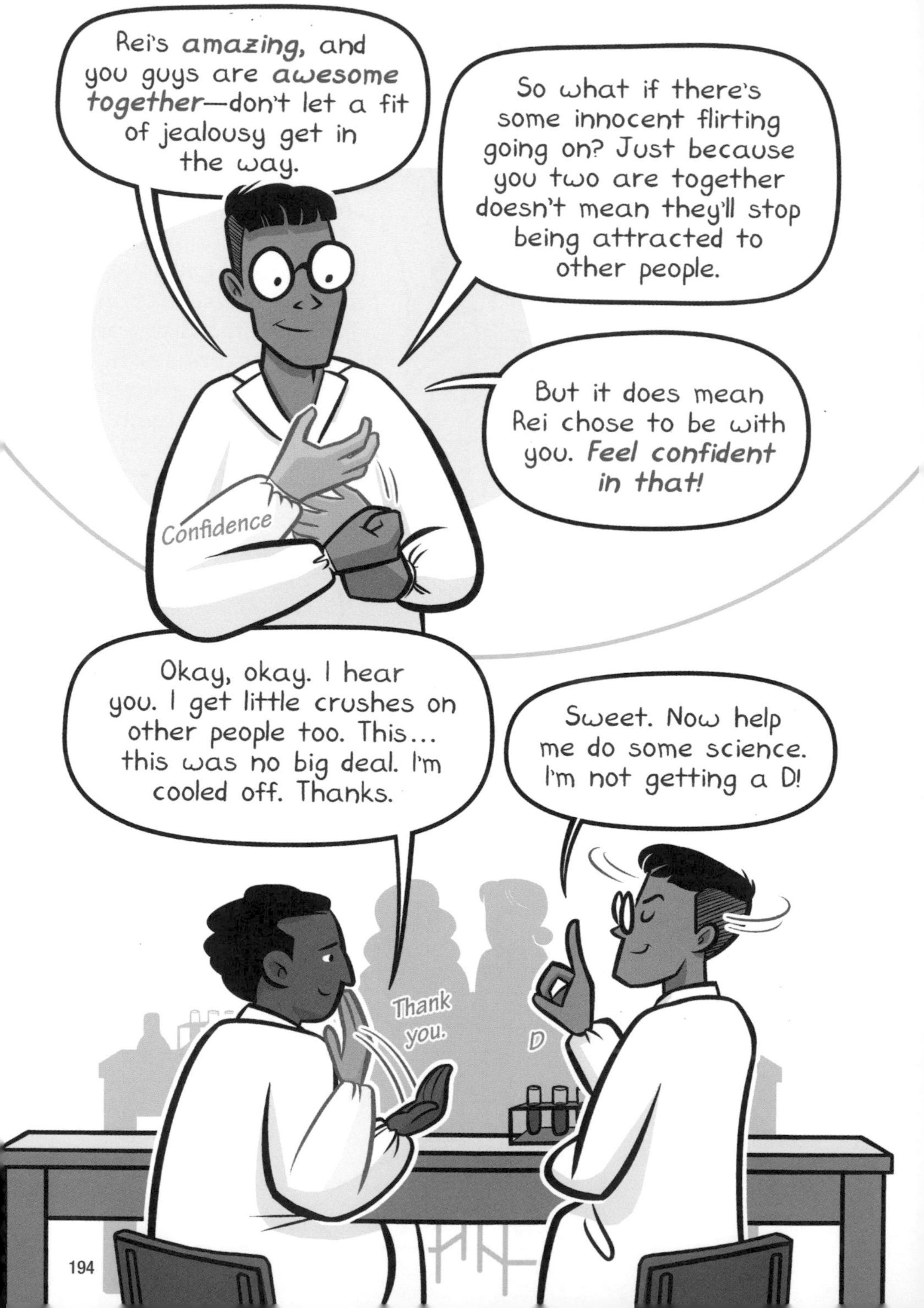
Rei's **amazing,** and you guys are **awesome together**—don't let a fit of jealousy get in the way.
So what if there's some innocent flirting going on? Just because you two are together doesn't mean they'll stop being attracted to other people.
But it does mean Rei chose to be with you. ***Feel confident in that!***
Confidence
Okay, okay. I hear you. I get little crushes on other people too. This... this was no big deal. I'm cooled off. Thanks.
Thank you.
Sweet. Now help me do some science. I'm not getting a D!
D

What is . . .
rejection?

What do you do when you get rejected? How do you apologize if you screw up? Should you ever ghost someone? What kinds of behavior are abusive? How do you do better?

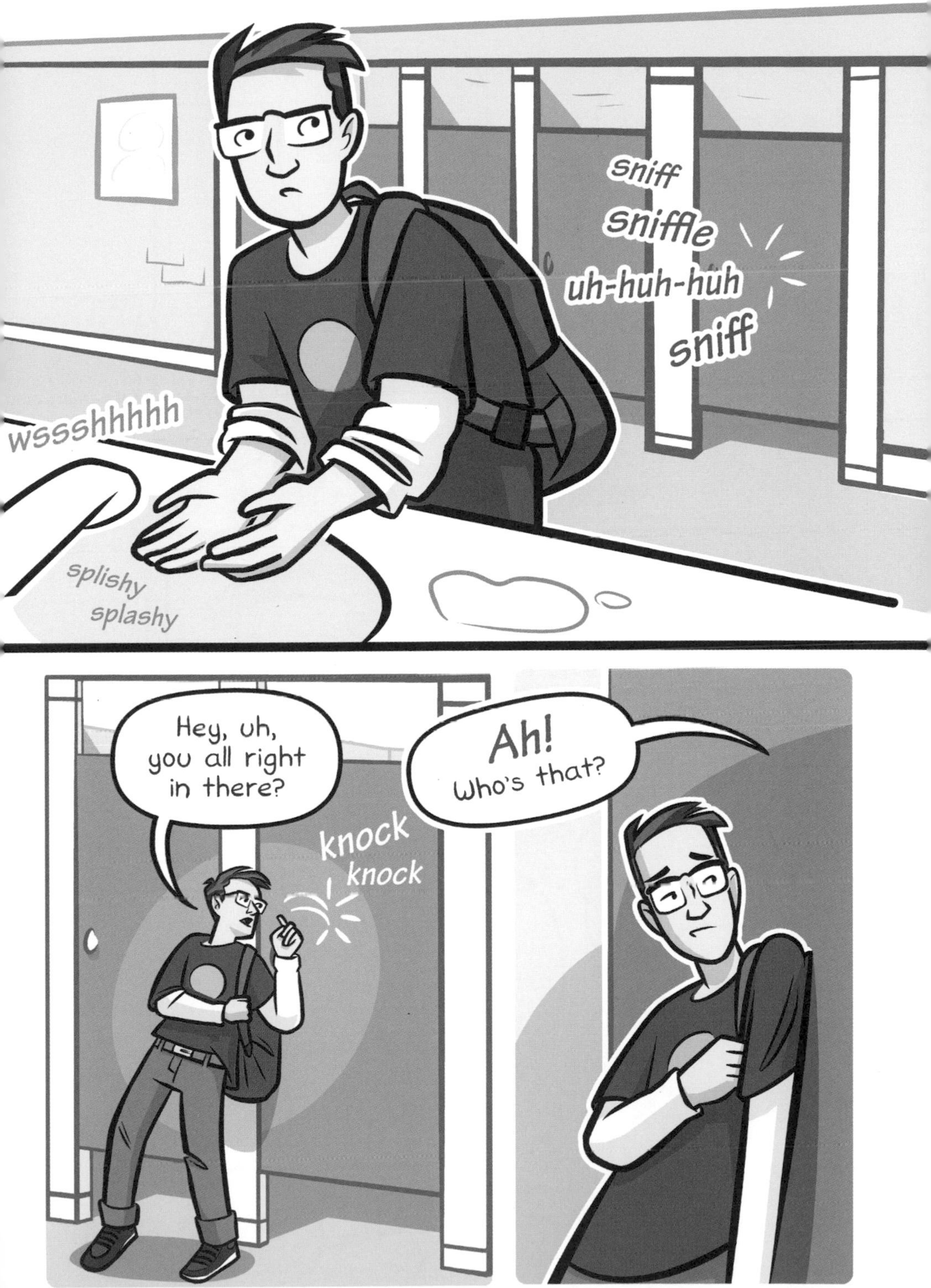
sniff
sniffle
uh-huh-huh
sniff
wssshhhhh
splishy
splashy
Hey, uh, you all right in there?
knock
knock
Ah!
Who's that?

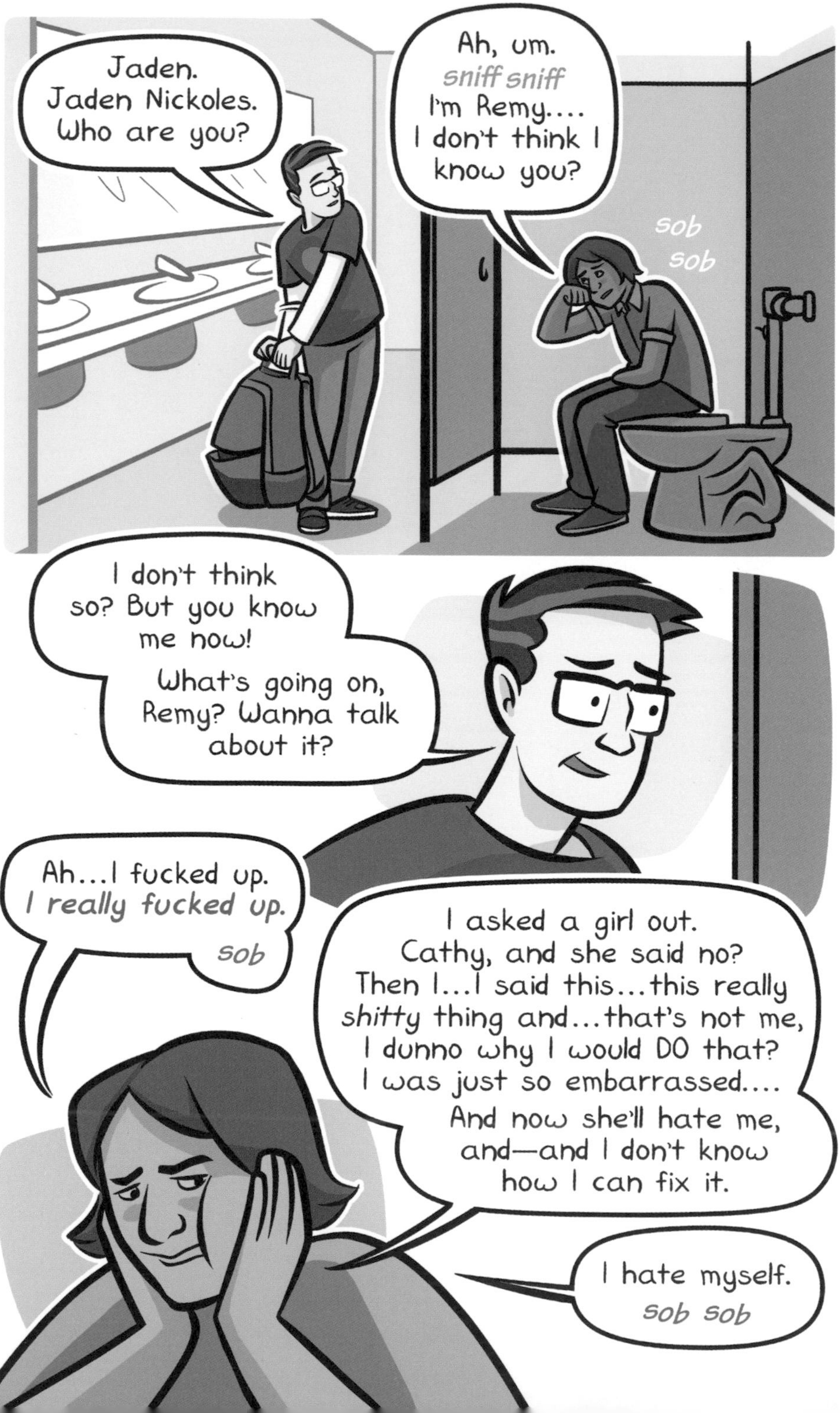
Jaden. Jaden Nickoles. Who are you?
Ah, um. sniff sniff I'm Remy.... I don't think I know you?
sob sob
I don't think so? But you know me now!
What's going on, Remy? Wanna talk about it?
Ah...I fucked up. I really fucked up.
sob
I asked a girl out. Cathy, and she said no? Then I...I said this...this really shitty thing and...that's not me, I dunno why I would DO that? I was just so embarrassed....
And now she'll hate me, and—and I don't know how I can fix it.
I hate myself.
sob sob

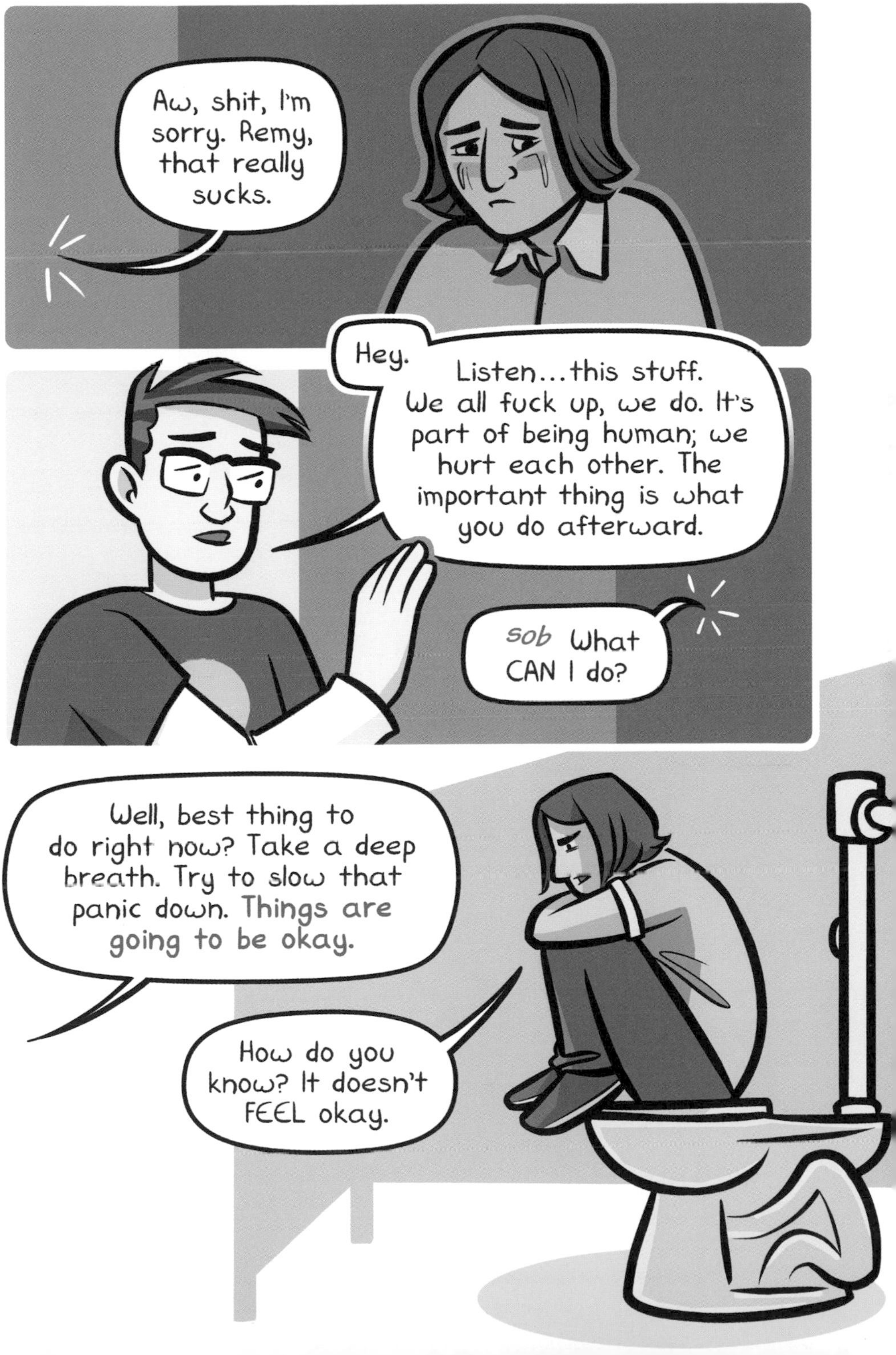
Aw, shit, I'm sorry. Remy, that really sucks.
Hey.
Listen...this stuff. We all fuck up, we do. It's part of being human; we hurt each other. The important thing is what you do afterward.
sob What CAN I do?
Well, best thing to do right now? Take a deep breath. Try to slow that panic down. Things are going to be okay.
How do you know? It doesn't FEEL okay.

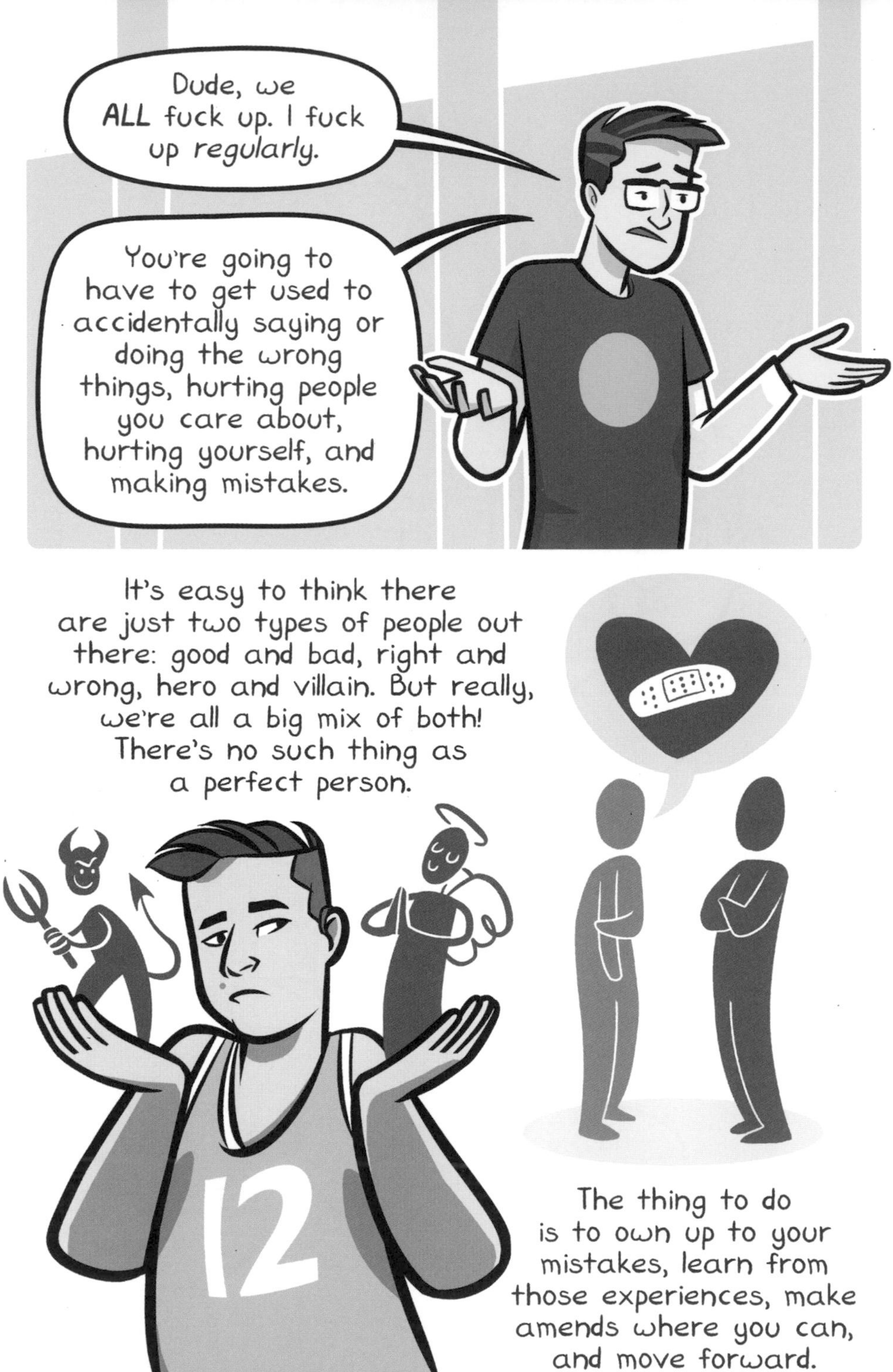
Dude, we ALL fuck up. I fuck up regularly.
You're going to have to get used to accidentally saying or doing the wrong things, hurting people you care about, hurting yourself, and making mistakes.
It's easy to think there are just two types of people out there: good and bad, right and wrong, hero and villain. But really, we're all a big mix of both! There's no such thing as a perfect person.
12
The thing to do is to own up to your mistakes, learn from those experiences, make amends where you can, and move forward.

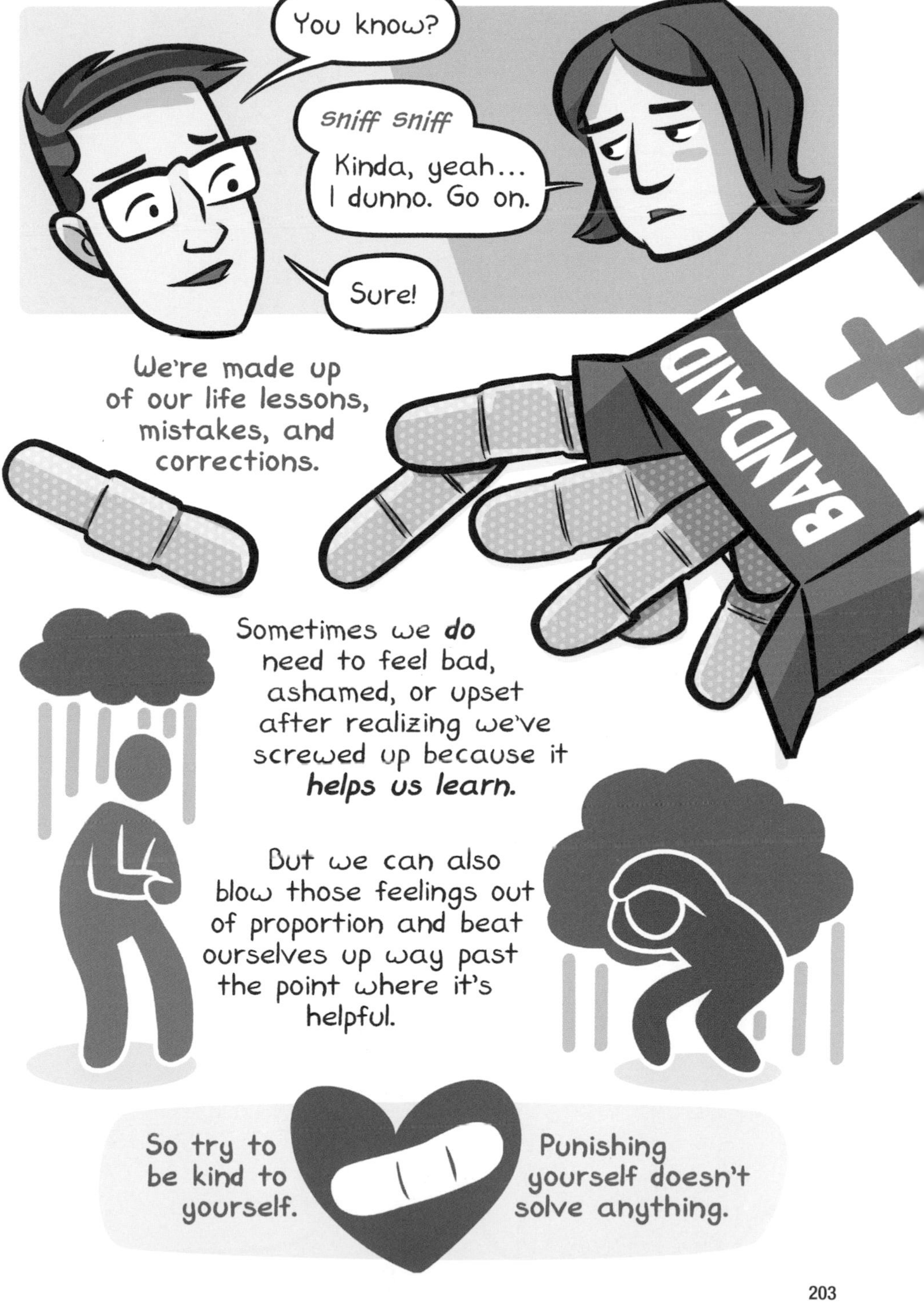
You know?
sniff sniff
Kinda, yeah... I dunno. Go on.
Sure!
We're made up of our life lessons, mistakes, and corrections.
BAND-AID
Sometimes we **do** need to feel bad, ashamed, or upset after realizing we've screwed up because it ***helps us learn.***
But we can also blow those feelings out of proportion and beat ourselves up way past the point where it's helpful.
So try to be kind to yourself.
Punishing yourself doesn't solve anything.

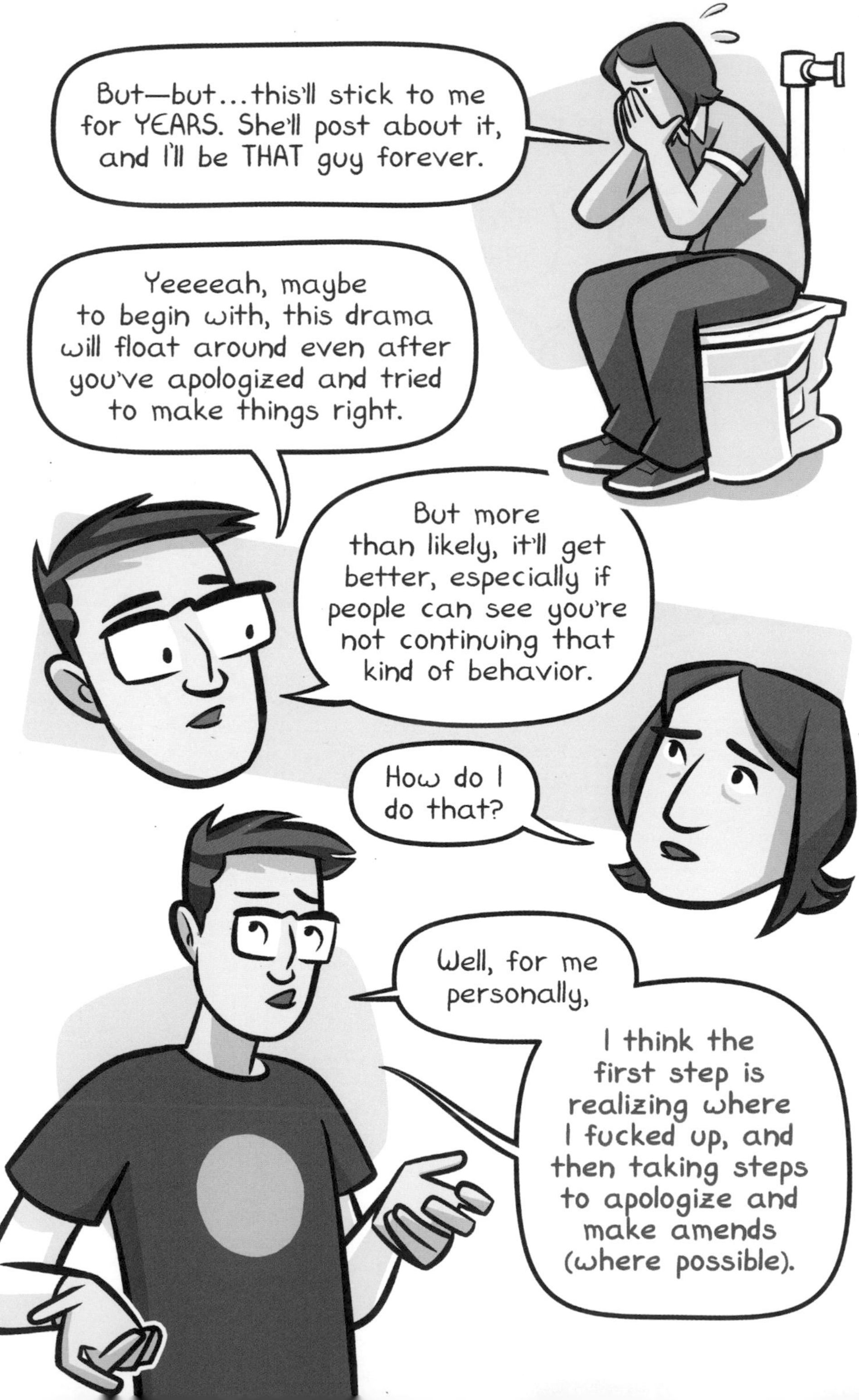

But—but...this'll stick to me for YEARS. She'll post about it, and I'll be THAT guy forever.
Yeeeeah, maybe to begin with, this drama will float around even after you've apologized and tried to make things right.
But more than likely, it'll get better, especially if people can see you're not continuing that kind of behavior.
How do I do that?
Well, for me personally,
I think the first step is realizing where I fucked up, and then taking steps to apologize and make amends (where possible).

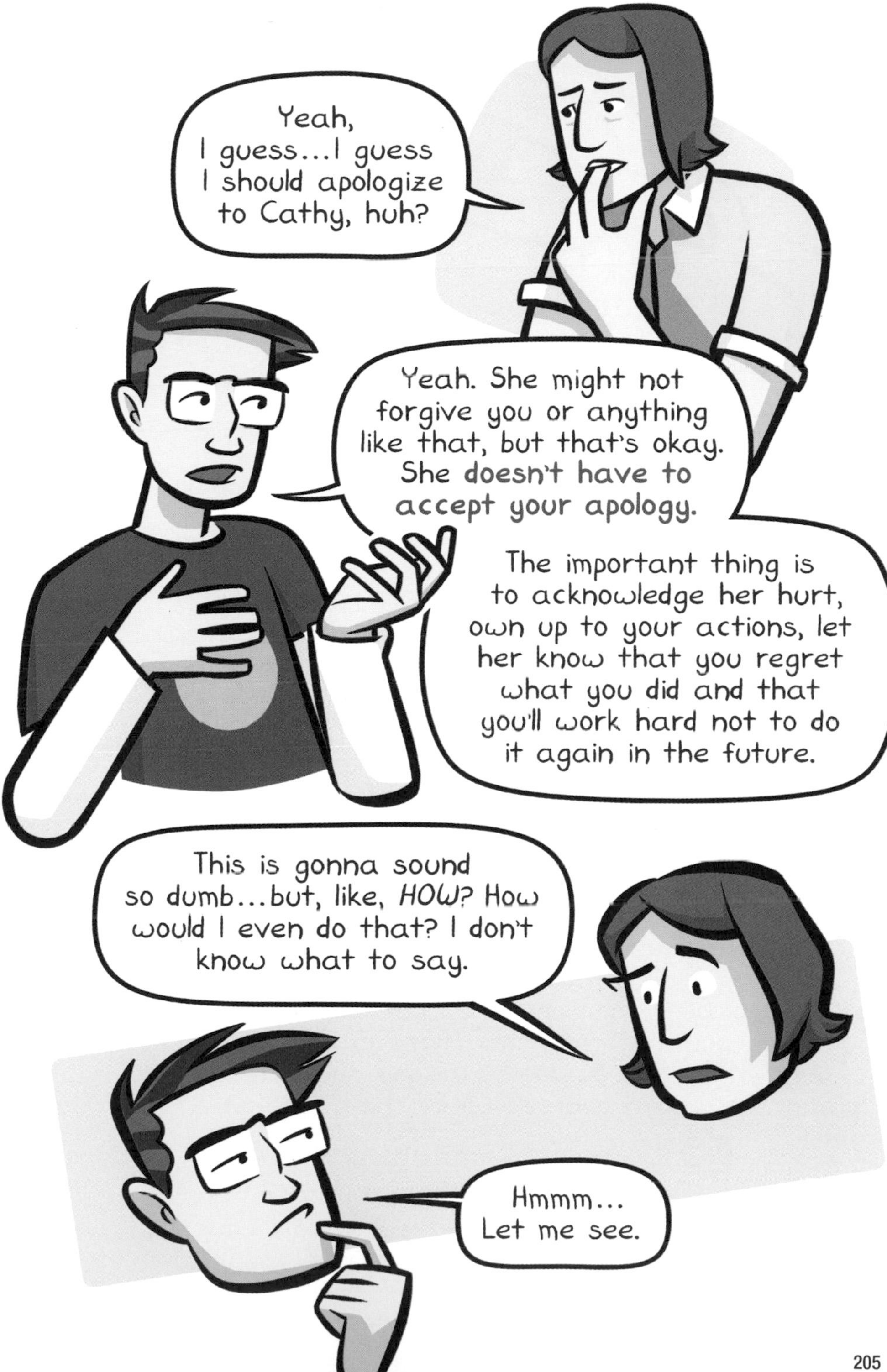
Yeah, I guess...I guess I should apologize to Cathy, huh?
Yeah. She might not forgive you or anything like that, but that's okay. She **doesn't have to accept your apology.**
The important thing is to acknowledge her hurt, own up to your actions, let her know that you regret what you did and that you'll work hard not to do it again in the future.
This is gonna sound so dumb...but, like, *HOW*? How would I even do that? I don't know what to say.
Hmmm... Let me see.

Jaden's Apology Recipe

1 Be Fast!
You'll want to apologize as soon as you realize you've messed up. Waiting makes things worse.

2 Express Remorse
Start with an "I'm sorry" or "I apologize." Be sincere and honest. Don't make any justifications for your actions, and stay away from following up with "but" or "because."

3 Admit Responsibility

Show some empathy and understanding to the person you've affected. "I know that I hurt you...."

4 Make Amends (if possible)
Earnestly offer to make it right: no token gestures. Offer a kindness that feels appropriate for the hurt you caused. Say something like, "Let me make it up to you...." Sometimes there IS nothing that can be done, but you should still open yourself up to their requests.

5 Commit to Changing Your Behavior
Help rebuild trust. Assure them that you'll change and learn from your mistakes. Honor your promise, and try to learn and grow from this. "From now on, I'll be better...."

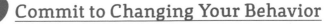

Weeeeell, you have to **respect what a person says!** If they said no, then they said no. There's no wiggle room there. Don't persist, don't pressure, and don't harass someone into changing their mind. AND same goes if they're vague or uninterested. Take that as a no too.

Think about how YOU would want to be treated in their shoes. What if somebody you didn't like asked you out on a date? You'd say no, and you'd want your no to be respected, right? So respect theirs.

After you get a no (or just not a definite YES), it's time to move on. Mentally drop the idea and stop thinking about the two of you together.

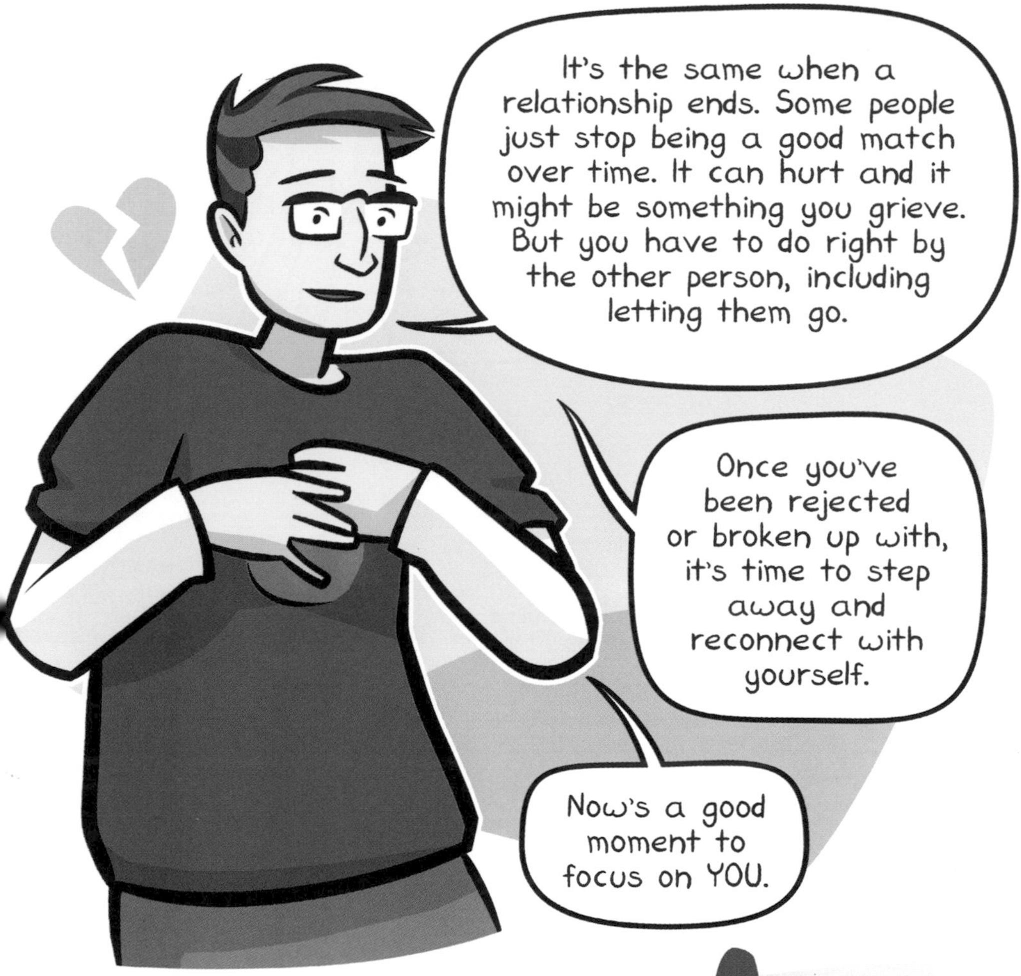
It's the same when a relationship ends. Some people just stop being a good match over time. It can hurt and it might be something you grieve. But you have to do right by the other person, including letting them go.
Once you've been rejected or broken up with, it's time to step away and reconnect with yourself.
Now's a good moment to focus on YOU.

Look inward.
What would be good for your heart?
What'll recharge you?
What do you need to do to feel happy with yourself?
Follow some of those paths, and see how it goes.

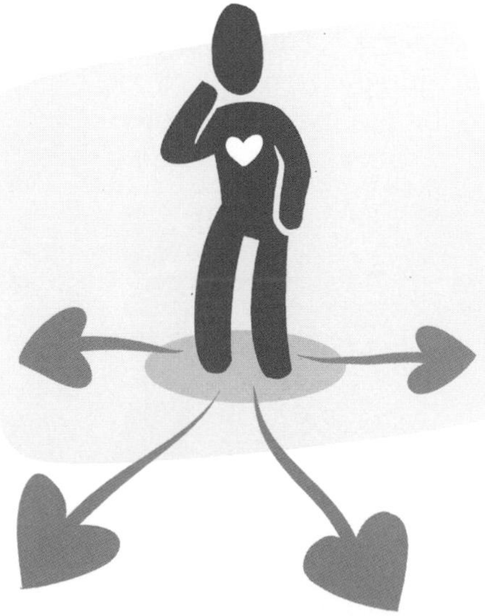

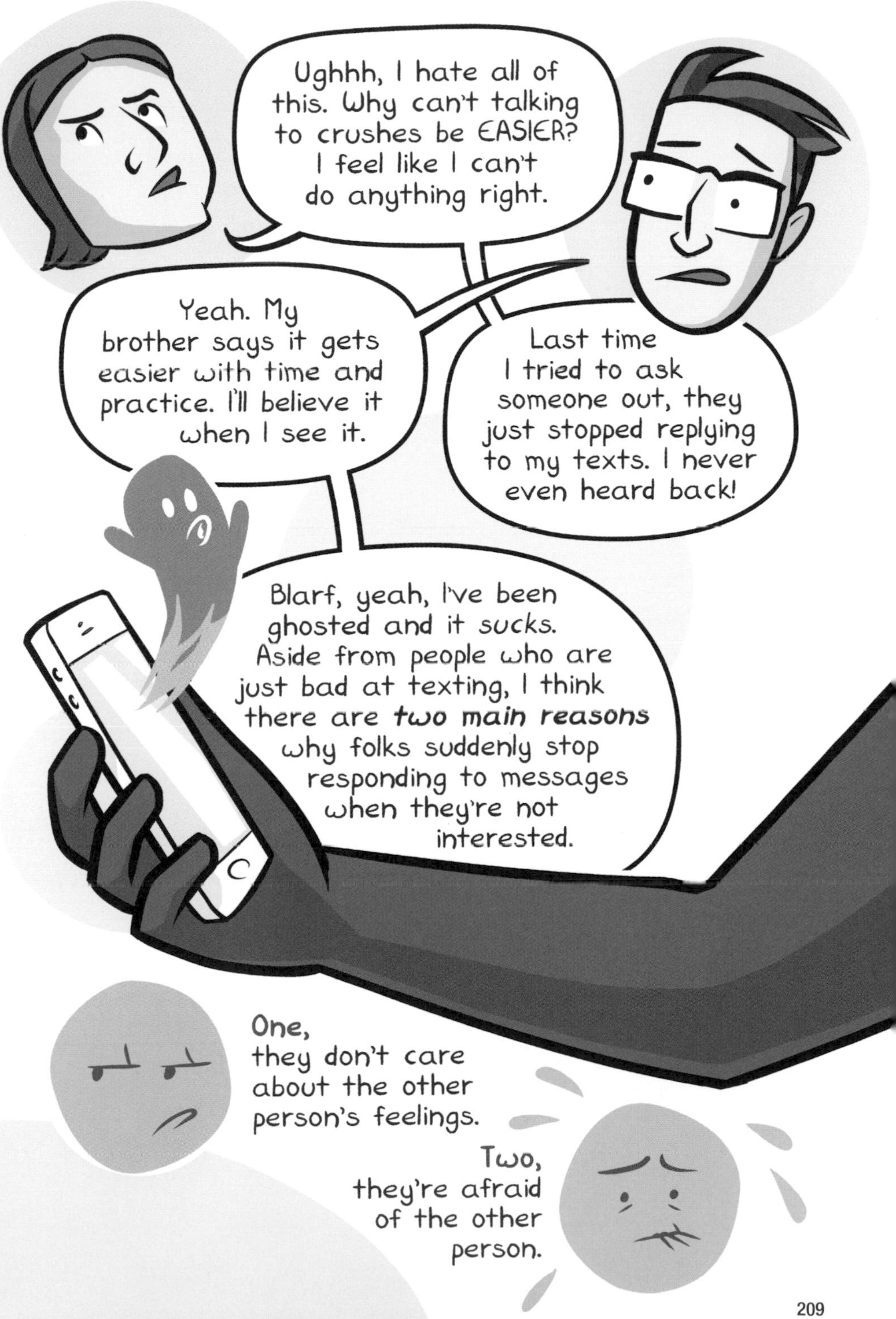

Ughhh, I hate all of this. Why can't talking to crushes be EASIER? I feel like I can't do anything right.
Yeah. My brother says it gets easier with time and practice. I'll believe it when I see it.
Last time I tried to ask someone out, they just stopped replying to my texts. I never even heard back!
Blarf, yeah, I've been ghosted and it *sucks*. Aside from people who are just bad at texting, I think there are ***two main reasons*** why folks suddenly stop responding to messages when they're not interested.
One, they don't care about the other person's feelings.
Two, they're afraid of the other person.

If you suspect someone has ghosted you because they're afraid of you, then fair enough. Reach out to some trusted people in your life and explore why somebody might feel this way about you.

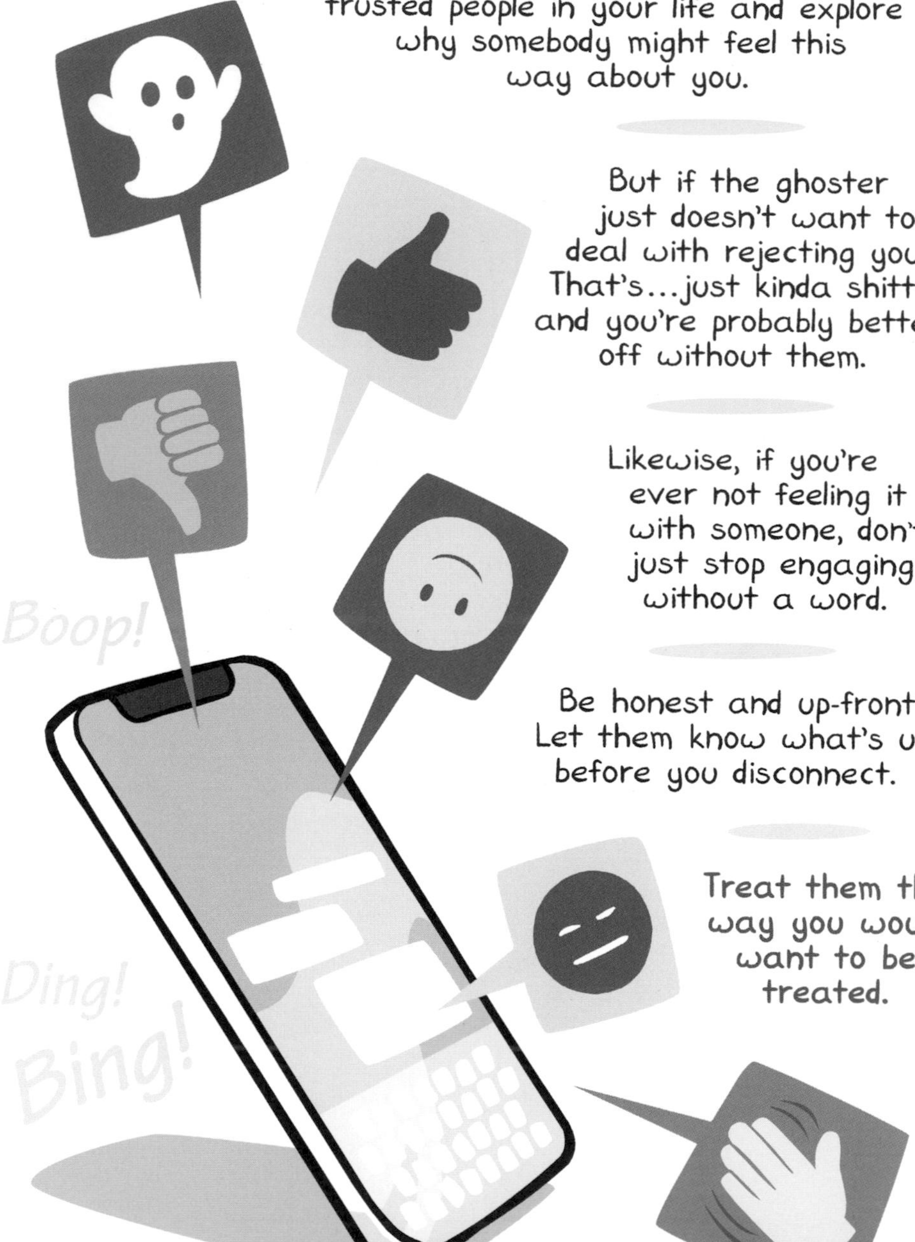
Boop!
Ding!
Bing!

But if the ghoster just doesn't want to deal with rejecting you? That's...just kinda shitty, and you're probably better off without them.

Likewise, if you're ever not feeling it with someone, don't just stop engaging without a word.

Be honest and up-front. Let them know what's up before you disconnect.

Treat them the way you would want to be treated.

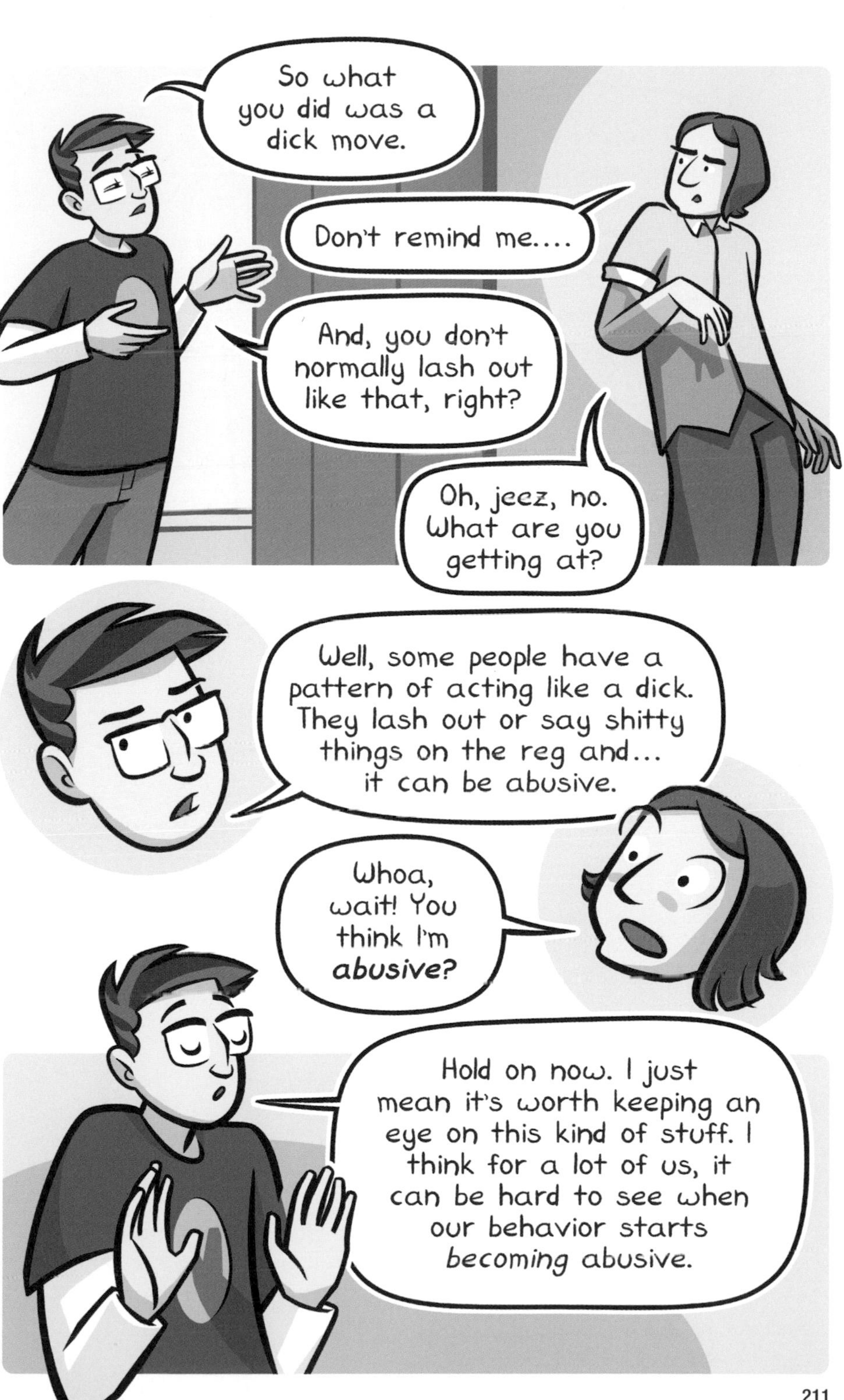
So what you did was a dick move.
Don't remind me....
And, you don't normally lash out like that, right?
Oh, jeez, no. What are you getting at?
Well, some people have a pattern of acting like a dick. They lash out or say shitty things on the reg and... it can be abusive.
Whoa, wait! You think I'm *abusive?*
Hold on now. I just mean it's worth keeping an eye on this kind of stuff. I think for a lot of us, it can be hard to see when our behavior starts *becoming* abusive.

...What are you counting as abusive here? How would I recognize it?
Well, sometimes it *can* be hard to tell if you're treating others like crap, or even if you're *being* treated like crap.
Abuse can be a difficult thing to see clearly.
It has many different forms, from **subtle to violent** and **unintentional to deliberate.**
But it's almost always about power and control.
Abuse is never a simple matter. It's a deep and complex subject. But still, let's take a look at some questions and behaviors that might help you recognize it.

Are You in an Abusive Situation?
Ask Yourself...

Are you often told that your feelings, thoughts, and voice aren't important?

•

Does your world revolve almost exclusively around another person?

•

Do you get called degrading names, get put down, or get overly criticized?

•

Do you feel manipulated and cornered?

•

Do you get accused of lying or cheating, or are you made a scapegoat for another person?

•

Are you feeling isolated and singled out, or confined and removed from the people you care about?

•

Do you experience anxiety, depression, and insomnia?

•

Do you feel pressured or forced into choices and actions you don't want to be a part of?

•

Are you in constant fear of making another person angry?

•

Are you held to unrealistic standards or impossible demands and get punished for failing them?

Are the things and people you love held hostage or damaged and hurt?

•

Do you minimize or ignore the negative actions of others or even cover up for them?

•

Are you the target of sexism or bigotry? Is your gender used against you?

•

Do you often hear concern and worry from the people around you?

•

Are you threatened verbally or physically?

•

Are you the target of another person's anger? Do you get shouted at or have things thrown at you?

•

Do you suffer shakes, the inability to stop crying, or blackouts?

Are You Being Abusive?
Ask Yourself...

Do you belittle, degrade, or make others feel lesser and weaker than you? Do you need to feel superior over others?

•

Do you have the need to control a person? Are you possessive of them?

•

Do you feel unreasonably jealous?

•

Do you blackmail others? Do you hold people or things hostage to get what you want?

•

Do you force others to do things even when they've said no, or scare them into saying yes?

Do you often accuse the people in your life of betrayal?

•

Do you find yourself separating people from their friends, family, or community?

•

Do you threaten others verbally, physically, or even just with your body language?

•

Do you often feel insecure, angry, and explosive?

•

Is there rage inside you that feels like it has nowhere to go?

•

Are you often physical with another person or objects—do you take out your frustrations by slamming doors, shouting, throwing, and hitting?

•

Do you have a history of bullying?

•

Do you burn through relationships with friends and family members?

•

Do you often hear concern and worry from the people around you, especially about how you treat others?

•

Do you experience tantrums, blind rages, or blackouts?

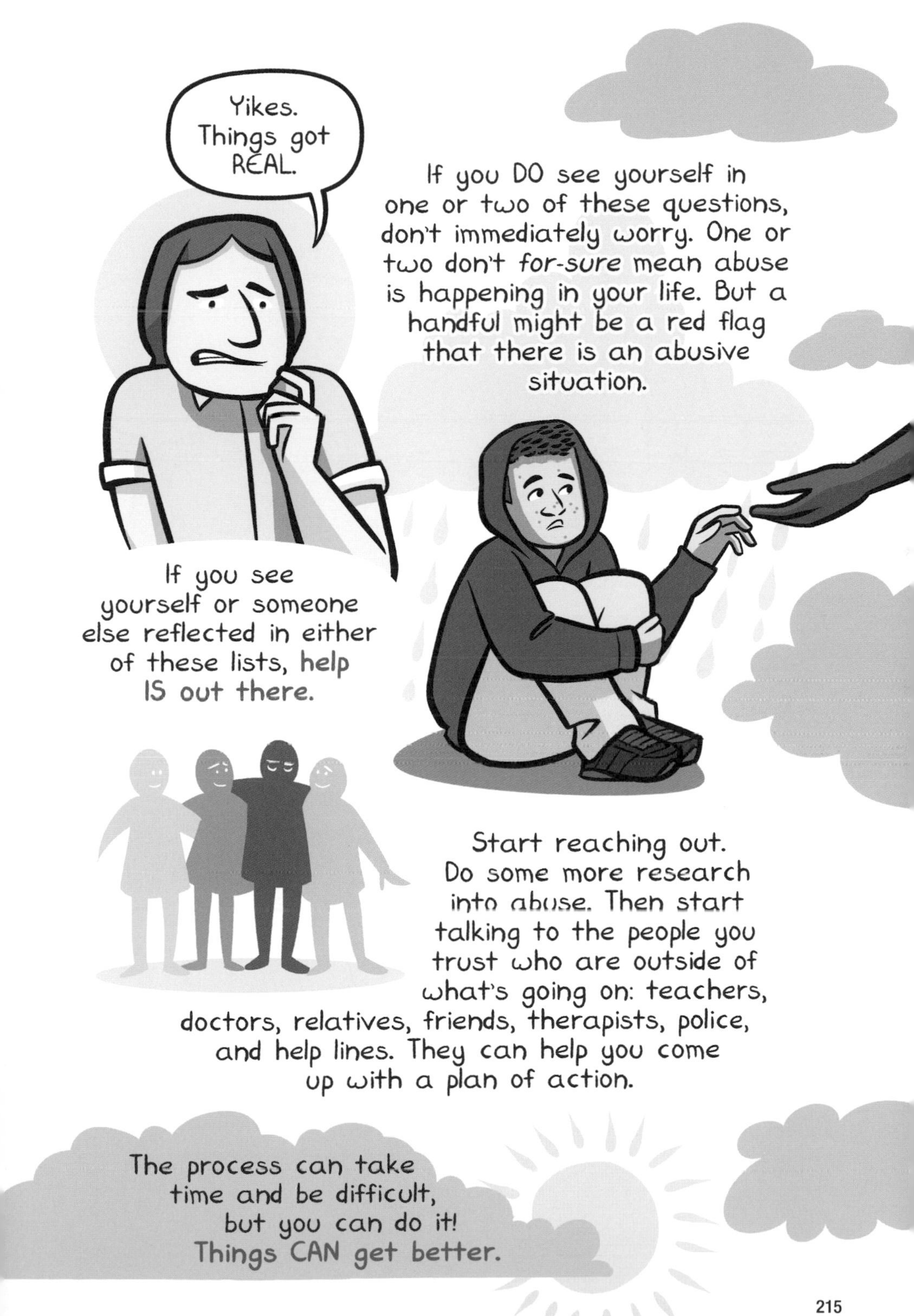
Yikes. Things got REAL.
If you DO see yourself in one or two of these questions, don't immediately worry. One or two don't *for-sure* mean abuse is happening in your life. But a handful might be a red flag that there is an abusive situation.
If you see yourself or someone else reflected in either of these lists, **help IS out there.**
Start reaching out. Do some more research into abuse. Then start talking to the people you trust who are outside of what's going on: teachers, doctors, relatives, friends, therapists, police, and help lines. They can help you come up with a plan of action.
The process can take time and be difficult, but you can do it!
Things CAN get better.

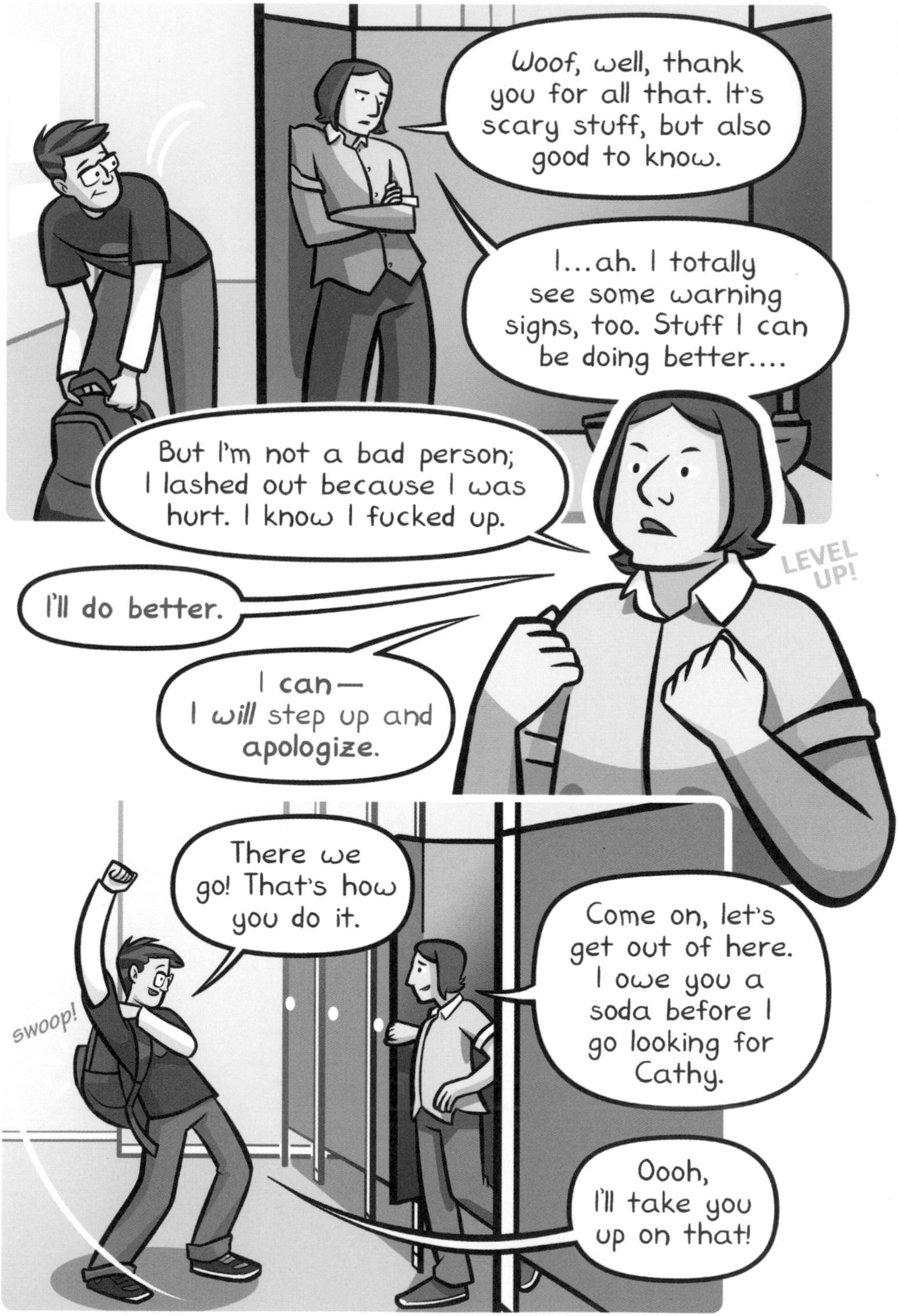

Woof, well, thank you for all that. It's scary stuff, but also good to know.
I...ah. I totally see some warning signs, too. Stuff I can be doing better....
But I'm not a bad person; I lashed out because I was hurt. I know I fucked up.
LEVEL UP!
I'll do better.
I can— I *will* step up and **apologize**.
There we go! That's how you do it.
SWOOP!
Come on, let's get out of here. I owe you a soda before I go looking for Cathy.
Oooh, I'll take you up on that!

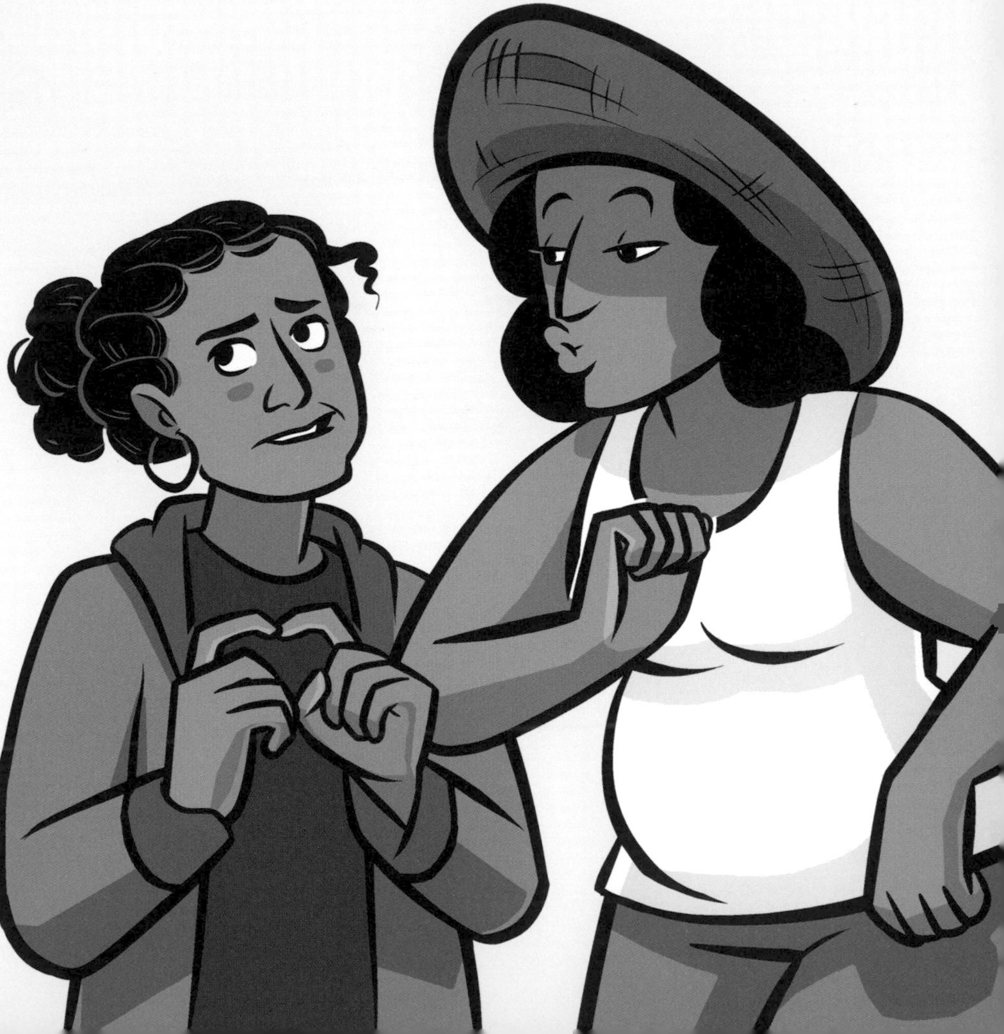

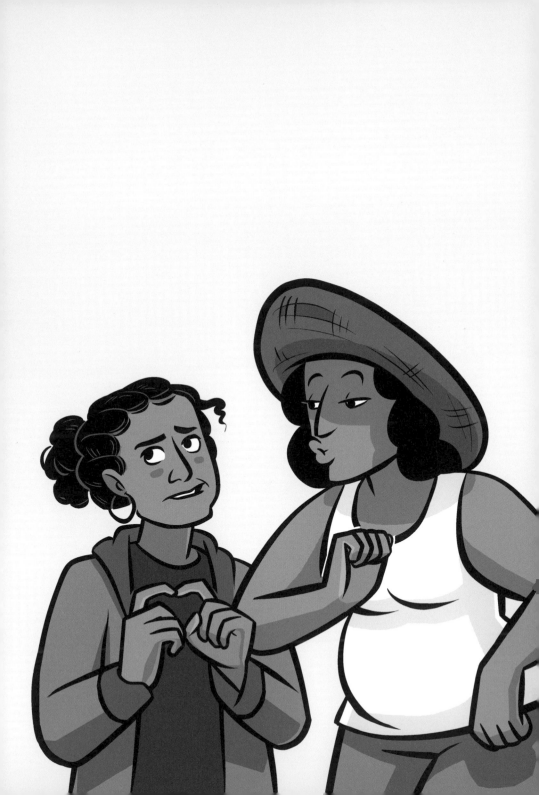

What is . . .
next?

How do you get help? Where do you find resources? What sort of connections and community can help you deal with all the many things in this book? What now?

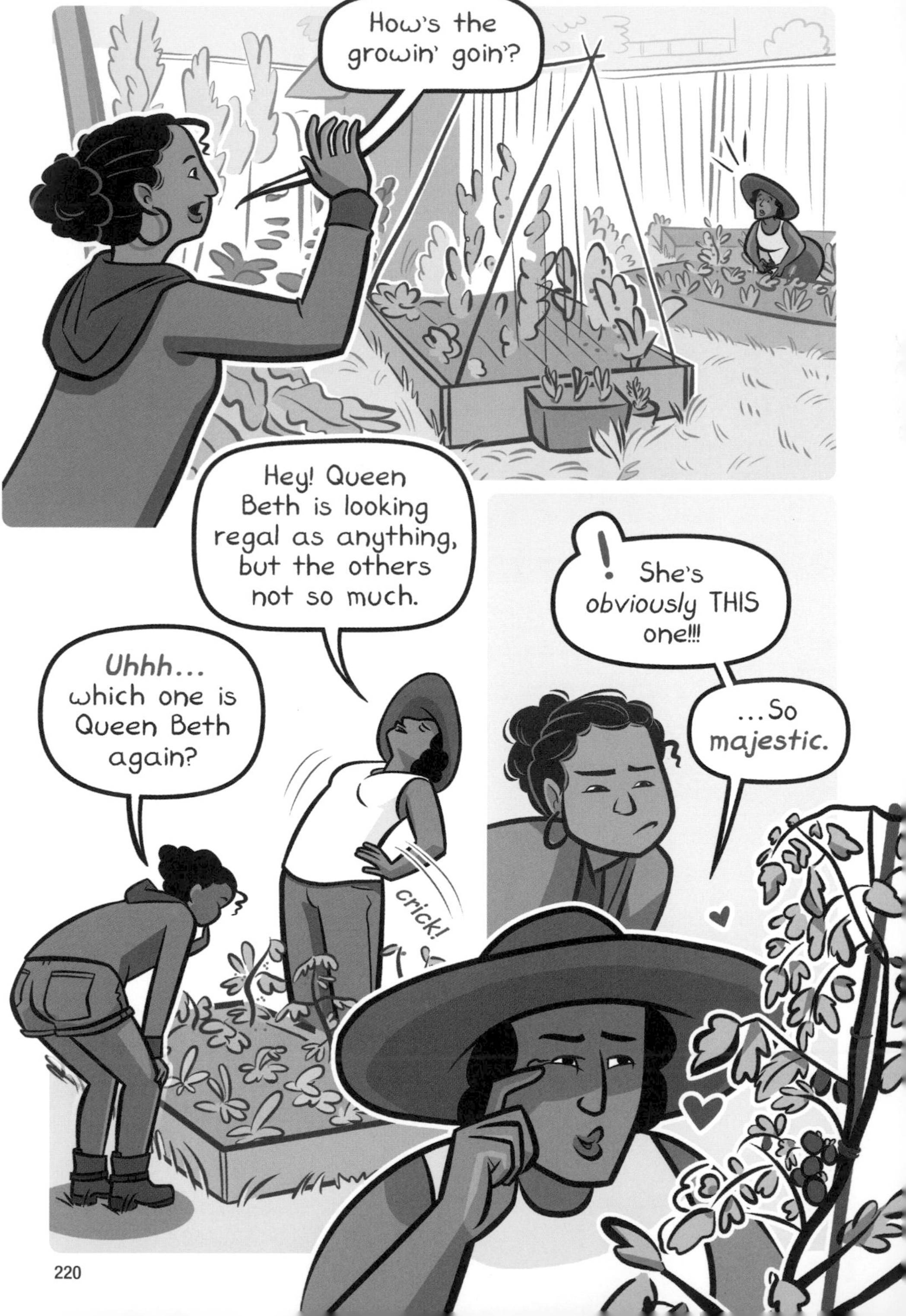
How's the growin' goin'?
Hey! Queen Beth is looking regal as anything, but the others not so much.
Uhhh... which one is Queen Beth again?
crick!
! She's obviously THIS one!!!
...So majestic.

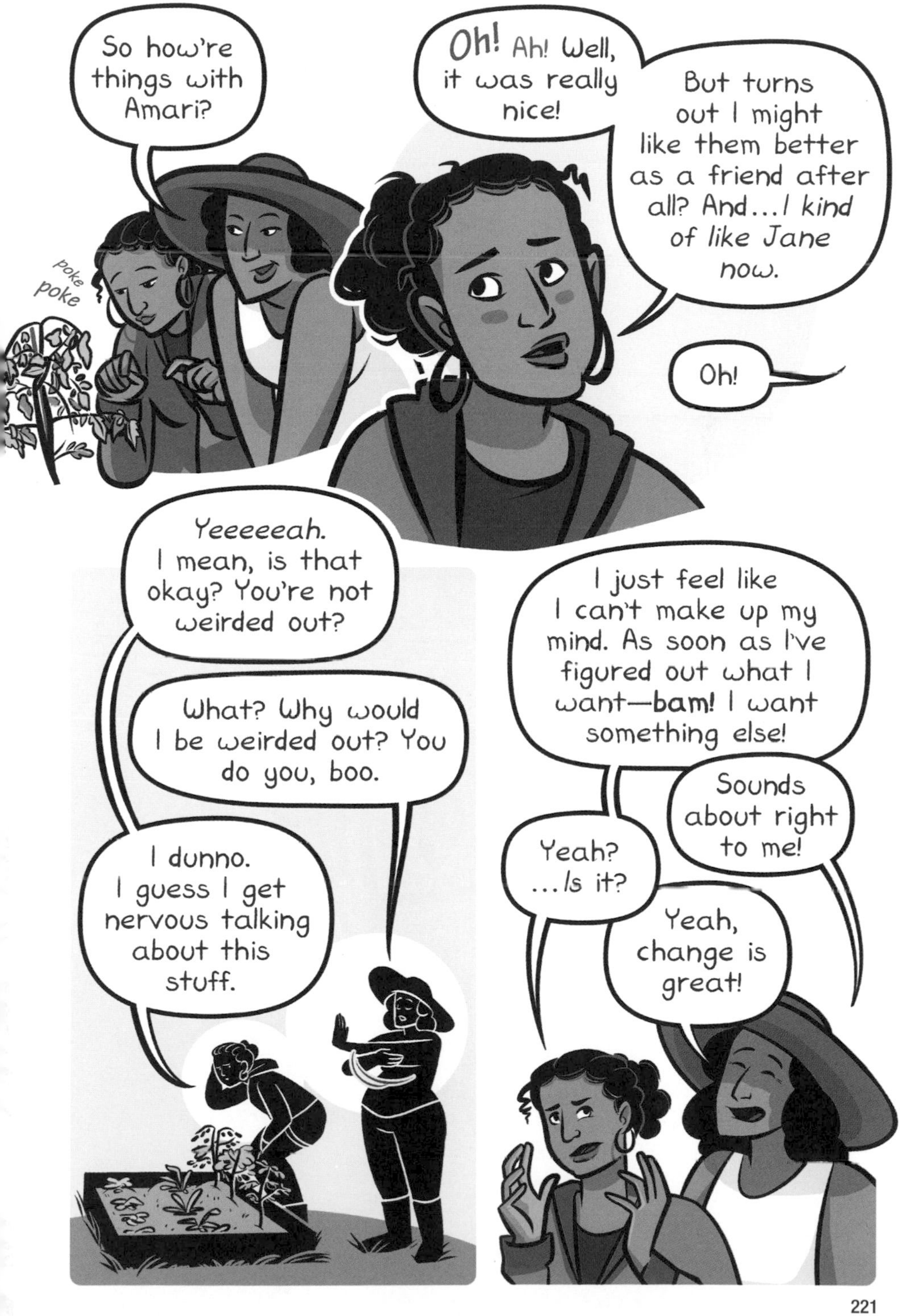
So how're things with Amari?
poke poke
Oh! Ah! Well, it was really nice!
But turns out I might like them better as a friend after all? And...I kind of like Jane now.
Oh!
Yeeeeeah. I mean, is that okay? You're not weirded out?
What? Why would I be weirded out? You do you, boo.
I dunno. I guess I get nervous talking about this stuff.
I just feel like I can't make up my mind. As soon as I've figured out what I want—**bam!** I want something else!
Sounds about right to me!
Yeah? ...*Is* it?
Yeah, change is great!

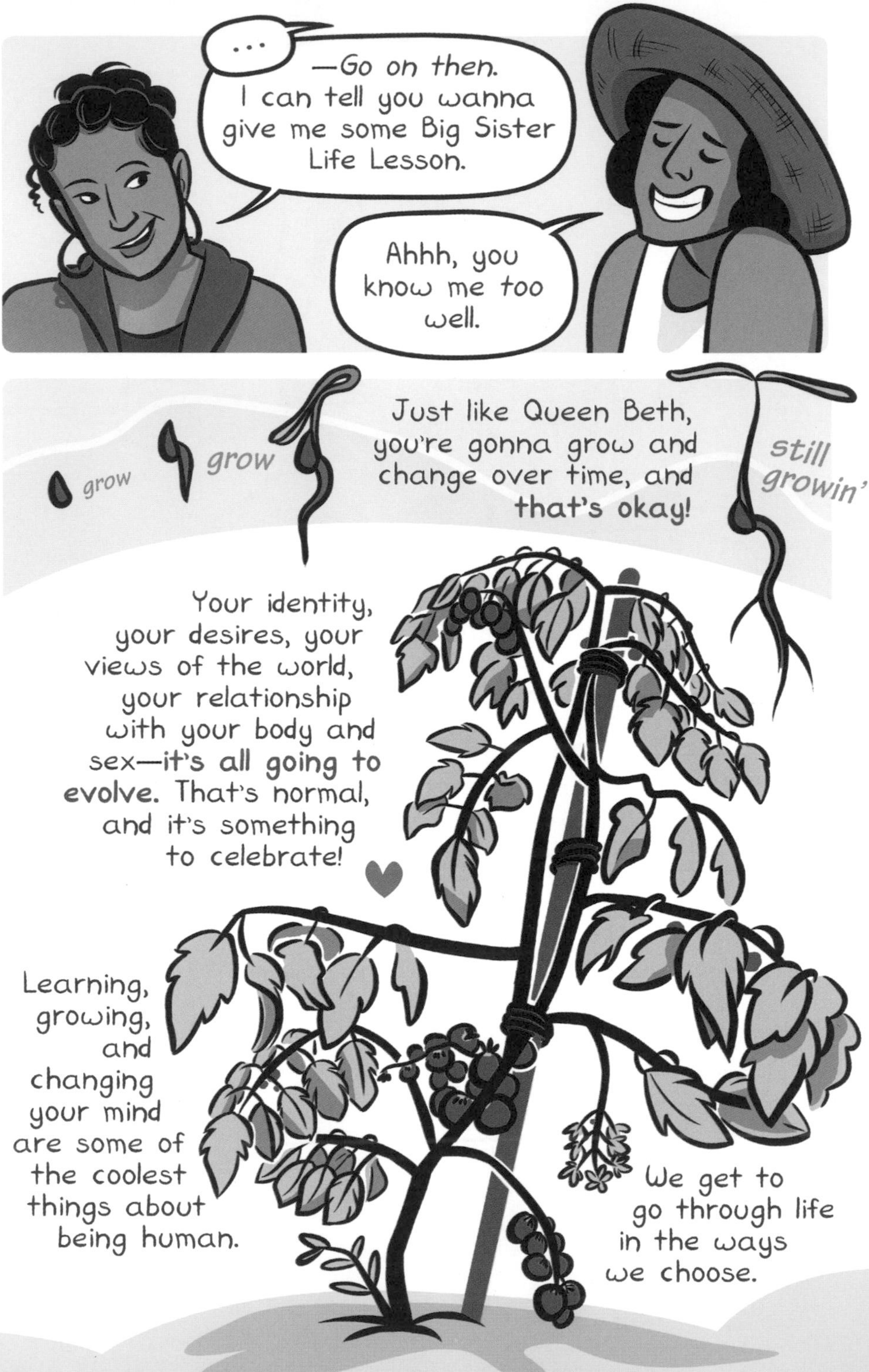
...
—Go on then. I can tell you wanna give me some Big Sister Life Lesson.
Ahhh, you know me too well.
grow
grow
Just like Queen Beth, you're gonna grow and change over time, and **that's okay!**
still growin'
Your identity, your desires, your views of the world, your relationship with your body and sex—**it's all going to evolve.** That's normal, and it's something to celebrate!
Learning, growing, and changing your mind are some of the coolest things about being human.
We get to go through life in the ways we choose.

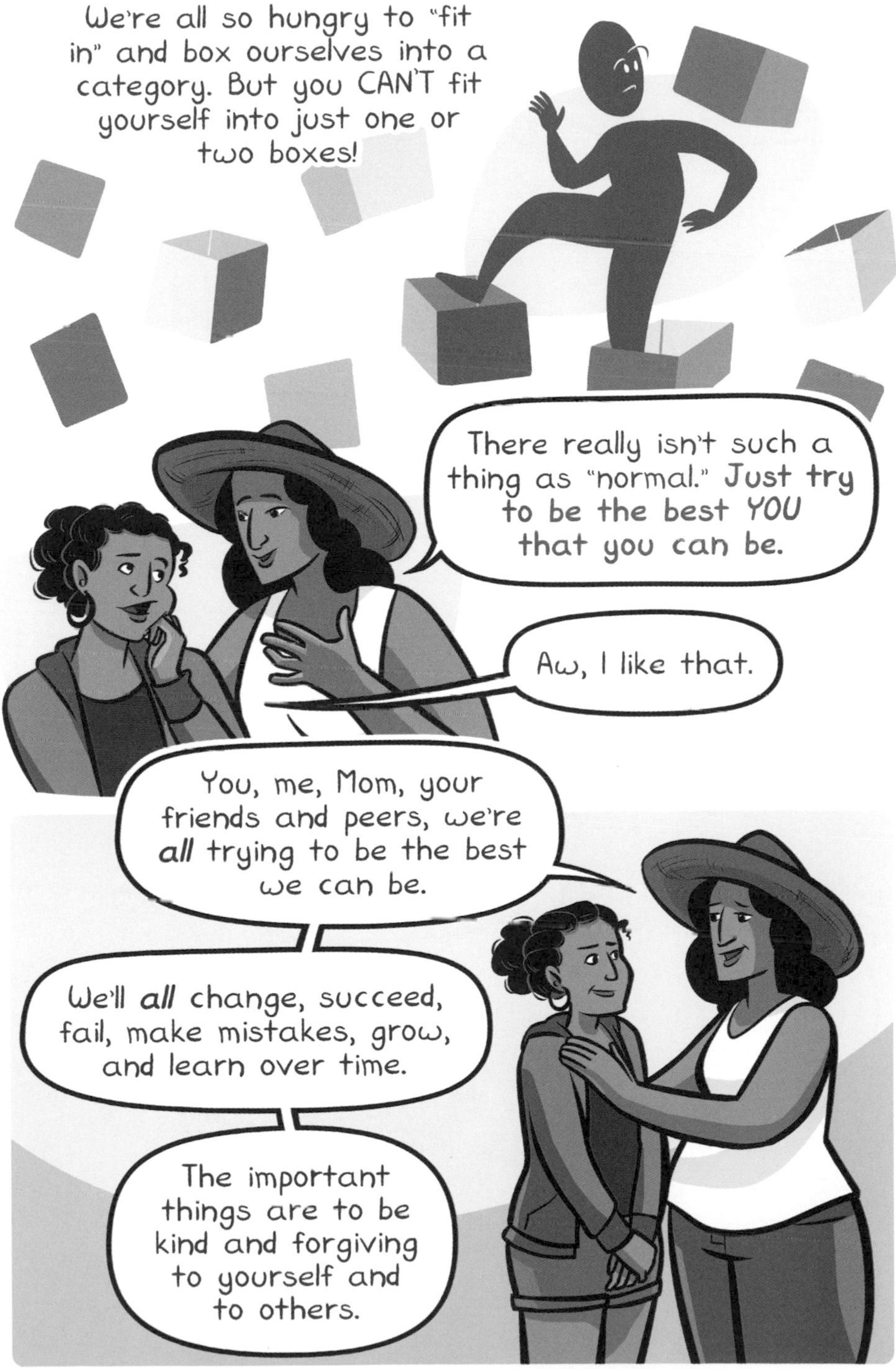
We're all so hungry to "fit in" and box ourselves into a category. But you CAN'T fit yourself into just one or two boxes!
There really isn't such a thing as "normal." Just try to be the best YOU that you can be.
Aw, I like that.
You, me, Mom, your friends and peers, we're *all* trying to be the best we can be.
We'll *all* change, succeed, fail, make mistakes, grow, and learn over time.
The important things are to be kind and forgiving to yourself and to others.

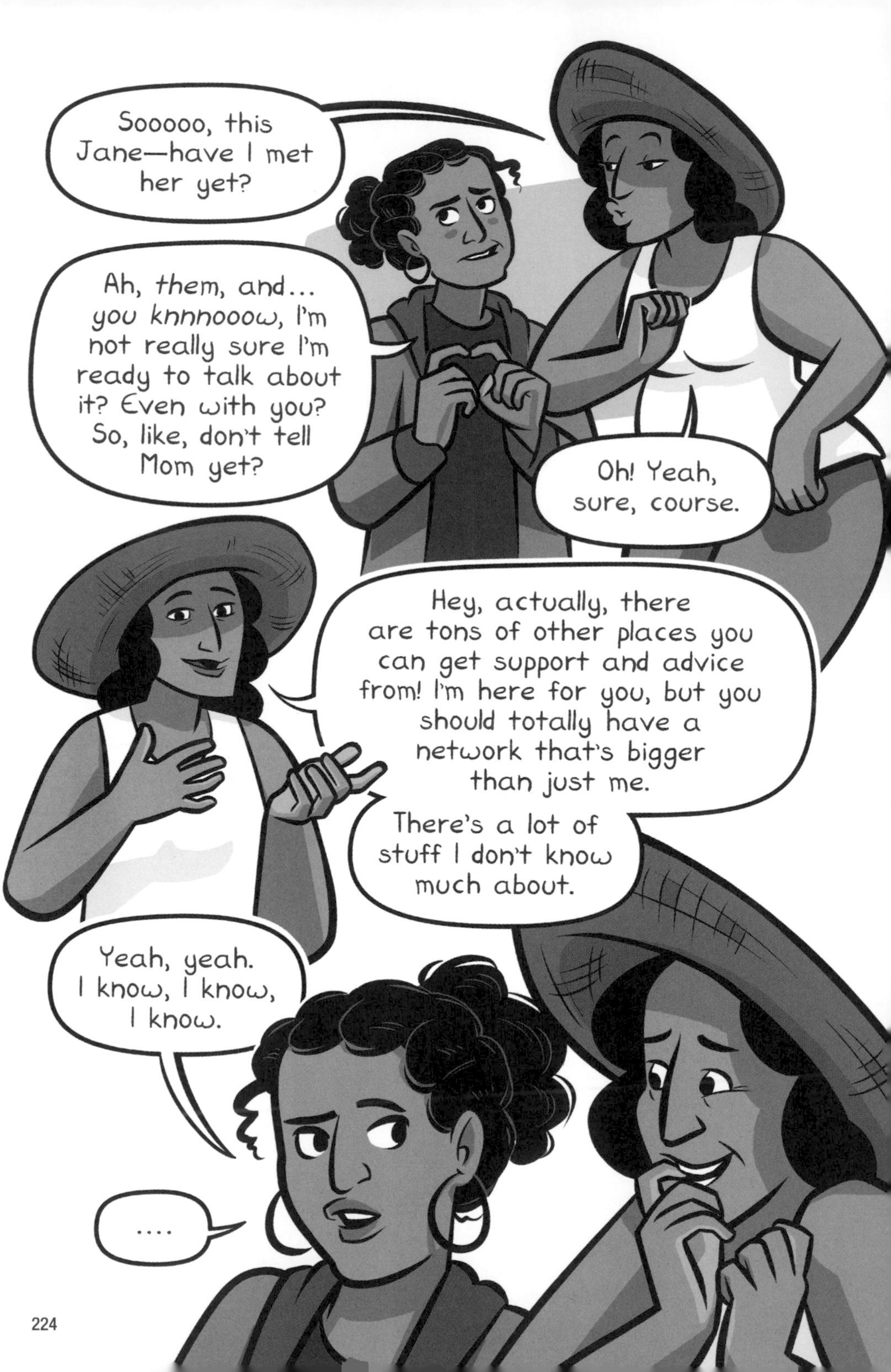
Sooooo, this Jane—have I met her yet?
Ah, *them*, and... you knnnooow, I'm not really sure I'm ready to talk about it? Even with you? So, like, don't tell Mom yet?
Oh! Yeah, sure, course.
Hey, actually, there are tons of other places you can get support and advice from! I'm here for you, but you should totally have a network that's bigger than just me.
There's a lot of stuff I don't know much about.
Yeah, yeah. I know, I know, I know.
....

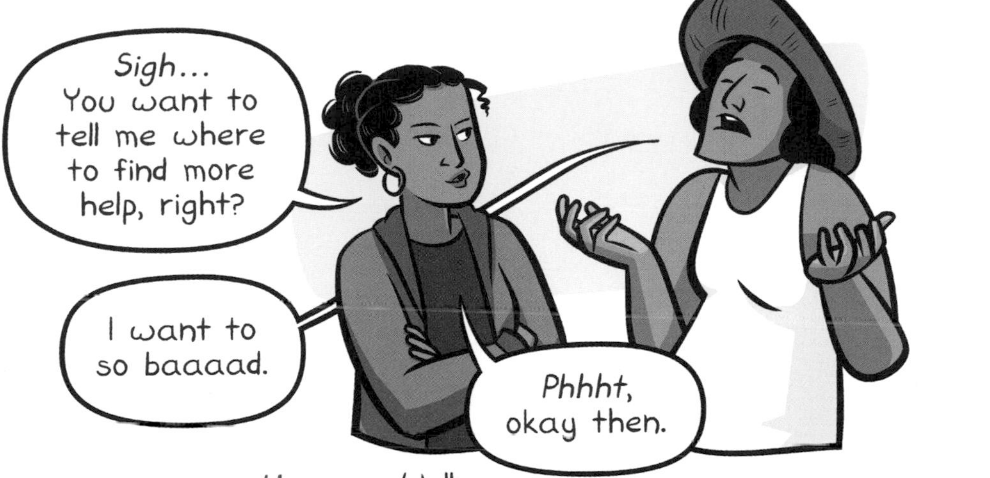
Sigh... You want to tell me where to find more help, right?
I want to so baaaad.
Phhht, okay then.

Yesss... Well, whether you're happy and healthy or knee-deep in crisis, having a group who has got your back can be crucial. Outside advice and fresh perspectives can help you in all kinds of decision-making.

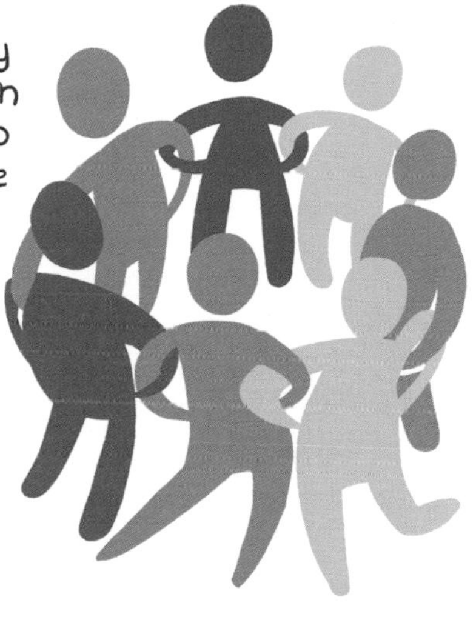

Finding and building that network takes time and looks different for each person.

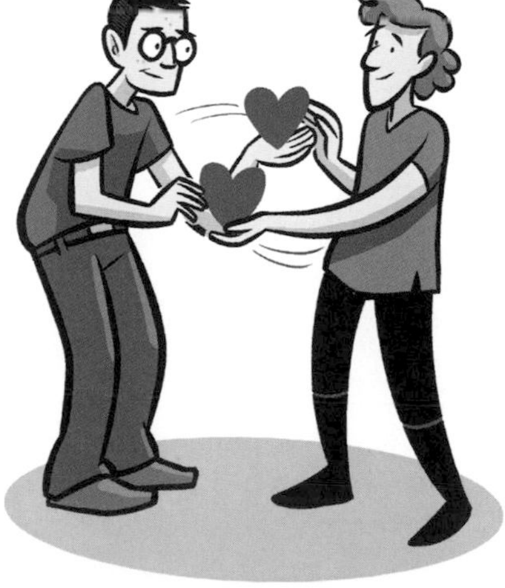

Remember, though, it's not just all about *you* and *your* needs.

Being a good friend or family member means being there *for each other*. So make sure to ***give*** as good as you ***get***.

A healthy relationship should be nourishing to everyone involved.

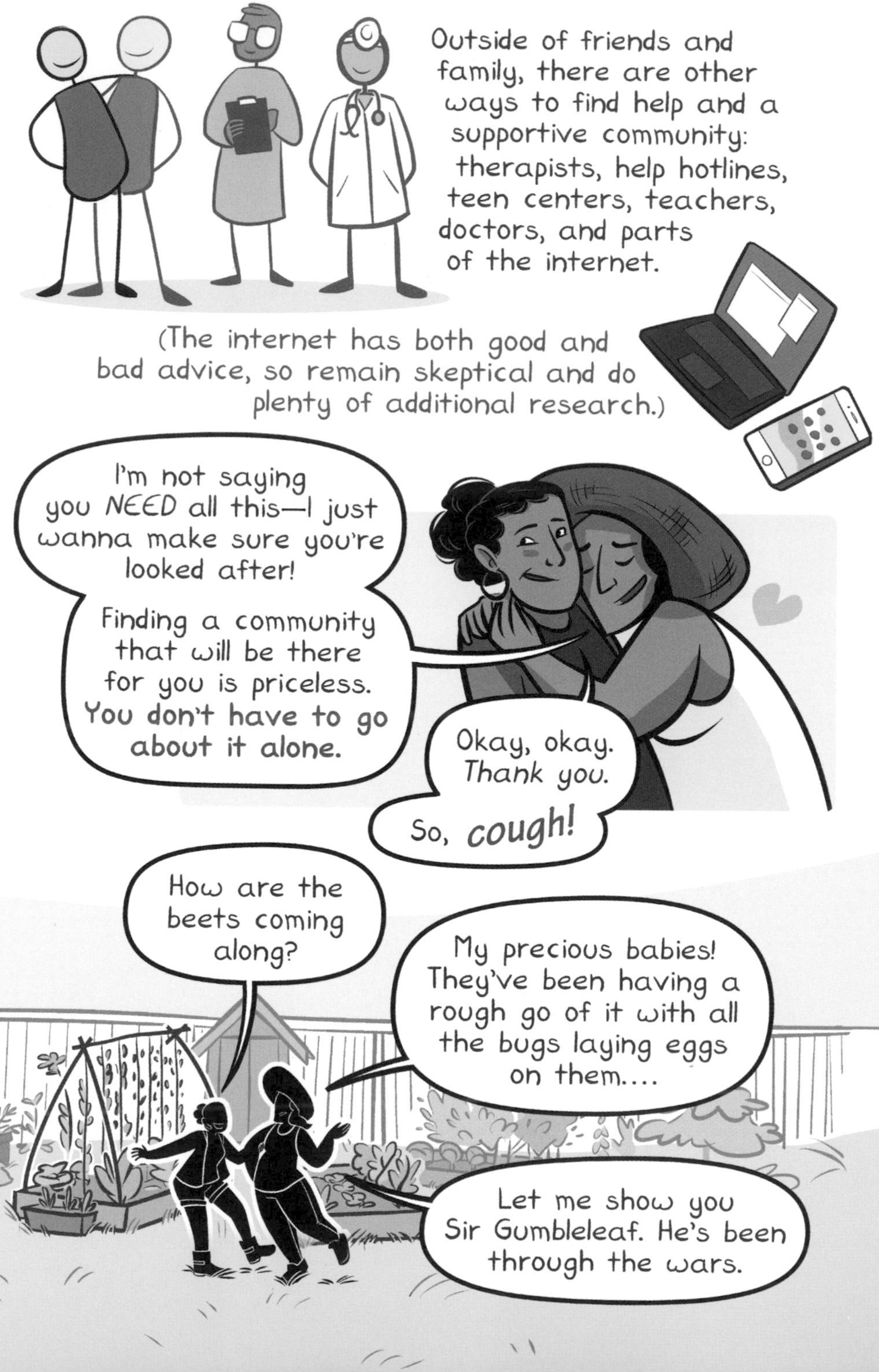
Outside of friends and family, there are other ways to find help and a supportive community: therapists, help hotlines, teen centers, teachers, doctors, and parts of the internet.
(The internet has both good and bad advice, so remain skeptical and do plenty of additional research.)
I'm not saying you *NEED* all this—I just wanna make sure you're looked after!
Finding a community that will be there for you is priceless. **You don't have to go about it alone.**
Okay, okay. *Thank you.*
So, **cough!**
How are the beets coming along?
My precious babies! They've been having a rough go of it with all the bugs laying eggs on them....
Let me show you Sir Gumbleleaf. He's been through the wars.

Further Reading

There's so much more to learn when it comes to sex; no single book can have all the answers. Thank goodness there are so many amazing resources available for you to check out!

It's Perfectly Normal
by Robie Harris and Michael Emberley

This heavily illustrated book goes back to the basics of sex and relationships. While it's meant for children, it's a great beginner's guide!

S.E.X.: The All-You-Need-to-Know Sexuality Guide to Get You Through Your Teens and Twenties
by Heather Corinna

This is THE sex ed book for teens. Comprehensive and nuanced, this weighty tome is an invaluable guide and a BIG read. Grab it when you feel ready to level up your education.

Come as You Are
by Dr. Emily Nagoski

This mind-blowing book is required reading for everyone who wants to understand how and why their sexual desire works the way it does (or doesn't).

Drawn to Sex (series)
by Erika Moen and Matthew Nolan

A collection of the short, fun comics we've made over the years with focused, condensed explanations of the world of sex.

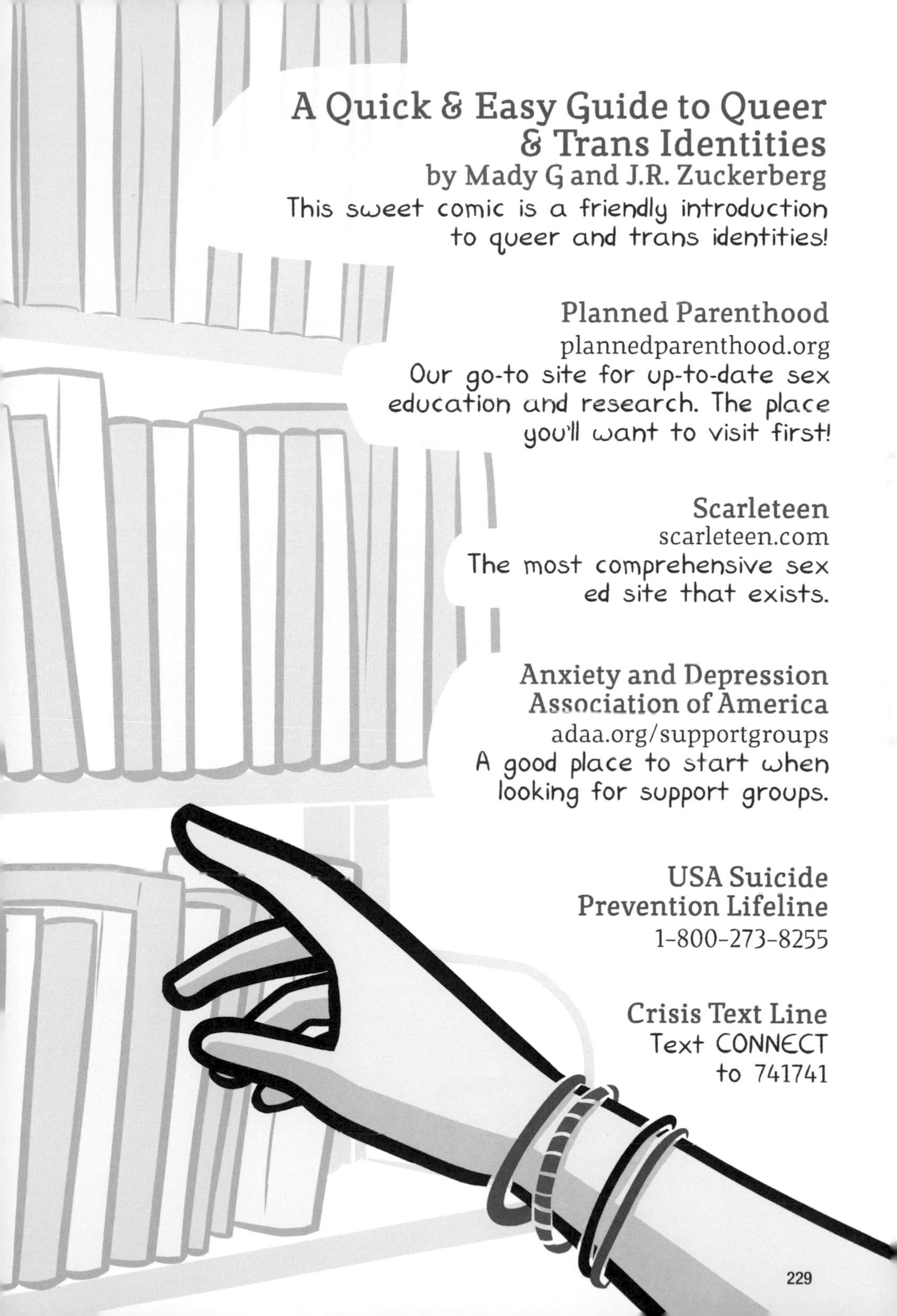

A Quick & Easy Guide to Queer & Trans Identities
by Mady G and J.R. Zuckerberg
This sweet comic is a friendly introduction to queer and trans identities!

Planned Parenthood
plannedparenthood.org
Our go-to site for up-to-date sex education and research. The place you'll want to visit first!

Scarleteen
scarleteen.com
The most comprehensive sex ed site that exists.

Anxiety and Depression Association of America
adaa.org/supportgroups
A good place to start when looking for support groups.

USA Suicide Prevention Lifeline
1-800-273-8255

Crisis Text Line
Text CONNECT to 741741

Authors' note

Sex education isn't JUST about how bodies smoosh together; it's about learning what it means to be a human who engages with other humans.

Really, sex education is ***relationship*** education, because while we're not all going to have sex, we are all going to have relationships with the people around us. When you learn about the wide world of sex, relationships, and intimacy, you learn more about yourself and others, which helps you to be a better person and to do better by others.

When we were teens learning about sex, the materials we encountered tended to be dry, dense, and hard to read, the helpful information locked away in thick tomes or behind scholarly texts. We wanted to make something welcoming and accessible, something that felt like a conversation between friends. Most of all, we wanted to make the kind of book we would have sought out as young adults. We're two comic nerds who love human stories and writing from the heart, so we decided to create a book that put that first and foremost.

We knew we had to cover the fundamentals—stuff about body parts and birth control and protection—but we wanted to focus more on the harder stuff, the interacting-with-other-people and figuring-out-what's-right-for-you stuff, like communication and consent and sexting and fucking up and fantasies and discovering yourself and exploring with a partner.

A great frustration for us both while developing this book is that we wish we could have covered so many more subjects and given more time to the ones we did. But if we had, the book would still be in progress, and it would be so thick that you'd never pick it up! If a topic near and dear to you didn't make the cut, it doesn't mean that it's not important—in fact, we probably agonized over the decision not to include it. Even on the day that Erika was drawing the final page, we were still having conversations about fitting in more topics.

We hope you find something in our book that's helpful, whether on the physical smooshing-bodies-together side or the interpersonal humans-engaging-with-humans side, or both! Hold on to the things that feel right to you; discard what doesn't. We support you changing your mind and growing over time.

You're awesome.

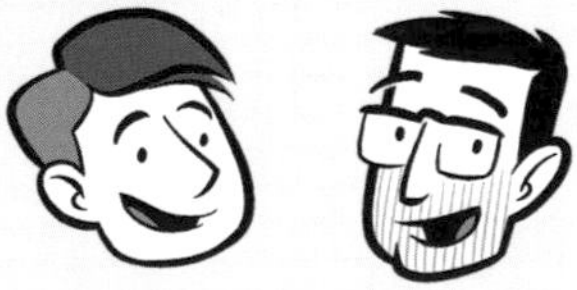

Good luck,
Erika and Matt

Index

Acknowledgments

Thank you to all the friends and family who supported us during the year of work we put into this book. We wouldn't have been able to complete the book or have it look so good without the help of Maria Frantz. A huge thank-you to our colleagues at Helioscope, who are both our professional peers and our extended family. And so much gratitude to all the guest artists we hired to cover our web comic updates while we worked on this book.

We also want to thank and celebrate the Adult Outpatient Services Intensive Treatment Program at Portland's Providence (and any other IOPs out there), which helped us when things felt insurmountable. We hope everyone who needs these resources can find and access them.

Finally, an acknowledgment to our cat, Flapjack, who helped us at every stage, only to pass away at the very end. We miss you, buddy.

About the Authors

Erika Moen and Matthew Nolan are both full-time professional cartoonists and comic book creators. They've been married for twelve years and have worked together for the past eight. They reside in Portland, Oregon. Together they run a sex-education-focused web comic called *Oh Joy Sex Toy*, which has won an assortment of accolades over the years and was even featured in the Tate Modern museum in London, England.